P9-EDT-639

THE AMERICAN HERITAGE

PUBLISHED BY AMERICAN HERITAGE PUBLISHING CO., INC., NEW YORK
BOOK TRADE DISTRIBUTION BY SIMON AND SCHUSTER, INC., NEW YORK

HISTORY OF
THE INDIAN WARS

by Robert M. Utley
and Wilcomb E. Washburn

Editors: Anne Moffat and Richard F. Snow

AMERICAN HERITAGE BOOKS

EDITOR-IN-CHIEF
Ezra Bowen

———

THE AMERICAN HERITAGE HISTORY OF
THE INDIAN WARS

EDITOR
Anne Moffat

TEXT EDITOR
Richard F. Snow

ART DIRECTOR
Murray Belsky

ART ASSISTANTS
Kay Sabinson
Elaine Golt Gongora

PICTURE EDITOR
Linda Silvestri Sykes

ASSISTANT PICTURE EDITOR
Jane Sugden

COPY EDITOR
Helen C. Dunn

ASSISTANT TEXT EDITOR
Jane Colihan

———

AMERICAN HERITAGE
PUBLISHING COMPANY, INC.

CHAIRMAN OF THE BOARD
Samuel P. Reed

PRESIDENT AND PUBLISHER
Rhett Austell

EDITORIAL ART DIRECTOR
Murray Belsky

Library of Congress Cataloging in Publication Data

Utley, Robert Marshall, 1929-
   The American Heritage history of the Indian wars.

   Includes index.
   1. Indians of North America—Wars. I. Wash-
burn, Wilcomb E., joint author. II. Title. III. Title:
History of the Indian wars.
E81.U74   973'.04'97   77-23044
ISBN 0-8281-0202-3
ISBN 0-8281-0203-1 de luxe

Book Trade Distribution Simon and Schuster, Inc.
ISBN: 0-671-22980-X (regular)
0-671-22981-8 (de luxe)

HALF-TITLE PAGE: *Lieutenant Powhatan H. Clarke, whose air of bravura was caught
in this drawing by Frederic Remington, fought Apaches with the 10th Cavalry during
the 1880's. He received the Medal of Honor for rescuing a wounded soldier.*

Harper's Weekly, MARCH 22, 1890

TITLE PAGE: *Geronimo, standing in front of the horse, leads his small but tough band of
Apache warriors to a peace conference in Mexico with General George Crook in 1886.*

NATIONAL ANTHROPOLOGICAL ARCHIVES,
SMITHSONIAN INSTITUTION

Contents

A Very

Real Nightmare

No American on the frontier was totally free from the specter of massacre. This nightmare vision, as interpreted on these pages by nineteenth-century painters, might take any form, from the death and mutilation of a single individual such as Jane McCrea (left)—who was murdered in New York in 1777 by Indians far less muscular and handsome than these—to the obliteration of wagon trains, armed troops, or whole towns. Fortunately for most frontier people, the nightmare was no more than that: a dreadful thought of something that never happened. But for the unfortunate few, there was no bright morning after.

The scene in this painting is more fable than fact; history
records few occasions when massed Indians attacked wagon trains.
MUSEUM OF ART, UNIVERSITY OF MICHIGAN

Sixty settlers were slaughtered in the Schenectady massacre of 1690,
but their razed homes were cabins, not these impressive brick dwellings.
SCHENECTADY COUNTY HISTORICAL SOCIETY

In this panorama Custer makes his last stand against ordered phalanxes of Indian cavalry—rather than the mounted mob he actually faced.
COLLECTION OF PETER H. TILLOU

PART I

The EAST

1492–1850

Almost from the moment white settlers set foot in
the New World, their relations with Indians were
characterized by hostility and violence. The first
part of this volume recounts the history of Indian-
white conflict beginning in 1492 with the arrival of
Columbus and ending in 1850 with the final subjugation
of all Indian tribes east of the Mississippi River.
The map at right—which includes present-day
state boundaries for clarity—locates the major
battles, forts, and tribes discussed in Part I.
Below, Virginia settler John Smith and a Pamunkey
warrior take aim at one another in an illustration
from Smith's 1617 work *Generall Historie of Virginia.*

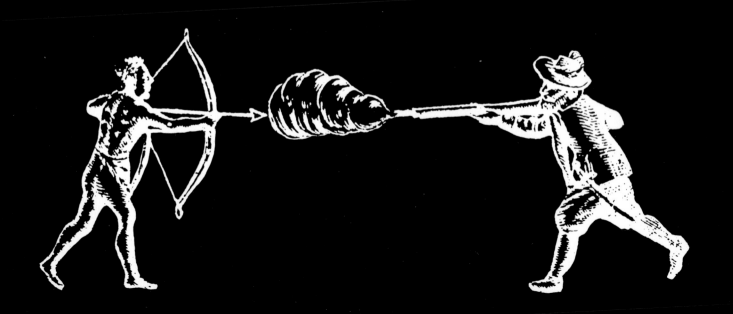

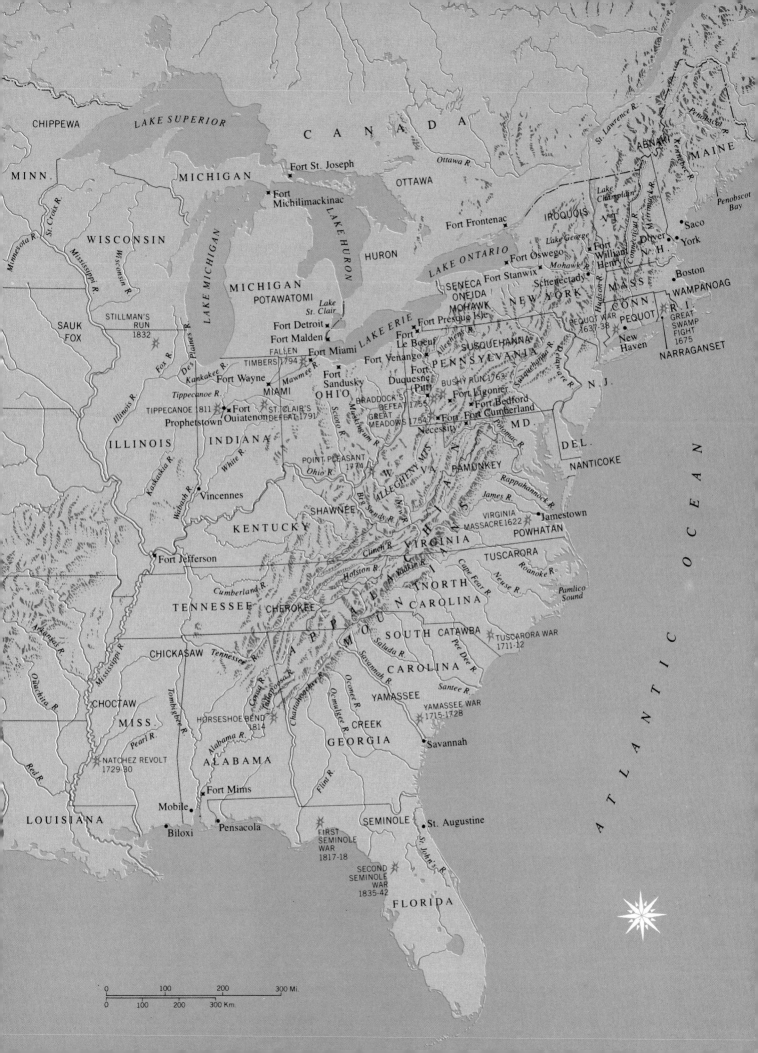

CHIPPEWA

LAKE SUPERIOR

C A N A D A

MINN.

MICHIGAN

OTTAWA

Fort St. Joseph

St. Lawrence R.

ABNAKI

Kennebec R.

Penobscot R.

MAINE

Ottawa R.

Fort Michilimackinac

LAKE HURON

Fort Frontenac

IROQUOIS

VT.

Penobscot Bay

WISCONSIN

Lake Champlain

Merrimack R.

Saco

N.H.

Dover

York

Connecticut R.

Fort William Henry

Lake George

MASS.

Boston

LAKE ONTARIO

Fort Oswego

Fort Stanwix

SENECA

ONEIDA

MOHAWK

Schenectady

Mohawk R.

Hudson R.

WAMPANOAG

CONN.

R.I.

PEQUOT WAR 1637-38

PEQUOT

GREAT SWAMP FIGHT 1675

NEW YORK

New Haven

NARRAGANSET

SAUK FOX

Minnesota R.

St. Croix R.

Mississippi R.

Wisconsin R.

LAKE MICHIGAN

MICHIGAN

POTAWATOMI

Lake St. Clair

Fort Detroit

Fort Malden

LAKE ERIE

Fort Miami

STILLMAN'S RUN 1832

Fox R.

Des Plaines R.

FALLEN TIMBERS 1794

Kankakee R.

Fort Wayne

Maumee R.

Fort Sandusky

MIAMI

OHIO

Fort Presque Isle

Fort Le Boeuf

Fort Venango

Allegheny R.

PENNSYLVANIA

SUSQUEHANNA

Fort Duquesne (Pitt)

BUSHY RUN 1763

Fort Ligonier

Susquehanna R.

Delaware R.

N.J.

Illinois R.

Tippecanoe R.

TIPPECANOE 1811

Prophetstown

Fort Ouiatenon

ST. CLAIR'S DEFEAT 1791

Scioto R.

Muskingum R.

BRADDOCK'S DEFEAT 1755

GREAT MEADOWS 1754

Fort Necessity

Fort Bedford

Fort Cumberland

Potomac R.

MD.

DEL.

Kaskaskia R.

ILLINOIS

INDIANA

White R.

Wabash R.

Vincennes

Ohio R.

POINT PLEASANT 1774

W. VA.

ALLEGHENY MTS.

New R.

Big Sandy R.

PAMUNKEY

NANTICOKE

Rappahannock R.

James R.

VIRGINIA MASSACRE 1622

Jamestown

SHAWNEE

KENTUCKY

Clinch R.

VIRGINIA

POWHATAN

TUSCARORA

Roanoke R.

Fort Jefferson

Holston R.

Yadkin R.

NORTH CAROLINA

Cape Fear R.

Neuse R.

Pamlico Sound

Cumberland R.

APPALACHIAN MOUNTAINS

TENNESSEE

CHEROKEE

SOUTH CAROLINA

CATAWBA

TUSCARORA WAR 1711-12

Pee Dee R.

Arkansas R.

CHICKASAW

Tennessee R.

Saluda R.

Savannah R.

Santee R.

Ouachita R.

Mississippi R.

YAMASSEE

YAMASSEE WAR 1715-1728

CHOCTAW

Coosa R.

Tallapoosa R.

Chattahoochee R.

Ocmulgee R.

Oconee R.

CREEK

MISS.

HORSESHOE BEND 1814

GEORGIA

Savannah

NATCHEZ REVOLT 1729-30

Alabama R.

Tombigbee R.

Pearl R.

ALABAMA

Flint R.

Red R.

Fort Mims

Mobile

Pensacola

SEMINOLE

St. Augustine

LOUISIANA

Biloxi

FIRST SEMINOLE WAR 1817-18

St. John's R.

A T L A N T I C   O C E A N

SECOND SEMINOLE WAR 1835-42

FLORIDA

0   100   200   300 Mi.

0   100   200   300 Km.

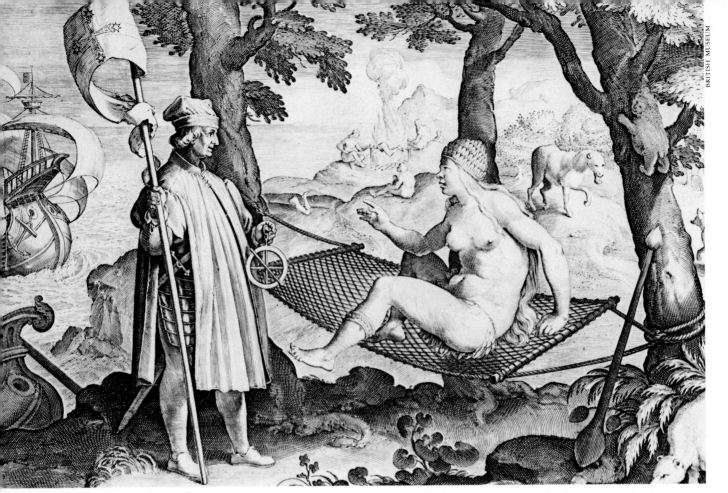

Amerigo Vespucci encounters America—depicted as an Indian woman in a sixteenth-century engraving.

1: Opening Guns

The morning of Good Friday, March 22, 1622, began much like any other in the English settlements scattered for a hundred miles up and down the James River in the colony of Virginia. On many of the plantations unarmed groups of Indians arrived early and, as was customary, were invited into the houses, where they were given breakfast and began to barter fish, furs, turkeys, and deer for glass beads and other trinkets.

Up the river at Henrico, the westernmost town of the colony, clergyman George Thorpe was at his devotions. Thorpe, whom one contemporary described as a "most sufficient gentleman, virtuous and wise," had left the King's Privy Chamber to establish a school in the New World and to convert the Indians there to Christianity. He was delighted with his progress; he felt that he had gained the trust and friendship of the natives and had even built a house "after the English fashion" for Opechancanough, leader of the powerful Powhatan Confederacy of Tidewater Indian tribes.

A few miles beyond, at Falling Creek, a hundred skilled workmen were building the iron foundry that the Virginia Company had sent them from England to establish. And all along the river men and women were planting tobacco and corn, sawing timber, making bricks, feeding livestock.

The sun reached the angle of eight o'clock, and fury burst upon the settlers with terrible suddenness. The Indians in the houses grabbed the weapons of their hosts, whom, as one report put it, "they basely and barbarously murthered, not sparing eyther age or sexe, man, woman or childe."

Thorpe was among the first to be killed. One of his servants sensed what was about to happen and tried to warn him to defend himself, but Thorpe, refusing to believe the man, was cut down without resisting.

The Indians swarmed into the foundry, killed the mill master and his men, burned the buildings, and wrecked the machinery. (Later the Virginia Company was able to salvage no more than a pair of tongs, a shovel, and one bar of iron.) Men and women taken by surprise in the fields were immediately put to death. But where people had time to resist, they generally survived.

At one plantation, for instance, a boy frightened off the attackers simply by discharging a musket into the air, and the settlers in a home nearby successfully defended themselves with spades, axes, and brickbats.

Jamestown was saved by an Indian boy named Chanco, the Christian servant of a Mr. Pace. Chanco's brother had ordered him the night before to kill Pace, but the boy could not bring himself to do it, and he told his master of the danger. Pace secured his home for the coming fight and then, before daylight, rowed across the James River to alert the governor. When the hour came, the capital was ready.

Even so, the assault was effective enough to wipe out one third of the entire colony. "There fell . . . three hundred forty seven . . . and not being content with taking away life alone, they [the Indians] fell after againe upon the dead, making as well as they could, a fresh murder, defacing, dragging, and mangling the dead carkasses into many pieces, and carrying some parts away in derision, with base and brutish triumph."

This bloody attack—the worst yet experienced by the English in the New World—devastated the settlers at a time when they thought they could count on peaceful relations with the Indians. The immediate cause was the death of Nemattanow, an Indian executed by the English in retribution for the murder of a man named Morgan. But in fact the war that, erupted with the 1622 massacre was no more fought over a single Indian than the First World War was fought over a Central European archduke.

The source of the conflict was foreshadowed by the first European footstep on the shores of the New World, when Columbus waded onto the beach of a beautiful Caribbean island, certain that he had landed on the edge of the rich and fabled Orient. That landing was the real beginning of the four-hundred-year chronicle of idealism, illusion, courage, cruelty, and greed that brought native Americans and European invaders together in a struggle for possession of a continent.

The treasures of the East—silk fabrics, jewels, spices, porcelain objects—together with such phenomena as gunpowder and the printing press, had long roused the envy and admiration of Europe. Compared with the Orient, Europe was an underdeveloped region: its population was minuscule beside that of China, Japan, and India, its economy was weak and limited, and its rural nation-states petty and fragmented. Europeans were designated "barbarians" by the haughty Chinese and Japanese—clever barbarians, perhaps, but barbarians nevertheless.

The bewilderment of the early explorers at finding a new continent was evident in their refusal to believe that they had found it. Columbus, who named the inhabitants of the New World "Indians" in the belief that he had reached India, persisted in this conviction until his dying day. Carrying diplomatic letters to the Great Khan politely and respectfully stating his peaceful intentions, Columbus searched fruitlessly for signs of vast cities and silk-clad philosophers in the jungles of Cuba.

He finally decided that while he had reached Asia, he was still on its outskirts, among the lands in the "Sea of India" described by Marco Polo as inhabited by naked men with simpler societies than those of the Chinese and Japanese. When Columbus's men showed their weapons to the hospitable natives of the island of Guanahani (which Columbus renamed San Salvador), the "Indians" cut themselves on the sharp blades of the Spanish swords from ignorance of their character. The New World had not yet entered its Age of Iron. Its weapons were still those of the Stone Age.

The disparity between the military strength of Europe, represented by gunpowder, steel, and the horse, and that of the New World, whose inhabitants fought with bows and arrows and wooden clubs, was immediately apparent to the European soldiery, who quickly saw the human population of the New World as a resource to be exploited. The attitude was prefigured in Columbus's journal entry of October 14, 1492, suggesting the establishment of a fortress, "though I do not see that it would be necessary, for these people are very simple as regards the use of arms, as your Highnesses will see from the seven that I caused to be taken, to bring home and learn our language and return; unless your Highnesses should order them all to be brought to Castile, or to be kept as captives on the same island; for with fifty men they can all be subjugated and made to do what is required of them."

This ease of conquest was not lost on the hardhanded crew that Columbus ordered to establish a Spanish city at La Navidad on Hispaniola while he returned to Spain to carry news of the discovery. He had barely departed when the soldiers set out after women and gold. With their leader safely beyond the horizon, they roamed the island, descending on villages and taking golden ornaments from the natives at sword point.

In time the Castilians would formalize this sort of robbery into the system of *repartimientos* and *encomiendas*—which meant that the natives labored in gold mines and on plantations in return for which their masters were supposed to instruct them in the Christian faith. It was little more than slavery; women murdered their own children rather than have them live under the conquistadors.

The Spanish also had a leaning toward gratuitous cruelty. Bartolomé de Las Casas, the first priest to be ordained in the New World, worked long and fruitlessly against the bloody excesses of his countrymen, of which he gave this stark description: "Overrunning Cities and Villages, where they spared no sex nor age; neither would their cruelty pity Women with childe, whose bellies they would rip up, taking out the Infant to hew it in pieces. They would often lay wagers who should with most dexterity either cleave or cut a man in the middle, or who could at one blow soonest cut off his head. The children they would take by the feet and dash their innocent heads against the rocks, and when they were fallen into the water, with a strange and cruel derision they would call upon them to swim. Sometimes they would run both Mother and Infant, being in her belly, quite through at one thrust.

The Aztec emperor Montezuma, whose family ruled central Mexico for 150 years prior to Hernando Cortes's invasion, looks every inch the regal warrior in this sixteenth-century painting. The Aztecs charged the Spanish with murdering him during the siege of the capital in 1520. Actually, Montezuma had been stoned by his own people as he urged an end to the fighting. Cortes always claimed that Montezuma had died as a result of the pelting of the Aztec mob.

"They erected certain Gallowses, that were broad but so low, that the tormented creatures might touch the ground with their feet, upon every one of which they would hang thirteen persons, blasphemously affirming that they did it in honour of our Redeemer and his Apostles, and then putting fire under them, they burnt the poor wretches alive."

Though they lacked the terrifying weapons and horses of the invaders, the natives rebelled against this tyranny when they dared. The garrison left at La Navidad was the first to feel their wrath. One night the Indians surprised ten Spaniards asleep in their huts, each with several women sleeping around him. Some of the Spaniards were killed outright; the others were driven into the ocean and drowned. Emboldened by their success, the natives hunted down the rest of the soldiers, who were out freebooting around the countryside. When Columbus returned in 1493, not one was left alive.

Though La Navidad was wiped out, the Spanish built new cities. Within a generation of establishing their first foothold in the islands of the Caribbean they were moving into the vast, unexplored continent beyond. The first two ships to drop anchor in the 1520's off the coast of what would become the Carolinas found there a "gentle, kindly, hospitable" people whom the sailors named the Chicoreans. They invited scores of these Indians aboard ship, offered them a look at the lower decks, and while the visitors were inspecting the holds, locked them in and set sail for Santo Domingo, where the Chicoreans were sold as mine slaves. Other slavers pursued these easy pickings, and by the end of the seventeenth century the tribe had disappeared from the face of the earth, as had the inhabitants of many of the West Indian islands.

In 1529 Pánfilo de Narváez, a red-bearded, one-eyed roughneck, came fresh from pillaging in Mexico to try his luck in the Gulf Coast villages. He opened negotiations with the natives around Tampa Bay by luring

Aztecs counterattack Spanish soldiers under Lieutenant Pedro de Alvarado, whom Cortes left to hold the captured capital while the main body of Spanish troops campaigned to the east. The Indians in this contemporary drawing are members of an elite warrior class; note the leader of the charge dressed as an eagle, and the combatant at the far right in a jaguar costume. In such encounters, however, even the best native fighters were no match for Europeans armed with crossbows and harquebuses.

The most despised enemy of any given Indian tribe was likely to be the tribe next door. And this fraternal warfare, kindled by centuries of established hatred, continued after the arrival of Europeans—who were often enlisted by ambitious chiefs as mercenaries in fights with other aborigines. One of the earliest intra-Indian wars witnessed by white men swept back and forth over Florida in the sixteenth century when King Outina, who ruled some forty villages in the St. Johns River region, marched against neighboring villages. Though Outina's men were far better organized than most warrior armies, in other respects they fought in conventional Indian ways that dismayed Outina's French allies. For example, they broke off fighting at sunset no matter how crucial the moment in battle. After an engagement was over, whichever side had killed the first man, rather than the most men, claimed victory. Surviving prisoners were then turned over to women and children, who tortured the losers to death.

CEREMONIES

Led by three scouts, King Outina, enclosed by a marching quadrangle of warriors, heads for battle.

OF WAR

To declare war, tribesmen plant arrows festooned with locks of hair outside the enemy village stockade.

Outina's army, aided by the French, fights Chief Potanou's.

In a rare night action, revengeful raiders shoot burning moss fastened to arrowheads onto enemy rooftops.

Victorious warriors scalp dead foes, then chop off limbs for trophies.

their chief and his family into the Spanish camp, cutting off the chief's nose, and ordering his mother torn apart by dogs. Narváez went on to take his army of four hundred men up the coast. Eventually he overplayed his hand and saw his command destroyed by Indians, exhaustion, exposure, and disease. Only four soldiers survived the expedition.

Hernando de Soto's subsequent march through the southeastern part of the country in 1540–42, and Coronado's expeditions in the southwest in the same period, showed the inland tribes that they could expect the worst from the bearded white men. Both Coronado and De Soto assumed that the local Indians should provide food, guides, and porters to carry their supplies and facilitate their search for portable wealth. When they suspected that a guide was deceitful, they killed him; if they thought an Indian ruler was less than cooperative, they often seized him to extort further concessions from his followers. The Spaniards burned villages and enslaved or killed their hosts in the conviction that terror and intimidation could serve their purposes better than any policy of kindness and accommodation. In these practices they merely followed on a smaller scale the practices of Cortés in Mexico and Pizarro in Peru. Unfortunately for the Spanish the country north of the Rio Grande could not provide the riches in gold, silver, and slaves that Central and South America afforded. Nevertheless, the pattern of extortion and terror continued.

And always, as the conquistadors cut their way through the New World, disease went with them, continuing the slaughter where the swords and the primitive guns (called harquebuses) left off. Smallpox, measles, and a score of other illnesses ravaged the Indians, who had had no chance to build up the immunities developed by Europeans during the terrible epidemics of the Middle Ages. Estimates of Indian population vary widely, but the first Spanish tribute rolls in Mexico indicate a native population of fifteen million. By the early 1600's the number had dwindled to about two million.

Such, then, was the groundwork the Spanish had prepared for other European settlers who came later. It was a legacy of unnecessary cruelty and death bequeathed by sword and disease. In 1570 the essayist Montaigne looked upon these works and despaired: "So many goodly cities ransacked and razed; so many nations destroyed or made desolate; so infinite millions of harmless people of all sexes, status, and ages, massacred, ravaged, and put to the sword; and the richest, the fairest, the best part of the world turned upside down, ruined, and defaced for the traffic of pearls and peppers! Oh, mechanic victories, oh, base conquest!"

When the English came to establish their first permanent colony at Jamestown in 1607, they too hoped to find gold and a passage to India. But they also sought furs, sassafras (then believed to be a cure for syphilis), and anything else that could make a profit for the Virginia Company of London, the joint-stock operation that was financing the colony. This English foray into the Virginia wilderness had been designed with political and economic ends in mind. A few pious remarks were made about introducing the Indian to Christianity, but there was little real missionary zeal.

Nor could the English have spread the gospel at sword point, even had they wished to. The first years of the colony were wretched ones. Of the nine hundred settlers who arrived during the first three years, only one hundred fifty remained alive in 1610. Most of the dead were taken by disease and starvation, not by Indians. There were a few bloody squabbles, but for the most part the Indians, who could so easily have extinguished the flagging settlement, let it alone.

These forbearing natives were members of an Algonquian confederacy of Indians, some two hundred villages and thirty-two tribes with a total population of about ten thousand. This "empire," as it has been called, had been stitched together by a determined chieftain named Wa-hun-sen-a-cawh, whom the colonists called King Powhatan after the town where he lived.

Powhatan's Indians not only permitted the settlement to survive, but actually helped the English during the first desperate winters. Captain John Smith, the principal military agent at Jamestown, wrote, "It pleased God (in our extremity) to move the Indians to bring us Corne, ere it was halfe ripe, to refresh us, when we rather expected . . . they would destroy us. . . ." But it is significant that, to Smith, it was the English God rather than the Indians' generosity that got the corn to his table.

The English showed little hesitation about attacking the Indians, for whatever reason. Once tobacco began to be cultivated after 1614 to meet the growing demand in England, the pressure on Indian lands increased. Tobacco cultivation exhausted the soil quickly, forcing the planters to move on to new fields. And it was far easier for the colonists to take over fields that the Indians had already cleared than to go through the tedious labor of felling trees and grubbing stumps. Captain Smith had set the pattern for Virginia's conduct toward the Indians in the period when the colonists seized rather than grew their crops. As he wrote, "The Warres in *Europe, Asia,* and *Africa,* taught me how to subdue the wilde Salvages in *Virginia . . . .*" Arrogant, truculent, possessed of immense physical courage, Smith was perhaps the quintessential seventeenth-century military commander. Once, having gone upriver to barter for corn with Opechancanough, the half brother of Powhatan, he found himself surrounded by hundreds of well-armed Indians. Coolly assessing the situation, Smith seized Opechancanough by his scalp lock, stuck a pistol in his ribs, and thrust him out in front of the throng. "Here I stand," he bellowed, "shoot he that dare. You promised to fraught my ship [with corn] ere I departed, and so you shall; or I meane to load her with your dead carcasses. . . ." He got the corn.

Powhatan clearly perceived the English intentions and yet hoped against hope for a peaceful accommodation. Smith quotes Powhatan in a conversation of 1609: "Captain *Smith,* (saith the king) some doubt I have of your comming hither . . . for many do informe me, your comming is not for trade, but to invade my people and possesse my Country." Powhatan went on to sketch the advantages of peace over war, when he would be "so hunted by you that I can neither rest eat nor sleepe, but my tired men must watch, and if a twig but breake, everie one crie, there comes Captain *Smith:* then must I flie I knowe not whether, and thus with miserable fear end my miserable life. . . ."

The tactics used by the English in their warfare with the Indians crossed the foggy dividing line between strategic deception and outright immorality. Early instructions from the Virginia Company's London directors advocated taking Powhatan prisoner as a means of bringing him under control. If that proved impossible, Sir Thomas Gates, who became governor

In this gruesome impression by engraver Théodore de Bry, published twelve years after the Virginia massacre of 1622, Indians mutilate settlers near houses surrounding Jamestown while other warriors travel by canoe to assault the town. Survivors of the massacre bitterly abandoned any pretense of peaceful coexistence and resolved that Indians had to be exterminated.

in 1611, was urged to make tributaries of as many chiefs as possible, and even to put to death the Indian priests. In one case, Gates lured Indians into the open by having his soldiers beat a drum and dance; when the Indians came out, Gates slaughtered them. The seizure of Pocahontas (see page 28) by Samuel Argall in 1613 provided another instance of English deception, though it brought years of relative peace to the fledgling colony.

Despite all such provocations, Powhatan worked to avoid violence. Then in 1618 he died, and Opechancanough succeeded him as ruler of the confederacy. Powhatan's half brother pledged his help and friendship to the colonists; but he smarted from the humiliations and extortions his people continued to receive, and he bided his time.

That time came early in March of 1622 shortly after the planter named Morgan went inland to trade with the Indians and never returned. The Englishman's servants, thinking that Nemattanow had done Morgan in, put the Indian to death. Nemattanow had been a man of some standing, and Opechancanough threatened vengeance. The colonists responded with threats of their own.

The case against Nemattanow, even as reported by John Smith, seemed flimsy. The Indian was said to have returned to Morgan's friends and servants wearing the dead man's hat on his head, hardly something a murderer could be expected to do. Then, according to Smith, Nemattanow ". . . so moved their patience, they shot him." That bare sentence suggests the Indian's outraged rejection of the implication that he was guilty, and it is not hard to imagine a series of other fatal misunderstandings in the emotionally charged atmosphere in which the information about Morgan's murder was transmitted.

A few months before the massacre Opechancanough had assured the English that "he held the peace so firme, the sky should fall or [ere] he dissolved it. . . ." But now, to Governor Francis Wyatt, he openly talked of revenge. Visiting the far-flung tribes of his confederation, he engineered a coordinated attack to be launched all along the James River at the same hour. It took him two weeks to complete the arrangements.

On March 20, according to Smith, Opechancanough guided some planters "with much kindnesse through the woods, and one Browne that lived among them to learne the language" was sent home in safety. Two days later, on Good Friday, the storm broke on the unsuspecting settlers.

Though they may not have realized it as they waited grimly for casualty reports from the outlying settlements, the English in Jamestown had reached a turning point in their relations with the Indians. Whatever actual and potential good will had previously existed went up with the smoke of the burning settlements. From that time on, the predominant English policy would be one of extermination. "It is infinitely better," wrote Wyatt, "to have no heathen among us, who were but as thornes in our sides, than to be at peace and league with them. . . ."

The colonists set about rooting the natives out of the entire Tidewater area. Regular patrols attacked neighboring Indian villages again and again. Disease broke out in the colonists' ranks, but they persevered with their offensive. "With our small and sicklie forces," wrote one of them, "we have discomforted the Indians round about us, burnt their houses, gathered their corn and slain not a few; though they are as swift as Roebucks, like the violent lightening they are gone as soon as perceived, and not to be destroyed but by surprise or famine." By January, 1623, the Virginia Council of State could report that more Indians had been killed in the previous year than had been slain since the beginning of the colony.

As the campaign wore on, the colonists resorted to measures ruthless enough to draw a rebuke from the Virginia Company itself. The chiding came when the company got word that Governor Wyatt had tried to poison Opechancanough during a feigned peace conference. The attempt was bungled, and, though two hundred Indians became violently ill and many were slaughtered, Opechancanough escaped. The council responded to the company's protests: "Wee hold nothing inuiste [unjust] . . . that may tend to theire ruine. . . . Stratagems were ever allowed against all enemies, but with these neither fayre Warr nor good quarter is ever to be held, nor is there other hope of theire subversione, who ever may informe you to the Contrarie."

For fourteen years, through the chilly winters and the malarial summers, the English continued their lethal pressure against the Indians. Finally, in 1632, the military efforts of both settlers and natives ground to a halt through mutual exhaustion. Each side grudgingly recognized the authority of the other in its own territory, and a weary, sullen truce settled over the Tidewater.

The respite lasted little more than a decade. Opechancanough, very old now but still canny and capable, went up and down the river in 1644, once again organizing an attack against the English. It came on the morning of April 18, and the few colonists who could recall the events of 1622 must have reacted with particular shock as they got word of the assault that had rolled over the isolated, scattered settlements.

But it was not quite like 1622. For one thing, the Indians backed off after their first offensive. Nobody knows why this curious lethargy settled over the attackers—perhaps some omen discouraged them—but rather than pressing home their initial advantage, they disappeared into the forest. And while they killed upward of four hundred settlers, Virginia's white population then stood at eight thousand. The attack, though costly, was not devastating.

The colonists had a new royal governor, the brilliant and dashing Sir William Berkeley, who wasted no time in launching a counterattack. He dispatched small groups of well-armed men who penetrated deep into Indian territory, burning fields and destroying natives wherever they could be found. In June the General Assembly passed an act calling for "perpetuall warre with the Indians" guilty of the attack.

Seeking assistance from the mother country, the assembly sent Sir William, whose connections at court were known to be good, over to England to procure a supply of arms and ammunition from His Majesty. The mission was not particularly successful, for Berkeley found his country locked in a bloody civil war—in which he briefly joined, fighting with the forces of Charles I against those of Parliament.

When he returned to America in June of 1645, the conflict with the Indian confederation was still unresolved. Although several forts had been built and expeditions continued to be sent into hostile country, Opechancanough remained a threat to the colony's existence. By March, 1646, the assembly had wearied of the apparently interminable fighting, and con-

This engraving from John Smith's Generall Historie of Virginia *shows King Powhatan chairing a tribal gathering. According to Smith, Powhatan held the power of life and death over the thirty-two tribes in his confederacy, and all subchiefs paid him "eight parts of ten tribute of all the commodities which their country yieldeth."*

sidering "the almost impossibility of a further revenge upon them, they being dispersed and driven from their townes and habitations, lurking up and downe the woods in small numbers, and that a peace (if honourably obtained) would conduce to the better being and comoditie of the country," Captain Henry Fleet, the colony's interpreter, was authorized to take sixty men, find Opechancanough, and make peace.

But before Fleet could move, Berkeley happened to learn the whereabouts of the Indian leader and set off with a troop of soldiers to raid his headquarters. Opechancanough was captured and taken to Jamestown. When the Indian leader, who was nearly a hundred years old and virtually blind, heard "a great noise of the treading of people about him . . . he caused his eye-lids to be lifted up; and finding that a crowd of people were let in to see him, he call'd in high indignation for the Governour, who being come, Opechancanough scornfully told him, that had it been his fortune to take Sir William Berkeley prisoner, he should not meanly have exposed him as a show to the people." Stung by the rebuke, Berkeley ordered him treated with appropriate courtesy. The governor's order was not obeyed. Opechancanough was shot in the back by one of his guards.

A peace of sorts with Necotowance, Opechancanough's successor, was finally made by the assembly in October, 1646. Necotowance acknowledged his dependence upon the king of England and agreed that his successors might be appointed or confirmed by the king's governors. Twenty beaver skins were to be presented annually to the governor as a sign of the nation's subjection. Boundaries were set between Necotowance's land and the English settlements, with each side forbidden to enter the other's territory except as authorized by the governor. For the first time the legal right of Virginia's Indians to the lands they occupied was formally recognized. The policy of "perpetual enmity" and the campaigns of extermination were replaced, at least temporarily, by a policy of mutual right.

The defeat of Opechancanough, whose federation had formed the only major obstacle in the Tidewater area, cleared the way for English expansion up to the rapids, or "heads" of navigation, of Virginia's rivers and set the stage for later migration into the rolling Piedmont area leading to the great Appalachian barrier. Because of the Civil War in England, which culminated in the execution of Charles I in 1649, controlling this expansion proved difficult. Although Governor Berkeley persuaded the assemblies of the late 1640's to restrict and even displace English settlements that were too scattered for their own safety or that impinged on the rights of the native inhabitants, the pressure of Virginia's growing population proved impossible to throttle. When Parliament sent a fleet to reduce the colony to obedience to the new Commonwealth government in January, 1652 (Virginia had declared itself loyal to King Charles), Berkeley was forced to retire from government. And his strict control over expansion was abandoned by a series of interim governors.

As local landowners—often important officials in the county governments—moved west up the tidal estuaries and north up the Eastern Shore in search of new tobacco lands, they often appropriated, by whatever means proved easiest, land that belonged to local Indian tribes. Restraints on their incursions were negligible, and the records of the minor wars that resulted are virtually undocumented in colonial archives. The surviving fragmentary accounts show that local officials were frequently empowered

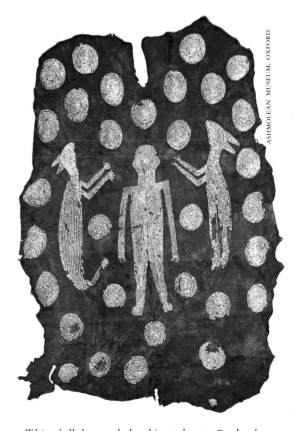

This shell-decorated deerskin, taken to England from Jamestown early in the 1600's, is believed to be one of the ceremonial cloaks that Powhatan wore on visits to various tribes, from which he collected his annual tribute in person.

27

Ætatis suæ 21. Aᵒ.1616.

An Anglicized Pocahontas posed for her portrait on a London visit with John Rolfe.

A NEW WORLD PRINCESS

The single most famous Indian during the early years of European settlement in North America was not a fearsome warrior chief but a diminutive maiden named Pocahontas. Almost single-handedly she forged one of the few eras of peace between the Indians and the hated European colonists. In the process she created a legend that endures to this day—a legend that if anything understates the reality of this extraordinary young woman.

Pocahontas was a genuine Indian princess, daughter of a chief named Powhatan, who by the time English settlers had founded the Virginia colony of Jamestown in 1607 had consolidated the region's warring Algonquian tribes into North America's first Indian empire.

Perhaps because of her station and ebullient nature ("Pocahontas" meant frisky in Algonquian), she was fascinated by—rather than fearful of—the pale, bearded foreigners who traveled on floating islands and carried sticks that boomed like thunder. At any rate, when in 1608 she met her first Englishman, a captive white chief named John Smith, the thirteen-year-old princess behaved in a most unusual fashion.

As her father's bodyguards brandished clubs over Smith's head, Pocahontas leapt forward and placed her head protectively over his. Startled by this bold act, Powhatan released Smith, who subsequently wrote that his benefactress "under God, was the instrument to preserve this colony from death, famine and utter confusion."

Apparently not all Jamestown's residents shared John Smith's enthusiasm for the Indian princess. In 1613, when Pocahontas was eighteen, Governor Sir Thomas Dale kidnapped her. Dale's intention was to use the princess as barter: he would return her to Powhatan if the Indian king would return English prisoners and arms he had seized.

During a year of haggling over conditions for the trade, Pocahontas was introduced to English woolen clothes and the English language, instructed in the Christian faith, and—as befitted a saved heathen—baptized. Her new name: Lady Rebecca. But Lady Rebecca refused to be inhibited by the stuffy English name or customs. Instead she startled staid colonists by performing handsprings nude in the streets.

Smitten by this beautiful "unbeeleeving creature," a strict Calvinist named John Rolfe wooed and then married her. An unexpected dowry was Powhatan's declaration of peace between his tribesmen and the English. Rolfe, meanwhile, had—like Powhatan's warriors—begun to plant tobacco, providing the colony with a cash crop.

In 1616 Rolfe took his Indian princess to London, where she created another sensation. Ben Jonson penned her into one of his plays, and she was presented—with a befeathered "guard"—to King James I and his court. Dressed in a tightly corseted gown with high lace collar, Pocahontas sat through a masque (an allegorical play performed by masked actors) that doubtless was as confusing to her as her Elizabethan clothes were uncomfortable. For Rolfe there was discomfort of another sort. A commoner, he had married into a royal family without the consent of James I.

The English sovereign soon forgot the indiscretion, however, and Pocahontas and John Rolfe returned to their lodgings in London's fittingly named Belle Sauvage Inn.

The following March, weakened by the cold and damp English weather, Pocahontas died. Her death at age twenty-one in the town of Gravesend was noted in this spare Puritan epitaph: "Rebecca Wrolfe wyffe of Thomas Wrolfe gent. A Virginia Lady borne was buried in the Chauncell."

to raise men to punish the "injuries and insolencies" received from neighboring Indians.

The "injuries and insolencies" that caused conflict on the frontier were usually rooted in simple trespass either by English cattle or hogs onto the unfenced cornfields of the Indians or by the Indian habit of moving freely over open fields that the English regarded as sacred private property. The Indians often killed strayed domestic animals belonging to the English and felt no responsibility for enclosing their own cornfields against such marauders. The English, on the other hand, wedded to the concept of mine and thine, demanded recognition of a definition of property that was alien to the natives.

Some attempts were made to see the Indians' position—if only to alter it. Thus the assembly of March, 1656, noting that the danger of war was caused by "our extreame pressures on them and theire wanting of something to hazard and loose beside their lives," provided that for every eight wolves' heads brought in by the Indians their "King or great man" should be given a cow. "This will be a step to civilizing them and to making them Christians," the act concluded; "besides it will certainly make the comanding Indians watch over their own men that they do us no injuries, knowing that by theire default they may be in danger of losing their estates." But these early efforts at implanting European values were largely ineffective and constantly marred by violence.

That same March of 1656, the assembly sent Colonel Edward Hill and a hundred men to remove certain "foreign" Indians (members of independent, nontributary tribes) who had occupied the area around the falls of the James, which the English considered theirs because "in a just warr [the previous inhabitants] were formerly conquered by us." Tottopottomoi, the king of the Pamunkeys, allied himself with Hill against the intruders and marched with a hundred of his warriors to assist the English colonel.

Despite the assembly's instructions that he expel the intruders without the use of force, Hill put to death five of the kings who came out to parley with him. As a contemporary writer put it: "This unparalleled hellish treachery and anti-christian perfidy more to be detested than any heathenish inhumanity cannot but stink most abominably in the noestrils of as many Indians, as shall be infested with the least scent of it, even to their perpetual abhorring and abandoning of the very sight and name of an English man, till some new generation of a better extract shall be transplanted among them."

Tottopottomoi was killed while aiding his English friends in the fight that followed Hill's treacherous act. Although the colonel, by a unanimous vote of the burgesses and council, was found guilty of "crimes and weaknesses" and suspended from all his offices, he did not disappear from the Virginia political scene.

The assembly that censured Hill also repealed an act making it lawful to kill an Indian committing a trespass. Since the trespass could be proved simply by the oath of the person doing the shooting, the assembly pointed out that killing Indians, "though never so innocent," had come to be of "small account" with the colonists. Hoping to prevent such incidents from triggering larger conflicts, the assembly attempted to provide some protection for the increasingly harassed natives. In trying to regulate land grants,

Not long after the founding of Jamestown, tobacco—distributed in Europe under such labels as the one above—emerged as the cash crop that made the Virginia colony profitable. Pocahontas's husband, John Rolfe, was largely responsible. In 1613 he sent part of his crop to London, where it was tested by experts and deemed superior. Four years later the George *sailed for England with 20,000 pounds of tobacco, prompting a boom in the demand for land in Virginia.*

it also stipulated that none be made to any Englishman until the Indians in the area had first been guaranteed fifty acres for each warrior. But such measures, however well meaning on the surface, only point up the aggressive pressures that drove the Indians to war or extinction.

By 1671 Governor Berkeley, who had been called back to his post by the Virginia assembly even before the Restoration of Charles II, was able to report to the Lords of Trade and Plantations that "the Indians, our neighbours, are absolutely subjected, so that there is no fear of them." Of the ten thousand that had once dominated the Tidewater area, only three or four thousand remained, of whom a bare seven hundred twenty-five were warriors. The English population, on the other hand, stood at forty thousand.

Far from being a threat, the remaining natives were wholly dependent on the colonists, and, as Berkeley pointed out, they were a good buffer against "foreign" tribes.

Nevertheless, another serious spate of fighting did erupt in Virginia. Though the so-called Indian war of 1675–76 was seen by some as a vast and concerted effort to drive the English into the sea, it in fact grew out of a characteristic incident of hostility at an outlying frontier settlement. A party of Nanticoke Indians of Maryland, claiming that a Virginia planter named Thomas Mathew had never paid for some goods he had gotten from them, crossed the Potomac and took some of his hogs. The English went after the Indians, killed several of them, and retrieved the hogs. The Nanticokes, in turn, sent out a war party that killed Mathew's herdsman, a man named Hen.

A fatal chain of revenge had thus been forged. George Brent and George Mason, the local militia captains, set off with thirty Virginians in pursuit of Mathew's killers. Crossing the Potomac into Maryland and surrounding an Indian cabin, Brent called upon the Indians to parley. When they did, Brent grabbed one Nanticoke chief by the hair and accused him of murdering Hen. When he broke out of Brent's grasp, the frightened chief was shot. Whether he had had anything to do with Hen's murder was never established.

A fight immediately broke out between the chief's companions and the English in which ten Indians were killed. Nearby, Mason had surrounded another cabin, whose sleeping inhabitants came pouring forth upon hearing the shots of Brent's men. Fourteen were killed before Mason realized that he was engaged with a party of Susquehannocks, a tribe with which the colony was on good terms. "For the Lords sake Shoot no more," Mason shouted, "these are our friends the Susquehanoughs."

The attacks by Brent and Mason stimulated the aggrieved Indians to retaliate heavily against outlying English settlements. On August 31, 1675, Governor Berkeley instructed Colonel John Washington (great-grandfather of George Washington) and Major Isaac Allerton to "call together the severall Malittia officers" of the regiments between the Rappahannock and Potomac rivers and make "a full and thorough inquisition" of the true causes of the various murders and raids "and by what Nation or Nations of Indians donne." After the investigation, the two officers were to demand satisfaction and "if they find cause" to raise men and punish the natives responsible.

Washington and Allerton brushed aside this proposal. Instead of conducting any serious inquiry, they immediately wrote to the Maryland authorities stating that they had been authorized simply to summon the militia and asking for all the men the colony could give them. Maryland sent two hundred fifty horse and dragoons under Major Thomas Trueman to rendezvous with Washington late in September.

On September 26 the combined force of Marylanders and Virginians surrounded the main fort of the Susquehannock Indians, a solid defensive position consisting of tightly linked palisades bulwarked by earthworks. Trueman invited five of the Susquehannock chiefs out to parley. Informed that they were suspected of the recent frontier murders, the chiefs denied all responsibility. The English did not believe them. Although they had come out under a flag of truce, the five chiefs were led away and murdered.

The Marylanders subsequently claimed that Washington and the Virginians had done the deed; the Virginians insisted that Trueman and the Marylanders were responsible. Trueman was impeached by the lower house of the Maryland general assembly and found guilty, but he was let off with a light fine. The upper house insisted that the penalty would satisfy neither heathen nor English consciences, but the lower house refused to alter its decision, claiming that "the Unanimous Consent of the Virginians and the generall Impetuosity of the Whole feild" had forced Trueman to act as he did "to prevent a mutiny of the whole Army."

Some aspects of the incident, like others in the colonial period, evoke memories of My Lai during the Vietnam War. The Maryland upper house, in rejecting the reasoning of the lower house, noted that at Trueman's trial it too plainly appeared "that his first Commands for the killing of those Indians were not obeyed and that he had some difficulty to get his men To obey him therein and that after they were put to death not a man would owne to have had a hand in it. . . ."

Governor Berkeley's reaction was characteristic: "If they had killed my Grandfather and Grandmother, my father and Mother and all my friends, yet if they come to treat of Peace, they ought to have gone in Peace." He ordered another investigation, this one to determine whether the Virginians shared responsibility for the killings. The results seemed to exonerate Washington and his men. But by now the theft of a few hogs was involving the entire colony in a bitter conflict with a powerful nation of formerly friendly Indians.

The remaining Susquehannocks withstood the continuing siege of their fort by the combined Virginia-Maryland force. Then one night the Indians slipped out with their women and children, killing ten sleeping English guards on the way. Once free of the siege, they continued to take a calculated revenge upon the perfidious English. For the Indians, this revenge was not merely casual retribution for specific injustices. It represented a strong moral principle in Indian life. To fail to repay an injustice was not charity or mercy, but itself injustice.

In a raid on the outlying settlements along the Rappahannock and Potomac rivers, the Susquehannocks killed thirty-six people. Having thus exacted their vengeance, they sent a message to the governor asking why the Virginians, theretofore friends, had become such violent enemies. In the absence of appropriate restitution, the Susquehannocks noted, they had killed ten of the common English for each one of their chiefs, a

INDIAN CITADELS

CHAMPLAIN, SAMUEL DE, *Voyages et Descourertes*, 1620, JOHN CARTER BROWN LIBRARY, BROWN UNIVERSITY

This sketch by Samuel de Champlain shows his mixed force overwhelming an Iroquois palisade near the mouth of the Richelieu River.

CHAMPLAIN, SAMUEL DE, *Voyages et Descouvertes*, 1620, JOHN CARTER BROWN LIBRARY, BROWN UNIVERSITY

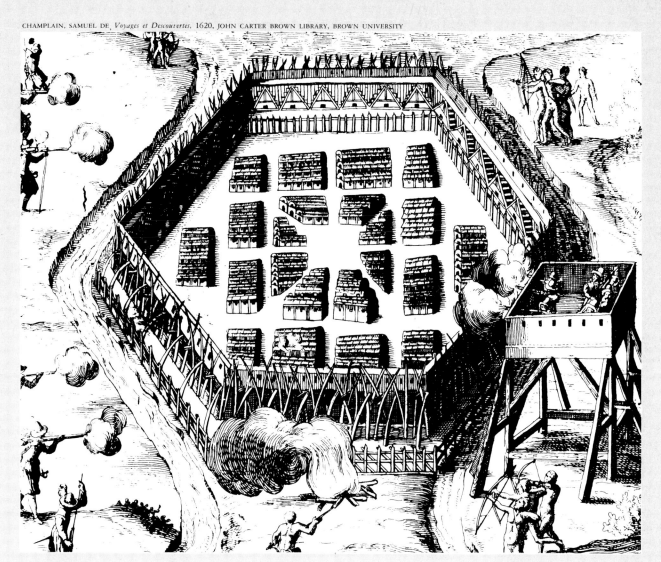

A rain of stones and "arrows thick as hail" threw back the Huron and French force assaulting this Iroquois fort near Lake Oneida.

Though most skirmishes in the Indian wars were fought wherever and however the hostile forces happened to meet, some warrior bands, when under attack, withdrew into redoubts like the Iroquois stockade opposite. Others fortified their villages or even constructed walled towns. The most common village fortification among eastern tribes was a stake fence of the type shown at right. It was a simpler version of the Pequot fort attacked and burned in Connecticut in 1637. Far more formidable was the palisaded Onondaga town above, whose thirty-foot walls and stout defenders held off a mixed force of French and Indians for some six days before the battered attackers abandoned the siege and limped home.

BRITISH MUSEUM

The Carolina Algonquian town of Pomeiock had one small break in its stockade.

After an Indian insurrection in 1644, the Virginia legislature issued medal passports "to be worn by the Indians when visiting settlements." This 1661 medal (above, the front; below, the back), the oldest one in existence, was worn by the chief of the Patomacs.

ratio they thought appropriate. Now they were willing to restore peace with the Virginians if the latter would compensate them for injuries inflicted and would withhold aid from the Marylanders. But the Susquehannock demand, however justified, was rejected by the English as derogatory "both to honour and intress." The war continued.

Berkeley now found near panic among outlying settlers. Though not yet affected by the war, they were terrified by rumors of wholesale slaughter in the northern reaches of the colony. When the governor's efforts to protect the colony by mobilizing militia failed to stem the fear, groups of colonists demanded more radical measures, requesting that they be allowed to form independent irregular forces. A proud and aging governor, given to command, did not take criticism the way a twentieth-century politician might. Frustrated in his attempts to make one such group see the importance of maintaining the regular military structure, Berkeley handed the would-be vigilantes their petition and "bid a pox take us."

At this explosive point, trouble built upon trouble with the appearance of a strange young demagogue named Nathaniel Bacon, a cousin of Berkeley's and a newcomer to the territory. One contemporary described him as "indifferent tall but slender, blackhair'd and of an ominous, pensive, melancholy Aspect, . . . of a most imperious and dangerous hidden Pride of heart. . . ." He was a proud, scornful man, and he hated Indians.

One day, while he was drinking with some of his companions and bemoaning the Indian attacks, he learned of a group of frontiersmen who, disgusted with Berkeley's cautious policies, wanted to march against the Indians. Bacon went to see the frontiersmen, and they promptly began urging him to join them. Flattered by the invitation and reckless with drink, Bacon agreed. In his acceptance were the roots of what was to become known as Bacon's Rebellion, the first significant revolt against royal authority in the New World—and an extension of the Indian campaign into a civil conflict.

In his subsequent unauthorized forays Bacon never came to grips with any Indians denominated "hostile" or "enemy" by the assembly. His victories—such as they were—were exclusively against Indians friendly to the colony. On his first outing he went to the island camp of the Occaneechi Indians, who lived along the Roanoke River near the present Virginia-North Carolina border, and told them he intended to fight the hostile Susquehannocks. The Occaneechis, knowing of a nearby encampment of Susquehannocks, offered to do the job for Bacon as a token of their friendship for the English. The Occaneechis returned with Susquehannock prisoners and captured furs and presented Bacon with the prisoners. Bacon demanded the booty as well and then tried to seize as slaves certain Manakin Indians who had helped the Occaneechis from within the Susquehannock camp.

When the Occaneechis refused this extraordinary and unjustified demand, Bacon's men attacked them, grabbed as much of the Occaneechi beaver skins and Susquehannock spoils as they could, and beat a hasty retreat to the English settlements. There they were received by the unthinking colonists as heroes, though, as Governor Berkeley put it, "that very action wherein [Bacon] so much boastes was Rashly foolish and as I am informed Treacherously carried to the dishonor of the English nation."

Berkeley sought to bring the young rebel to heel, but Bacon, after being captured and pardoned by the governor, returned to Jamestown with a rowdy army demanding that the assembly name him commander in chief of all the forces raised to fight the Indians.

Bacon stood before the State House and shouted, "God damne my Blood, I came for a commission, and a commission I will have before I goe." Berkeley appeared, denounced Bacon as a rebel before his men, and refused his demands. Bearing his breast to Bacon, the seventy-year-old governor contemptuously challenged him: "Here! Shoot me, foregod, fair Mark, Shoot."

There was no shooting, but Bacon's men eventually cocked their pieces and aimed at the burgesses who were leaning out of the windows of the assembly house watching the incredible contest of wills. "Dam my Bloud," cried Bacon, "I'le Kill Governr Councill Assembly and all." One of the terrified legislators began to wave his handkerchief, calling, "You shall have it, You shall have it," and soon the cowed assembly passed an act giving Bacon the authority he sought.

Thus commissioned, Bacon set out on his final sally, a raid against the queen of the Pamunkey Indians. This ruler was unswervingly loyal to the Crown, but she and her people were Indians, and that was sufficient provocation for Bacon. Fleeing his threatened attack, the queen led her tribe into the Great Dragon Swamp, between the Rappahannock and Potomac rivers. When her hiding place was discovered, she ordered her subjects to escape as best they could without raising a hand against the English. Some of them made it; the rest were killed or captured.

In the meantime, Governor Berkeley announced that Bacon's commission had been extorted and was therefore wholly illegal and once more declared him a rebel. When he got wind of Berkeley's most recent proclamation, Bacon broke off fighting Indians and turned his army against Jamestown, where he resorted to a stratagem for which southern gentlemen have never to this day been able to forgive him. He seized the wives of loyalist councilors and put them on the parapets to shield his men while they constructed siege lines. Aided by this screen of "white aprons" he took the city and put it to the torch.

Jamestown was eventually retaken by Berkeley's loyalists. Bacon died on October 26, 1676, of what was described as the "bloody Flux" and the "Lousey Disease; so that the swarmes of Vermyn that bred in his Body he could not destroy but by throwing his shirts into the Fire as often as he shifted himself." Upon his death, an "honest minister," as Berkeley described him, wrote this epitaph: "Bacon is Dead I am sorry at my hart / That lice and flux should take the hangman's part." His rebellion died with him, and shortly afterward there were English warships in the James River making sure that Bacon's followers would not again forget their proper allegiance.

The queen of Pamunkey was honored for her loyalty in the face of Bacon's assaults and given a frontlet inscribed with the name and royal arms of Charles II.

The Susquehannocks, having gained an unusually satisfying revenge against the Virginians, returned to their northern haunts, where, in the eighteenth century, they would fight a losing battle to maintain a footing in the great valley they had once dominated.

Governor Sir William Berkeley ruled Virginia for nearly thirty years until a rebellion led by a young cousin, Nathaniel Bacon, proved his undoing. King Charles II, displeased with Berkeley's handling of Bacon's Rebellion, recalled him to England. Berkeley died there shortly after his arrival, while preparing a brief that he hoped would justify his actions to the king.

A Murderous Clash of Cultures

When Europeans first came to the New World their confrontations
with the natives varied according to each nation's purposes. The
Spaniards were after booty and converts to Catholicism and pursued
each ruthlessly. Bartolomé de Las Casas, a dissident priest who
watched the Spanish burn this Cuban native chief alive in 1512,
wrote that during the ordeal the chief confessed that "he had
no mind to go to Heaven for fear of meeting with such cruel and
wicked company as they were; but would much rather go to Hell."

Eskimos in kayaks and atop the cliffs of Baffin Island attack English sailors searching for the Northwest Passage in 1577.

In March, 1621, the Pilgrims signed a treaty with the Wampanoags, shown greeting the newcomers in this symbolic painting.

While Spain plundered and proselytized in the New World, the English first concentrated on finding the Northwest Passage to the Indies. Although some of the early English explorers clashed with natives (left), most of their conflicts were with the crews of tempting Spanish treasure ships. When the English began to colonize early in the seventeenth century, however, the settlers were confronted by wary and powerful native forces. Jamestown and Plymouth colonists moved quickly to make peace and trade agreements with local Indians. But in truth, most Englishmen regarded the Indians as the "dregs of mankind" and tended to treat them accordingly—with predictable results (below).

John Smith seizes Pamunkey chief Opechanca-nough during a 1608 skirmish over trade. The chief yielded, and the shaky peace was saved.

*An Indian pleading "Come over and help us" forms the
centerpiece of Massachusetts Bay colony's 1675 seal.*

2: A New Golgotha

Captain John Smith, while prisoner on a French pirate ship in 1615, wrote *A Description of New England* about the bountiful land he had explored the previous year. Published in 1616, the book's title struck a responsive chord in English ears. So did Smith's description of the New England coast, which had previously been known more for its forbidding than its inviting character. Smith's New England coast was lined "all along [with] large corne fields, and great troupes of well proportioned people." When the Pilgrims, dissatisfied with the religious intolerance of the Old World, began to think of immigration to the New, Smith offered his services to them. They declined in order "to save charges," he noted, "saying my books and maps were much better cheape to teach them, than myselfe." By the time the Pilgrims had arrived on the New England shore most of the "corne fields and salvage gardens" were still there, but many of the natives had disappeared.

Of the approximately twenty-five thousand Indians living between the Penobscot River and Narragansett Bay, perhaps one third had succumbed to a series of mysterious plagues that struck in the years between Smith's voyage and the Pilgrims' landing. Smallpox, measles, and other European diseases to which the Indians lacked immunity had depopulated the land. The pious English interpreted this phenomenon as an expression of God's providential concern for His people. The real source of the providence was more likely the explorers and fishermen who had visited the coast since the beginning of the century and perhaps even before.

The natives were enslaved as well as infected. One brutal sea captain named Thomas Hunt, whom a contemporary dismissed as "a worthless fellow of our nation," kidnapped twenty-four friendly Indians during a voyage in 1614, took them to Málaga in southern Spain, and sold them into slavery. Through such contact the coastal societies were devastated and disillusioned. One observer of the destruction wrought by European diseases along the New England coast noted that "the bones and skulls . . . made such a spectacle . . . that, as I travailed in that Forrest nere the Massachusetts, it seemed to mee a new found Golgotha."

Not surprisingly, the decimated natives at first showed little sign of themselves near Plymouth. On the first Christmas Day at the colony the Pilgrims heard distant shouting and saw smoke rising some miles away. But when Miles Standish, the chief military man in the community, went to investigate, he found only empty huts.

Still, the Pilgrims, desperately weak from their voyage, lived in constant fear of attack. Their first real meeting with an Indian, however, was most amicable. The Plymouth leaders had gathered in March of 1621 to discuss defenses when "a certaine Indian came bouldly amongst them, and spoke to them in broken English, which they could well understand. . . ." This astonishing apparition was Samoset, a Maine Indian who had picked up the English tongue from coastal traders. The Pilgrim Fathers sat listening all afternoon and on into the night while he told them of the nearby tribes.

The natives nearest the Pilgrims were Wampanoags. Samoset left promising to return with some members of the tribe, and within a few days he was back with Massasoit, the grand sachem, or chief, of the Wampanoags, and an Indian named Tisquantum. This latter, whose name was shortened to Squanto by the Pilgrims, had been kidnapped, taken to England by a ship captain, and later returned to his native country. He was, in the words of Governor William Bradford, "a spetiall instrument sent of God for their good beyond their expectation." His English was even better than Samoset's, and he instructed the Pilgrims "how to set their corne, wher to take fish, and to procure other comodities, and was also their pilott to bring them to unknowne places for their profitt. . . ."

Squanto performed his first service to the colonists by arranging a treaty between them and Massasoit. In some pomp (a green carpet was laid on the ground for the comfort of the seated negotiators) the Pilgrims and Wampanoags agreed to avoid any injury to each other and to aid each other in repelling attacks by outside enemies.

The treaty proved a durable document. The peace it brought the Pilgrims allowed them to get their community firmly established and to learn something of the ways of their strange new allies. In 1621 the powerful Narraganset tribe sent the colony a bundle of arrows tied up in a rattlesnake skin, which Squanto interpreted as "a threatening and a challenge." Governor Bradford removed the arrows, filled the skin with powder and shot, and returned it to its owners with the message that if they wanted war, they were welcome to begin it when they pleased. The Narragansets backed down.

A harsher example of Pilgrim sternness came two years later, when

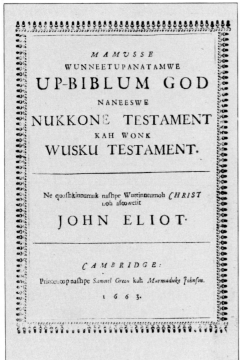

The Reverend John Eliot (right, a 1659 portrait) of the First Church of Roxbury was one of the few Puritans to take seriously the "royall intention" in the Massachusetts Bay charter: "To wynn the natives of the country to the knowledge and obedience of the onlie true God and Savior of mankinde." He established a settlement eighteen miles up the Charles River at Natick for converted "Praying Indians" and worked for ten years on his monumental Algonquian translation of the Bible (above, the title page).

Bradford got word of a planned attack on the settlement of Wessagusett, a new community up the coast from Plymouth. The colonists there were a seamy lot who had courted trouble by various abuses, including stealing corn from the neighboring Massachuset Indians. Nevertheless, the people of Wessagusett were Englishmen, and their fate was linked to that of the Pilgrims, so Plymouth sent Captain Standish to the settlement. There, under the guise of conferring with Witawamet, chief of the Massachusetts and the suspected ringleader of the rumored attack, Standish lured him and his tribesmen from the woods into the open. At a signal from Standish, the English immediately killed all the Indians except Witawamet's eighteen-year-old brother, whom they hanged a little later. The Massachusetts thus humbled, the Pilgrims took Witawamet's head back to Plymouth and mounted it on the wall of their fort, where it grinned a warning to all Indians who would conspire against Englishmen.

Standish's solution did not sit well with John Robinson, the spiritual mentor of the Pilgrims, who wrote from Holland, "Oh, how happy a thing had it been, if you had converted some before you killed any!" "Besides," he noted prophetically, "where blood is once begun to be shed, it is seldom staunched of a long time after." The behavior of the Pilgrims' military leader is reminiscent of the bullying tactics of Captain John Smith in Virginia. Thomas Prince, the eighteenth-century historian, observed that Standish "spread a Terror over all the Tribes of *Indians* round about him. . . ."

Whether Standish's tactics were harmful or helpful to the colony, Plymouth survived and prospered during its first decade of existence. In the next decade, however, major decisions relating to war and peace in New England would be taken out of Plymouth's hands by the dominance of the settlers who came in 1630 and founded the Massachusetts Bay colony. The "Great Migration" from Europe that began that year was under the leadership of well-educated and well-established men such as John Winthrop. In proportion to its population the Massachusetts Bay colony had more university graduates than England itself. Its aims were godly; its leaders shrewd. And it was powerful; by the middle of the decade there were eight thousand people living in Massachusetts Bay, while Plymouth had not grown beyond six hundred.

. Like their Plymouth counterparts, the Massachusetts Bay settlers landed in an area that had been cleared by the plague. Although welcomed by the surviving Indians, the new arrivals were frightened by reports of native cruelty. They feared men who, in their warfare, liked nothing more than to "tormente men in ye most bloodie maner that may be; fleaing some alive with ye shells of fishes, cutting of[f] ye members and joynts of others by peesmeale, and broiling on ye coals, eate ye collops of their flesh in their sight whilst they live; with other cruelties horrible to be related."

Fear of this sort of treatment was evident in the instructions that Captain John Endecott, the agent of the New England Company in the Massachusetts Bay colony, received from overseas. "We trust you will not be unmindful of the mayne end of our plantation by indevoringe to bring the Indians to the knowledge of the gospell," the communication began. But it concluded by reminding Endecott of the Virginia massacre, which had resulted from being "too confident of the ffidellitie of the salvages."

The Massachusetts colonists were anything but confident. When, for example, on an early spring night in 1631 a man in Watertown innocently fired his musket into the air to scare wolves away from his cattle, the whole colony went on alert. People who lived within earshot spread the alarm, and before morning drums were beating in Boston and settlers were grabbing for their weapons.

Into this atmosphere of anxiety and mistrust flowed a steady stream of new settlers. And as the colonists migrated away from the ordered settlements of the bay into the Connecticut valley, the causes of a future war began to take shape.

Most of the New England tribes were of the Algonquian linguistic family. Among those tribes were the Pequots (who with the Mohegan Indians were related to the Mahican Indians of the Hudson River area, whence they had originally come). By 1634 the Pequots, who jealously guarded their prerogatives against both the Narragansets on Narragansett Bay and the Dutch who had established trading posts up the Connecticut River, were confronted by English colonists in what the Pequots regarded as their domain along the lower reaches of the Connecticut valley.

Into this volatile situation sailed one Captain John Stone. A coastal trader, Stone had managed to make himself unwelcome in every settle-

BACQUEVILLE. *Histoire de L'Amerique Septentrionale*, 1722

The first Indian nun in North America was Tekakwitha, a Mohawk converted by French Jesuits. Loyal to her new faith in spite of persecution by her own people, she served them under the name "Lily of the Mohawks."

ment north of Virginia. He had tried to steal a ship in New Amsterdam, had drawn a knife on the governor of Plymouth, had spoken "contemptuously . . . and lewdly" to officials in Massachusetts Bay, and had still found time along the way to be charged with drunkenness and adultery. With that gaudy record, Stone might as easily have been done in by white men as red. Unfortunately it turned out to be the latter. One day while his ship was riding at anchor at the mouth of the Connecticut River a band of Indians — not Pequots but members of a tribe dominated by the Pequots — swarmed aboard and massacred all hands.

Though Stone was a highly unsatisfactory martyr, English blood had been spilled, and the Massachusetts Bay authorities demanded that the Pequots surrender the murderers to English justice. Already at war with the Narragansets and Dutch, the Pequots found it prudent to be conciliatory toward this potential third enemy. They agreed to a treaty by which they promised to hand over Stone's murderers along with a heavy indemnity. At the same time, Pequot spokesmen insisted that Stone's killers had acted in retaliation for the murder of their chief, who had been kidnapped by a white trader and sent back dead after his ransom was paid. Whether the original deed had been committed by the Dutch or the English — the Pequots asserted that they could not tell one European from another — the Indians' act of retaliation was at worst a tragic misunderstanding for which the Pequots begged pardon and offered reimbursement.

The new treaty failed to avert war. The Indians paid part of the indemnity but reported that those of Stone's assassins who remained alive had fled and could not be taken. In July, 1636, word came that another trading captain named Oldham had been killed by natives off Block Island. Again the killers were not Pequots. Block Island was inhabited by Narragansets, but the English managed to include the Pequots in their plan of retaliation. Although Canonicus and Miantonomo, the Narraganset leaders, were quick to condemn and make reparations for the Block Island murder and pledged neutrality in the dispute with the Pequots, the Bay colony ordered Captain Endecott to take a force of ninety colonists and put to the sword all the men on Block Island. Once the Block Island males had been exterminated and the women and children taken for slaves, Endecott was to sail to Pequot territory on the Connecticut River, where some of the murderers of Oldham were rumored to have fled, and demand the killers of both Stone and Oldham along with a thousand fathoms of wampum for reparation.

Endecott carried out his orders with merciless efficiency. His men tracked down the few Block Islanders they could find and, disappointed at running out of Indians to kill, chopped up the natives' pet dogs. Leaving the ravaged island behind him, Endecott then sailed for Saybrook, at the mouth of the Connecticut River, where stood a fort manned by Connecticut settlers.

Lieutenant Lion Gardiner, commanding the fort, received Endecott sullenly. "You come hither," Gardiner complained, "to raise these wasps about my ears, and then you will take wing and flee away." Ignoring Gardiner's protests, Endecott sailed a few miles northeast to Pequot Harbor at the mouth of the Pequot (now Thames) River, where the Indians greeted him warmly, crying, "What cheer, Englishmen, what cheer, what do you come for?" When Endecott told them, the Pequot emissary sent to determine his purpose begged him to wait until the Pequot chiefs arrived on

Among the many tribes that resisted conversion by European missionaries, the Iroquois were particularly vengeful toward French Jesuits. In this detail from a composite engraving of Iroquois murders, they work their slow torture on Jean de Brébeuf, a missionary to the Hurons whom they kidnapped and murdered in 1649.

the scene so that the matter could be discussed in peace. Endecott, professing to see the Pequot request as a stratagem to deceive him, refused all demands for parley and "spent the day burning and spoyling the Countrey."

His job done, Endecott sailed away, leaving Lieutenant Gardiner to watch his own prediction come true. The Pequots, having tried to avoid a fatal confrontation, now saw that the English intended to start a war. They came in force and invested the little fort at Saybrook, where they "made many proud challenges, and dared them out to fight." A party from the fort went out, was nearly surrounded, and got back only with difficulty. One group of settlers fared worse. Three were killed outright, one was roasted to death, and one came floating past the fort a few days later with an arrow in his eye. Gardiner readied his works for a siege.

The Pequots, on their part, prepared for the war that was obviously coming by sending ambassadors to urge the Narragansets to join them against the English. Massachusetts Bay got wind of the Pequot embassy and sent to Rhode Island begging help from the clergyman Roger Williams, who was famous for his rapport with the natives. Williams had not long before been expelled from Massachusetts for his heretical teachings, and he must have taken a sour pleasure in the request. Nevertheless he responded nobly, at once setting out by canoe for Narraganset headquarters. "Three days and nights," he wrote, "my business forced me to lodge and mix with the bloody Pequot ambassadors, whose hands and arms, methought, wreaked with the blood of my countrymen . . . and from whom I could not but nightly look for their bloody knives at my own throat also."

The Pequot spokesman insisted that if the Narragansets sided with the English, the English were sure to turn on them once the Pequots were out of the way. But Miantonomo, the chief of the Narragansets, had no love for the Pequots, and Williams prevailed upon him to reject the Pequot offer and ally himself with the English against them. Not long afterward, in March of 1637, the Narragansets formalized the treaty with a gift to the Bay colony—forty fathoms of wampum and a Pequot hand.

Late in April two hundred Pequots attacked a group of colonists who were working in a field near Weathersfield, up the Connecticut River from the Saybrook fort. Nine settlers, a woman and child among them, were killed. The Indians paddled past the fort with the clothing of the murdered settlers held up on poles in a grim parody of English sailing ships.

While Massachusetts Bay and Plymouth worked to coordinate their attacks on the Pequots, Connecticut forces under Captain John Mason of Windsor, an able soldier who had seen action campaigning with the English in the Lowlands, were the first in the field.

On May 10 Mason set out from Hartford with ninety colonists and sixty Mohegans (a splinter group related to the Pequots but allied with the English) under Chief Uncas. The English were a little nervous about the loyalty of these Indian allies, but Uncas soon reassured them. No sooner had he reached the Saybrook fort than the Mohegan chief attacked a nearby Pequot party and returned with four heads and one prisoner. According to a contemporary account, the captive scornfully "braved the *English,* as though they durst not kill a *Pequot.*" Mason's soldiers disabused the prisoner of this idea by tying one of his legs to a post and, manning a

SCHOOLCRAFT, HENRY, *Indian Tribes of the United States*, 1857

Chippewa and Fox Indians battle for control of Lake Superior. By the late 1660's the Chippewas dominated the lake.

SEAMEN IN WAR PAINT

Sleekly muscled, war-painted, galloping across plains on lean ponies, moving stealthily through deep green pine forests: this is how the popular imagination saw the American Indian. When he was associated with water at all, he was usually envisioned paddling a frail-looking canoe down a sun-dappled stream.

In fact, many American Indians were more at ease on water than on horseback. And they ventured onto every conceivable body of water—including the oceans. Indeed, Indian seafarers produced the New World's first navies and its first true admirals—men who came to be respected and even feared by able British sailors.

The Indians of the East Coast and Great Lakes were accomplished seamen long before the first English settlers arrived in Virginia, Maine, Massachusetts, and Newfoundland in their great sailing ships at the beginning of the sixteenth century. They learned the sea and the lakes

and their ways because they had to in order to survive. Hunters of land animals in the winter when such game was easily tracked and killed, these Indians had to turn to the water in the summer for food.

Time not spent providing food was used to wage war—a brutal pastime that developed the aboriginal navies into formidable fighting forces. Indians quickly learned that they could strike enemy villages with almost total surprise if they attacked by boat. Frequently back-and-forth raids of this sort touched off naval battles involving hundreds of shallow-draft canoes, each having a complement of warriors who seemed to defy the laws of gravity as they stood erect to shower arrows on one another.

It was these maritime Indians that colonists encountered when they sought to establish themselves along the East Coast. In their first brushes with the invaders, the Indians relied primarily on surprise

attacks. A good example of such tactics occurred in 1631 when swarms of canoes slipped into Massachusetts Bay at night, disgorged at dawn war-painted "marines" who sacked and burned the settlements, then slipped back to the birchbark fleet and escaped before a counterattack could be mounted.

The English retaliated by destroying Indian villages and crops and by fortifying their own outlying towns. As warfare with the whites intensified, the Indian navy men adopted portions of the white technology. Some canoes sprouted crude hide sails and wooden tillers, which together provided more maneuverability and in some cases enabled the Indians to strike more quickly at their enemies.

In time the Indians even took on the role of privateer, preying on English ships, some of which were captured on the high seas. A New England Indian named Mugg excelled at this form of warfare to

PEABODY MUSEUM OF SALEM

Penobscots built this bark canoe, the oldest in existence, early in the 1800's.

such a degree that the English dubbed him "Rogue Mugg."

Mugg was a brilliant naval strategist and ship handler, a sort of Indian Nelson who feared neither the English nor their cannon-armed ships. While King Philip's War raged to the south, Mugg's attacks on towns and shipping climaxed in 1676 when he sacked the present-day Maine settlement of Black Point. That deed done, Mugg lay in wait as a thirty-ton English ketch approached the ruins. When the ship's crew disembarked as a landing party, a contingent of Mugg's warriors pinned them down ashore, while another group of Indians in a canoe slipped up to the ketch and cut its anchor line. As the empty ketch drifted away, Mugg put aboard a prize crew, sailed off, and

LAHONTAN, BARON DE, *New Voyages to North America*, 1703, RARE BOOK DIVISION, NEW YORK PUBLIC LIBRARY

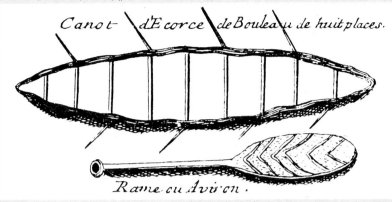

Canot d'Ecorce de Bouleau de huit places.

Rame ou Aviron.

A 1684 diagram shows a paddle and paddlers' positions in an Iroquois canoe.

rogue admiral intended, according to a contemporary account, to blockade and "burn Boston."

Although Mugg did attack the fishing towns, he was killed during a skirmish. His death did not end

THOMAS GILCREASE INSTITUTE OF HISTORY AND ART, TULSA

Warriors adapted the white man's sail to their war canoes.

proceeded to lay up his captive ketch for the winter.

The ketch became the nucleus of a small but formidable navy that also included two smaller armed craft called scallops (each of which could carry eighty men) and several other boats. With this force Mugg planned to sweep through the Massachusetts fishing communities in the spring, capture more vessels, and with an overwhelming fleet destroy the coastal trade. Then the

the naval war, however. In the following months thirteen English ketches were seized around Salem alone by other so-called tawnies, whom the proud English hated to concede capable of such feats. The worst humiliation, however, was yet to come.

In 1724 two English men-of-war sailing off the coast of New Hampshire engaged an Indian-manned schooner that had "driven the Fishermen from the Sea." The Indian

captain deftly sailed between the English warships and then "crossed the T"—the classic naval maneuver whereby one ship crosses the bow of its enemy in order to bring the full force of broadside cannon to bear. A single shot felled one English ship's captain, mate, and two seamen, while another carried away the man-of-war's mainsheet and shrouds, thereby disabling it. Having pulled the beard of the best the English had to offer, the Indian captain sailed away and—despite English efforts to hush up the embarrassing episode—into history. His victory was the high point in the naval history of the eastern Indians, who, lacking the technology to build ships to compete with the English navy, were gradually dominated by superior force.

WILLIAM L. CLEMENTS LIBRARY, UNIVERSITY OF MICHIGAN

Hurons build a canoe early in the 1700's.

rope tied to the other leg, tearing him to pieces. Captain John Underhill arrived on the scene with a small contingent of Massachusetts soldiers in time to dispatch the terribly maimed captive with a pistol shot.

Mason and Underhill joined forces and moved against the main settlement of the Pequots. Though Mason was under orders to launch an amphibious assault against the chief Indian fort on Pequot Harbor, he decided that such a move was too risky. Instead, he proposed a flanking maneuver against a second Pequot fort up the coast on the Mystic River; this would allow the English to sail past the main stronghold and debark in Narraganset territory, where native allies could be recruited to help in the attack.

The English obtained six hundred Narraganset and Eastern Niantic warriors under a chieftain named Ninigret for the expedition. Though some of the latter melted away as the army moved toward the fort, Mason still had a strong force when he approached the Pequot camp on the evening of May 25. Mason asked the nervous Narragansets to remain in an outer circle around the fort while the English undertook to show them how Englishmen could fight. The captain and his men went to sleep that night listening to the Pequots noisily celebrating the arrival of a hundred fifty warriors who had just come in from outlying villages to help fight the English.

Mason stormed the fort at dawn. The English forces crept to within a few feet of the palisades, fired a hasty volley, and swarmed inside through the two entrances at opposite ends of the camp. Though taken by surprise, the Pequots fought fiercely and stubbornly, "with a resolution that would have done honour to Romans," as the historian Benjamin Trumbull later put it. As the struggle continued, Mason abandoned his plan to seize the camp intact for its booty, grabbed a firebrand, and set it aflame. As the eighty closely packed huts, which housed eight hundred Indians, went up in smoke, the Pequots poured out of the stockade to meet death from English and Narraganset swords and muskets. Others — hundreds of them — remained huddled inside the huts and were burned, women and children, old and young, "in promiscuous ruin."

The massacre was over in half an hour. According to Underhill, his Narraganset allies were appalled by the ferocity of the settlers. "*Mach it, mach it,*" they cried, "it is naught, it is naught, because it is too furious, and slaies too many men." Something of the shock the Narragansets must have felt at this glimpse of how the settlers waged war is indicated by Underhill's assessment of native tactics. "They come not near one another," he wrote, "but shoot remote, and not point-blank, as we often do with our bullets, but at rovers, and then they gaze up into the sky to see where the arrow falls, and not until it is fallen do they shoot again. This fight is more for pastime, than to conquer and subdue enemies. . . . They might fight seven years and not kill seven men."

The English suffered only slight losses in the attack — two men killed and about twenty wounded. Behind the English terror tactics was a theological imperative. "*In a word,*" as Captain Mason put it, "the Lord *was as it were pleased to say unto us,* The Land of Canaan will I give unto thee tho' but few and strangers in it. . . ." Underhill found the justification equally simple: citing David's war, he noted that "we had sufficient light from the word of God for our proceedings."

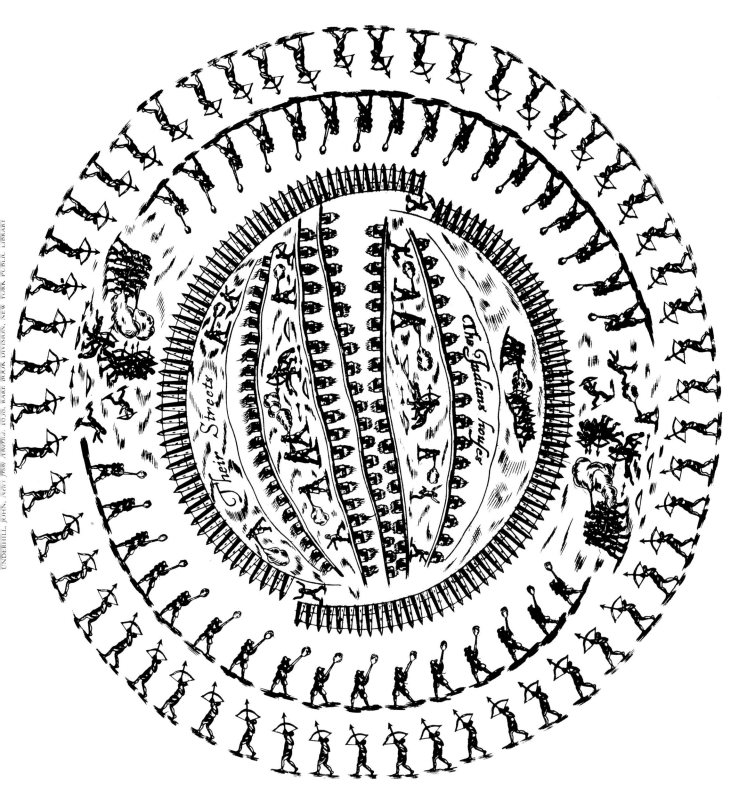

A year after a 1637 massacre of Pequots at their fort near the Mystic River in Connecticut, English captain John Underhill published this woodcut to show how he and Captain John Mason had carried out the slaughter. Surrounding the fort with soldiers and Narraganset allies, they set it afire, trapping some 800 Pequot men, women, and children. Those who escaped were picked off by the ring of besiegers. Shocked by the incident, William Bradford, governor of Plymouth colony, wrote that "it was a fearfull sight to see them thus frying in the fyer, and the streams of blood quenching the same, and horrible was the stinck and sente of her."

CHAOS IN NEW NETHERLAND

Of all the Europeans who swarmed into seventeenth-century America, the Dutch were the most pragmatic in their approach to the aborigines. To be sure, like their fellow colonizers, the English Puritans and Spanish Catholics, they gave lip service to the ideal of "Christianizing the savages." But the burghers of the Dutch West Indies Company were far more interested in making money.

In pursuit of this goal, they established friendly relations with the Indians shortly after their arrival on Manhattan Island in 1624. By the third decade of the seventeenth century the fur trade with these Indians had made the little colony of New Netherland and its capital, New Amsterdam, one of the most powerful European footholds in the New World.

This productive tranquillity was to be short-lived, however. In 1637 an incompetent sop named Wouter Van Twiller was replaced as governor of New Netherland by one Willem Kiefft. As it turned out, Kiefft was an even worse administrator than Van Twiller. The new governor's idea of dealing with the Indians was to extort from them a levy of corn, wampum, and especially fur for the "protection" afforded by New Amsterdam.

This protection was sadly wanting, for in February, 1643, an inebriated Kiefft ordered the execution of eighty peaceful Wappinger Indians who had sought sanctuary on nearby Staten Island from marauding Mohawks. The governor is reported to have "laughed right heartily" as New Amsterdam matrons used the severed heads of Indian men, women, and children for a grisly game of kickball.

The mutilated Wappingers were the lucky victims. A captive from another tribe was publicly skinned, then forced to eat his own flesh. He continued to wail his death chant even as his captors castrated him, ceasing his song only when soldiers bashed his brains out with clubs.

News of these atrocities spread quickly among the tribes surrounding New Amsterdam. They attacked and burned outlying Dutch villages, slaughtering settlers who knew nothing of Kiefft's butchery. Then the Indians struck New Amsterdam itself, prompting the town's defenders to throw up a wall along a street at its north end (today's Wall Street in lower Manhattan). Only with the help of English volunteers were the fifty Dutch militiamen able to drive off the attackers.

Hundreds of Indians were killed in this battle and subsequent fighting—seven hundred in one attack on a Westchester encampment in 1644. But despite such military successes, New Amsterdam's entrepreneurs and their directors back in Holland were growing weary of a war that was costing them their lucrative fur trade.

Finally, in August, 1645, Kiefft was replaced as governor of New Netherland by a peg-legged soldier of fortune named Peter Stuyvesant. Stuyvesant managed to secure an uneasy peace with the Indians, enabling New Amsterdam's merchants to pursue once more their profitable bartering for furs.

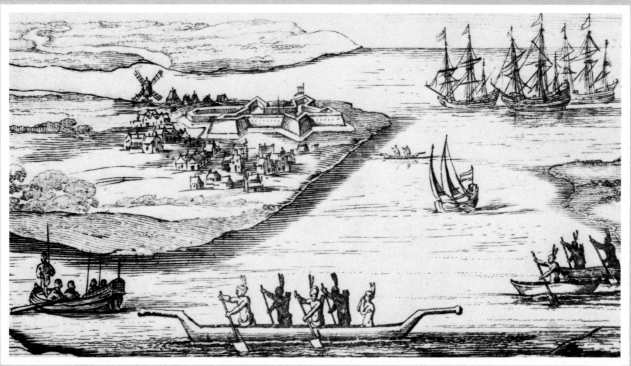

The earliest known view of New Amsterdam shows Indians in fur-laden canoes heading for Manhattan to trade during the 1630's.

Stunned by the total victory of the English, the remaining Pequots in the area fled, led by Sassacus, their sachem. But they were slowed down by women and children, and the pursuing English trapped them in a swamp near New Haven. Old men, women, and children were allowed to come out unmolested. Eighty warriors refused to surrender and tried to break through the English cordon on July 14. Twenty of them made it; the rest retreated back into the swamp. When the colonists went in to ferret them out, they found the natives huddled close together on the ground. The English charged their muskets with ten or twelve balls apiece and tore apart the beaten Indians at close range.

Among those who had escaped was Sassacus, but there was no sanctuary for him or his followers. Other tribes, getting word of what the white soldiers could do, were quick to send the victors Pequot heads in hopes of placating them. Sassacus's head arrived early in August, sent by the Mohawks he had approached for asylum.

The few beaten remnants of the tribe sued for peace, which they got on harsh terms. The Treaty of Hartford, signed on September 21, 1638, stipulated that they be divided as vassals among the settlers' Indian allies: eighty to Uncas and his Mohegans; eighty to Miantonomo and his Narragansets; twenty to Ninigret and his Niantics. The name of the tribe was to be erased from the lexicon even of the surviving Pequots, who were forced to assume the identity of their new hosts and denied the right to live in their old homeland. In the same treaty the English, now in a position of dominance, forbade the Mohegans and Narragansets to war against each other without the permission of the colonists.

In the first few years after the end of the Pequot War rumors kept cropping up—frequently emanating from Uncas—which implied that the Narragansets were plotting with the Mohawks or by themselves against the English. In 1640 Miantonomo was called to Boston to be examined and to prove his innocence. He was denied the right to bring Roger Williams as his interpreter—Williams was still under a decree of banishment—and was forced to speak to Governor Thomas Dudley through a Pequot interpreter. Miantonomo was outraged; unlike Uncas he regarded himself as a prince, subordinate to the king of England but not at the beck and call of every colonial governor.

The unpleasantness passed for the moment, only to surface again in 1642 when Connecticut heard rumors of a conspiracy against the English in which Miantonomo was again the prime suspect. Governor Winthrop of Massachusetts Bay admitted that such reports were made almost yearly and had invariably proved to be "raised up by the opposite factions among the Indians." Yet in the climate of fear that existed, no rumors could be discounted. The proud Miantonomo was again summoned to Boston, where, Winthrop noted, in his answers "he was very deliberate and showed good understanding in the principles of justice and equity, and ingenuity withal." But Miantonomo was not content to be submissive and accept the English acknowledgment that the accusations against him were false. "He demanded that his accusers might be brought forth, to the end, that if they could not make good what they had charged him with, they might suffer what he was worthy of, and must have expected, if he had been found guilty, viz., death." The Massachusetts leaders declined to give him satisfaction on this score, though they did dissuade the Connecticut men from starting a war that would have brought trouble down on all the colonies. The arms of some of the neighboring Indian nations were temporarily confiscated, and a number of hostages seized, but war was averted.

In 1643 a fight broke out between Uncas's Mohegans and the Narragansets, and Miantonomo was captured. The Narragansets offered to ransom him. Always careful to cultivate the English authorities, Uncas asked for their advice. After mature deliberation, the commissioners of the United Colonies (representatives of Massachusetts Bay, Connecticut, Plymouth, and New Haven who met after 1643 to coordinate their policy toward the Indians) authorized Uncas to put Miantonomo to death, but in his own jurisdiction and without undue cruelty. So, as Uncas's men led Miantonomo through the woods outside Hartford on their way home one of them dispatched the Narraganset leader with a blow from behind. Historian Charles McLean Andrews was to call the act a "cold-blooded murder . . . for which the colony [of Connecticut] must always bear the blame."

Pressure now increased upon the Narragansets, who continued to protest their innocence of all charges of plots and conspiracies. Their stubbornly independent attitude continued to annoy the colonial authorities. The Narraganset sachems, Pessicus and Canonicus, "having ourselves been the chief Sachems, or Princes successively, of the country, time out of mind," protested their frequent summonses to appear before the Boston magistrates. They noted that "neither yourselves nor we are to be judges; and both of us are to have recourse, and repair unto that [the king's] honorable and just Government."

In July of 1645, on the occasion of yet another outbreak of violence between the Narragansets and Uncas, the United Colonies voted to raise an army against the Narragansets. Under the threat of colonial preparations for war the Narragansets gave in, and by a treaty of August 28, 1645, they acknowledged their guilt for various misdeeds, paid an indemnity, and granted their claim to all the Pequots' old country to the English colonies.

Following the humbling of the Narragansets, there was a lull in New England's warring with the native inhabitants. But when trouble inevitably came again, it came in torrents the settlers could scarcely have imagined, and from their old friends the Wampanoags.

Chief Massasoit, the staunch ally of the Pilgrims, died in 1661 at the ripe age of eighty-one. He was succeeded by his son Alexander, who was at once ordered to Plymouth by the governor there to acknowledge his loyalty. He went reluctantly, trudging through the heat of midsummer, and was sick by the time he arrived. On the way home he died. Among the many Indians who believed that Alexander had been poisoned was his twenty-four-year-old brother, the new chief of the Wampanoags. His Indian name was Metacom, but the English called him King Philip.

Philip was summoned to Plymouth and Boston too frequently for his liking. At one point he told the English in exasperation: "Your governor is but a subject. I shall treat only with my brother, King Charles of England. When he comes, I am ready." But Philip was unable to sustain his independent stance. Plymouth, for example, insisted that he obtain the colony's consent before he disposed of any of his land; Philip insisted on his right to sell land as he chose. Suspicions rose rapidly on both sides, with the hot-tempered Philip becoming more and more convinced that the Plymouth settlers were planning a war against him, and the settlers equally fearful

WHITE MAN'S ARMS

For fifty years after the white man's arrival in North America, his superiority over the Indian in weaponry applied only in rare pitched battles, where the sword and matchlock firearms could be effectively used against a massed foe. In the guerrilla fights of Virginia and New England forests, however, these weapons proved inadequate. The musket was so heavy that it had to be supported in a forked rest (above), took two full minutes to load, and misfired about three times in ten. Moreover, the "match" of burning hemp used to light the gunpowder went out in rain or wind—and made the musketeer an easy target at night. Even the pistol took almost a minute to fire and, lacking a sight, was notoriously difficult to aim.

By the mid-1660's New Englanders had imported enough new flintlocks to gain an edge over the enemy. Set off by the scraping of flint on steel, these weapons could fire two shots per minute and misfired only one time in ten.

Seventeenth-century arms, from the left: Plymouth colonist's flintlock; Indian fighter Benjamin Church's sword; powder flask; brass-barreled pistol; ceremonial halberd from John Alden's home

MASSACHUSETTS HISTORICAL SOCIETY

PILGRIM SOCIETY, PLYMOUTH

PILGRIM SOCIETY, PLYMOUTH

that the Wampanoags were plotting against them.

Early in January of 1675 John Sassamon, a Harvard-educated Indian whom one contemporary described as a "very cunning and plausible" man, "well skilled in the English language," was found dead beneath the ice of a pond near Plymouth. The colony coroner ruled that Sassamon had been the victim of foul play, though others believed that the bruises around his neck could have been caused when he slipped through the ice. Three Wampanoags were haled into Plymouth colony court, found guilty of murder, and executed. Two of them vigorously protested their innocence before their execution. The other, hopeful of a reprieve when the rope with which he was being hanged broke during his execution, charged Philip with killing Sassamon as part of a plot against the English.

Philip was furious at the Plymouth authorities for taking into their own hands a matter he regarded as strictly a Wampanoag concern. Brought before the Pilgrim authorities, he behaved haughtily. Since his involvement could not be proved and since no evidence of any hostility toward the English could be demonstrated, he was dismissed. Though guarding his irritation at the time, Philip was outraged. Some contemporary observers concluded that his so-called conspiracy stemmed from his desire to revenge himself on the English at this time.

Philip's sense of grievance was aggravated as he reflected on the fact that when the English first came, his father had been a great man and the English as a "little child," yet Massasoit had protected them from other Indians, given them land and corn, and showed them how to plant. Now, Philip noted, the English had a hundred times more land than the Wampanoags and treated them with contempt.

A proud and aggrieved man, Philip had sought to preserve the Wampanoags' independent status as established in the original treaty between his father and the first Pilgrim settlers. His efforts had become increasingly futile as the English forced him to bend to their laws and as the several colonies asserted jurisdiction over portions of his domain. Philip's was the unenviable position of several Indian leaders before him — and many after — whose options were limited to self-destruction either by acquiescence or by resistance.

Shortly after Sassamon's accused murderers were executed, the Wampanoag sachem, fearing that the English intended to destroy him, readied his nation for war. As tensions mounted, some of the whites in the outlying settlements abandoned their farms for the safety of Plymouth; others stayed behind. In Swansea, one of these semideserted villages, some scavenging Indians, appropriating property left by fleeing owners, were fired upon by settlers who had remained. One Indian was killed. The first blood was thus drawn by the English, not by the Indians. The natives went to the local garrison and asked why the colonists had shot their fellow tribesman. The English wanted to know whether he had died. When the Indians, hoping that the settlers might attempt to make amends for the incident, answered that he had, a lad of the garrison replied that the death was of no consequence. The Indians, furious, went away and the next day killed the Englishman who had shot the Indian, his father, and five other settlers. The war had now begun in earnest — but not as the result of a conspiracy on the part of either Indians or English. The events of the struggle show that Philip was hardly masterminding a campaign to drive the English into the sea; his actions were haphazard and inexplicable except as reactions to circumstances beyond his control.

Plymouth forces rapidly moved into King Philip's homeland of Mount Hope, a thin, rocky peninsula that stretched into Narragansett Bay. Among the officers commanding the Plymouth soldiers was a thirty-five-year-old captain named Benjamin Church. This was a stroke of good fortune for the colonists, for Church was that rare creature, a trained soldier who was at once intelligent and flexible.

Moving his men onto the peninsula, Church discovered that the Indians had melted away, probably east across the bay to the Pocasset country. Some of the soldiers interpreted their departure as a great victory for colonial arms. A grand council was held, and its members resolved to build a fort on the peninsula to hold the ground they had won. Church disagreed, urging a campaign of rapid pursuit. "The enemy were not really beaten out of *Mount-hope* Neck," he wrote, "though 'twas true they fled from thence; yet it was before any pursued them. It was but to strengthen themselves, and to gain a more advantagious post."

With their dubious victory behind them, the Massachusetts and Plymouth contingents split up. The Massachusetts men marched west to investigate rumors that some Wampanoags had taken refuge with the Narragansets. Arriving in the Narraganset territory of western Rhode Island, the Massachusetts troops on July 15 forced some of the minor leaders of the tribe to sign a treaty requiring them to hand over any Wampanoags they were sheltering and to confirm grants of their land to the English. Then, convinced that the Narragansets had been coerced into good behavior once and for all, many of the Massachusetts men marched to rejoin the Plymouth forces, which had finally located Philip's men in the Pocasset swamp country, across the bay from Mount Hope.

Before the Massachusetts contingent arrived, however, three dozen men under Captain Matthew Fuller and Benjamin Church landed on the Pocasset shore after crossing the bay in boats from Rhode Island. Prior to settling down for the night, the force split into two groups in hopes of catching the Indians in an ambush. But, as Church wrote in disgust, men in Fuller's detachment, "being troubled with the epidemical plague of lust after tobacco, must needs strike fire to smoke it." An enemy party saw the lights and ran off. The next morning Church was further annoyed when the soldier in charge of provisions explained that he had somehow contrived to leave all the rations behind.

Grumbling, Church's men went forward with empty stomachs. Before long they came to the edge of an abandoned vegetable garden, where they were greeted by a powerful volley of musketry. The startled soldiers saw that the ground above them "seemed to move, being covered over with Indians, with their bright guns glittering in the sun, and running in a circumference with a design to surround them."

Greatly outnumbered, Church fell back to the shore, where his men threw up a hasty breastwork, took cover behind it, and commenced to fight a savage battle that lasted all through the hot afternoon. With dusk coming on and their powder running low, many of the soldiers thought themselves as good as dead. But just then salvation appeared in the form of a sloop from Rhode Island, which ran down toward them and pulled them off their desperate beachhead.

INDIAN ARMS

Before the arrival of the white man the Indians had no steel or iron weapons, and for 350 years afterward their arms were an odd mixture of stone-age and modern technology. Once tribes felt firsthand the effects of the flintlock, they made it a high-priority demand in trade agreements with whites, and many New Englanders traded the guns—or sold them outright for personal profit—before seeing the error of their ways. Warriors who could not get their hands on a firearm continued to use the bow and arrow, a weapon that some may even have preferred for its ability to let fly a barrage of shots in quick succession. To make arrows more damaging on impact, Indians sharpened the stone or bone—and later iron or steel—heads and fastened them loosely to the shaft so that they would remain in the wound. For hand-to-hand combat, they converted bayonets into knives and hatchets into war tomahawks and began attaching metal blades to weapons of their own devising.

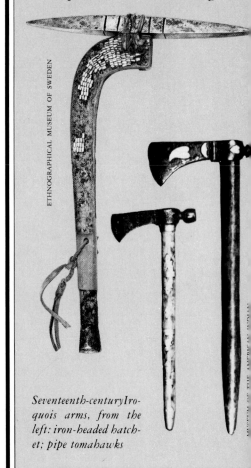

ETHNOGRAPHICAL MUSEUM OF SWEDEN

Seventeenth-century Iroquois arms, from the left: iron-headed hatchet; pipe tomahawks

Left to right: Bayonet-knife captured in 1675; Mahican war club with metal blade; Iroquois wooden war club

A few days later, on July 19, Church went back into the Pocasset swamp, now accompanied by the newly arrived Massachusetts men. After a long, wearing fight the English drew back, leaving seven or eight dead behind them. They had failed to dislodge Philip's men and, as one contemporary observer put it, had learned a costly lesson about "how dangerous it is to fight in such dismal Woods, when their Eyes were muffled with the Leaves, and their Arms pinioned with the thick Boughs of the Trees, as their Feet were continually shackled with the Roots spreading every Way in those boggy Woods. It is ill fighting with a wild Beast in his own Den."

Once the English had withdrawn from the half light of the swamp, they settled down to surround the area, hoping that Philip would come out and surrender. Instead he escaped, and the war, which had thitherto been confined to the region adjacent to the Wampanoag homeland, spread throughout New England.

Early in August Indians attacked the isolated town of Brookfield, Massachusetts. The settlers barricaded themselves in a house while, one of them wrote, "they did roar against us like so many wild bulls, sending in their shot amongst us till towards the moon rising, which was about three of the clock; at which time they attempted to fire our house by hay and other combustible matter. . . . They continued shooting and shouting . . . scoffing at our prayers as they were sending in their shot upon all quarters. . . ." The terrified settlers were besieged for forty-eight hours before English troopers galloped in to save them.

Often English nervousness brought previously peaceful tribes into Philip's "conspiracy." In September, for instance, Captain Samuel Moseley was sent to protect the area near the Merrimack River on Massachusetts's northern frontier and to determine the attitude of the local Indians. As they pressed up the Merrimack valley he and his men entered the territory of the Pennacooks, who had long been firm friends of the English. Fearing a confrontation, Wannalancet, their sachem, withdrew his tribesmen to the north. Moseley managed to construe this retreat as a sign of guilt and put a Pennacook village to the torch. Wannalancet refused to strike back, anxious to avoid bloodshed that might lead to more serious consequences for his people.

In the Connecticut valley similar English suspicions led to attempts to disarm the Indians who lived in a camp near the village of Hatfield. Ordered by the local authorities to turn in their arms on August 24, the Indians slipped away from their camp and headed north. Pursued and overtaken between Hatfield and Deerfield, the Indians refused to surrender to the uncertain mercies and intentions of the colonists. In the fight that followed, nine English were killed, and the Indians resumed their journey north.

The Connecticut authorities, who had cautioned the men of Massachusetts against alienating the Narragansets in July, were equally annoyed at the excessive demands of the Massachusetts men on the Indians of the Connecticut valley, which, they believed, helped to precipitate and spread the war in the area.

Even the most harmless natives fell under suspicion. "Praying Indians," Christian converts who lived in villages near the Puritan settlements, were constantly threatened. When the authorities placed John Hoar of Concord in charge of one band of loyal Indians, he found it necessary to build a workhouse for them and to lock them in at night for their own protection. But the edgy colonists were not satisfied and forced the unoffending Indians into exile on the bleak, barren, storm-lashed islands in Boston Harbor. Soon there were four hundred natives on Deer Island alone, grubbing out a miserable existence by digging shellfish at low tide. Even then, they had more than cold and starvation to fear: the authorities were barely able to check an expedition of thirty or forty men who wanted to exterminate the Deer Island exiles.

Fortunately for the English, and despite their clumsiness in dealing with neighboring Indians, not all the tribes joined Philip's men. Such skilled rangers as Captain Benjamin Church persuaded the authorities to enlist Indian allies to be the eyes and ears of the colonial forces. Church recruited friendly Indians and used them effectively as scouts, interpreters, and warriors. He forced his own men to live and fight as the Indians fought: stealthily, rapidly, lightly. Almost as many Indians remained loyal to the English as went with Philip. And the success of English arms was directly proportionate to the number of Indians engaged on the English side.

Early in November Plymouth, Massachusetts, and Connecticut decided together that the time had come to strike a blow against the Narragansets. Although the tribe had turned over to the settlers a number of Wampanoags, the English claimed that they were violating the July 15 treaty. On December 19 a thousand men under the command of Governor Josiah Winslow of Plymouth set off through a snowstorm to attack the main Narraganset fort near Kingston, Rhode Island.

Despite their heavy leather jerkins, the soldiers suffered terribly from the cold as they moved forward. As the short, bitter day waned, the soldiers at the head of the leading column came upon the most formidable Indian fort any of them had ever seen. Its thick log walls were protected by yards of brush and tree limbs and surrounded by marshland, which, fortunately for the attackers, was frozen solid.

Without waiting for the main body of the army to come up, two companies charged forward across the muck of the swamp. They had chosen as their objective the one weak corner of the fort where the palisade was not quite completed. Nevertheless, they had a hot time of it. Two of their captains fell under the Indian musketry, and though a few men managed to scramble through the brush and into the fort, they were soon driven out.

Seeing the first effort fail, the doughty Benjamin Church led thirty men stumbling toward the breach through the twilight. As they fought their way into the fort Church went down, struck by three bullets. Though he had been hit in the hip and thigh, the weather was so brutal that he particularly regretted the shot that had torn through his pocket and "pierced . . . and wounded a pair of mittens that he had borrowed of Capt. Prentice [which] being wrapped together, had the misfortune of having many holes cut through them with one bullet."

The battle went on around him, soldiers and Indians trampling the bloody snow, and then the Indians began to give way. When Church heard someone ordering that the wigwams be set afire he protested. His men had come a long, cold way and would need shelter during the night and food the following day. But despite his pleas to General Winslow to continue the fight without firing the camp, it was fired nonetheless. Perhaps three hundred warriors and an equal number of women and children were killed.

The Token and Atlantic Souvenir. 1842

In 1829 a tragic play about the extinction of the noble savage, based upon the life of King Philip, opened at New York's Park Theater to rave reviews. A few years later Frederick S. Agate painted this heroic image of actor Edwin Forrest in the lead role. Since no contemporary illustrations of Philip exist, Forrest had to rely on his imagination for costuming.

CAPTIVE AMONG "BLOODY HEATHEN"

Title page of Mary Rowlandson's diary

Among all the calamities that might befall settlers on the frontier, capture by Indians — with the attendant possibility of death by torture — was the most feared. A powerful and harrowing account of eleven weeks and five days in captivity was recorded in the diary of a courageous Massachusetts colonist named Mary Rowlandson.

"On the 10th of February, 1676, came the Indians with great numbers upon Lancaster," she wrote. One wounded settler, "though he begged of them his life, promising them money . . . they would not harken to him, but knocked him on the head, stripped him naked, and split open his bowels.

"At length they came and beset our house, and quickly it was the dolefulest day ever mine eyes saw." The house was set afire, and Mrs. Rowlandson took her "children, and one of my sisters took hers, to go forth and leave the house, but as soon as we came to the door and appeared, the Indians shot so thick that the bullets rattled against the house as if one had taken a handful of stones and threw them, so that we were forced to give back."

As the flames grew hotter, the settlers again ran from the house. They had gone only a few steps when Mrs. Rowlandson's brother-in-law fell dead at her feet, and "the bullets flying thick, one went through my side, and the same, as would seem, through the bowels and hand of my poor child in my arms." Mrs. Rowlandson and twenty-four other English survivors were herded away by the Narragansets allied with King Philip.

The first night in captivity was spent in the snow without sleep as the Indians' "roaring, and singing, and dancing, and yelling . . . made the place a likely resemblance of hell." After nine days of forced marches through deep snow, Mrs. Rowlandson's daughter "like a lamb departed this life." Her mother had little time to mourn, however, for shortly afterward her Narraganset captor sold her as a slave to a Sagamore, who used the genteel Englishwoman as a maidservant and — when the need arose — as a pack horse. When she complained that a load was too heavy, her mistress "gave me a slap in the face and bid me be gone."

After three weeks in captivity, Mrs. Rowlandson found that her English manners had deserted her. Seeing that a young captive girl was too weak to eat her ration of boiled horse's hoof, Mrs. Rowlandson "took it of the child, and eat it myself, and savory it was to my taste." And when her master's child died, she noted dryly, "there was more room [in the wigwam]."

Yet her captors suffered almost as much as she did, especially from lack of food, and thus made use of every morsel. Even old bones "were cut into pieces at the joints, and if they were full of worms and maggots they would scald them over the fire, to make the vermain come out, and then boil them, and drink up the liquor, and then beat the great ends of them in a mortar, and so eat them."

After eight wearying shifts of camp, required to elude pursuing English soldiers, Mrs. Rowlandson was ushered before King Philip. "He bade me come and sit down, and asked me whether I would smoke." She would not, observing testily that "surely there are many who may be better employed than to sit sucking a stinking tobacco-pipe." Unperturbed, Philip then "spake to me to make a cap for his child." She did, but as a devout minister's wife she refused to work on the Sabbath, which so enraged a woman with Philip's band that she threatened to "break my face" with a tomahawk.

Summoned again before King Philip, she received heartening news: the Narraganset chief would free her if she could raise a ransom of twenty pounds, two coats, half a bushel of corn, and some tobacco. Then Philip got roaring drunk. He puffed around after his wife "round the wigwam . . . but she escaped him; but having an old squaw, he ran to her, and so through the Lord's mercy we were no more troubled that night."

After many more days of hunger and hardship, the ransom raised by friends in Boston arrived, and Mrs. Rowlandson was freed.

"Affliction I had, full measure, pressed down and running over," she recorded in her diary. She vowed never again to place undue importance on the material benefits accorded a minister's wife. "The Lord hath showed me the vanity of these outward things," she wrote, "that they are . . . but a shadow, a blast, a bubble, and things of no continuance."

The attackers lost seventy men, among them seven of the fourteen company commanders. Having deprived themselves of shelter, the English withdrew, nursing their wounds, to the house of a Richard Smith at Wickford.

Although the Great Swamp fight effectively destroyed the main body of the Narrangansets, it loosed the remnants against the English. Throughout the winter of 1675–76 many New England tribes, now thoroughly roused, ravaged the frontiers. The town of Lancaster was so badly mauled that it was subsequently abandoned; Medfield, less than twenty miles from Boston, was burned; a company of Plymouth colony men, cut off and surrounded, was annihilated.

But even in their grimmest hours, the colonists were fortunate that several powerful warrior tribes remained aloof from Philip's cause. In midwinter the desperate English called upon Governor Sir Edmund Andros of New York to induce the Mohawks to attack Philip, who in December had moved his base of operations to the area northeast of Albany. The Mohawks struck Philip's forces so vigorously that he was forced to return to New England.

The significance of the role of the Iroquois—and particularly the Mohawk nation—in King Philip's War has been overlooked by most historians partly because of the absence of detailed sources and the confusion surrounding those that do exist. Nevertheless, as the historian Francis Jennings has pointed out, it was the crushing blow dealt by the Iroquois, acting at the request of the English, that "lost the war for Philip." The Mohawk victory prevented the remnants of Philip's forces from finding any sanctuary outside New England and forced the Wampanoag leader to return to do unequal battle with the colonial forces on his home ground.

If the Mohawks began Philip's fall, the increasing number of friendly Indians operating with the English forces ended it. In July Captain Church's mixed band of Indians and English captured Philip's wife and nine-year-old son. When he got the news, Philip is reported to have cried out, "My heart breaks; now I am ready to die. . . ." There was much debate about what to do with the pair. The Plymouth authorities, after consulting several godly ministers, spared their lives but sold them into slavery abroad.

On August 11 an Indian approached the English, saying that he had just

Paul Revere engraved portraits of King Philip and Benjamin Church, Philip's most successful adversary, in the 1770's, but he made no attempt to discover how they actually looked. Philip's portrait (below) seems deliberately frightening. For the Church portrait, Revere copied a likeness of English poet Charles Churchill and then added a powder horn. The three key battle scenes reproduced here are from nineteenth-century textbooks and correspond to contemporary written accounts.

Metacom, or King Philip, by Paul Revere

Indians setting fire to Brookfield, Massachusetts (August, 1675)

English force charging Narragan.

come from Philip's camp on the southwestern side of Mount Hope. Philip had killed one of the man's kinsmen for suggesting that he surrender, and the embittered deserter was willing to lead Church to the camp.

Shortly after midnight Church skillfully deployed his forces around the rocky outcropping where the Wampanoag sachem was asleep with his ten remaining followers. There was no sentry; Philip was through with the rigors and heartbreaking discipline of war. He had apparently come home to die.

At the discharge of a musket, Church's men fell upon the camp. The startled Indians tried to escape, and one, running through the forest, was brought down by a shot fired by an Indian auxiliary. When the soldiers examined the body, they were elated to find that the fallen Indian was King Philip.

Church, surrounded by his cheering men, went to view the corpse. Whatever thoughts may have been in his head at that moment, all he could say later of the man who had fought so long and so hard for his people's self-respect was that he looked like "a doleful, great, naked, dirty beast." Church ordered that Philip's body be butchered. His head and one hand were given to the Indian who shot him. His body was quartered and hung upon four trees.

The war was over, but New England would take years to recover from its ravages. Word of the colonists' plight spread far; in Dublin the churches collected money from their parishioners to send a relief ship. Six hundred English were dead, twelve hundred houses burned, eight thousand head of cattle killed. Edward Randolph, an agent sent over by King Charles II to assess the situation, estimated that some three thousand Indians had lost their lives "who if well managed would have been very serviceable to the English: which makes all manner of labour dear."

Many of the surviving Wampanoags were sold in the slave markets of the West Indies and Spain at a going price of about thirty shillings each. The other tribes of southern New England were broken and humiliated. A Frenchman who visited the region a decade after the war wrote, "There is Nothing to fear from the Savages, for they are few in Number. The last Wars they had with the English . . . have reduced them to a small Number, and consequently they are incapable of defending themselves."

DRAKE, Biography and History of the Indians of North America, 1851

CULVER PICTURES

rt (December, 1675)   *Benjamin Church by Paul Revere*   *An Indian slaying King Philip, ending the "conspiracy" (August, 1676)*

The Warrior at Home

Although warfare was the consuming passion of most eastern tribesmen, their ritualized fighting did not occupy much of their time. When not at war they hunte fished, feasted, danced, or like the sixteenth-century Indians shown here near the St. Johns River in Florida, they played at warrior's games: running races to improve their endurance, tossing balls at a treetop target, and firing arrows at various distant objects.

SERVICE HYDROGRAPHIQUE DE LA MARINE

The sixteenth-century Virginia Indians above hollow out the inside of a canoe with seashells. Europeans judged the boats to be as seaworthy as theirs. At left, seventeenth-century upper New York State Indians fish successfully using crude spears and nets.

64

European explorers found natives along the length of the Atlantic coast hunting and fishing with some proficiency in spite of primitive tools and weapons. Their methods varied, but hunting was nearly always a group effort. Sometimes they set fire to an area, enclosing the game or driving it into the water, where it could be killed easily by canoemen. Perhaps the most imaginative scheme was to hide inside the skin of a deer, approach a watering hole, and shoot an unsuspecting animal with a bow and arrow. Most often the men fished—sometimes with weirs and hooks, sometimes with spears and hooks—from canoes. With no iron tools, they made canoes by burning down a tree trunk and scraping off successive layers of bark with seashells until the boat had a strong, smooth bottom.

Sixteenth-century Florida Indians hunted for deer by draping themselves in deer-skins (below); Penobscots in Maine used deer masks like the one shown at right.

Each year the Carolina village of Secotan
hosted a great feast whose religious dances
shocked Europeans with symbolic pantomimes
of fertility and war. Here, spear-wielding
warriors and mature women dance and sing in a
circle of poles carved as human heads while
three virgins cluster at a center pole.

At a Florida war council Indian women prepare a powerful drink called cassina. Only warriors were permitted to sample it, and men who failed to keep it down were left behind.

Widows scatter their hair, cut off just below the ears, over the graves of their husbands killed in a Florida battle. Tribal law forbade remarriage until their hair reached their shoulders.

This thunder medicine bundle gave its Potawatomi owner the power of thunder—a mighty messenger between heaven and earth—in peace as well as in war.

The Hurons presented this peace-treaty wampum belt to the Iroquois at the headwaters of the Ottawa River in 1612. The square stands for the Huron nation, and the white stripes mean peace.

In this 1624 engraving Hurons carry war dead into a feast of honor.

The most dramatic ceremonies in nearly every eastern tribe — and sometimes
in separate societies within a tribe — were those that preceded and
followed battle. Most had religious connotations and were conducted by
shamans, who functioned as soothsayers and magicians in some societies
and as highly trained priests in others. A tribal council decided whether
to go to war, often by unanimous, rather than majority, agreement.
Warriors killed in action received especially elaborate services and
were often buried with funeral gifts to ease their life after death.

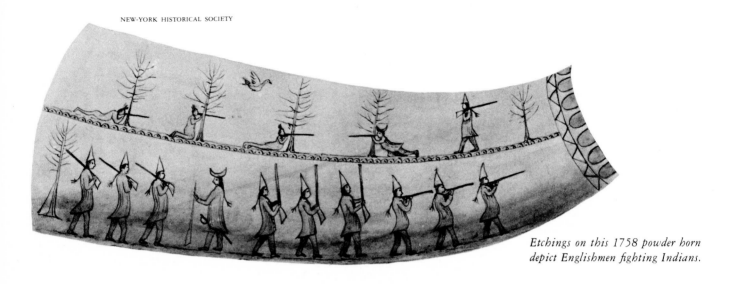

Etchings on this 1758 powder horn
depict Englishmen fighting Indians.

3: War in the Forest

Sixteen eighty-nine has been called by the military historian Douglas Edward Leach the "year of the great divide, marking as it does the beginning of a series of four major wars whose outcome would shape the whole future of North America." That year saw the start of the titanic struggle between predominantly Protestant Britain and Catholic France that lasted for seven bitter decades. In America the long series of skirmishes, pitched battles, and anxious truces would be popularly remembered as the French and Indian Wars, a name implying that the Indians were pawns of their European allies.

They were not. Caught between two warring nations whose customs were equally incomprehensible to them, the North American natives were again and again forced to pick sides. Some tribes chose to fight with the French, and some with the English, but all the tribes fought for their own best interests as they saw them. And although the war was a clash between European rivals, Indians were in it from the first; in fact, the war actually began in America in 1688, while Europe was at peace and England still had a Catholic king.

Although it had at first been sluggish in colonizing the New World, by the 1680's France had established strong bases in Montreal, Port Royal, and Quebec. The British had forestalled French expansion north of Quebec by opening a trading post at Hudson Bay in 1670, but the St. Lawrence and Ottawa rivers gave France access to the immense reaches of land in the interior of the continent. The English had a long Atlantic coastline, but the French meant to see that their ancient rivals stayed behind the Appalachian mountain barrier.

The English, in turn, were ever on guard against French encirclement, and none was more vigilant than the autocratic Sir Edmund Andros, who as New York's governor had persuaded the Mohawks to side with his English settlers during King Philip's War. James II of England had appointed Andros governor of all the northern colonies from New Jersey to Maine, with orders to prevent any French encroachments. This Andros did with hawkish efficiency.

In April of 1688 he moved north with a company of soldiers to Penobscot Bay, where a Frenchman with the resonant name of Jean Vincent de l'Abadie, baron de St. Castin kept a trading post at what is now Castine, Maine. Castin had established his post on land Andros felt had been granted to the duke of York and had gotten rich from the fur trade. He had married the daughter of a chief and was well loved by members of the Abnaki confederacy of eastern Indians. As an observer wrote in 1684, they were the "most powerfull, politick, warlike and numerous nation of Indians since the Narragansetts are broken, and influence and steer all others that inhabit the English Plantations or Colonies."

The Abnakis were furious when Andros and his men descended on their friend Castin's trading post, plundered his home, and demanded his submission to James II. When, a little later, English settlers at Saco, Maine, seized sixteen Indians in retaliation for the killing of some cattle at nearby North Yarmouth, the natives responded by capturing as many settlers as they could lay hands on.

In September the nervous English began erecting fortified stockades at North Yarmouth. Having received a report that a large number of natives were approaching, the soldiers fled, only to stumble onto the party of Indians, who had brought a number of English captives along, evidently for the purpose of negotiating a settlement of their grievances. Although nobody wanted a fight, the English tried to free the captives, and in the scuffling "one Sturdy and Surly Indian," as the indefatigable Puritan chronicler Cotton Mather described him, "held his prey so fast, that one Benedict Pulcifer gave the Mastiff a Blow with the Edge of his Broad Ax upon the Shoulder, upon which they fell to't with a Vengeance, and Fired their Guns on both sides, till some on both sides were Slain." In this manner, Mather said, "the Vein of New-England first opened, that afterwards Bled for Ten years together!" Blood had been spilled, however blindly and unnecessarily; by the values of both Indians and settlers blood spilled had to be avenged.

The Indians attacked the outlying settlements, burned, killed, captured, and plundered. With the onset of winter they withdrew into the woods. Governor Andros arrived on the scene with a thousand men in November and built forts at Pemaquid and what is now Brunswick. But, as Mather noted in disgust, Andros's men killed no Indians until the spring, when Andros returned to Boston, where he was promptly deposed in the backwash of a Protestant revolt in England that dethroned the Catholic king James II. Andros went home to Britain, and the war whose opening moves he had managed continued without him under the name of King William's War, after the new English monarch.

Meanwhile France sought to bolster its situation in America by appointing a vigorous governor for New France. The choice was Louis de Buade, comte de Frontenac, a tough old soldier and a good one (he had been made a brigadier general at the age of twenty-seven). Frontenac had been governor once before, in 1672—court gossip said that he had gotten the job because he became too intimate with the king's favorite mistress.

He had handled his duties with energy and skill, but he was quarrelsome and overbearing and in ten years made himself so thoroughly unpopular that he had been recalled. Now, however, the situation demanded Frontenac's knowledgeable toughness, and the French king reappointed the seventy-year-old autocrat.

Frontenac set sail from France armed with an ambitious battle plan: to invade the English colonies through Lake Champlain and Lake George to Albany, where, after concluding an alliance with the Iroquois, he was to move down the Hudson and with the help of a French fleet capture New York. But the old commander never got the chance to put this grand design into operation.

When he arrived at Quebec, Frontenac found the colony stunned by a savage Iroquois attack that had devastated the settlement of Lachine, six miles upriver from Montreal, during the night of July 25–26. The settlers, taken in their beds, had had no time to resist; the Indians killed 200 of them immediately and took another 120 prisoner. The ferocity of the attack was typical of the Iroquois. When Jacques Bruyas, the French missionary to the Iroquois, told his charges that all their desires would be satisfied in heaven, they badgered him with "impertinent questions as that they would not believe that there were no wars in heaven; if one would meet human beings there and if there one would be looking for scalp locks." Bruyas deplored their "passion to kill," so that "they are willing to travel 300 leagues to have the opportunity of taking a scalp lock."

Demoralized by so ruthless an enemy, the French had abandoned their fort at Cataraqui on Lake Ontario. Frontenac, far from being able to send a campaign roaring down the Hudson valley, had to content himself with small-scale sallies against English settlements on the frontier, a strategy he called *la petite guerre*—which we would call guerrilla warfare. To fight his "little war," Frontenac began to forge such Indian allies as he had into efficient units that attacked under the direction of French officers.

In the meantime, the English continued to have their share of Indian trouble. After Andros's departure from Maine the Indians continued their assaults on outlying settlements and then mounted a major expedition against Dover, New Hampshire. There they killed thirty English, among them the trader Major Richard Waldron, an old enemy from King Philip's War. Local Indians of the Pennacook, Ossipee, and Pigwacket tribes attacked the seventy-five-year-old patriarch. While he lay dying they cut off his fingers, one by one, asking him mockingly whether his fist, which he had often put onto the scales as a makeweight against their furs, would weigh a pound now. Then they took turns slashing his chest, saying, "See! I cross out my account."

The Indians maintained the pressure on the frontier throughout the summer until finally the English abandoned all their posts east of Falmouth (present-day Portland). The general court at Boston sent six hundred soldiers north to help secure the frontier, but the expedition accomplished little more than Andros had the year before.

Then, as winter came on, Frontenac, with characteristic energy, decided to add to the English miseries with a three-pronged attack on Albany and the borders of New Hampshire and Maine. The Albany party, composed of 160 Canadians and 100 Indians, set off from Montreal early in 1690. In arctic weather they struggled down Lake Champlain to the frozen southern

With reason, European immigrants feared the bellicose Iroquois above all other eastern Indians. These natives gained their fearsome reputation early; when a London publisher brought out a history of America in 1698, he called this scene of torture and murder "Unheard of Crueltys of the Iroquois." The inset shows a later engraving of one of their warrior chiefs in full regalia.

BRYANT, *A Popular History of the United States.* 1897

Hannah Dustin prepares to kill her sleeping Abnaki captors in this nineteenth-century version of the redoubtable farm woman's escape.

tip of Lake George, then took to the woods. By the time the French and Indians reached the Hudson they decided that Albany was too difficult a prize and instead chose to attack the closer settlement of Schenectady. Even so, they had a dreadful march through half-frozen swampland before they got within striking distance on the afternoon of February 8. They waited until dark and then approached the village, where, to their astonishment, they found the open gates guarded only by two snowmen.

The party swept into the sleeping town and for two hours hacked men, women, and children to pieces. When the carnage ended, sixty villagers were dead. "No pen can write, and no tongue express," said one contemporary, "the cruelties that were committed."

Frontenac's other two blows fell with equal strength, at Salmon Falls, New Hampshire, where thirty-four died, and in mid-May at Falmouth, where hundreds of Abnaki Indians joined the French in an attack on Fort Loyal. After a stiff defense, the commander of the fort surrendered on the promise that the garrison would not be harmed, then marched out to see a hundred English murdered by the Indians.

By the time Fort Loyal fell, the English colonies had managed to mount a counterattack in the form of a naval assault on Port Royal in Acadia under the command of Sir William Phips. A curious figure, Phips was the twenty-first child of a Massachusetts farming family and had made his fortune by recovering a huge treasure from a Spanish ship sunk in the Bahamas. His flotilla of fourteen vessels easily took Port Royal and Phips went home a hero, whereupon he was immediately given command of a far larger expedition against Quebec. He got the fleet there, but then the operation fell apart. The English could not dislodge the French defenders — who commented in journals that they were watching the bumblings of a bunch of amateurs — and in November, with smallpox spreading among his men, Phips went home. Fortunately for him, the authorities chose to blame the debacle on the "awful frown of God" rather than on any possible mismanagement by Phips.

The English did better the next year with a land campaign against the Maine frontier, in which Massachusetts enlisted the indestructible Benjamin Church. This old warrior had grown quite fat in the fifteen years since he brought down King Philip, but like Frontenac he retained his vigor and his military judgment. Arriving in Saco with three hundred soldiers in September of 1691, Church harried the Indians so effectively that most of them retired inland. Although his men fought no decisive battles, they shook their opponents badly. In October several Abnaki sachems sued for a truce, and on November 29 they signed a document by which they agreed to bring in all English captives, warn the English about French plots, and do them no harm until May 1, 1692.

Whatever relief the treaty gave the weary, frightened settlers did not last long. On February 5, 1692, Indians and Canadians fell upon the town of York in Maine, killed forty-eight inhabitants, and took about seventy prisoners. From this fresh beginning the savage dialogue of raid and counterraid, deception, and bad faith continued for years. New Hampshire, Maine, and Massachusetts all suffered as the Indians burned towns and butchered settlers with a sort of ghastly monotony, which the great nineteenth-century historian Francis Parkman described as "a weary detail of the murder of one, two, three or more men, women or children, waylaid in fields, woods and lonely roads, or surprised in solitary cabins."

On March 15, 1697, a party of Abnakis struck the town of Haverhill, Massachusetts, in a raid different from a score of others only because it marked the beginning of the extraordinary saga of a farm woman named Hannah Dustin. Mrs. Dustin's eighth child had been born the week before, and she was resting in her house when the attack came. Her husband, who was working in the fields nearby, told his children to run to a fortified house and then tried to fight his way through to his wife. He failed, and the natives carried off Mrs. Dustin, her baby, and the nurse who was caring for them.

As the Indians escaped with their captives silently through the forest the infant began to cry, and in a cruel but characteristic response a warrior grabbed the child and smashed its head against a tree. A little later the Indians killed some of the captives and divided up the rest amongst themselves. Mrs. Dustin and the nurse were handed over to a group of two warriors, three women, and seven children. This party led them north through the woods for more than a month, the Indians, who were Catholic, pausing twice a day to say their rosaries.

At last, on the night of March 29, Mrs. Dustin and the nurse rose silently from the campfire, got hold of hatchets, and set about murdering their sleeping captors. They killed all but two, an old woman and a boy who fled into the forest. Mrs. Dustin must have been an extremely practical woman: Massachusetts was offering a bounty on dead Indians, and so, despite her six-week ordeal and the horror of the recent butchery, she carefully scalped all her victims. Then she and the nurse made their way home to Haverhill, where Mrs. Dustin found that her husband and children had also survived the raid. Massachusetts gave her £25 for her night's work.

Though the European end of the war between France and England wound down with the signing of the Treaty of Ryswick in September of 1697, in the colonies spasms of frontier violence continued. Part of the reason for the continuing hostilities was the English colonists' very real horror of their opponents. In the Puritan cosmology, civilized Europeans and barbarous Indians represented opposite and antagonistic poles. Thus to see Frenchmen not only living the life of the native warrior, but united with him in some sort of spiritual brotherhood, appalled and bewildered the English. Cotton Mather, in *Decennium Luctuosum* (Woeful Decade), his account of the war, speaks grimly of the "Half Indianized French, and Half Frenchified Indians." The terror and awe that these mixed parties inspired is clearly shown in the way individual accounts of English captives dominate Mather's narrative. Writing of the ordeal of one woman taken by the Indians, Mather intoned: "Read these passages without Relenting Bowels, thou thyself art as really Petrified as the man at Villa Ludovisia (an Italian statue). . . . I know not, reader, whether you will be moved to tears by this narrative; I know I could not write it without weeping."

In 1702 Europe began to fight anew, and the deadly raids in the colonies turned back into a full-scale war, named this time after Queen Anne, who had just taken the throne upon William's death. As before, New England bore the brunt in America. (New York escaped the worst horrors because of the protection provided by its Iroquois subjects—as New Yorkers referred to the Indians when they were out of earshot—or allies, a nicety of phrasing employed during negotiations.)

The worldly, power-loving Joseph Dudley, Massachusetts's new governor, had been made responsible for keeping peace with the Abnakis, which he did in schizophrenic fashion, alternately wooing and scorning them. At a conference in Casco, Maine, he claimed to have 1,250 men under arms and compared the Indians to wolves, able to disturb men but not capable of doing any real harm. "I value them not," he said, "no more than the paring of my nails." Then, changing his tune, he announced that several chiefs among the Indian delegations "are fit to be made Officers to bear commission from the Queen of England, to bear Rule among you, who shall be my Officers, and shall be Rewarded from time to time. . . ." Several of the Indian leaders declared that they would resist the overtures of the French, but the meeting broke up with the peace still fragile.

Then in August of 1703 a party of Englishmen plundered the house of St. Castin's son, an Abnaki chief. Enraged by this affront, the Indians responded. Less than six weeks after Dudley's peace conference, two hundred miles of New England frontier were in flames.

Despite his boasts, the best Dudley could do was to field an army of 360 men, which advanced as far as Saco, with the Indian forces melting away before it unharmed while the raids continued unabated. To the staggered colonists, it all seemed a repetition of King William's War. Indeed, many of the same towns suffered, among them Deerfield, Massachusetts, the northernmost settlement of the string of villages along the Connecticut River.

Oglethorpe presenting Creek Indians to the trustees of Georgia

NOBLE SAVAGES ON TOUR

To most who settled in the New World, Indians were terrifying and brutal adversaries. But to Europeans at a safe remove from the terror, native Americans were exotic curiosities, romanticized by philosophers into Noble Savages. Colonial leaders lost little time in turning this fascination to their own advantage.

In 1710 four Mohawks, including the war-painted chief at right, were sent on a voyage to England to help their British sponsors win Queen Anne's support for an attack on the French in Canada. In 1734 James Oglethorpe, who had founded the colony of Georgia the previous year, took Creek dignitaries to London (above) to prod British trustees who were losing interest in the project.

Probably the oddest example of a colonist who capitalized on the Indian craze abroad was William Augustus Bowles, left, a Maryland-born white man who masqueraded as an Indian in England to help win support for his plan to drive the Spanish out of Florida.

Bogus redskin William Augustus Bowles

A Mohawk in court dress

Indians attack Deerfield, Massachusetts, in this illustration from the Reverend John Williams's Redeemed Captive Returning to Zion, *the book in which the Deerfield cleric told of his adventures as a prisoner. A contemporary best seller, it made the raid famous throughout the colonies. The inset shows one of the grisly scenes that took place inside the houses.*

Deerfield had already had its share of grief. Almost wiped out during King Philip's War and badly mauled during King William's, by the winter of 1704 the community had recovered and become a prosperous village of 41 houses and some 270 people.

Remembering the past, the townspeople had posted a sentry, but he was either asleep or absent on the last night of February, 1704, when a party of fifty French and two hundred Abnakis and Caughnawagas trudged toward the village through deep snow. They attacked two hours before dawn and killed many settlers in their beds. But some villagers, awakened by the screams and shouting, fought back. The militia sergeant, Benoni Stebbins, had time to order his seven men to barricade the windows of his house, which had been otherwise bulletproofed by means of brick walls. The militiamen drove off an attack of about fifty Indians, and though Stebbins died at the window where he had posted himself, his house withstood the onslaught. Most of the villagers, however, thrown into panic by the whooping death that had come on them out of the night, died or were captured. By dawn the fighting had ended, leaving some fifty settlers dead and more than a hundred prisoners.

The French and Indians bullied their captives north along the forest trails toward Canada. Among the survivors of the brutal trek was John Williams, a Deerfield clergyman whose immensely popular account of his sufferings, *Redeemed Captive Returning to Zion*, kept alive the memory of the Deerfield raid long after similar atrocities had been forgotten. His wife, who had just borne a child, was too weak to keep up with the rest of the party. When Williams tried to help her the Indians drove him away,

and they killed her a little later when she flagged trying to cross an icy river. But another Indian carried Williams's daughter Eunice nearly every step of the three-hundred-mile journey. Eventually the French ransomed most of the prisoners, but Eunice Williams never came home. Adopted by the Caughnawagas, she married the warrior who had saved her life. Years later she visited her one-time neighbors in Deerfield, but the gulf had grown too wide, and she returned to the forest.

The news of the Deerfield raid brought Benjamin Church stamping into Boston, furiously demanding that Dudley give him a force to lead against Acadia. By this time Church was so old that he had to have a soldier walking beside him to help him over fallen logs along the line of march. But he got 550 men up into French territory, where he terrorized some settlements, telling the inhabitants that if any more English villages suffered Deefield's fate he would return with a thousand Indians to repay the compliment to the French. Church wanted to attack Port Royal, but his officers restrained him, and he sailed back to Boston after throwing some bombastic threats at the well-defended French stronghold.

The English colonists took another ill-fated stab at Port Royal in 1706 and then appealed to the mother country for help. Committed as she was to a costly European land war, Queen Anne had few troops to spare. Finally, in hopes of generating some sympathy and publicity, the colonists sent several Mohawk chieftains to the English court in 1710. Outfitted by a London theatrical costumer in what he thought barbarian warlords should wear, the four Indians made a magnificent spectacle. The queen was delighted with them, the archbishop of Canterbury gave them Bibles, fash-

One of the worst butcheries of southern settlers took place on November 28, 1729, when Natchez Indians, enraged at white incursions into the Mississippi Valley, struck French Fort Rosalie at the site of present-day Natchez, Mississippi. The warriors killed two hundred fifty men and took three hundred women and children prisoner. The French retaliated quickly, recaptured the prisoners, and destroyed the Natchez nation. But the campaign was so costly that the joint stock company which owned Louisiana had to surrender its charter, and its holdings became a royal colony. This view of the attack is from a diorama painted more than a century later.

ionable artists of the day painted their portraits, crowds followed them through the streets, and the nobility vied for the privilege of entertaining them. The next summer the long-awaited troops arrived from England, and in September Port Royal fell and with it Acadia.

Emboldened by their success, the British moved against Quebec the next year, but they had to retire at the end of a timid and badly mismanaged campaign. Despite this British fiasco, old King Louis XIV of France, tired and debt-ridden, ended the war by accepting the Treaty of Utrecht in 1713. The treaty ceded Hudson Bay and Acadia to the English, but left the bounds of France's Canadian empire in doubt. By a treaty of July 13, 1713, the Eastern tribes sued for a separate peace with the New Englanders, acknowledging their "past rebellions, hostilities, and violations of promises" and promising to become loyal subjects to Queen Anne. The Abnakis, however, had little idea of what being a British subject meant, and their oath of loyalty was too tenuous a thing to withstand the English incursions on their land that began nearly as soon as the treaty was signed.

While the Northern colonies enjoyed the brief respite from frontier raids that came with the Treaty of Utrecht, warfare was ripping through the Carolinas. The white traders there had done much to bring the fighting

on themselves. Like Indian traders everywhere, they tended to be rough, unprincipled men who duped the Indians and debauched them with liquor. Adding to these abuses, the traders also sold Indians as slaves. The Tuscaroras, who had settled inland along the coastal rivers of North Carolina, suffered most, and though they did not at first retaliate, their discontent was obvious enough to make the settlers uneasy. By 1710 relations had become so tense that the Tuscaroras sent messengers to Pennsylvania asking permission to migrate there. The Pennsylvania authorities said that they could settle provided they had a note from the North Carolina government attesting to their previous good conduct. The Carolinians refused outright.

Less than a year later a group of Swiss colonists organized by a promoter named Baron Christoph von Graffenried went to occupy a tract of land at New Bern, at the confluence of the Neuse and Trent rivers in North Carolina, only to find an Indian town on the site. Von Graffenried complained to the surveyor-general, who told him that the colonists held clear title to the land and suggested they drive off the Indians without payment. That was poor advice; on September 22, 1711, the Tuscaroras responded with a dawn attack on settlements between the Neuse and Pamlico Sound.

During the bloody morning they killed nearly two hundred settlers, among them eighty children. The survivors fled to the coastal towns, and the usual sequence of raids and counterraids began. Von Graffenried had earlier been captured, and in order to spare New Bern from attack—and as a condition of his release—he promised not to make war on the Indians. But one of his settlers, a foolish man named William Brice, decided that the baron's pledge showed contemptible softheartedness and took matters into his own hands by capturing the chief of one of the smaller tribes allied with the Tuscaroras and roasting him alive. The Indian attacks increased in fury.

North Carolina sent to South Carolina for help, which arrived in the form of Colonel John Barnwell, a tough Irish-born soldier, who came leading a force of thirty settlers and five hundred Indians. Barnwell handily neutralized the resistance of tribes allied with the Tuscaroras and devastated their communities. In March of 1712, with his forces strengthened by a contingent of North Carolinians, Barnwell launched an assault on the fort of the Tuscarora king Hancock, which failed when the North Carolina men panicked and broke. Then the Indians exposed some of their white prisoners in view of Barnwell's lines and tortured others in hopes of forcing the Carolina troops to negotiate. Barnwell agreed to call off his men if the prisoners were released. He took fifty of them safely back to New Bern, where he discovered that the North Carolina assembly was vexed because he had not destroyed the Tuscarora fort. Whereupon Barnwell went back, forced the Tuscaroras into a treaty and then, on his way home, immediately violated it by seizing a group of Indians as slaves. So the war broke out afresh in the summer of 1712.

Again North Carolina begged its southern neighbor for help, and in November a seasoned Indian fighter named Colonel James Moore arrived with thirty-three whites and a thousand friendly natives. Joining with North Carolina troops, he struck the main Tuscarora force late in March of 1713 and smashed it. Moore's men killed several hundred Indians and captured four hundred more, whom he sold into slavery at £10 each to help pay for the campaign. Most of the surviving Tuscaroras began a long, slow retreat to the north, where they eventually joined the Iroquois confederacy.

The last feeble Indian resistance in the Carolinas ended when Tom Blount, the chief of the Tuscarora faction loyal to the English, signed a peace treaty on February 11, 1715. But no sooner had peace come to North Carolina than war began in South Carolina. Like the Tuscaroras, the Yamassees, a Muskhogean tribe that had moved into South Carolina, had suffered the exploitation of traders. On Good Friday, April 15, they avenged themselves in a well-coordinated attack similar in every respect to the great Virginia massacre of 1622. The assault left the outlying settlements north of present-day Savannah, Georgia, in flames and took the lives of a hundred settlers. South Carolina's governor Charles Craven, commanding his colony's militia, moved quickly and by June had driven the Yamassees from their villages. That autumn, on a follow-up expedition, he hit them so hard that they fled to Spanish Florida. The English appropriated the Yamassee lands for the new colony of Georgia.

Although he had gotten the Yamassees out of the way, Craven still feared the powerful Creeks and tried to counterbalance them by inducing the equally strong Cherokee nation to join the English. Although divided into two factions, the proud Cherokees, under the prodding of the English, broke with their southern neighbors and joined the Carolinians in curbing the Creeks. Thus, a measure of peace returned to the Carolinas.

In New England the brief span of peace was drawing to a close. The Abnakis had pledged their allegiance to Queen Anne, but their true loyalties lay with the French. Provoked by the English settlers who kept pushing into their territory, the Indians were urged on by French agents who kept them well supplied with ammunition. One of these men, a Jesuit priest named Sebastian Rale, had lived for years among the Norridgewock tribe on the Kennebec River in Maine. A trusted adviser who spoke their own tongue, Rale incited the Indians to strike back at the English who were dotting Abnaki lands with blockhouses and farms. In the autumn of 1721 his charges began attacking isolated farmsteads.

The Massachusetts authorities reacted particularly strongly to these raids; Rale, living among the Indians in their forest home, was the embodiment of all the English feared and loathed. In 1723 a force of 230 men moved up the Penobscot and burned the mission town of Passadumkeag, but they failed to capture the soldier-priest. The next summer another expedition struck north at Rale's headquarters in the town of Norridgewock and took the village completely by surprise. The English held their fire while the Indians got off a wild, scattered volley, then killed 26 of the panicked natives with a well-aimed fusillade. The surviving Norridgewocks jumped into the river and swam to safety, but Rale refused to surrender, forcing the English to shoot him although they had hoped to take him alive.

His death had the predictable results: the Abnakis struck back not only along the Maine frontier but in Massachusetts and New Hampshire as well. The English counterattacked with forces raised by the colonial governments and with companies of volunteers who offered to fight Indians in return for pay, scalp bonuses, and booty. Captain John Lovewell, a resident of Dunstable, raised one such company after the Indians burned his Massachusetts border town in the autumn of 1724. He petitioned the General Court in Boston to pay five shillings a day for his volunteers. The court would not put up more than two and a half, but it offered a bounty of a hundred pounds on every male Indian scalp. Late in February of 1724, Lovewell and his eighty-seven men surprised a small encampment of ten Indians, killed them all, and went home to collect a thousand pounds.

Cheered by his success and the easy money, Lovewell immediately embarked on a summer campaign accompanied by forty-seven volunteers. On May 8 the company sighted a single Indian on the shore of Saco Pond. Lovewell gave chase, suspecting that he had been posted to lure the company into an ambush but confident that the English could handle any assault. He was wrong. A large party of Indians ambushed the company and boldly closed to within a few yards of the English. "The battle continued fiercely throughout the day," said a contemporary account, "the Indians roaring and yelling and howling like wolves, barking like dogs, and making all sorts of hideous noises; the English frequently shouting and huzzaing, as they did after the first round." But the shouting and huzzaing died away as one Englishman after another went down. Lovewell himself died late in the afternoon, and though the Indians finally abandoned the field, they left only a few of their opponents unhurt.

The survivors retreated at once, leaving the badly wounded behind, among them a lieutenant who asked that his gun be charged and left with him. "The Indians will come in the morning to scalp me," he said, "and I'll kill one more of 'em if I can." Only fourteen soldiers eventually made it home to receive barren solace from such ministers as the Reverend Thomas Symmes of Bradford, who declaimed that the reason "so many brave men should descend into battle and perish" was clearly the general backsliding and irreverence of New Englanders, which had aroused the wrath of a vengeful God. Nevertheless, further English campaigns in Maine once more forced Abnaki chiefs to the treaty table in 1725, where they again acknowledged their submission to England.

Except for an occasional isolated atrocity, the New England frontier remained quiet for the next two decades, then boiled up again in 1744 when England went to war over who should succeed to the throne of Austria. This time George II gave his name to the struggle in the colonies, and King George's War saw the frontiers again convulsed from New York to Maine by Indian raids and white counterraids. The most significant part of the colonial war, however, was not the Indian fighting but an extraordinary expedition, mounted by New Englanders without any help from England, against the great fortress-rock of Louisburg, the anchor of France's right flank in the New World. Built on Cape Breton Island, the fort guarded the approaches to the vital St. Lawrence River with the strongest concentration of cannon in North America. Nevertheless, 4,200 Massachusetts militiamen took it in June of 1745. England, astonished and de-

This map of Fort Duquesne, the bulwark of French strength in the Ohio valley, was published in 1758, the year English troops under General John Forbes took the fort.

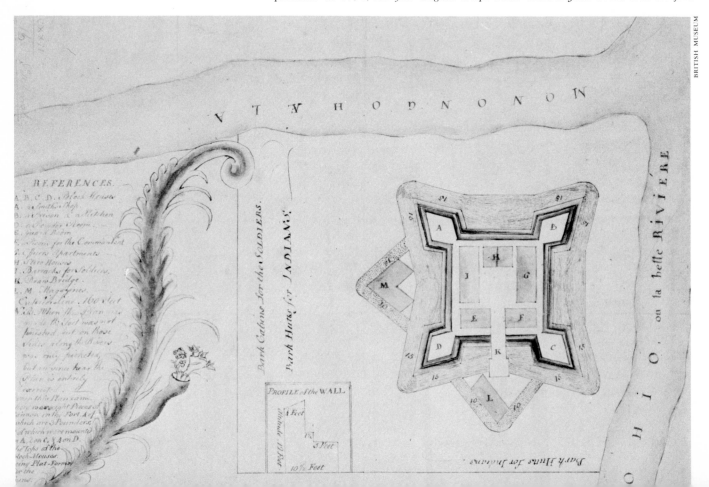

lighted at this unprecedented triumph of provincial arms, repaid Massachusetts for the cost of the expedition but then enraged the colonists by handing the fort back to the French in return for Madras when the treaty of Aix-la-Chapelle ended the European phase of the war in 1748.

The peace that followed King George's War was a truce, a brief respite before the culminating struggle for supremacy in North America that would have bagpipes and French battle horns challenging one another in virgin pine forests. This final clash of arms would come to be known as the French and Indian War, an inadequate title that fails to distinguish it from all the wars, large and small, that preceded it. Lawrence Henry Gipson, the most thorough historian of the climactic struggle, chose a far better name — the Great War for Empire.

As before, Indian support would be crucial to both French and English in the coming fight, and one who saw that fact clearly was a cheerful, indefatigable Irishman who had come to America in the 1730's to manage his uncle's estates in the Mohawk valley. His name was William Johnson, but the Iroquois knew him as their brother Warraghiyagey — "He-Who-Does-Much." He opened a small trading post in 1738 and immediately won a reputation among the Indians as one of the few white men who would deal fairly with them. By the 1750's this reputation had made him the largest trader in the area. He kept his home, which he shared with his wife, a Mohawk woman, open to his Indian friends at all times. In 1756 he wrote of the people he knew so well: "Whoever pretends to say, as some have fatally imagined, that the American savages are of little or no account to our interest on that continent, and that, therefore, it is not of great consequences, whether or no we endeavour to cultivate friendship with them must be so extremely ignorant, or else so wilfully perverse, that it would be wasting time to expose the absurdity of such preposterous suggestions."

Johnson's conviction was borne out by the demography of North America on the eve of the war. The French, concentrated in a thin line stretching down the St. Lawrence from Louisburg through the Great Lakes and down the Mississippi valley to the Gulf of Mexico, numbered only about fifty-five thousand souls in 1754. But their Indian neighbors in the Great Lakes region alone could field perhaps as many as seventy thousand warriors.

The English colonies, with well over a million white inhabitants, enjoyed an overwhelming superiority in numbers, but the population was confined to the seaboard. The French controlled the interior, largely by dint of their policy of befriending Indians whenever possible rather than fighting them. In some cases the French commitment to coexistence became so strong that one observer wrote, "Those with whom we mingle do not become French, our people become Indian." Despite close ties, the French were never wholly successful in their efforts to secure their southern flank with allies in the southeastern tribes. They formed strong bonds with the numerous and powerful Choctaw Indians who occupied the lands along the coast north of the French bases at Biloxi and Mobile, but they never won over the Chickasaws, who lived to the north of their ancient Choctaw enemies in lands east of the Mississippi River. The English retained Chickasaw loyalty, and despite a series of hard-fought battles, the French never subdued the tribe.

The engraving on Johnson's testimonial

HEAVEN-TAUGHT FRONTIERSMAN

The Mohawks made Irish fur trader William Johnson a blood brother; the Iroquois made him a chief. British soldiers who served under him during campaigns against the French called him "the heaven-taught general." The Irishman's power over all these diverse people hinged on his uncanny ability to get along with Indians.

As Superintendent of Indian Affairs for the Northern Colonies, Johnson fed and clothed whole tribes who came to him for help—a beneficence often paid for out of his own pocket. When any Indian showed special loyalty, Johnson promptly rewarded him with a medal and printed testimonial (above). He adhered to a policy of honest trade, and he not only allowed Indians to buy rum, but stuck by his agreements even after they got drunk on it.

Johnson made his own home (below) the center of all negotiations and seems to have allowed his Indian friends the run of the property. A young ensign staying with Johnson noted in his journal, "Sir Wm. continually plagued with Indians about him—generally 300–900 in number—spoil his garden and keep his house always dirty." But Johnson's own writings indicate that his affection was genuine, and many historians consider his success in enlisting the Iroquois to the British cause critical to the outcome of the French and Indian War.

An 18th-century portrait of Johnson

Indians gathered on the lawn at Johnson's home

Nevertheless, by the mid-1750's the French had seized the initiative and begun advancing into the Ohio valley just when Virginia speculators were beginning to take a strong interest in the same rich region.

Robert Dinwiddie, the determined sixty-year-old governor of Virginia, saw which way the wind was blowing and in October of 1753 sent a twenty-one-year-old militia major named George Washington to the recently begun Fort Le Boeuf (now Waterford, Pennsylvania) to tell the French commander there that his garrison was on English lands. Washington arrived after a long, cold journey. Having received him courteously, the commander bluntly informed Washington that he was on French soil and that thenceforth any Englishmen who set foot in the Ohio valley would be taken prisoner.

Acting promptly on Washington's news, Dinwiddie sent a small force of men to build a fort at the crucial junction of the Monongahela and Allegheny rivers—where Pittsburgh stands today—and early in April of 1754 dispatched 120 reinforcements under Washington.

The undertaking was wretched from the beginning. Hacking their way across Pennsylvania's endless ridges, the men under Washington soon became exhausted. Supplies of food and arms failed to arrive; what did get through was the disheartening news that the men Washington was marching to support had been chased from the fort by the French. But most serious of all was the failure of Washington's command to enlist the aid of more than a handful of friendly Indians. Dinwiddie knew the value of Cherokee, Catawba, and Chickasaw support for the expedition, but those Indians had long been accustomed to dealing with South Carolina, whose governor was outraged that Virginia might think of enlisting "his" Indians without first getting his permission. So Washington began his march without Indian support and only belatedly received native detachments.

On May 24 Washington reached a place called Great Meadows, where a Mingo chief known as the Half-King told him that the French were nearby. Washington took forward a detachment of forty men and, joined by a dozen of Half-King's warriors, surprised a party of thirty-three Frenchmen. The English killed ten, and the rest surrendered after a brief defense during which, for the first time in his life, Washington heard bullets whistling past him, a sound he described as "charming." The French later charged that Washington had murdered innocent soldiers in time of peace; the young militia officer responded that they had brought it upon themselves by shadowing his forces in a surreptitious and apparently hostile manner. Whatever the truth, the Great War for Empire had begun—begun, as Gipson put it, in an "isolated mountain ravine on the western slopes of the Alleghenies." It would spread like a forest fire "to leap over oceans, to illuminate continents, and to end by reducing to ashes the bright dreams of Frenchmen of a great future in the New World."

Washington fell back on Great Meadows, where he had his men throw up a stockade he named Fort Necessity. Reinforcements had brought the strength of his command up to about four hundred, a considerable improvement, but nowhere near enough to hold off the nine hundred French troops who moved out from Fort Duquesne to avenge the death of their comrades. They attacked the English fort on July 3, fighting in a steady downpour that turned Washington's entrenchments to soup and rendered his swivel guns useless. With nearly half his men dead, sick, or wounded, Washington surrendered. He and his men were allowed to march from the fort with full honors of war. The French could afford to be generous — they had swept the English from the Ohio valley.

The English struck back the next year. This time there would be no inept campaign by provincial troops, but a well-planned attack by two regiments of British regulars under the command of General Edward Braddock. A tough, competent officer, Braddock had spent forty-five of his sixty years in the army. He was brave, popular, and considerate of his men. If he had a failing, it was his confident determination to prove that his troops had nothing to fear from "naked Indians . . . [or] Canadians in their shirts."

Braddock moved out of Fort Cumberland, Maryland, at the head of some twenty-five hundred men in June. There were no Indians with him as he plunged into the hundred miles of forest that separated him from Fort Duquesne; Governor Dinwiddie had promised the support of the southern tribes, but their help had failed to materialize. The French, on the other hand, had successfully courted their Indian allies and sent them to harry the English settlements along the route of Braddock's march. Braddock had such trouble chopping his way through the dense forest that at last he detached some fifteen hundred of his best troops and led this flying column quickly toward the fort. He had little fear of the French: Fort Duquesne had only eight hundred defenders, and they would be powerless against the British artillery. On July 7 Braddock's men made camp less than ten miles away from their objective.

The French, however, had no intention of waiting for the British to roll over them. On July 8 a captain named Hyacinth de Beaujeu took a detachment of two hundred men out of the fort and persuaded an equal number of reluctant Indians to join him by crying, "I am determined to go against the enemy! What! Will you allow your father to go alone?"

On the morning of July 9 the British army splashed across the Monongahela with the fifers shrilling out "The Grenadiers March." Washington, who had resigned his command and was serving without pay as an aide to Braddock, thought it the most splendid sight he had ever seen. As the troops pushed on through the woods they suddenly heard war whoops. The English vanguard formed a skirmish line, sent a volley crashing into de Beaujeu's troops, and then fell back. The Indians and French scattered to the ravines that ran along both sides of the English forces. Posting themselves behind trees, they raked the milling, panicked British with a murderous crossfire. As the English in the van fell back, they collided with troops coming up, and in the confusion men began to drop by the hundreds. Braddock, wildly and vainly trying to rally his men, had five horses shot out from under him before he was himself brought down with a mortal wound. The slaughter went on for three hours.

With British troops flinging away their muskets and fleeing and the drums rattling out retreat, Washington found a wagon, got Braddock into it, and pulled the stricken general away from the carnage. The afternoon had cost the French fewer than 60 casualties; of the 1,373 English noncoms and privates involved, only 459 escaped being killed or wounded, and three quarters of the 86 officers became casualties. "Who would have thought it?" the wounded Braddock kept muttering. He died two days later, and Washington had him buried in an unmarked grave in the road so that the Indians would not mutilate his remains.

The debacle threw Virginia into a panic and left the frontier of Virginia, Maryland, and Pennsylvania open to French and Indian raids. To the north the English had better luck, thanks to the efforts of William Johnson, whom the king had appointed superintendent of northern Indian affairs. Johnson led three thousand New Englanders against Crown Point, a French stronghold at the southern end of Lake Champlain. The French marched to meet him and, getting word of their advance on September 8, Braddock sent forward a detachment of a thousand militiamen and two hundred Mohawks under Chief Hendrick, a canny old warrior who had visited Queen Anne in 1710. Hendrick was dubious about the detachment: "If they are to be killed, too many; if they are to fight, too few." The command marched straight into an ambush where French musketry ripped it apart. Chief Hendrick was among those killed.

The survivors fled back to the English lines, where, incredibly, Johnson succeeded in rallying them behind a log barricade. When the French regulars attacked, the provincials beat them off. Johnson never got to Crown Point, but he did build Fort William Henry on Lake George and received a knighthood for his part in the campaign.

In the spring of 1756 a formidable new commander named Louis Joseph, marquis de Montcalm joined the French in America. Short, nervous, brilliant, and brave, Montcalm moved quickly and skillfully. He threw three thousand troops at Oswego, the English fort on the south side of Lake Ontario, and captured it in August of 1756. His victory encouraged the western Indians, whom the English had hoped to secure as allies, to support the French. One Indian delegation to Montreal said, "We wanted to see this famous man who tramples the English under his feet. But you are a little man, my father. It is when we look into your eyes that we see the greatness of the pine-tree and the fire of the eagle." Throughout the colonies Indians began to pull away from any associations they might have had with the English. In January of 1757 Washington, training a Virginia regiment, wrote that "the French grow more and more Formidable by their alliances, while our Friendly Indians are deserting Our Interest."

The year 1757 dawned bleakly for the English. Seven years before, the French had had eight hundred regular troops in America; now they had sixty-six hundred. Everywhere, England was on the defensive. In the spring Montcalm prepared to attack Fort William Henry. He recruited two thousand Indians from the upper Great Lakes, and, sensitive to the diplomatic niceties required, presented many of them with belts of wampum in the name of the king of France. At last the French and Indians marched toward Lake George eight thousand strong, destroying several British parties on the way. The Indians scalped and even practiced cannibalism on some of the English dead, behavior the French justified on the grounds that they could not prevent it without losing the Indians.

Montcalm besieged the fort early in August. The hopelessly outnumbered garrison put up a spirited defense before surrendering. Montcalm allowed the men to keep their arms and promised to protect them from his Indian allies. But the English had no sooner left the fort than the Indians fell on them and, berserk with plundered brandy, began to strip and murder the captives. Unable to check the chaos, Montcalm finally bared his breast

The acerbic Brigadier General George Townshend, who served under Wolfe in North America, drew these caustic caricatures, indicating that he thought little of the Indians and not much more of his sovereign, King George II.

to the Indians and cried, "Since you are rebellious children who break the promise you have given to your Father and who will not listen to his voice, kill him first of all." His officers finally restored some order, but not before two hundred of the two thousand prisoners had been murdered. Montcalm's Indian allies immediately abandoned him, and the French destroyed Fort William Henry and then withdrew to their posts at Ticonderoga, Crown Point, and Montreal.

These events had marked the nadir of British fortunes in the war; the next year saw the British taking the offensive and redressing the balance with powerful strokes. On July 26 Louisburg fell to twelve thousand British regulars under Lord Jeffrey Amherst, and a month later a provincial force of thirty-six hundred men captured Fort Frontenac, on the north side of Ontario, giving the British control of the lake. Indians took only a minor part in these battles, but they were to play a major role in the campaign that began to take shape in the Ohio valley late that spring. Rankling over their two ill-starred attempts to seize Fort Duquesne, the British had appointed General John Forbes to lead a new assault. Though only fifty-one, Forbes, wracked with disease, was a dying man—he had to be carried on a litter— but his capacity for intelligent, meticulous planning had not deserted him. Forbes's campaign differed from the earlier failures of Washington and Braddock not only in the general's choice of a new route, but in his vigorous efforts to secure Indian support.

That support was difficult to get and to control. Washington, commanding the Virginia regiment, wrote in disgust: "The Indians are mercenary; every service of theirs must be purchased; and they are easily offended, being thoroughly sensible of their own importance." The natives often arrogantly demanded food, supplies, and presents, and sometimes left in a huff when they felt the provisions were inadequate. But they were not drawing regular military pay, and despite the moralizings of the frustrated white commanders, they could hardly be expected to serve Europeans in a European manner for no good Indian purpose.

By April 10, 1758, more than five hundred southeastern Indians had gathered at the English camp, eager to go into the field on scalp-seeking parties. As summer came on, however, and the campaign failed to get under way, they became disgusted and went home, carrying their presents with them. By July most of the Cherokees and Catawbas had drifted away.

When Forbes finally moved out of the main supply base he had built at what was to become Bedford, Pennsylvania, he had few Indian allies with his five thousand provincial troops and fourteen hundred Scots Highlanders. Newcomers arrived, however, including some Cherokees under their chief Little Carpenter, whose demands Forbes met, though he termed them "sordid and avaricious." The army moved forward with care, leaving a string of fortified posts behind it. Despite their precautions, the English suffered a setback in September when Forbes sent out some eight hundred Highlanders to scout around Fort Duquesne. The Scots got themselves badly cut up, losing a third of their number. The French had relied heavily on their Indian allies in the fight, and the natives were shaken by the number of casualties they had sustained. When more of them were killed in a skirmish in October, they began to leave the French camp. They were sick of dying for their allies, and they had begun to get word of a series of peace conferences between English and Indians in Philadelphia.

SACRED GIFT OF THE SUN

The 150-year-old Cree pipe shown above was handed down for ten generations and solemnized two peace agreements. The decoration of beads, fur, and feathers—similar to those of the pipe in the scene at left—was prescribed by custom so that other tribes could recognize the pipe's peaceful symbolism.

According to tradition, tobacco fire in a pipe bowl was related to the supernatural power of the sun. To invoke the pipe's power, Indians smoked tobacco prepared by a conjurer in a special dawn ritual. Facing the sun, he kneaded the tobacco while speaking the tribe's intentions aloud. Then, by smoking the prepared tobacco during ceremonies of dancing and chanting, tribes petitioned the gods for the destruction of enemies, or health and good luck, or needed rains. To call the gods to witness a treaty, a tribe's members blew smoke to the sky and the earth, and to the four points of the compass. Conjurers could put a good or evil wish into the tobacco and cast a spell by blowing the smoke on the chosen person.

As a sacred and powerful object the pipe was carefully kept from sources of pollution. Pregnant women were considered impure, and their husbands were not allowed to smoke a ceremonial pipe.

Chitimacha Indians, who lived near Grand Lake, Louisiana, carry a peace pipe similar to the Cree pipe above (an artifact with the bowl missing) as they approach seated French delegates at the start of their ritualized peace ceremony in 1718.

Among the Cherokees who cast their lot with the English was Chief Outacite, shown in a nineteenth-century portrait wearing the silver gorget (below), engraved with the royal arms of George III, that his allies presented to him.

Forbes and the colonial authorities had convened the conferences to recapture the allegiance of the Delawares, Shawnees, and Mingos and to reassure the western Indians that the English did not intend to dispossess them of their lands. At the same time, Christian Frederick Post, a Moravian missionary who had twice been married to Indian women, carried out a delicate mission in the country of the western Indians, assuring them of English good will and inviting the Delawares to return to their original home in the Susquehanna valley. Post managed to counter a good deal of legitimate skepticism: "You intend to drive us away and settle this country," the Indians said, "or else, why do you come to fight in the land that God has given us?"

"I am your flesh and blood," Post replied, "and sooner than I would tell you any story that would be of hurt to you, or your children, I would suffer death . . . I do assure you of mine and the people's honesty."

Some five hundred Indians, Iroquois among them, attended another treaty conference at Easton, Pennsylvania, in October, where several colonial governors discussed and redressed many native grievances. The proceedings, subsequently ratified by the king of England in Council, returned land west of the Appalachians—which had been deeded to the Pennsylvania proprietors by the Iroquois—to the other tribes that lived on it. Colonel Henry Bouquet, Forbes's chief of staff, issued a proclamation prohibiting English movement west of the mountains without special authorization. The Easton treaty, Bouquet said, was a blow that "knocked the French in the head."

When, a little later, a French officer from the threatened Fort Duquesne approached an Indian camp with a string of wampum and offered it to one of the Delaware chiefs with whom Post was conferring, the Indian refused it. The Frenchman thereupon threw the belt to a nearby group of Delawares, who treated it like a snake, kicking it from one to the other until one of them picked it up with a stick and flung it away.

By November 24 the English forces had advanced to within a few miles of Fort Duquesne. As they approached they heard a terrific explosion, and when they arrived at the fort the next day they found it gutted and the defenders gone. Inside the ruined fort the English troops came upon a row of stakes on which were fastened the heads of Highland troops who had been taken in the earlier engagement, each with a Scottish kilt tied beneath it.

For all its savagery, there was a note of despair in the grisly taunt. The French were losing the war, and they knew it. The final blow came the following September, when British troops under General James Wolfe faced off against French regulars commanded by Montcalm on the Plains of Abraham, near Quebec. Both commanders died in the battle—surprisingly brief, considering all the years and wars that had led up to it—but Wolfe lived long enough to know that he had won. The peace treaty would not materialize for three years, but after Quebec, New France never had a chance.

Still, the fighting went on. While Wolfe was taking Quebec, the back country of the Carolinas was again in an uproar. The Cherokee nation, about ten thousand strong and scattered through some forty villages along the frontiers of Virginia, North Carolina, South Carolina, and Georgia, had taken up the hatchet against the English. The war apparently began

With this florid document, the French governor of Louisiana concluded a treaty of friendship with Cherokee chief Oconostota in 1761.

when Cherokee warriors, returning home from Forbes's campaign against Fort Duquesne, appropriated several horses they found running wild in the woods. A group of frontiersmen, claiming the horses as their own, ambushed and killed a dozen of the Cherokees. The Cherokees retaliated by murdering twenty or thirty settlers, and soon a full-scale war engulfed the frontier. The fighting lasted for two years, ending in the winter of 1761 after a long, devastating campaign conducted against the Indians by regular and provincial troops. The harsh terms of the treaty included the establishment of a boundary line between Indian and white settlements.

Three years before, when the English had set up a similar line, they had done so in hopes of placating a valuable ally. The contrast between that boundary and the one forced on the Cherokees at gunpoint indicated how the native Americans had fared in the war. No matter which side the Indians chose, their true interests lay in a continued stalemate between the English and the French. With the French forces driven from the New World, the natives could no longer be of any use to the colonists. Just as much as the French, the Indians lost the long struggle that had begun with a bloodless scuffle at a Maine trading post seventy years before.

Pawns
in a
Bloody Game

As France and Britain struggled for supremacy in the seventy-year conflict that culminated with the Great War for Empire, both nations sought the allegiance of the Indians. By force and flattery, by bribery and cajolery, the European powers finally succeeded in getting most of the tribes to pledge their loyalty to white monarchs an ocean away. Here, during King William's War, New France's tireless and intractable governor, Count Frontenac, watches as his native allies torture a prisoner during a punitive expedition against the Iroquois. For all his determination, Frontenac could never bring the Iroquois into his camp.

ONONDAGA HISTORICAL ASSOCIATION

General William Johnson's 1755 victory
over Baron Ludwig Dieskau's French
regulars at Crown Point—shown in
this contemporary engraving as a tidy
set-piece battle—actually was a
desperate business of confused fighting
behind hasty barricades. Johnson's
Mohawk allies stood by his militia
and played an important part in the
action. But Dieskau's Caughnawagas
simply sat down to watch the outcome.
The colonists routed the regulars
and captured their leader, who paid
the amateur fighters a rueful
tribute: "In the morning they fought
like good boys, about noon like
men and in the afternoon like devils."

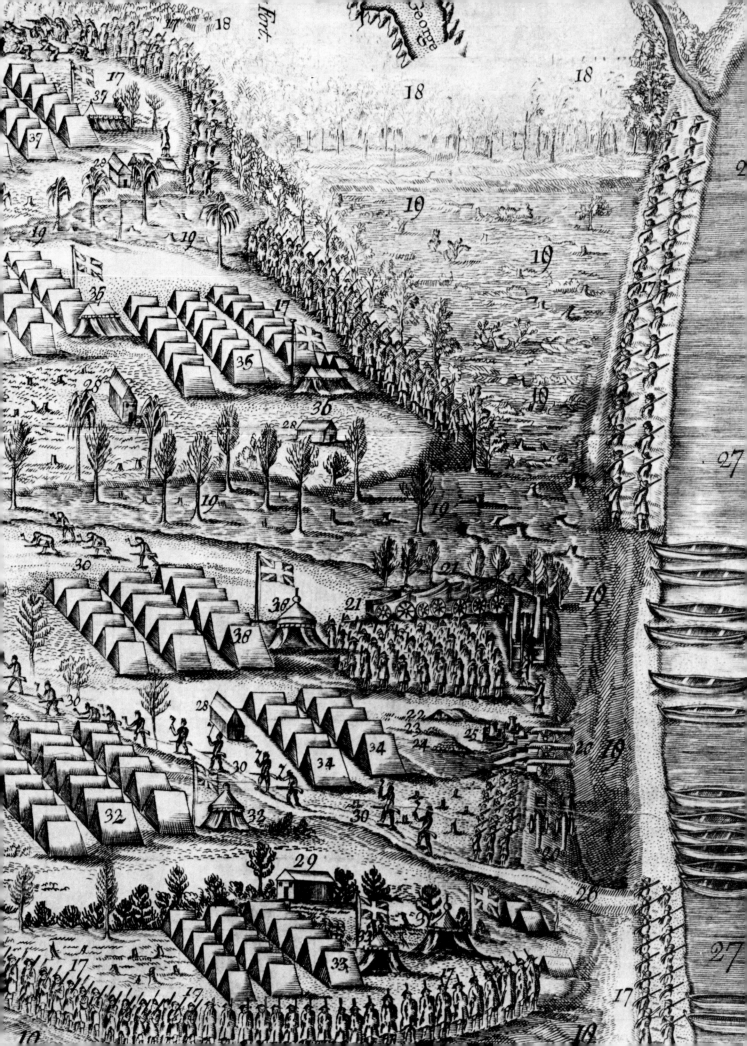

Fighting as they fought best, Indians could
break armies. In this painting of the last,
terrible moments of General Edward Braddock's
command, the doomed British regulars struggle
to maintain their formations against a hidden
enemy. The disgust and bafflement that the
news of the debacle stirred in England prompted
the wit Horace Walpole to write, "Braddock's
defeat remains in the situation of the longest
battle that ever was fought with nobody."

In his hour of triumph, British
general James Wolfe dies on the plains
of Quebec in Benjamin West's heroic
vision of the final defeat of New
France. Although Indians had little
to do with this particular campaign,
West probably included his brooding
warrior as a tribute to the part
the Iroquois played in the war.
NATIONAL GALLERY OF CANADA, OTTAWA

4: A Time of Rebellion

When the governor of French Canada surrendered to Lord Jeffrey Amherst, the British commander in chief in America, on September 8, 1760, among the French concessions were the several forts in the western Great Lakes area, most notably Detroit and Michilimackinac—now Mackinac Island. General Amherst immediately dispatched Major Robert Rogers, with two companies of his Rangers, to accept the surrender of these posts and to raise the British flag over them. The twenty-nine-year-old Rogers seemed the right man for the job. A superb scout, he had consistently fought and beaten the Indians on their own terms.

As he penetrated the western territories, Rogers was met by chiefs of the various tribes that inhabited the region. Though allied with the French during the war, the Indians of the old Northwest did not consider themselves any less the owners of the lands on which the forts had been built. Indeed, the European forts were seen by the Indians as convenient places to trade furs for valuable European goods and to obtain powder and guns as part of the tribute Europeans paid to Indians for their cooperation (the Europeans regarded the process as "gift giving"). The forts existed, in Indian eyes, not in European territory, but in Indian country; the natives had merely allowed the Europeans to use a little waste ground to build these establishments.

For the Europeans, on the other hand, the peace that emerged in the great struggle between the French and English largely ignored the Indian. France and England dealt with each other in the framework of European diplomacy. They dealt separately with the native inhabitants of North America.

This stark woodcut is from a broadside telling about U.S. General St. Clair's defeat of 1791.

When Robert Rogers arrived at the lakes, he was met by a delegation of chiefs at the mouth of the Detroit River on November 27. The Ottawa chief Pontiac was probably among the group of Ottawas, Hurons, and Potawatomis that halted Rogers's party. As Rogers noted in his journal, Pontiac "demanded my business into his country and how it happened that I dared to enter it without his leave." Rogers adroitly replied that his mission was to remove the French from the area and that he had no designs against the Indians. He gave the Indians some belts of wampum signifying his friendly intentions, and Pontiac in turn offered him the pipe of peace, which they both smoked. The Indian leader granted the Englishman permission to pass through the country, even giving assurances that he would be protected while doing so.

Though the Indian chiefs did not see themselves as conquered allies of the French, they realized that they had to come to some arrangement with the English. Rogers reported that Pontiac indicated his willingness to "reign in his country in subordination to the King of Great Britain, and was willing to pay him such annual acknowledgement as he was able in furs, and to call him his uncle." On the other hand he warned Rogers that if the English neglected him, he would shut off their route into the interior. Pontiac's whole demeanor, Rogers said, indicated that "he was far from considering himself as a conquered Prince, and that he expected to be treated with the respect and honour due to a King or Emperor, by all who came into his country, or treated with him."

On November 29, 1760, in a colorful ceremony, the French flag came down at Fort Detroit, the British flag went up, and French soldiers were sent off to be exchanged. Rogers dispatched troops to occupy some of the smaller French forts in the area, among them Fort Miami on the Maumee River and Fort Ouiatenon on the Wabash. Then he set off with a detachment to try to reach Fort Michilimackinac before the winter ice closed the lakes to travel. Meanwhile, Captain Donald Campbell, one of the many Scots officers in the British army, took command of Fort Detroit.

The shift from French to British control did not change the life of the fort at first. The French *habitants*, who lived along the river on either side of the fort, continued to gather there to chat and exchange news with the garrison. The surrounding Indians, many of them converted to Catholicism during the French regime, continued to barter with the traders for blankets, kettles, knives, and guns. At the commandant's quarters lively parties with card playing and dancing lasted into the small hours of Sunday.

But there was one significant—and fatal—difference between the old French regime and the new English one. The French had secured the loyalty of their Indian allies by consistently giving them ammunition and provisions. Campbell, however, under severe orders from Amherst to withhold such gifts, could not play the political and economic role expected of him. He begged for greater latitude, and Sir William Johnson, the knowledgeable superintendent of northern Indians, supported his plea. "It is very necessary," Johnson wrote Amherst, "and will always be expected by the Indians, that the commanding officer of every post have it in his power to supply them in case of necessity with a little clothing, some arms and ammunition to hunt with; also some provisions on their journey homewards, as well as a smith to repair their arms and working utensils, etc."

Amherst, determined to stop the practice of supplying the Indians gratis, replied, "I do not see why the Crown should be put to that expense. Services must be rewarded; it has ever been a maxim with me. But as to purchasing the good behavior either of Indians or any others, [that] is what I do not understand. When men of whatsoever race behave ill," he concluded, "they must be punished but not bribed."

Amherst's blindness made war between Great Britain and the Indians of the old Northwest almost inevitable. The Indians might have accepted his tightfisted policy had they not also worried that, as the French had often told them, the English intended to take away their lands. When, after the war, Amherst gave some Seneca land near Niagara to some of his officers as a reward for service, his action not only expressed the English attitude of proprietary right toward Indian land but violated a treaty between the Six Nations and the colony of New York. Though it was overruled in London, the grant had given the aggrieved Senecas clear evidence of their uncertain tenure in their own country.

In addition to such tangible affronts, the Indians began to sense the contempt and hostility that pervaded the English attitude toward them. Indians were no longer welcome in the forts, and interracial mingling, especially intermarriage, was discouraged. In sum, the English acted as though they had no obligation toward the inhabitants of the country — with predictable consequences.

By the summer of 1761 war belts — strings of wampum that one tribe sent another when seeking help in a coming war — had begun to be passed among the Indians of the area. The Senecas urged the Delawares and Shawnees in Pennsylvania and Ohio, and the Ottawas, Hurons, Chippewas, and Potawatomis near the Great Lakes, to join in an assault on the British forts at Detroit, Pittsburgh, Presque Isle, Venango, and Niagara. But European intelligence of Indian plots was surprisingly good, largely because of the difficulty of bringing all potential Indian participants to the same point of view, and Captain Campbell got word of the preparations in time to alert the endangered posts.

In response to the growing threats to the western forts, Amherst decided to reinforce Detroit with troops under Major Henry Gladwin, a tough and fearless officer who had been wounded during Braddock's campaign in 1755. Amherst ordered Gladwin, in June of 1761, to proceed to the west and help the local commanders prepare to defend the forts against possible Indian attack. Conferences with the Indians soon followed, with Sir William Johnson present. But although officers on the spot wanted to supply the Indians with adequate amounts of ammunition and gifts, Amherst's stern orders, frequently reiterated, prevented them from doing so.

Yet this policy was never clearly stated to the Indians, who only gradually discovered its true nature. Campbell, writing Colonel Henry Bouquet, commander of Fort Pitt (the English name for Fort Duquesne), noted that "the general says the Crown is to be no longer at the expense of maintaining the Indians, that they may very well live by their hunting, and desires to keep them scarce of powder." Campbell wondered whether Bouquet was observing the general's policy; for his part, he feared its consequences. "I assure you they only want a good opportunity to fall upon us if they had encouragement from an enemy."

Agents and traders who knew the Indians best began to hear rumors of

further conspiracies against the English. These rumors were aggravated by reports of an Indian known as the Delaware Prophet, who, in a peculiar crying manner, was urging the Indians to throw off their dependence on the white man and his goods, even to the point of rejecting the use of firearms. The road to Heaven, the Prophet said, was being blocked by the white people, and it could be opened only by a change of heart on the part of the Indians and, probably, war.

Early in 1763 war belts again appeared among the Hurons, Ottawas, Senecas, Potawatomis, Delawares, Shawnees, and Miamis, presaging an attack on the English. In the interpretation of many nineteenth-century historians, the imperious Ottawa chief Pontiac, whom Rogers claimed to have met on his mission, was the instigator of the so-called conspiracy from its inception. But to later scholars Pontiac's role in the initial stages of the war was less apparent. Although he gradually assumed the leadership of the attack that followed, in the beginning Pontiac was probably just one of many tribal leaders who decided that war with the English was necessary to preserve the Indian position in the North American interior.

By an ironic coincidence, Britain and France signed a formal peace in Europe at the same time the first new Seneca war belt turned up among the Miamis. By April Pontiac was gathering support from the Potawatomis and Hurons as well as from his own Ottawas. Calling a grand council for April 27, he exhorted his fellow Indians to attack. He spoke of a message the "Master of Life" had communicated to the Delaware Prophet: give up the white man's liquor, cleave to only one wife, abandon the white man's

In the wake of the Great War for Empire in 1760, Major Robert Rogers (above, left) set out for Detroit to take over the old French territory. Along the way he met with some Chippewa chiefs and got them to sign this treaty, ceding to the English a tract of land near Detroit. During his foray Rogers met Chief Pontiac (above), who three years later set the Northwest aflame.

British colonel Henry Bouquet, who won the decisive victory at Bushy Run, also took part in the peace negotiations that followed Pontiac's Rebellion. In this Benjamin West engraving, he meets with the Indians in 1764.

weapons and clothes and go back to using the skins of animals. As interpreted by Pontiac, the Master of Life had also urged his Indian children to "drive off your land those dogs clothed in red who will do you nothing but harm." Here Pontiac conveniently overlooked the Prophet's strictures against all white men by excluding the French from his condemnation. He told his audience that in four days he would go with his young men into the fort, ostensibly to entertain the garrison with a ceremonial dance, but in fact to spy preparatory to another visit when he would attempt to seize the place. Finally, he asked the Potawatomis and Hurons to return to their villages and prepare for war.

Pontiac's visit to the fort went off as scheduled, and the chief announced to Major Gladwin, who had taken command of the garrison the summer before, that he would return in a few days for a second visit. In the meantime he held another council on May 5 and again harangued his audience, comparing the English unfavorably to the French and detailing his plan for the assault on the fort. The Indians would carry sawed-off muskets, as well as tomahawks and knives, into the stockade under their blankets while other bands would surround it and prevent any reinforcements from coming up the Detroit River. But Pontiac's plan, scheduled for two days from the meeting, did not long remain a secret. Somebody—perhaps a young Indian maiden called Catherine who was in love with Gladwin, perhaps the daughter of a French friend of Pontiac's—told the commander of the scheme. Other signs, such as reports that Indians were filing off the barrels of their guns or borrowing files from the French inhabitants, seemed to lend credence to the warnings.

Gladwin's garrison, two under-strength companies of Royal Americans and one company of Queen's Rangers, probably did not number more than 120 men. But they were ready on Saturday morning, May 7, 1763, when Pontiac and about 300 Indians appeared, each with his blanket thrown over his shoulder to conceal the weapons he carried. Although Gladwin left the gates of the fort open as usual, there were doubled guards on sentry duty, each with fixed bayonet. Moreover, only Gladwin and his second in command, Captain Campbell, were waiting, both armed, for Pontiac and his chiefs at the council table in Campbell's house. The other officers were ready at their posts among the men. Pontiac, noting the preparations for trouble, protested that the English had listened to some "bad birds" who had given Gladwin information accusing Pontiac of plotting against him.

Abandoning his plan, Pontiac withdrew his men from the fort after desultory talks. Some of his followers were furious and accused him of having lost his nerve at the last moment. He tried again the following day, but Gladwin would admit only the chiefs. To allay suspicion, Pontiac then sent messengers to the Hurons, Potawatomis, and French, asking them to come and play an innocent game of lacrosse. Outside the fort the game went on until Sunday evening, when Pontiac announced that he would return the next day with his warriors for another council. But Gladwin again sent messengers to inform the chief that only he and a few of his chiefs might come to council.

His plan of a surprise attack frustrated and his leadership called into question by his followers, Pontiac decided to strike outside the fort. He sent a war party to the farmhouse of a Mrs. Turnbull, who lived within

Bouquet demanded severe concessions from the Indians. Here, in another West engraving, he supervises the return of white prisoners taken during Pontiac's Rebellion. The scene is Fort Pitt, which Bouquet himself had earlier relieved.

107

*An unknown British officer did this sketch of
the garrison town of Detroit in 1794. French-
held until 1760, for the next thirty-six years
Detroit belonged to the English, who used it
during the Revolution as a base for raids against
the American frontier. Opposite is a French
drawing of an Indian of the Great Lakes area.*

sight of the fort. The braves killed and scalped three people there and went
on to attack other wilderness settlements. On May 10 Pontiac called a
conference at which both French and Indian leaders discussed the situation.
The French, more nervous than the Indians about the possible consequences of the attacks, persuaded Pontiac to offer Gladwin a truce during
which terms of peace could be presented. The Indian leader sent several
of the French and four of the Indian chiefs to the fort to request that Captain Campbell be sent out to negotiate. Gladwin, sensing treachery, refused
to order Campbell out but finally permitted him to go of his own volition,
fortified by French assurances that his character as an ambassador would be
respected. Gladwin's misgivings proved sound when the Indians seized
Campbell as a hostage.

Pontiac then sent threatening messages to Gladwin ordering him to surrender the fort, while his war parties continued to ambush outlying settlers.
Gladwin rejected the demands out of hand and insisted that Campbell be
returned before he would discuss any terms of settlement. Pontiac, meanwhile, sent war belts to the Miamis and other Indian nations and messengers
to the French in Illinois to urge their support for his cause.

The French, however, were becoming leery of Pontiac, who began to
receive complaints from the *habitants* that his warriors were plundering
French farmers. A delegation of French settlers, noting that "we are all
brothers and the children of your Great Father, the King of France," told
Pontiac that when the king returned, as they hoped he would, "he will
regard you as rebellious children and traitors, and instead of petting you
he will make war upon you. . . ." Pontiac, in response, apologized for the
rough handling some of the petitioners had received from his young men,
but he called upon them to remember how he had defended the French
against their Indian enemies many years earlier. "I am the same French
Pontiac who helped you seventeen years ago; I am French, and I want to
die French. . . ." He urged the *habitants* to help him carry out his plan.
"I do not demand your assistance, because I know you could not give it; I
only ask you for provisions for myself and all my followers."

Pontiac then began to make war in earnest, and the series of English

forts stretching throughout the Great Lakes country began to fall, one by one, to his men. First to go was Sandusky, on the south shore of Lake Erie. On May 16 a group of Ottawa and Huron chiefs requested and immediately received permission to enter the fort, whose commander, Ensign Christopher Pauli, knew them. During the council the chiefs seized him while their men butchered the fifteen-man garrison. Pauli himself survived only because he roused the interest of a widow who adopted him to replace her lost husband.

On May 28 Lieutenant Abraham Cuyler of the Queen's Rangers, en route from Niagara with supplies for the Detroit garrison, put in at Point Pelee on the western end of Lake Erie. His command consisted of ten *bateaux* (flat-bottomed pointed-end French craft that could be propelled either by sails or by oars) and ninety-six men, none of whom had heard that hostilities had broken out. While camped on the shore, the party was rushed by Indians who had been quietly watching from the nearby woods. The natives seized eight of the *bateaux* along with valuable supplies, but Cuyler and several of his men escaped with the two remaining boats. Another detachment of eighteen soldiers and two boats coming south from Fort Michilimackinac was also captured. Success seemed to crown all of Pontiac's endeavors. The English fort among the Miamis (near Fort Wayne, Indiana) was the next outpost to fall. Although aware of Indian hostility, Ensign Robert Holmes, commanding, was decoyed out of the fort by his mistress, a Miami girl, and killed. His eleven men attempted to hold the fort against the Indians, but on the threat of annihilation they soon surrendered.

On June 1 Pontiac's men reached Fort Ouiatenon (Lafayette, Indiana) and asked Lieutenant Edward Jenkins, commander of the fort, to come outside to a cabin to meet several chiefs in council. No sooner had Jenkins entered the cabin than he was seized and bound; his garrison of twenty surrendered.

Fort Michilimackinac fell next. Unaware of the troubles at Detroit Captain George Etherington and his thirty-five men left the fort to watch a game of lacrosse being played by the Chippewas against some visiting

RAMPAGES OF THE PAXTON BOYS

Exasperated by a long series of Indian raids on frontier settlements in Pennsylvania, a mob of so-called Paxton Boys (from the town of that name) vented their anger on an innocent Conestoga Indian village. On the morning of December 14, 1763, they brutally hacked four villagers to death and shot two more. Though the Conestogas remained peaceful, and the original grievances against them had been trumped up in any case—one vigilante claimed an Indian had melted his pewter spoons—the Paxton Boys swooped down on them again some two weeks later at the Lancaster jailhouse (right) where the Conestogas had gone to place themselves under government protection. Fourteen more were killed there.

Emboldened, the bully-boys decided in February, 1764, to march on Philadelphia and finish off the Indians living there. Rumors of impending slaughter swept the staid city, and the Quaker citizens uncharacteristically took up arms. The cartoon below depicts the ludicrous anticlimax of the mobilization, as the aroused Quakers prepare to fire on the horsemen entering at right, who were actually German butchers coming to the city's aid. The real Paxton Boys were encamped outside Philadelphia. There, a delegation led by no less a personage than Benjamin Franklin parleyed with the rowdies and persuaded them to go home—with a promise that thenceforth they would receive a bounty for their Indian scalps.

Philadelphia Quakers hastily form a battle line near the Court House to stand off the Paxton mob.

In the prison yard in Lancaster, Pennsylvania, men from nearby Paxton hack and stab Conestoga Indians.

Sauks. During the game, by prearrangement, one of the Indians hurled the ball into the stockade and immediately the players rushed in headlong past the sentries to retrieve it. Once inside, they dropped their lacrosse sticks, grabbed weapons smuggled into the fort earlier by their women, and proceeded to kill twenty soldiers and one trader. Nearby French families saved a few Englishmen by hiding them in their homes while the Indians went about the countryside slaughtering.

After the fall of Michilimackinac, the attacks shifted to the Pennsylvania forts and those closer to the eastern settlements. Fort Pitt, Fort Ligonier, and Fort Bedford were all besieged. Most of them held, but in mid-June a force of Senecas dealt a crushing defeat to Fort Venango (Franklin, Pennsylvania) and annihilated the fifteen- or sixteen-man garrison. The Senecas then moved on to Fort Le Boeuf (Waterford, Pennsylvania), where half the garrison of thirteen men escaped after the Indians burned the works on June 18. Supported by Ottawas, Hurons, and Chippewas, the Senecas next struck Fort Presque Isle (Erie, Pennsylvania). With the fort in flames from burning arrows, the thirty defenders surrendered on the promise that they would be permitted to withdraw safely to Fort Pitt. But the victors broke their pledge and divided up the prisoners among the four tribes.

While the Senecas celebrated their victories, a party of Delawares approached Fort Pitt on June 24 and demanded its surrender. But they had picked a tough adversary in a Swiss soldier of fortune named Simeon Ecuyer, who was commanding the 338-man garrison in Bouquet's absence. Captain Ecuyer flatly rejected the Indian demand and then sent the Delawares a present of two blankets and a handkerchief from the fort's smallpox hospital. The brutal trick apparently worked. The Indians backed off and subsequently a white captive of the Delawares testified that the tribe was being decimated by the disease.

The fall of the other British forts in the interior at last impressed Amherst with the seriousness of the challenge, and when the news arrived overseas the king's ministers hastened their deliberations on proclaiming a limit to white settlement beyond the Appalachians. The famous Proclamation of 1763, issued on October 7, prohibited such movement—and might have prevented the spread of war had it been issued earlier.

Though the English forts all around Detroit had fallen rapidly to the Indians, Detroit itself, under the cool and unbending Gladwin, held out. Pontiac tried many stratagems to take it, but he ruled out a frontal assault, which would have cost many men. He kept the place surrounded and continued to harass it with a persistence not at all typical of Indian warfare. As the celebrated historian Francis Parkman later put it, the history of the American Indian "cannot furnish another instance of so large a force persisting so long in the attack of a fortified place."

But Gladwin held, and while awaiting reinforcements he periodically sent detachments out from the fort to harry its Indian assailants. On July 4 one such foray killed two Indians, one of them the nephew of Wasson, chief of the Saginaw Chippewas. Outraged, Wasson demanded that Pontiac turn over Captain Campbell, still a prisoner, to his revenge. In an action for which Pontiac must accept the blame—though he may have been temporarily absent when it occurred—Campbell was released to Wasson, who promptly killed and scalped him. The body, thrown into the river, floated down to the fort and further enraged the defenders.

In the meantime, Bouquet was marching west from Carlisle, Pennsylvania, with a relief force of some 460 men, including the Highlanders 42nd Regiment, which had already become renowned as the Black Watch. The troops had gotten to within thirty miles of Fort Pitt when, at a place called Edge Hill, a mixed force of Delawares, Shawnees, Mingos, and Hurons fell upon the advance guard. In a rough fight that lasted all through the afternoon of August 5, Bouquet's men held the hill but could make no headway against their foes. When the sun went down the thirsty, battered force found itself surrounded.

The next day the confident Indians saw the crest of the hill defended by only a thin line of men. Abandoning their cautious tactics, they rushed from the cover of the forest, breached the line, and then recoiled in astonishment and terror as two companies that Bouquet had concealed smashed into their flanks. The attack disintegrated, and the Indians fought their way back into the forest as best they could. Bouquet's set-piece victory cost him fifty men killed and sixty wounded, but the Indians undoubtedly lost an equal number of men, among them two Delaware chiefs. Bouquet camped that night at nearby Bushy Run, which gave its name to the battle. Four days later the relief column marched into Fort Pitt.

As usual in an Indian war, the frontier settlers suffered terribly. One contemporary estimate claimed that as many as two thousand English died during the bloody spring and summer, and those who escaped came pouring into the eastern towns, where their grim tales added to the atmosphere of hatred and resentment. The Quaker-dominated Pennsylvania assembly steadfastly refused to support aggressive measures against the natives, but such reasoning seemed ridiculous to the hot-blooded Presbyterians on the frontier. The frenzy reached its climax with the massacre of a group of unoffending Conestoga Indians in Lancaster County on December 14, 1763. Aroused by unsupported assertions linking some of the Conestogas with the natives who had perpetrated the frontier massacres, a group of fifty-seven vigilantes surrounded the village and scalped, hacked, stabbed, and mangled the three men, two women, and one young boy who were present. The rest of the Indians were out peddling the baskets, brooms, and bowls that they manufactured for sale to the whites.

The magistrates of Lancaster gathered the survivors and put them in the workhouse there for their own protection, while Governor John Penn, son of the commonwealth's founder, issued a proclamation condemning the killings and forbidding any further violence. Despite the proclamation, the vigilantes assembled again on December 27, broke into the workhouse, and killed the fourteen remaining Indians while they knelt in prayer, children clinging to their mothers as they received their judgment. "Men, women and little children were every one inhumanly murdered in cold blood!" Benjamin Franklin wrote in his stinging *Narrative of the Late Massacres in Lancaster County*, published immediately after the event. Franklin noted that the bodies had been finally buried in a hastily dug hole. "But the wickedness cannot be covered, the guilt will lie on the whole land, till justice is done on the murderers. The blood of the innocent will cry to Heaven for vengeance." The outraged Franklin spoke of the absence of any connection between those attacked and those committing depredations on the frontier. "The only crime of these poor wretches seems to have been

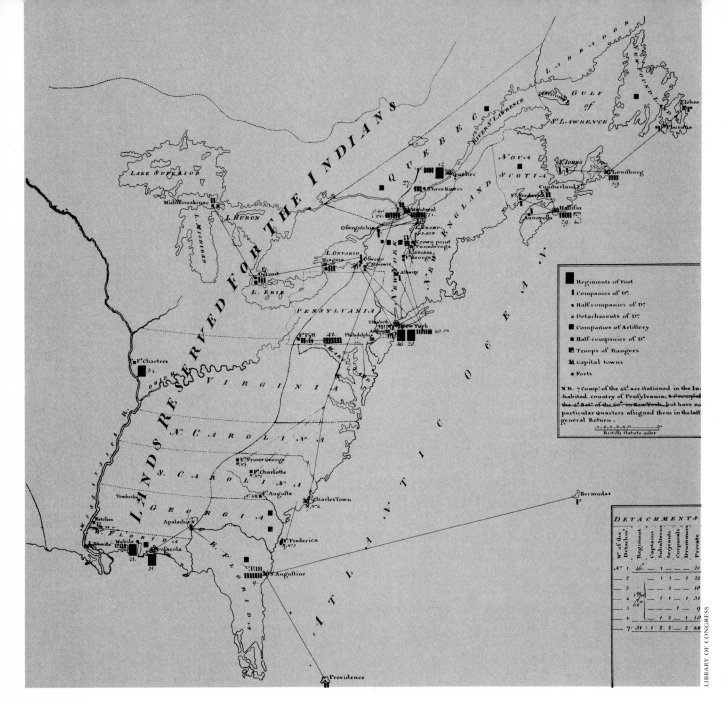

The 1767 edition of a map issued annually by the British to indicate the distribution of their troops in North America also shows the vast trans-Appalachian region granted to the Indians. The colonists generally ignored the restrictions against settling the reserved land.

that they had a reddish-brown skin and black hair, and some people of that sort, it seems, had murdered some of our relations." "Unhappy people!" Franklin exclaimed, "to have lived in such times, and by such neighbours... they would have been safe in any part of the known world, except in the very neighbourhood of the *Christian White savages* of Peckstang and Donegall."

Meanwhile the real war was coming to an end. Gladwin's stern defense of Detroit had permitted Amherst's reinforcements to come to his relief. The Indians, faced with the prospect of continued hostilities, started losing their unity. Indian bands began to make terms with Gladwin and pull out of the war, and eventually the flickering hope of substantial French military involvement died. Even Pontiac was at last forced to agree to peace on October 3, 1763. Although Amherst had been determined to eradicate the Indian vermin—if necessary by the further use of smallpox-infected blankets—a more conciliatory policy emerged with Pontiac's submission.

Two punitive expeditions had penetrated the interior regions, but the Indians had suffered no significant defeat and Pontiac was still a free man, chastened but not humbled.

In the next two years he visited French settlements in Illinois, and rumors began to spread of renewed resistance to English rule in the interior. But as English power in the area became more firmly established, Pontiac came increasingly to forget his French allegiance and to embrace the English.

Pontiac's death came as a shameful anticlimax to his life. A Peoria Indian shot him in the back as they were both leaving a store in Cahokia in 1769. Although the motive for the killing was obscure, suspicion inevitably fell on the English at Fort de Chartres, within whose protective walls the Peorias fled.

With Pontiac died perhaps the last real chance for the American Indian to blunt or even turn back the tide of English settlement. Later Indian leaders would attempt to unify and to repel the invader, but none who followed Pontiac would come as close to success.

Despite Pontiac's defeat, the natives continued to believe that the European forts in the interior were merely islands in an Indian sea, existing by Indian sufferance for Indian benefit. The English, thoroughly jangled by Pontiac's War, confirmed this belief through a series of treaties, negotiated between 1763 and 1775, that created a virtually continuous boundary between the colonists and the Indians stretching from Lake Ontario to Florida. But no proclamation or treaty could keep the English on their side of the Appalachians, and by early in the 1770's they had begun to establish settlements in Kentucky.

Among those not particularly impressed by the boundary was Virginia's bluff, strong-minded governor, the earl of Dunmore, who granted land beyond the line to veterans of the Great War for Empire and thereby triggered a brief, ugly confrontation afterward known as Lord Dunmore's War. In 1774 the Shawnee Indians, who were most affected by the settlements built by Dunmore's veterans, started attacking them. Dunmore immediately sent volunteers into the troubled area. When one party was ambushed on the Kentucky River in July, the governor ordered out fifteen hundred militia to chastise the Shawnees.

Meanwhile the Shawnees had appealed to the Iroquois for support. The Iroquois were concerned not only because they had a long-standing relationship as "elder brothers" of the Shawnees, but because Senecas as well as Shawnees had suffered violence as the whites moved into the disputed areas. Sir William Johnson, still at his post as superintendent of the northern Indians, strove to keep the Iroquois from allying themselves with the Shawnees against the English. In the midst of a conference with the Iroquois, Sir William died on July 11, 1774. His nephew and son-in-law, Colonel Guy Johnson, stepped into the breach and continued the conference, being confirmed as his uncle's successor both by the Iroquois, with whom he had long worked, and by General Thomas Gage, commander in chief of British forces in America. The conference was successfully concluded with the Iroquois renewing their covenant with the British and rejecting the pleas of the Shawnees to come to their assistance. So the Shawnees were left alone to face the invasion of their territory by Virginia militia. On October 6, at Point Pleasant, where the Great Kanawha

River meets the Ohio, a large force of Shawnees led by their chief, Cornstalk, crossed the Ohio before daybreak and took the Virginians by surprise. In a fierce wilderness battle that lasted the whole day, the Virginians lost fifty killed and twice that many wounded; but by dusk the Shawnees were beaten, and soon afterward Cornstalk made peace with Dunmore.

Lord Dunmore's War represented something more than the old story of whites usurping native territory. For in giving away Indian land, Dunmore had flouted not only the Shawnees, but the king of England as well. The years and miles that separated the colonists from their sovereign had worked a change; the king and his ministers had told them to stay east of the Appalachians, and they had ignored the order. Dunmore remained loyal to the Crown for the rest of his days, but, significantly, most of the men who fought his battle at Point Pleasant sided with the rebels when the Revolution began the next year.

As the Revolution broke over America, the Indians were not at first directly involved in the colonists' struggle against the mother country. When a group of Boston citizens dressed as Indians boarded British ships and threw their cargoes of tea into Boston Harbor, Guy Johnson explained the resulting crisis to the Iroquois, gathered in conference in January, 1775. He called it a dispute "solely occasioned by some people, who notwithstanding a law of the King and his wise Men, would not let some Tea land, but destroyed it, on which he was angry, and sent some Troops with the General [Thomas Gage], who you have long known, to see the Laws executed and bring the people to their sences, and as he is proceeding with great wisdom, to shew them their great mistake, I expect it will soon be over."

In this period the Indians were not asked to take sides, and indeed they were reluctant to do so. The Oneidas informed Governor Jonathan Trumbull of Connecticut, "We are unwilling to join on either side of such a contest, for we love you both—old England and new. Should the great King of England apply to us for our aid—we shall deny him—and should the Colonists apply—we shall refuse." But while the powerful Iroquois were staying aloof, some of the minor tribes were being drawn into the vortex. During the winter of 1774–75, George Washington recruited soldiers from among the Stockbridge, Passamaquoddy, St. John's, and Penobscot Indians. The Continental Congress, meeting in July, 1775, organized an Indian department modeled on the British superintendencies, though creating three (northern, middle, and southern) rather than two, as in the British system. The Congress also drafted a speech that could be delivered by the commissioners to any nations in their district. The Congress asserted that the disturbances were "a family quarrel between us and Old England. You Indians are not concerned in it. We don't wish you to take up the hatchet against the king's troops. We desire you to remain at home, and not join on either side, but keep the hatchet buried deep."

Yet both sides began to make unofficial efforts to elicit the support of the Indians. In May, 1775, Ethan Allen of Vermont urged the Iroquois to join him against the king's troops: "I know how to shute and ambush just like Indian and want your Warriors to come and see me and help me fight Regulars You know they Stand all along close Together Rank and file and my men fight so as Indians Do and I want your Warriors to Join with me and my Warriors like Brothers and Ambush the Regulars, if you will I will Give you Money Blankets Tomehawks Knives and Paint and the Like as much as you say because they first killed our men when it was Peace time."

By July the British too were inviting the Iroquois to "feast on a Bostonian and drink his Blood." As a preliminary substitute for the real thing, the British provided a roast ox and some wine. By the autumn of 1775 General Gage had instructed Guy Johnson and John Stuart (his superintendent in the southern department) to bring the Indians into the war when opportunity offered.

With British and Americans both pressing the Iroquois to join their sides, the Indians found themselves in an increasingly difficult position. In the summer of 1776 the Tory colonel John Butler, soon to be hated by the Revolutionists as the leader of the infamous Butler's Rangers, exhorted the Iroquois to join the king's forces against the colonists. Reiterating the argument that the French had used during the earlier conflict, Butler warned that the colonists' "intention is to take all your Lands from you and destroy your people, for they are all mad, foolish, crazy and full of deceit— They told you last Fall at Pittsburgh that they took the Tom Hawk out of your Hands and buried it deep and transplanted the Tree of Peace over it. I therefore now pluck up that Tree, dig up the Tom Hawk, and replace it in your hands with the Edge toward them that you may treat them as Enemies."

But the Iroquois rejected the British advice. Chief Cawconcaucawheteda, or Flying Crow, told them: "You say their Powder is rotten—We have found it good. You say they are all mad, foolish, wicked, and deceitful—I say you are so and they are wise for you want us to destroy ourselves in your War and they advise us to live in Peace. Their advice we intend to follow."

As it turned out the Iroquois were drawn into the war, but not as a unit by one side. Instead the famous unity of the league, which had given the Iroquois such commanding strength in previous years, was broken. Four of the Six Nations—the Mohawks, Cayugas, Senecas, and Onondagas —finally entered the war on the British side, while the Oneidas and Tuscaroras joined forces with the Americans. In July, 1776, Colonel Guy Johnson returned from England with Thayendanegea, the Mohawk chief known to the whites as Joseph Brant, who had accompanied him on a visit to the mother country. Brant had been lionized by London society; his portrait had been painted by George Romney, and he came home dedicated to the British cause. Arriving in New York, which was then under siege by Washington, Brant fought gallantly at the Battle of Long Island and then slipped through the American lines, returning to his homeland, where he urged his tribesmen to join the king's cause against the rebellious colonists. The decision of four of the six formerly confederated nations in favor of the British took place at a great congress in July of 1777, at which Colonel Butler supplied the Indians with rum, provisions, and arms.

The commitment and division of the Six Nations was sealed in blood shortly thereafter when, on August 6, 1777, the American general Nicholas Herkimer, with Oneida and Tuscarora support, went to the relief of beleaguered Fort Stanwix, at the head of the Mohawk River in upstate New York. At Oriskany he faced British troops supported by Indians from the other Iroquois nations. Though the British checked Herkimer's advance, their native allies suffered heavy casualties, and seventeen of the thirty-

In 1774 Colonel Guy Johnson, shown here in a portrait by Benjamin West, succeeded his uncle, Sir William Johnson, as Superintendent of Northern Indian Affairs. An able and tireless administrator, he did much to keep the Iroquois loyal to the British during the Revolution.

117

three Indians killed were Senecas. Among the casualties were several chiefs. Measured in terms of Indian values, where avoidance of casualties on one's own side rather than inflicting of casualties on the other, or taking territory, was the highest accomplishment, the battle was a disaster. But even more agonizing was the fact that brother was fighting brother. The great peace of the Iroquois Confederacy had finally been dissolved.

Shortly after Oriskany the Oneidas and Tuscaroras again proved helpful to the patriot cause by joining General Horatio Gates's army in time to blunt British General John Burgoyne's thrust down the Hudson valley from Canada. During this campaign the Indian followers of Burgoyne murdered Jane McCrea, a comely American girl. The incident, immediately seized upon by American propagandists, helped rouse the colonists to the sentiment made famous by Thomas Jefferson in the Declaration of Independence: that the king had "endeavoured to bring on the inhabitants of our frontier the merciless Indian savages, whose known rule of warfare is an undistinguished destruction of all ages, sexes, and conditions."

During 1778 and 1779 combined British-Indian sorties led by Butler and Brant evoked memories of French and Indian raids during the previous century. Striking silently out of the forest when least expected, the attackers devastated outlying communities such as that at Cherry Valley, New York. The familiar scenes of burning houses, scalped victims, and terrified prisoners were repeated again and again.

General Washington, stung by the effectiveness of the Tory-Indian raids, determined to teach the Iroquois a lesson. In a brilliant strategic and tactical move, he sent General John Sullivan into the supposedly inaccessible western reaches of the Iroquois country to destroy villages and cornfields. Rather than fighting his way through one Iroquois nation after another by the usual route of approach from the east along the Mohawk River, Sullivan went up the Susquehanna River from the south, directly into the territory of the Seneca nation, the most numerous and powerful of the Six Nations and guardian of the western gate of the confederacy. After trying the strength of the invading army, the Senecas prudently abandoned their villages and allowed Sullivan's army to wreak a havoc that deprived many of the natives of food and shelter for the succeeding winter.

The indirect effects of the campaign were devastating. Years later the Seneca chief Cornplanter said to Washington, "When your army entered the country of the Six Nations we called you Town Destroyer; and to this day when that name is heard our women look behind them and turn pale, and our children cling close to the necks of their mothers."

In the South the Indian war developed in much the same way it had in the North. English settlers had encroached on Indian lands despite treaty guarantees, and by 1775 the Cherokees were ready to go to war to preserve their homeland. When they attempted to warn immigrating colonists off Cherokee lands at Watauga and Nolichucky, British Indian agents merely provoked the colonials to indict them as instigators of Indian attacks on the settlements. For the most part the frontiersmen refused to withdraw from settlements in the Cherokee country. In April, 1776, American commissioners for Indian affairs tried to supplant the king's agents among the natives, but the Indians chose to maintain their tie with the king. In May, 1776, on the urging of a delegation of Shawnees, Delawares, and Mohawks from the North, the Cherokees took up the hatchet

and devastated white settlements on the frontier.

Thomas Jefferson, who had hoped that the interests of both red man and white could be accommodated on the American continent, now concluded that the Cherokees should be driven beyond the Mississippi. In a series of campaigns, colonial troops penetrated Cherokee country and burned native crops and houses. The Cherokees, like the Iroquois in the North, withdrew before the onslaught, and the troops laid waste their homeland.

The Creek Confederation leaned sympathetically toward the king but in the face of the destruction visited upon the Cherokees showed little eagerness to break the peace. When, however, a British fleet arrived off Georgia late in 1778 and captured Savannah, John Stuart, the Indian superintendent in Pensacola, sought to recruit a powerful force of English loyalists and Creeks. But because the admiral of the fleet had failed to give him advance word of the movement, Stuart was unable to bring the Indians into effective support of the British redcoats who arrived with the fleet.

The cost of maintaining an alliance with the southeastern Indians was staggering to the British. As one commentator put it, "Reason and Rhetoric will fall to the Ground unless supported by Strouds and Duffells. Liberality is alone with Indians true Eloquence without which Demosthenes and Circero or the more modern orators Burk and Barre might harrangue in vaine." In 1778 the British Parliament spent seventy-five thousand pounds sterling for gifts to the southeast Indians. The extent of the expenditure without significant results caused unfavorable comment in Parliament. Still, the southern tribes could bring some 10,000 warriors into the field (3,000 Cherokees, 3,500 Creeks, 3,100 Choctaws, and 475 Chickasaws) and could have played a key role in the war had they been properly led.

For example, the British missed a crucial opportunity to use the Choctaws against the Americans' Spanish allies. In the fall of 1779 General John Campbell, commanding the British forces at Mobile, called down several hundred Choctaws in anticipation of a Spanish attack that failed to materialize. The Choctaws, camped near the town, were poorly supplied and poorly paid by the British. By the time a Spanish fleet under Admiral Bernardo de Gálvez arrived on February 10, 1780, only eighteen Choctaws

An orator rather than a fighter, the Seneca chief Red Jacket worked his whole life to preserve the ancient customs of his people against the incursions of white society, technology, and religion. In the 1790's, protesting Seneca land sales, he said, "We stand a small Island in the bosom of the great waters. . . . They rise, they press upon us and the waves will settle over us and we shall disappear forever. Who then lives to mourn us, white man? None." His eloquence came too late to alter events. Gradually abandoned by his people, the tired, disillusioned old man died, a semialcoholic, in 1830. In a final irony, Chief Red Jacket was buried in a Christian grave.

Two luckless generals, Arthur St. Clair (top) and Josiah Harmar, both suffered defeat in the Ohio valley at the hands of Chief Little Turtle's warriors, Harmar in 1790, St. Clair in 1791.

remained. Campbell sent for the natives again, but it was too late: before any help could arrive the town fell to the Spanish.

Gálvez pushed on to Pensacola in March of 1780. This time two thousand Creeks arrived to support the British. Gálvez, afraid to attack such a formidable force, decided to wait and take the city after the Indians grew weary and returned home. After six weeks half of the Indians had left, but Gálvez's hopes of victory were frustrated by the arrival of a British fleet. Campbell had been saved by the British Navy—and, in this one case, by Indian allies.

Inland, the skilled fighter Lieutenant Colonel John Sevier led an expedition of three hundred North Carolinians against the Cherokees late in 1780. Joining forces with four hundred Virginians under Colonel Arthur Campbell, the force ravaged the Cherokee country as earlier expeditions had done in 1776. Even the central village of Chote was razed, and the Chickamauga towns destroyed.

In March, 1781, a Spanish fleet again appeared off Pensacola and disgorged an army of four thousand men. The force confronted fifteen hundred British soldiers supported by four hundred Choctaws and one hundred Creek warriors. The Indians bravely assaulted the Spanish siege lines and at one point actually broke through. But, as the Choctaws complained, their English allies failed to come to their support at this critical juncture. When the Spanish were reinforced by three thousand more men, the British situation became hopeless. On May 8, 1781, General John Campbell surrendered. Augusta and Savannah soon fell into American hands, and in 1783 the British evacuated St. Augustine.

At the war's end the Indian allies of the British were forced to make their peace with the Americans as best they could. The British were astonished to discover the depth of the commitment of some of their Indian allies. "If the English mean to abandon the land," one Indian put it, "we will accompany them—We cannot take a Virginian or Spaniard by the hand—We cannot look them in the face." The commandant of the St. Augustine garrison reported that "the minds of these people appear as much agitated as those of the unhappy Loyalists on the eve of a third evacuation; and however chimerical it may appear to us, they have very seriously proposed to abandon their country and accompany us, having made all the world their enemies by their attachment to us."

The Indians learned to their sorrow how they ranked in the hearts of their white allies when they got news of the preliminary peace articles. The negotiators in Paris had acted as though the natives did not exist. Trying to justify his countrymen's abandonment of their allies, the British statesman Lord Shelburne disingenuously proclaimed that "in the present treaty with America, the Indian nations were not abandoned to their enemies; they were remitted to the care of neighbours."

Although the Spanish negotiator at the Paris peace conference, the conde de Aranda, attempted to uphold the position that the territory between the Appalachians and the Mississippi, which England had "delivered to the American colonies," belonged to "free and independent nations of Indians, and you have no right to it," the American negotiators rejected the claim and asserted their sovereignty over the lands of the interior.

Stung by the criticism of their abandonment of the Indians, the British did what they could to help those who wished to live under the king's protection. When General Frederick Haldimand, military commander and governor of Quebec province, attempted to resettle some of the Iroquois on Canadian lands, his efforts met with the sympathetic approval of Lord North, the prime minister. North wrote: "These People are justly entitled to our Peculiar attention and it would be far from either generous or just in us, after our cession of their Territories and Hunting grounds, to forsake them."

As an additional gesture, Haldimand at first refused to turn over the British forts to the Americans as required by the final treaty of peace signed on September 3, 1783. He clung to the outposts and used them in bargaining not only to force the Americans to meet their treaty obligations toward the Tories, but also to slow the transition to American rule in the area. Not until 1796 did the British finally give up the forts.

In the years following the American Revolution, American negotiators sought to force the Indians to acknowledge their defeat and to recognize their submission to the victorious colonials. James Duane, a member of the Continental Congress, advised the governor of New York not to treat with the Iroquois as equals. "I would never suffer the word 'nation' or 'six nations' or 'confederates,' or 'council fire at Onondago' or any other form which would revive or seem to confirm their former ideas of independence. They should rather be taught that the public opinion of their importance has long since ceased."

But neither the Iroquois nor the Indians of the interior accepted American assertions of their defeat and subjection. Although their ally Great Britain might admit defeat, the Indians still regarded themselves as independent and continued to negotiate from a position of insistent pride albeit of somewhat diminished power. For some years the obstinacy of the Indians caused the Americans to send armies to enforce their claims.

In 1790 General Josiah Harmar set off into Indian country with some 1,400 men, all but 320 of them militia. Harmar was brave enough, but he drank heavily, exercised little control over his troops, and had no experience whatever fighting Indians. Facing him was a force of Miamis, Shawnees, Potawatomis, and Chippewas under the command of Little Turtle, a fearless and highly intelligent warrior. Little Turtle skillfully drew Harmar into the Maumee valley, burning a village here and there to convince the American general that the Indians were fleeing in terror. Then, deep in the forest, he turned on Harmar's scattered, disorganized forces, flanked them, and killed 183 soldiers. Harmar retreated—he got his men out only because Little Turtle let them go—and then had the gall to claim a victory.

Washington knew better and turned over command of the campaign to Harmar's superior, General Arthur St. Clair, governor of the Northwest Territory. The fifty-five-year-old St. Clair had fought well in the Revolution but, like Harmar, he was wholly ignorant of Indian warfare. He went blundering off into the wilderness in October of 1791, followed by as poor an army as ever took the field. Apart from two tiny regular regiments totaling six hundred soldiers between them, the two-thousand-man force was composed entirely of militia purchases, according to one account, "from prisons, wheelbarrows and brothels at two dollars a month." The pay did not make much difference, however, since the men never received it, and the corrupt and incompetent quartermaster's corps made sure that the soldiers went hungry. St. Clair had to detach regulars to guard the

Tough, competent General Anthony Wayne avenged the defeat of Harmar and St. Clair when he beat the Indians at Fallen Timbers in 1794.

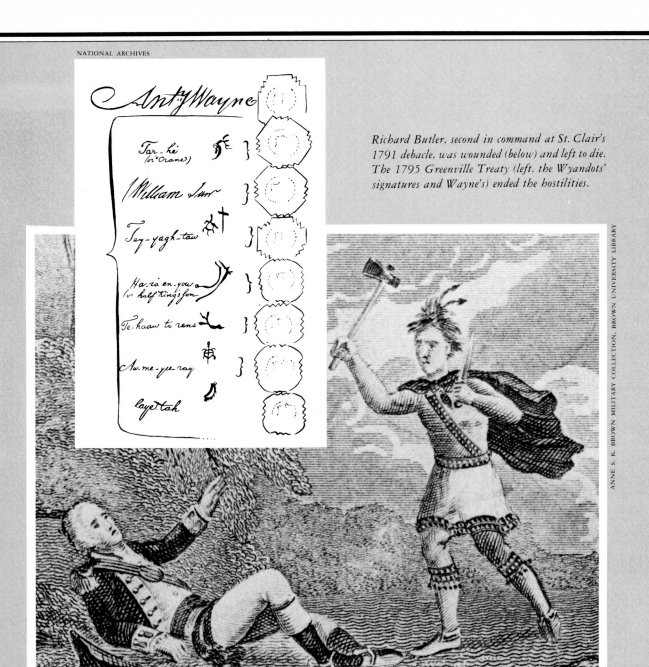

Richard Butler, second in command at St. Clair's 1791 debacle, was wounded (below) and left to die. The 1795 Greenville Treaty (left, the Wyandots' signatures and Wayne's) ended the hostilities.

STRUGGLE FOR THE NORTHWEST

In spite of efforts by the newborn U.S. government to encourage settlement of the Northwest Territory, hostile Indians discouraged significant migration. In 1790 warriors of the Miami Confederacy, led by Little Turtle, ambushed and defeated Josiah Harmar's troops. A year later Little Turtle trounced a larger force led by Arthur St. Clair.

President Washington then sent General Anthony Wayne to assert federal authority in the Northwest.

Wayne spent a year carefully drilling his men, a fact noted by Little Turtle: "We have beaten the enemy twice under different commanders. . . . The Americans are now led by a chief who never sleeps . . . we have never been able to surprise him . . . it would be prudent to listen to his offers of peace." Little Turtle's allies rejected his advice, and Wayne routed them in 1794, near present-day Toledo, Ohio.

A peace conference convened in

June, 1795, with representatives of the Shawnees, Wyandots, and the Miami Confederacy, among others, in attendance at Fort Greenville. They signed a treaty in August, giving up their lands in southeastern Indiana and southern Ohio, thereby opening the gates of the Northwest Territory to settlement. A Wyandot chief concluded sadly that "we . . . acknowledge the fifteen United States . . . to be our father . . . [we] must call them brother no more."

supply train from his own men. Morale was such that, by November 3, when St. Clair occupied the high ground on the upper Wabash River where he hoped to make a stand, six hundred of his men had deserted.

The general had chosen a good strong defensive position and, feeling secure there, had neglected to build any defenses or post adequate lookouts. When Little Turtle's attack struck early the next morning, the Kentucky militia in the advance units were taken completely by surprise. The Indians came forward keeping close to the ground, firing out of the forest. Though the Kentuckians had no idea how strong a force they were up against, they fled immediately, pouring back into the main camp and spreading panic there. Only the artillerymen kept their heads and stood by their pieces and fought. But the smoke was so thick in the heavy morning air that soon the gunners were firing blindly and ineffectually.

St. Clair finally managed to rally enough militiamen for a bayonet attack, but Little Turtle's men withdrew before it into the woods, picking off the soldiers until the assault melted away. St. Clair tried more charges, but, he noted, "in all of them many men were lost, and particularly the officers, which, with so raw troops, was a loss altogether irremediable." At last, with more than half his army down and completely surrounded, St. Clair ordered a retreat, and the remnants of his command fought their way through the Indian lines. "The camp and artillery were abandoned," the commander reported gloomily, "but that was unavoidable, for not a horse was left alive to have drawn it off. But the most disgraceful part of the business is, that the greatest part of the men threw away their arms and accoutrements, even after the pursuit (which continued about four miles) had ceased. . . . The rout continued quite to Fort Jefferson, twenty nine miles [away], which was reached a little after sunsetting."

St. Clair survived the battle to spend the rest of his life with the knowledge that he had been in charge of the worst disaster in the long history of the Indian wars. Only 580 of his men got home.

At last Washington picked a suitable commander for his Indian fighting forces in the Revolutionary War hero General "Mad Anthony" Wayne. A stern disciplinarian, Wayne bullied the army into shape and led it into the field so effectively that Little Turtle, assessing the quality of the man he was now up against, advised the Indians to seek peace. The other chiefs overthrew him and gave his command to Turkey Foot, a less skilled strategist. He took his braves into action at Fallen Timbers on August 20, 1794, and Wayne beat them soundly, losing only thirty-three men in the process.

Nevertheless, the Indians' strong showing in the earlier campaigns persuaded the Americans to drop the extreme position implying that the native tribes were subject to American authority. On August 3, 1795, the Treaty of Greenville resulted in the Indians' ceding the southeastern corner of the Northwest Territory together with enclaves beyond (Detroit and the future site of Chicago among them) in exchange for annuities amounting to $10,000.

"So ended," in the words of historian Samuel Eliot Morison, "almost twenty years of fighting: the last phase of the War of Independence." The way had been cleared for the advance of the American farmer and entrepreneur into the rich interior of the continent. This movement would, in turn, create another series of wars. But in the end, the outcome would be the same.

The Romantic Image

While the pioneers coped with the thousand perils of wilderness life—especially the dread of hostile Indians—a cheerful legend began to grow up around their efforts. Lithographs and books of the era often portrayed the settlers as plumply heroic types happily reaping the rewards of their toil in a new Eden. Reality came in such unpalatable forms as this 1796 attack on a Tennessee stockade; but many Americans preferred the ideal as offered by the artists in this portfolio, among them Currier & Ives, whose print "The Pioneer's Home" (inset) shows successful hunters bringing a deer from the fruitful wilderness, to an unguarded and presumably unthreatened cabin.

German-born artist Charles Wimar painted Jemima being carried across a Martian landscape.

In the summer of 1776 Indians kidnapped fourteen-year-old Jemima Boone, daughter of the redoubtable Daniel, and two of her playmates while they were canoeing near their home at Boonesborough, Kentucky. Terrified as they were, the girls managed to mark their trail with scraps of cloth torn from their dresses. Boone set out in pursuit and three days later got the captives back. This bit of bloodless derring-do delighted painters and print makers, who churned out some wonderfully imaginative and varied versions of the chase for generations. The three scenes on these pages were all done some three quarters of a century after the event.

126

Another Wimar production shows the girls being poled downriver by their captors.

Daniel Boone recovers the girls, who seem none the worse for wear, in this 1851 lithograph.

An immaculate soldier phlegmatically defends his lady in a print after an Alonzo Chappel painting.

*Militia major Samuel McCulloch escapes from a band of hostile Indians
in 1777 by leaping a precipice into Virginia's Wheeling Creek. This
1851 lithograph greatly exaggerates the audacity of the major's feat.*

Even the most brutal massacre could take on a certain mellow
quality when processed by the sentimentalists. The ennobling vision
at left purported to show the calamitous Creek attack on settlers
at Fort Mims. When it actually took place in 1813, the bloodletting
roused the entire country to horror and wrath. But by mid-century,
when this print and ones like it were being issued, the eastern
Indians had been safely subdued and shipped west, and the very real
horrors of pioneer life had become bathed in a romantic afterglow.

Seminole leader Osceola defies the whites in this contemporary lithograph.

5: Finale in the East

Where today are the Pequot? Where the Narraganset, the Mohican, the Pokanoket and many other once powerful tribes of our people? They have vanished before the avarice and oppression of the white man, as snow before a summer sun. . . ." So spoke the Shawnee chief Tecumseh in the early years of the nineteenth century, exhorting his people—and the people of all the eastern tribes—to make a final stand against the whites. He has been called "the greatest Indian who ever lived." And indeed he was the first native leader with vision enough to see that if white encroachments were to be stopped, the stopping could not be done by a single tribe, or even a confederation, but only by a great union of all the tribes to fight for their common homeland. He came too late to alter events, but he cast a long shadow over the Indians' last, desperate attempts to hold their lands east of the Mississippi.

Tecumseh was born in 1768 near present-day Dayton, Ohio, where the dispossessed Shawnees, buffeted by the Virginians on the east, the Iroquois on the north, and the Creeks on the west, had finally found a home. While still in his early teens, Tecumseh fought alongside the British in the Revolution, and later he stood with Little Turtle against Harmar and the next year St. Clair. He led raids against the border settlements until Anthony Wayne came with his regulars, and then he fought bravely at Fallen Timbers, where he lost a brother and witnessed the overwhelming defeat of his people.

Tecumseh refused to attend the subsequent council, which ended with the piratical Greenville Treaty, and retired brooding into Indiana, where he spoke against the white man and began to attract a following. Toward the turn of the eighteenth century he formed a strange friendship with a white woman named Rebecca Galloway, the blonde, blue-eyed daughter of an Ohio farmer. She taught him the Bible, Shakespeare, and world and American history. He learned of Alexander the Great, Caesar, and other empire builders, and certainly during this time he pondered the efforts of Pontiac and King Philip and the reasons they had failed. Eventually he asked Rebecca to marry him, and she consented on the condition that he abandon his Indian ways. Tecumseh thought it over for a month, then refused and bade her farewell, telling her that he could never leave his people.

About 1805 Tecumseh began to assert that no Indian tribe had the right to sell lands to the white man without the consent of all the tribes, and he gained a curious ally in Lalawethika, his indolent, drunken younger brother. Lalawethika had led a dissolute life until he fell into a trance from which he emerged insisting that he had communed with the Master of Life. He changed his name to Tenskwatawa—"the Open Door"—and began to preach the same message the Delaware Prophet had spoken in Pontiac's time: shun the white man's liquor, abandon his ways, return to the old customs. The reformed Tenskwatawa was so compelling a preacher that his word spread to tribes as far away as the plains of central Canada. When in 1808 he and Tecumseh established a religious community on the Wabash near its confluence with the Tippecanoe River, Delawares, Wyandots, Ojibwas, Kickapoos, and Ottawas came to settle and live there in austere harmony.

In this village, which came to be called Prophetstown, Tecumseh saw the nucleus of the great tribal union he hoped to forge. He left it to roam the Northwest Territory and then the South, taking his message to dozens of tribes. Many, cowed by the brutal reverses of the last decades, scorned him, but others listened and took up the cause. Tecumseh was successful enough that eventually General William Henry Harrison, governor of the Indiana territory, became alarmed.

Then in his late thirties, the tough-minded Harrison was an able soldier and a good administrator. He was also ambitious, and in the summer of 1809, while Tecumseh was away proselytizing, he decided to take more Indiana land from the Indians. Summoning some of the older chiefs to Fort Wayne, he plied them with liquor and extracted from them the cession of three million acres in return for seven thousand dollars and a small annuity. When Tecumseh heard of this his rage apparently heightened his eloquence, for he soon had a thousand warriors gathered in Prophetstown to enforce his declaration that any attempt to settle the hastily ceded land would be repelled.

Harrison did not underestimate his opponent. "The implicit obedience and respect which followers of Tecumseh pay him," he wrote, "is really astonishing and more than any other circumstance bespeaks him one of those uncommon geniuses which spring up occasionally to produce revolutions and overturn the established order of things. If it were not for the vicinity of the United States, he would perhaps be the founder of an Empire that would rival in glory Mexico or Peru."

With great caution, Harrison received Tecumseh at his headquarters in Vincennes in August of 1810. Arriving with four hundred warriors, the

Ignoring the protests of his subordinates, General William Henry Harrison spurs toward the thickest of the fighting at Tippecanoe. Since the predawn attack took the camp by surprise, nobody was as tidy as the heroic style of this Currier lithograph suggests, but Harrison did expose himself to danger throughout the battle. A soldier recalled that the officers "acknowledged that the cool undaunted bravery of the c. in c. [commander in chief] contributed more than even the courage of the army to defeat the ferocious . . . enemy. . . ." Harrison, in turn, was delighted with his green troops' showing; they behaved, he said, "in a manner that never can be too much applauded."

chief impressed at least one American officer, who wrote, "[Tecumseh] is one of the finest men I ever met—about six feet high, straight with large fine features and altogether a daring, bold-looking fellow."

Harrison invited Tecumseh to take a chair among the territorial officials gathered for the council, telling the Indian leader it was the wish of the "Great Father, the President of the United States, that you do so." Tecumseh spurned the offer and stretched out on the ground, saying, "My Father?—The Sun is my father, the Earth is my mother—and on her bosom I will recline!"

During the next three days Tecumseh recited his grievances to Harrison, who found them "sufficiently insolent and his pretensions arrogant." When Harrison foolishly tried to placate his knowledgeable guest by speaking of the "uniform regard to justice" shown the Indians by the whites, Tecumseh jumped to his feet. "Tell him he lies!" he shouted to the interpreter, while his warriors rose to stand around him.

"Those fellows mean mischief, you'd better bring up the guard," an official told a lieutenant, who ran to summon reinforcements. Tecumseh urged the reluctant translator to relay his message. When Harrison finally learned that he was being called a liar, he leaped to his feet and drew his sword, while the regulars closed ranks behind him. The tension of the moment ebbed, and Tecumseh later apologized, but the talks ended in an angry stalemate.

"Is one of the fairest portions of the globe," Harrison asked the Indiana legislature, "to remain in a state of nature, the haunt of a few wretched savages, when it seems destined, by the Creator, to give support to a large population, and to be the seat of civilization, of science, and of true religion?" When in July of 1811 Potawatomis killed some settlers in Illinois, Harrison saw an opportunity to make a show of force and acted quickly. Claiming that the murderers were followers of Tenskwatawa, he demanded that the Shawnees in Prophetstown turn them over to him immediately. Tecumseh refused and at once set out again to try to rally the southern Indians for the fight he knew was imminent.

In an extraordinary six-month journey, he visited the Carolinas, Mississippi, Georgia, Alabama, Florida, and Arkansas, begging the natives to abandon their petty tribal squabbles and join together to fight for their land while they still had land to fight for. Captain Sam Dale, a Mississippi Indian fighter, heard Tecumseh speak and was astonished by the chieftain's eloquence: "His eyes burned with supernatural lustre, and his whole frame trembled with emotion. His voice resounded over the multitude—now sinking in low and musical whispers, now rising to the highest key, hurling out his words like a succession of thunderbolts. . . . I have heard many great orators, but I never saw one with the vocal powers of Tecumseh." But for all his vocal powers, Tecumseh met a great deal of resistance; the younger warriors tended to support him, but the older chiefs, many of whom lived on government annuities, held back.

In the meantime, Harrison hoped that before Tecumseh returned "the fabrick which he considered complete will be demolished and even its foundations rooted up." In the fall of 1811 word came that Indians had stolen the horses of an army dispatch rider. This was the incident Harrison needed as an excuse to strike at the Indian community, and he put a thousand men on the march at once.

As the general moved with his army up the Wabash toward Prophets-town, emissaries of Tenskwatawa stepped from the forest and asked him for a council on the next day, November 7. Harrison agreed and went into camp on Burnet's Creek, three miles from the mouth of the Tippecanoe River. Uneasy about Tenskwatawa's intentions, he ordered his men to sleep on their arms, bayonets fixed and cartridges ready.

Tecumseh had told his brother to avoid a fight until he returned from the South, but with Harrison's army a few miles away, Tenskwatawa prepared to attack. He assured the Indians that, due to his magic, the white men would be as harmless as sand, and their bullets as soft as rain. In fact, he said, many of the whites were already dead. The confident Indians left Prophetstown bent on that rarity in Indian warfare, a night attack. They approached the American camp through a fine rain.

At quarter to four on the morning of the seventh, one of Harrison's sentries saw something stirring off in the darkness. He had time to get off a shot before the Indians killed him. The camp came awake to terrifying shouts and a fusillade of musketry that tore into the tents and kicked the campfire coals high in the air. In seconds the Indians had broken the army's lines in two places. "Under these trying circumstances," wrote Harrison, "the troops (nineteen-twentieths of whom had never been in action before) behaved in a manner that never can be too much applauded." Surprised and frightened as they were, men stood their ground, and companies stuck together even after their officers had been killed. Dashing along the line, Harrison saw a young soldier taking aim. "Where's your captain?" he demanded.

"Dead, sir."

"Your lieutenant?"

"Dead, sir."

"Your ensign?"

"Here, sir," the boy replied. Harrison told him to hang on, and he turned to rally the militia. Subsequently, Harrison's voice, according to one admiring regular, "was frequently heard and easily distinguished, giving . . . orders in the same calm, cool, and collected manner . . . which we had been used to . . . on a drill on parade. The confidence of the troops in the General was unlimited. . . ."

That confidence began to tell. Though the well-disciplined Indians came on again and again, Harrison's lines stiffened and held, and they stood intact when daybreak brought the attacks to a halt. Tenskwatawa's men kept up a sporadic fire on the camp all day long, but that night they went away, too demoralized even to return to their village.

On November 8 the army entered Prophetstown, took what supplies the men could carry, burned the rest, and started home. Harrison lost thirty-seven dead and one hundred fifty wounded in the Battle of Tippecanoe, but he had gained what he set out to gain, and more—thirty years later the victory would supply him with a campaign slogan that would put him in the White House.

Tecumseh returned early in 1812. Enraged at his brother for triggering the premature fight, he threatened to kill him and then sent him away. Tenskwatawa drifted west and soon dropped into obscurity. Taking stock of the debacle, Tecumseh realized that what he had worked to prevent would now begin: isolated tribes would seek vengeance one by one, and

A SCENE ON THE FRONTIERS AS PRACTICED BY THE HUMANE BRITISH AND THEIR WORTHY ALLIES!

Bring me the Scalps
and the King our Master
will reward you!

Reward for
16 Scalps.

Arise Columbia's Sons and forward press,
Your Country's wrongs, call loudly for redress,
The savage Indian with his scalping knife
Or tomahawk, may seek to take your life,

By bravery aw'd, they'll in a dreadfull fright
Shrink back for refuge to the woods in flight,
Their British leaders then will quickly shake
And for those wrongs shall restitution make.

with no unifying force behind them, they would be easy targets for the army. Standing in the ashes of Prophetstown, Tecumseh said, "I summoned the spirits of the braves who had fallen . . . and as I snuffed up the smell of their blood from the ground I swore once more eternal hatred — the hatred of an avenger."

But Tecumseh could no longer wreak his vengeance, as he had wished, at the head of a host of unified tribes. He needed an ally. And so, reluctantly, he turned to the Canadian garrisons where the British were getting ready for their second war against the Americans.

Though singularly unprepared for any sizable conflict, the United States declared war on June 18, 1812. A month later Brigadier General William Hull marched out of Detroit with twenty-two hundred men to invade Canada. Hull had been a daring and capable officer during the Revolution, but now he was slow, nervous, and, some said, senile. As Hull moved cautiously forward, Tecumseh harried his flanks with Wyandot, Chippewa, and Sioux warriors who had been drawn to the British cause by the magic of the chief's name. Hull, frightened by Tecumseh's minor prods, hurried back to Detroit, where he soon found himself besieged by Tecumseh and by British troops under Major General Isaac Brock. Brock, a pleasant and

This bitter cartoon attacks the British for offering bounties on American scalps during the War of 1812, while the optimistic doggerel beneath it assures Columbia's Sons that they can easily humble the British leaders.

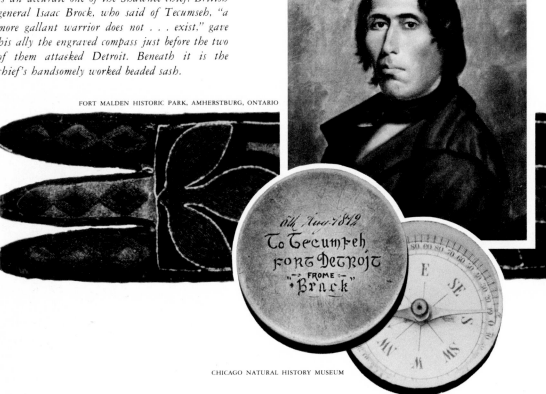

For years no contemporary image of Tecumseh was known to exist, but recent research indicates that the 19th-century portrait at right is an accurate one of the Shawnee chief. British general Isaac Brock, who said of Tecumseh, "a more gallant warrior does not . . . exist," gave his ally the engraved compass just before the two of them attacked Detroit. Beneath it is the chief's handsomely worked beaded sash.

6th Aug. 1812
To Tecumseh
Fort Detroit
FROME
"Brock"

capable officer, fully appreciated Tecumseh's abilities and took the Indian's advice over that of his own officers when the chief suggested an immediate attack on Detroit.

Hoping to convince Hull that thousands of warriors were lurking in the forest, Tecumseh marched his force of six hundred Indians three times through a clearing in sight of the fort. Always ready to believe the worst, Hull fell for the ruse. On August 16, without putting up any fight at all and without consulting his officers, the frightened old commander surrendered Detroit to a force less than half the size of his own.

For a brief, triumphant time Tecumseh, his band of Indians grown to fifteen thousand, ravaged the Northwest, snatching up American outposts. But two events soon dimmed the chief's fortunes: in October his friend and ally General Brock fell to an American bullet, to be replaced by the far less able Colonel Henry Proctor, and General William Henry Harrison took charge of a force forlornly named "the second Northwestern Army."

With eleven hundred men Harrison marched to recapture Detroit, and on his way he built Fort Meigs near the site of the Battle of Fallen Timbers. Tecumseh learned to his dismay what sort of man had succeeded Brock when the two of them went to attack Fort Meigs in the spring of 1813. Colonel Proctor was as cautious as Hull and harbored a wholehearted contempt for Indians.

When Fort Meigs failed to surrender immediately, Proctor chose to invest rather than storm it, allowing time for eleven hundred Kentucky reinforcements to come up. Tecumseh's warriors killed half of them, but Proctor, disheartened, lifted his siege a couple of days later. Late in July Proctor decided he had had enough of campaigning, and, to Tecumseh's immense disgust, withdrew his forces to Fort Malden on the Canadian side of the Detroit River. This was a wonderful stroke of luck for Harrison, who needed time to get his army organized. By September he had forty-five hundred men waiting to move on the word that Naval control of Lake

American cavalrymen burst through the English line in the charge with which Harrison opened the Battle of the Thames in Canada. While the faint-hearted British general Proctor fled the field, Tecumseh stood and fought—and died.

Erie was in friendly hands, and the British thereby cut off from their eastern supply bases.

Word came on September 10 in the form of a grubby note sent by Commodore Oliver Hazard Perry from the deck of his flagship: "DEAR GENL: We have met the enemy, and they are ours—two ships, two brigs, one schooner, and one sloop." Proctor, who had also heard about the battle, decided to abandon Fort Malden and retreat.

Tecumseh had something to say about that: "You always told us you would never draw your foot off British ground; but now, father, we see you are drawing back. . . . We must compare our father's conduct to a fat animal, that carries its tail upon its back, but when afrighted, he drops it between his legs and runs off. . . ." But though he could not shame Proctor into holding the fort, Tecumseh did persuade the colonel to make a stand on the Thames River, some eighty-five miles to the east. When they got there, with Harrison following close behind, Proctor was again vacillating. While the colonel faltered, Tecumseh chose a defensive position with the river on his left flank and a swamp on the right. When the dispositions had been made, the chief passed down the line, touching the hands of the British officers as he went. "[He] made some remark in Shawnee," one of them remembered, "which was sufficiently understood by the expressive signs accompanying, and then passed away forever from our view."

Harrison attacked on the morning of October 5, sending his cavalry headlong against the British line, a measure, he admitted, "not sanctioned by anything I had seen or heard of but I was fully convinced it would succeed." It did. The British lines disintegrated, but the Indians, posted in the swamp, poured out a volley that forced the Americans to dismount and come in after them on foot. Above the clamor of the frenzied hand-to-hand fighting, the soldiers heard Tecumseh roaring encouragement to his men. A few saw him, blood on his face, defending his hopeless vision to the last. Then he was gone, and soon after his Indians broke and fled.

That evening some vengeful Kentuckians stripped the skin from a body they thought was Tecumseh's. They were wrong; his body was never found. Later a few of the chieftain's followers said that they had carried the corpse off the field and buried it secretly. For years some believed that Tecumseh still lived, and in a sense they were right. Although Indian hopes for holding the Northwest had died with Tecumseh, he had spread his word in the South more effectively than he knew. Even while he was making his last stand on the Thames, Indians a thousand miles away who had been inspired by his rhetoric were beginning a struggle that would last nearly thirty years.

Early in the 1800's the Creeks lived in towns scattered through Alabama and Georgia. Although many of them remained neutral when the War of 1812 broke out, a remarkable chief named Red Eagle did not. Red Eagle had been born William Weatherford, the son of a Scottish trader. Though only one-eighth Indian, he chose to cast his lot with the Creeks and had been deeply impressed by Tecumseh's message. Late in August of 1813 he led a war party against Fort Mims on the lower Alabama River. The fort was little more than a flimsy stockade built around the home of a man named Samuel Mims, who had given shelter to some five hundred settlers seeking refuge there from the threat of Creek attacks.

On the morning of August 30 Major John Beasley, commanding the

After the Creek nation had been shattered by Andrew Jackson's troops at Horseshoe Bend on the Tallapoosa River—shown above in a contemporary map—one of the Creek leaders, William Weatherford, came into Jackson's camp alone and surrendered. Impressed by Weatherford's dignity and strength, Jackson let him go after the interview pictured in the engraving at left.

garrison's small force of Louisiana militia, had complacently left the main gate open and neglected to post sentries. The major paid for his confidence when, toward noon, Weatherford's men leaped out of the tall grass and came shouting toward the fort. Taken completely by surprise, the militiamen fought back as best they could, struggling for hours under the blazing sun. At last, with the house in flames from fire arrows, the defenders emerged to die at the hands of the victors, who massacred all but thirty-six who managed to escape.

When word of the slaughter reached Tennessee, the legislature there quickly authorized an army of 3,500 militia and $300,000 to suppress the Creeks and turned to a tough, profane, brawling ramrod of a man named Andrew Jackson to handle the job. Jackson was informed of the appointment on his sickbed, where he was recovering from severe wounds sustained in a duel. Though still too weak to get up, he said he would be on the march in nine days. Pale, haggard, his arm in a sling, Jackson nevertheless drove his men south at the rate of twenty miles a day. As the army approached Ten Islands on the Coosa River, Jackson learned that two hundred Creek warriors were staying in the nearby village of Tallushatchee. He sent a thousand men against the Indians, among them a rangy young frontiersman named Davy Crockett, who reported with satisfaction that "we shot them like dogs." The militia lost 5 killed in the fight; the Indians,

Shortly afterward word came that Weatherford was thirty miles away, laying siege to Talladega, a Creek fort held by Indians loyal to the United

A TOUGH AND TRICKY FOE

The proud man in the 1852 daguerreotype at left is Billy Bowlegs, a widely feared Seminole chief who took charge of two hundred surviving warriors after the surrender of the Seminole leader Osceola in 1838. Bowlegs began by leading his band in a daring nighttime raid on an army stockade, killing twenty-four soldiers. But after a subsequent year of bitter guerrilla warfare in the Florida swamps Bowlegs sued for peace. After rebuffing numerous cash offers to take his men out to present-day Oklahoma, Bowlegs finally made a bonanza of a deal with a corrupt Indian agent in 1858. He departed Florida with fifty slaves and "a hundred thousand dollars in hard cash."

At the outbreak of the Civil War Bowlegs and several other chiefs in Oklahoma sided with the Union. In a series of desperate battles two thousand warriors held off attacking Confederates. In December, 1861, after a month's fighting, the warriors retreated to the safety of federal camps in Kansas, where Bowlegs died several years later.

States. Jackson got his army on the march at once, and as his troops approached the fort the defenders waved and called out, "How-dy-do, brother, how-dy-do." There was little time for an exchange of pleasantries, however; Weatherford's men rushed from the woods, Crockett said, "like a cloud of Egyptian locusts, and screaming like all the young devils had been turned loose, with the old devil of all at their head." The army made short work of them. In fifteen minutes a third of Weatherford's thousand-man force had fallen under Jackson's disciplined musketry. The rest would have been done for too, but they had the good fortune to dislodge some shaky militia in the line and escaped into the woods.

However satisfying the victory, it did not feed Jackson's ill-supplied troops, and late in November the hungry, disgruntled soldiers started home. Jackson, still weak from his wounds and ravaged with dysentery, blocked their path and, bluffing with a rusted, useless musket, threatened to shoot the first man who stepped forward. The troops stayed, and in January of 1814 their nerveless commander had them marching south to Horseshoe Bend, where the Tallapoosa River swings in a wide loop. Across the neck of this peninsula, Weatherford's Creeks had built a sturdy log barricade. By the time Jackson arrived with two thousand troops, nine hundred warriors stood ready to oppose him. Jackson brought his artillery to bear on the position on the morning of March 27, but the shot sank harmlessly into the thick logs. Finally the general ordered a frontal assault, and he saw his men go forward into the teeth of heavy fire and swarm across the barricade. The Indians fought stubbornly all afternoon, but by nightfall the troops had virtually annihilated the Creek nation. More than five hundred warriors lay dead, but Weatherford was not among them.

A few days later a gaunt Indian, dressed in rags, appeared in the army camp and approached Jackson. "I am Bill Weatherford," he said.

Jackson took his visitor into his tent. "I am in your power," Weatherford told the general, "do with me as you please. I am a soldier. I have done the white people all the harm I could; I have fought them, and fought them bravely; if I had an army, I would yet fight, and contend to the last: but I have none; my people are all gone. I can now do no more than weep over the misfortunes of my nation."

Moved, Jackson replied, "You are not in my power. I had ordered you brought to me in chains. . . . But you have come of your own accord . . . I would gladly save you and your nation, but you do not even ask to be saved. If you think you can contend against me in battle, go and head your warriors."

Weatherford walked out of the camp a free man and never fought again.

Jackson acquitted himself less honorably during the treaty negotiations that followed. The Creeks came to the council so hungry, said Jackson, that they were "picking up the grains of corn scattered from the mouths of horses." On these wretched people, the general forced a treaty by which they gave up twenty-three million acres of their land. Though the Creeks would never again fight as a nation, many of them moved south to Florida, where they settled among the Seminoles, who also hated the whites.

For years Seminoles and whites had clashed along the Florida border, the white raids all the harsher because the Seminoles had long provided sanctuary for runaway slaves. By December of 1817 the squabbling had grown to such a pitch that Secretary of War John C. Calhoun ordered Jackson to

U.S. soldiers in camp at Tampa Bay, 1835

A detachment fording Lake Ocklawaha in central Florida

Troops burning a Seminole village

go back south and rectify the situation. Though treated to some governmental delicacy about invading Spanish Florida, Jackson ignored this concern and drove straight across the border, burning every Seminole village he could find. Then, taking time out from the campaign against the Indians, he seized the Spanish fort at Pensacola. With the Seminoles temporarily subdued and the Spanish in an impotent fury, Jackson headed back north. In a show of bravado, President John Quincy Adams sent the Spaniards an ultimatum demanding that they keep order in their territory or turn it over to those who could. The next year Spain ceded Florida to the United States.

After taking over the territory, the whites forced the Seminoles onto an inland reservation in central Florida, where, the Indians were promised, they would be given food, farming tools, and annuities. But many of them died of starvation the first winter, and their new lands, according to one observer, were "by far the poorest and most miserable region I ever beheld." Before long the angry Indians began to raid white settlements, and the settlers started to demand that the natives be removed to the west. American policy makers regarded the lands west of the borders of Arkansas and Missouri as of little use to whites and therefore a perfect place for the eastern Indian tribes to relocate. There they envisioned a line of forts establishing a "Permanent Indian Frontier," which would keep red men and white out of each other's way forever.

In the spring of 1832 James Gadsden, a young surveyor acting for Secretary of War Lewis Cass, met at Payne's Landing, Florida, with delegates from a few of the friendlier Seminole villages and presented them with a treaty. Couched in clouds of double talk, this remarkable document said

NATIONAL COLLECTION OF FINE ARTS

"For nearly two hundred miles," one discouraged soldier wrote of the frustrating campaign against the Seminole leader Osceola (standing at left), "we passed through an unknown region, cutting through dense hummocks, passing innumerable cypress-swamps and pine barrens . . . and, for the last three days, wading . . . up to our necks in water. Our privations have not been less than our fatigue, the men being almost naked, and one third of them destitute of shoes." General after general tried his hand at subduing the Seminoles, without success. Finally, after a series of futile and costly raids, General Thomas Jesup had to resort to a ruse to capture Osceola.

143

that, in return for $15,400 in cash and some blankets and frocks, every Seminole would be out of Florida in three years' time. Though Gadsden browbeat the Seminoles into signing the treaty, many of the tribes that had not been represented in the council repudiated it. In the spring of 1835, after a series of bitter negotiations, General Wiley Thompson, a Georgia militia officer whom the government had made an Indian agent, called the Seminole leaders to sign another document pledging them to leave Florida quietly. One by one the sullen chiefs put their marks on the paper until— according to a persistent story—one of them drew himself up before the table and plunged his hunting knife into the treaty. "That's your heart," he said, "and my work."

The rebellious Indian was Osceola, a Creek who had been born about thirty years earlier in Alabama. He had fought against Jackson during the War of 1812, and with his family he had been forced into Florida when the Creek nation disintegrated. For a while he helped the government agents police Indians on the reservation, but whatever loyalty he might have felt toward the United States evaporated after the Treaty of Payne's Landing. Though he was not a chief, Osceola's outspoken opposition to removal had gained him a sizable following by the end of 1834. Just how determined an enemy he was became doubly evident to General Thompson when, at the treaty council, Osceola continued to defy him.

"My brothers! . . ." the Indian declaimed, "the white man says I shall go, and he will send people to make me go; but I have a rifle, and I have some powder and some lead. I say, we must not leave our homes and lands. If any of our people want to go west we won't let them; and I tell them they are our enemies, and we will treat them so, for the great spirit will protect us."

Thompson had Osceola clapped in irons. The Indian roared and protested throughout the night, but the next day, seeing his one chance to gain his freedom, he agreed to sign. Then he went back into the swamp, and before long, as the Indians began to acquire more arms, Seminoles friendly to the United States asked for protection. By November Indian bands led by Osceola were attacking white settlements. In the next few months the raids grew into a full-scale war in which whites died by the hundreds— all because of the Treaty of Payne's Landing, which, an infantry officer wrote, "only adds another melancholy proof to the many on record, that hard and unconscionable terms, extorted from . . . [the Indians] while in distress, under promises never to be realized, has only served to whet and stimulate revenge and to give to old hostilities, not yet extinguished, greater exasperation and ferocity."

On December 28 Osceola avenged the humiliation he had suffered from Thompson by ambushing and killing the agent, while fifty miles to the south a band of Seminoles cut off and annihilated two companies of soldiers. Then, on New Year's Eve, Osceola dealt a decisive defeat to a force of three hundred regulars and five hundred Florida militia.

When news of the swift succession of calamities reached Washington, a new President—none other than Andrew Jackson—reacted with characteristic toughness. He appointed Major General Winfield Scott to lead the campaign against the Seminoles and ordered him to deal with them only on terms of unconditional surrender. Scott, as good a soldier as America had, was helpless against this enemy. There were only a few hundred Seminole warriors, but they fought skillfully in the swampy country, sallying out to cut up small groups of soldiers and disappearing before massed regulars. Scott blundered around for two months, accomplished nothing, and then was sent up to Alabama, where remnants of the Creek nation were beginning to make trouble. General Robert Call, the governor of Florida and a seasoned militia commander, took over and conducted an ineffective summer campaign that failed when fever decimated his ranks.

In December a confident new general named Thomas Sidney Jesup set out to try his luck. Jesup had fought Indians before and looked forward to the campaign. Within a year he was in despair, his career sinking into the Florida swamps, his failure against a few naked Indians a bitter joke throughout the United States. Finally, having decided to accomplish by deceit what he could not at bayonet point, Jesup asked Osceola to come and parley under a flag of truce. When the leader appeared, Jesup had him seized. Osceola, weary of the long war, offered no resistance. Jesup sent him off to St. Augustine and captivity between two files of troops. Too ill to walk, Osceola made the journey on horseback. Jesup gained little from

When word got out that Zachary Taylor was trying to hunt down Seminole Indians with dogs, newspapers throughout the North attacked the government for sanctioning such cruelty. In this 1837 cartoon, Secretary of War Joel R. Poinsett presents the colors to the "1st Regiment of Republican Bloodhounds" while Francis P. Blair, founder of the Washington Globe *and a strong supporter of the administration, encourages his "brethren-in-arms."*

his cheap ploy; the outraged Seminoles pressed their attacks with renewed vigor, and the commander found himself the butt of scorn in the press.

Drained by malaria and a throat disease, Osceola grew weaker and weaker. On January 30, 1838, he called for his battle dress, and, rising from his bed, he pulled on his shirt, leggings, and moccasins, and strapped his war belt around his waist. Then, according to Dr. Frederick Weedon, the post surgeon, he "called for his red paint, and his looking-glass, which was held before him, when he deliberately painted one-half of his face, his neck and throat — his wrists — the backs of his hands, and the handle of his knife, red with vermillion; a custom practiced when the irrevocable oath of war and destruction is taken." After recovering his strength for a moment, the dying leader "rose up as before, and with most benignant and pleasing smiles, extended his hand to me and to all the officers . . . and shook hands with us all in dead silence. . . . He made a signal for them to lower him down upon his bed, which was done, and he then slowly drew from his war belt his scalping knife, which he firmly grasped in his right hand, laying it across the other on his breast, and a moment later smiled away his last breath, without a struggle or groan."

The author of this touching account was not totally overcome by the dignity of the scene, for he immediately cut off Osceola's head and kept the grisly souvenir for years.

In May the tired and disgusted Jesup turned over his command to Colonel Zachary Taylor, a rigid and inflexible commander who was cut from the same cloth as Jackson — and who would follow the same road to the White House. "We must," Taylor said, "abandon general operations and confine ourselves to minute and specific ones." He proposed to divide

During the last, bloody hours of Black Hawk's brief war, the Sauk and Fox chief's men found themselves trapped on the banks of the Mississippi River between the six-pounder of the steamship Warrior *and the muskets of thirteen hundred vengeful Americans. The curious configuration of the landscape in this picture may be due to the fact that it was drawn from reports in Düsseldorf.*

Das Illustrierte Mississippithal. 1857

Florida into a grid of squares twenty miles on a side, each patrolled by its own garrison. Taylor took scores of Seminole prisoners and sent them west, and still the war went on. By now a good deal of public outcry had risen against it, which increased when Taylor tried to use bloodhounds to track down his stubborn opponents.

Gradually, one by one, Seminole chiefs began to surrender. In one extraordinary capitulation in 1841, a chieftain named Coacoochee and two of his followers, who had earlier plundered a trunk full of theatrical supplies, solemnly approached the army lines dressed as Hamlet, Richard III, and Horatio.

On that note, part tragedy and part farce, the long, expensive war petered out. The obdurate Seminoles had cost the United States twenty million dollars, had engaged more than thirty thousand soldiers, and had killed nearly fifteen hundred of them. And even then not all the Indians surrendered. More than four thousand Seminoles were eventually shipped west, but some bands, too weak to fight further but too proud to yield, fell far back into the swamps. When the United States entered the Second World War a century later, some of their descendants refused to register for the draft, explaining that they were not Americans but members of the Seminole nation, a sovereign state that never had been conquered.

While the government was trying to cope with the Seminoles, settlers far to the north in the Illinois country had been shaken by a brief, forlorn Indian revolt in which a warrior named Black Hawk took a last gamble against steep odds. Black Hawk, a chief of the Sauk and Fox Indians—two related tribes that had early joined together—was born in 1767 in a Sauk village on the site of present-day Rock Island, Illinois. He fought his first battle at fifteen, and by the time he reached his thirties he was ably directing armies of more than five hundred Sauk and Foxes against tribal enemies.

In 1804 the United States summoned some Sauk and Fox chieftains to St. Louis, and, after entertaining them lavishly in the grog shops, got them to sign a treaty by which, in return for the usual pittance, they ceded fifty million acres of land. Although Black Hawk's village was included in the cession, the chief was not alarmed at the time because he and his fellows thought the whites merely wanted to use the land for hunting. He subsequently signed a document reaffirming the 1804 treaty, but, he wrote, he "touched the goose quill to the treaty—not knowing . . . that, by that act, I consented to give away my village. Had that been explained to me, I should have opposed it."

Soon white settlers began to move into the territory. Black Hawk became bitter, and his anger and determination grew when he met Tecumseh and heard the great chieftain's compelling message. He fought alongside Tecumseh in the War of 1812 and was with him during his final hours.

In the years following the war, Black Hawk watched the settlers pouring into Illinois. Every year, returning from their winter hunting, the Sauk and Foxes found their lodges burned, their cornfields fenced in, their cemeteries plowed up. Again and again Black Hawk protested to the Indian agents at Rock Island, only to be told that he should move across the Mississippi.

At last, early in 1829, the chieftain returned from a poor hunt to find a white family settled in his own lodge. He got an interpreter and had him tell the squatters "not to settle on our lands—nor trouble our lodges or

Although sent east as a prisoner, Black Hawk still appeared proud and resolute when John Jarvis painted this portrait of him in 1833.

fences—that there was plenty of land in the country for them to settle upon—and they must leave our village, as we were coming back to it in the spring."

The family ignored the demand, more whites came to settle in the village, and in the summer the General Land Office announced that the area would be put up for public sale in October. For two tense summers Black Hawk returned to stay on his usurped lands. Finally, in April of 1832, the chief, who had spent the winter on the far side of the Mississippi, crossed the river with a band of a thousand men, women, and children, and headed toward his town. The frightened settlers appealed to the Illinois governor, John Reynolds, who, seeing an opportunity to increase his political popularity, called for volunteers to "repel the invasion."

Sixteen hundred men turned out in June and joined regular troops under General Edmund P. Gaines. Gaines, the commander of the Western Department of the Army, had fought well against the Creeks and Seminoles with Jackson, but his volunteers were a poor lot. In mid-May two hundred seventy-five of them under Major Isaiah Stillman overtook Black Hawk when the chief was away from his main camp and had only forty warriors with him. The odds were too great; Black Hawk sadly sent out a delegation to discuss terms of surrender. As the Indians approached the camp under a flag of truce, Stillman's half-drunk militia fired on them. Black Hawk decided that, if he had to die, he would die fighting. Marshalling his tiny force, he led what he was sure was a suicidal attack against the volunteers. As he ran shouting toward certain death, however, the volunteers broke and ran. The Indians gave chase for a while, but the soldiers kept right on going until they reached their main camp twenty-five miles away. They staggered in all night, babbling confused accounts of the action, which soon came to be called Stillman's Run.

Astonished and encouraged by this example of the fighting abilities of the army, Black Hawk went on to lead his people through the countryside burning farmsteads and taking scalps. The Illinois settlers responded with total hysteria. A Galena newspaper called for a "war of extermination until there shall be no Indian *(with his scalp on)* left in . . . Illinois," and throughout the states volunteer companies turned out to hunt down the Indians. One such company, the 1st Regiment of the Brigade of Mounted Volunteers, served under the amiable command of a New Salem boy named Abraham Lincoln. During his campaigning, Lincoln said, he never saw "any live, fighting Indians," though he had "a good many bloody struggles with the musquitoes." He did, however, witness the scene of a massacre, and the sight stayed with him for the rest of his life. Years later, in one of his very few autobiographical reminiscences, he spoke of coming upon five of Stillman's men, with "the red light of the morning sun . . . streaming upon them as they lay heads toward us on the ground. And every man had a round, red spot on the top of his head, about as big as a dollar where the redskins had taken his scalp. It was frightful, but it was grotesque; and the red sunlight seemed to paint everything all over. I remember that one man had on buckskin breeches."

With 150,000 settlers living in Illinois, Black Hawk never had a chance. He did as much damage as he could, but finally, with troops moving toward him on every side, he found himself with half his warriors gone and his back to the Mississippi. Before he could ford the river, the steamboat

AN IMPOSING PEACE ADVOCATE

Wearing a necklace of bear claws and a government peace medal, the venerable Sauk chief Keokuk— meaning "Watchful Fox"—stares stolidly out of this 1847 daguerreotype made when he was almost eighty. Keokuk was an astute politician and a forceful orator. He counseled his tribe to submit peacefully to the advance of white settlers in Illinois, reasoning that profits from trading and selling land to the whites outweighed the short-lived glory of trying to fight them off. In 1824 Keokuk even persuaded Secretary of War John C. Calhoun to pay the Sauks for land the U.S. had bought from another tribe.

Keokuk's influence kept most Sauk and Fox warriors neutral during the Black Hawk War. After Black Hawk's capture, the government installed the cooperative Keokuk as chief. He sold the tribe's land in Iowa and moved his people to a reservation in Kansas, where he lived peacefully and in some prosperity until his death in April, 1848, of "dysentery brought on by a drunken frolic."

GWY  JⱠᎤᎧᏓ.

CHEROKEE PHŒNIX.

VOL. I. **NEW ECHOTA, WEDNESDAY JUNE 4, 1828.**

EDITED BY ELIAS BOUDINOTT
PRINTED WEEKLY BY
ISAAC H. HARRIS,
FOR THE CHEROKEE NATION.

At $2 50 if paid in advance, $3 in six months, or $3 50 if paid at the end of the year.

To subscribers who can read only the Cherokee language the price will be $2,00 in advance, or $2,50 to be paid within the year.

Every subscription will be considered as continued unless subscribers give notice to the contrary before the commencement of a new year.

Any person procuring six subscribers, and becoming responsible for the payment, shall receive a seventh gratis.

Advertisements will be inserted at seventy-five cents per square for the first insertion, and thirty-seven and a half cents for each continuance; longer ones in proportion.

☞ All letters addressed to the Editor, post paid, will receive due attention.

AGENTS FOR THE CHEROKEE PHŒNIX.

The following persons are authorized to receive subscriptions and payments for the Cherokee Phœnix.

Henry Hill, Esq. Treasurer of the A. B. C. F. M. Boston, Mass.
George M. Tracy, Agent of the A. B. C. M. New York.
Rev. A. D. Eddy, Canandaigua, N. Y.

of said river opposite to Fort Strother, on said river; all north of said line is the Cherokee lands, all south of said line is the Creek lands.

ARTICLE 2. WE THE COMMISSIONERS, do further agree that all the Creeks that are north of the said line above mentioned shall become subjects to the Cherokee nation.

ARTICLE 3. All Cherokees that are south of the said line shall become subjects of the Creek nation.

ARTICLE 4. If any chief or chiefs of the Cherokees, should fall within the Creek nation, such chief shall be continued as chief of said nation.

ARTICLE 5. If any chief or chiefs of the Creeks. should fall within the Cherokees, that is. north of said line, they shall be continued as chiefs of said nation.

ARTICLE 6. If any subject of the Cherokee nation, should commit murder and run into the Creek nation, the Cherokees will make application to the Creeks to have the murderer killed. and when done; the Cherokee nation will give the man who killed the murderer, $200.

ARTICLE 7. If any subject of the Creek nation. should commit murder and run to the Cherokees, the Creeks will make application to the Cherokees to have the murderer killed, and when done the Creek nation will give the man who killed the murderer $200.

ARTICLE 8. If any Cherokees. should come over the line and commit murder or theft on the Creeks, the Creeks will make a demand of the Cherokees for satisfaction.

ARTICLE 9. If any Creeks should come over the line and commit murder or theft on the Cherokees, the

William Hambly,   (Seal)
his
Big ⋈ Warrior,   (Seal)
mark.
WITNESSES.
Major Ridge,
Dan'l. Griffin.
A. M'COY, Clerk N. Com.
JOS. VANN, Cl'k. to the Commissioners.

Be it remembered, This day, that I have approved of the treaty of boundary, concluded on by the Cherokees, east of the Mississippi, and the Creek nation of Indians, on the eleventh day of December, 1821, and with the modifications proposed by the committee and council, on the 28th day of March, in the current year. Given under my hand and seal at Fortville, this 16th day of May, 1822.
CHARLES R. HICKS, (Seal)
WITNESS,
LEONARD HICKS.

WHEREAS, The treaty concluded between the Cherokees and Creeks, by commissioners duly authorised by the chiefs of their respective nations. at General Wm. M'Intosh's on the eleventh day of December, (A. D.) one thousand eight hundred and twenty one, establishing the boundary line between the two nations, has this day been laid before the members of the national committee, by the head chiefs and members of council of the Cherokee nation, and Saml. Hawkins, Sah.naw, wee, Ninne,ho.mot.tee and Ia.des.le,af,kee, chiefs duly appointed and authorised by the head chiefs of the Creek nation, for a friendly explanation & full understanding of the constructions to be placed on the differ-

mitting murder on the subject other, is approved and adopted respecting thefts, it is hereby that the following rule be subs and adopted; viz: Should t jects of either nation go over and commit theft, and he, she be apprehended, they shall b and dealt with as the laws of t tion direct, but should the pe persons so offending, make their and return to his, her or their then, the person or persons so ed, shall make application to per authorities of that nation dress, and justice shall be rend far as practicable, agreeably and law, but in no case shall ei tion be accountable.

The 10th article is approv adopted, and all claims for the sidered closed by the treaty as lated in that article.

The 11th article is approve dopted, and it is agreed furth contracting nations will exte respective laws with equal ju wards the citizens of the othe gard to collecting debts due individuals of their nation to t the other.

The 12th article is fully a and confirmed. We do hereb er agree to allow those ind who have fell within the limit other, twelve months from t hereof, to determine whethe tions, or continue and become subjects of that nation; and it is also agreed that in case the citizens of either nation, who may choose to remove into the nation, of the other and become

CONSTITUTION
OF THE
CHEROKEE NATION,
MADE AND ESTABLISHED
AT A
GENERAL CONVENTION OF DELEGATES,
DULY AUTHORISED FOR THAT PURPOSE,
AT
NEW ECHOTA,
JULY 26, 1827.

PRINTED FOR THE CHEROKEE NATION,
AT THE OFFICE OF THE STATESMAN AND PATRIOT,
GEORGIA.

The highly civilized Cherokee nation published its own newspaper, the Phoenix, *written both in English and in Cherokee—the latter using an alphabet developed by the brilliant Indian leader Sequoyah. Moreover, the Cherokees had a written constitution (whose title page appears above) modeled on the Constitution of the United States. Its preamble—which expressed much of how all the tribes felt about their lands—read, in part, "We, the Cherokee people, constituting one of the sovereign and independent nations of the earth, and having complete jurisdiction over its territory. . . ." As usual, the whites did not listen.*

Warrior hove into sight with a detachment of soldiers and a six-pounder aboard. Black Hawk raised a white flag, but the jittery troops responded by opening fire. The Indians sought cover and fired on the ship until she retreated down the river to refuel. Then, early on the morning of August 3, 1,300 volunteers and regulars came storming up to the riverbank. The Indians tried to surrender, but the troops, inflamed by weeks of panic, set upon them clubbing, stabbing, and shooting. The massacre went on for eight hours. When the *Warrior* returned to add her six-pounder to the carnage, one observer saw the Mississippi "perceptibly tinged with the blood of the Indians who were shot in its margin and in the stream." The soldiers took only thirty-nine prisoners. Two hundred Sauk and Foxes somehow managed to thrash their way across the river only to be scalped or taken prisoner by hostile Sioux, who awaited them on the other side.

Black Hawk managed to survive the slaughter and escaped north to Wisconsin, where he fell in with some Winnebagos who turned him over to the authorities for a reward of a hundred dollars and twenty horses. The chief stayed in jail for a year, and then the government decided to send him on a tour around the country so that the curious could have a chance to get a look at him. He was burned in effigy in Detroit, but by the time he reached the eastern cities, which had not felt the strength of the Indian raids for years, he had become something of a celebrity. Cowed, amiable, his fighting days behind him, he smiled and nodded to the guests at hotel banquets, and they applauded him, a harmless relic of a gaudy past.

Black Hawk died in 1838, the same year that a final tragedy befell the eastern Indians. In the last confrontation of the war in the East, there were no raids, no battles, no skirmishes; there was simply a vast and relentless land grab. This one was directed against the Cherokees.

In the first decades of the nineteenth century the Cherokees had lived on forty thousand square miles of rich land in the valley of the Tennessee. Their communities prospered: they had ten sawmills, more than sixty smithys, eight cotton-weaving machines, eighteen schools, miles of public roads, sturdy houses, and their own newspaper, the *Phoenix,* which was published in both English and Cherokee. Alone among the Indian nations, they had a written constitution. And they lived in harmony with their white neighbors.

However, these peaceful, steady people were nothing but an irritant to the state of Georgia, which wanted their lands. In 1822 the state's politicians, invoking an 1802 treaty that promised Georgia Cherokee territory as soon as the Indians could be peaceably moved, pressed Congress into nullifying the natives' land titles. The Indians resisted, and soon Georgia hotspurs were raiding Cherokee territory. Rather than move toward war, the Cherokees took their case to the Supreme Court, which in 1832 ruled that the Indians had every right to their nation. President Jackson thought differently: "John Marshall has made his decision," he said, "now let him enforce it." Three years later the Georgians managed to assemble some five hundred Cherokees and forced on them a treaty by which the Indians promised to sell their land for five million dollars and relocate in the west. They had two years to get out.

Nearly sixteen thousand Cherokees signed a petition denying the treaty, but Jackson stuck by his guns, the document was ratified, and a removal deadline was set for May 23, 1838. Winfield Scott and John Ellis Wool, a regular army general, were sent to enforce the treaty. Both men found the duty repellent. "The whole scene since I have been in this country has been nothing but a heartrending one," Wool wrote, "and such a one as I would be glad to get rid of as soon as circumstances will permit. Because I am firm and decided, do not believe I would be unjust. If I could . . . I would remove every Indian tomorrow beyond the reach of the white men, who, like vultures, are watching, ready to pounce on their prey and strip them of everything they have or expect from the government of the United States. Yes, sir, nineteen-twentieths, if not ninety-nine out of every hundred, will go penniless to the West."

Tennessee volunteers under Brigadier General R. G. Dunlap began to build log pens for any Cherokees who might prove recalcitrant when the day came. Halfhearted to begin with, the Tennessee boys became thoroughly disgusted with their job after they began to attend Cherokee parties where they danced with bright, pretty, well-educated Indian girls. Finally Dunlap threatened to resign his commission, stating that he would not bring dishonor on his state "by aiding to carry into execution at the point of the bayonet a treaty made by a lean minority against the will and authority of the Cherokee people."

Still the preparations went on. By 1838 two thousand Cherokees had reluctantly moved west, but fifteen thousand remained behind, refusing

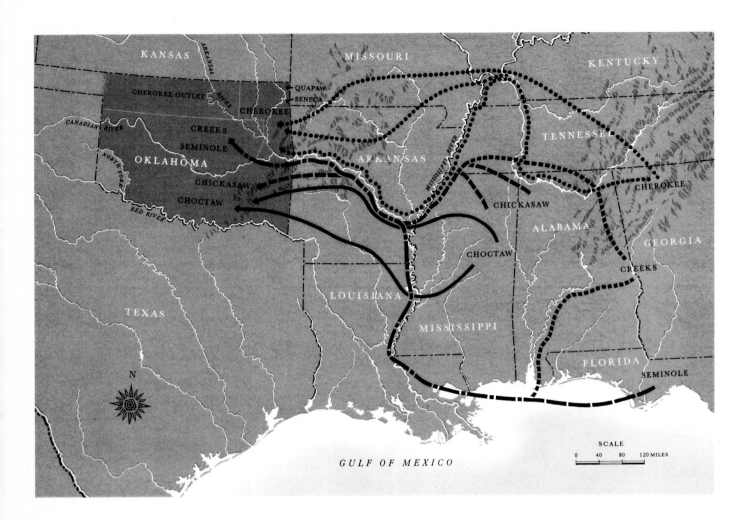

Though the Cherokees gave the name Trail of Tears to their seven-hundred-mile westward trek, Choctaws, Chickasaws, Seminoles, and Creeks also traveled bitter roads between 1820 and 1845. This map shows the routes the "Five Civilized Tribes" followed to their new homes in Indian Territory, the dark area on the map covering most of present-day Oklahoma. They were supposed to function as independent nations within Indian Territory; but the government used their allegiance to the Confederacy during the Civil War as cause for reclaiming much of their land.

to emigrate. As the day approached, Winfield Scott glumly told the seven thousand soldiers at his disposal that "every possible kindness . . . must . . . be shown by the troops, and, if, in the ranks, a despicable individual should be found, capable of inflicting a wanton injury or insult on any Cherokee man, woman, or child, it is hereby made the special duty of the nearest good officer or man, instantly to interpose, and to seize and consign the guilty wretch to the severest penalty of the laws."

Yet, on the sunny May morning when the soldiers set about their task, some of them raped, robbed, and murdered the Indians. In other villages, the task went a little better. One man who took part in the roundup wrote that "after all the warning and with soldiers in their midst, the inevitable day found the Indians at work in their houses and in their fields. . . . Two or three dropped their hoes and ran as fast as they could when they saw the soldiers coming into the fields. After that, they made no effort to get out of the way. The men handled them gently, but picked them up in the road, in the field, anywhere they found them . . . and carried them to the post. . . .

"Chickens, cats, and dogs all ran away when they saw us. Ponies under the shade trees fighting the flies with the noise of their bells; the cows and calves lowing to each other; the poor dogs howling for their owners; the open doors of the cabins as we left them—to have seen it all would have melted to tenderness a heart of stone."

The army kept the Cherokees penned up in concentration camps

throughout the stifling summer; many died, and many more fell ill. In the fall and early winter contingents started west, some in flatboats, some in wagons, some on foot.

A young private who watched one wagon train pull out wrote that "in the chill of a drizzling rain on an October morning I saw them loaded like cattle or sheep into six hundred and forty-five wagons and started toward the west. . . . When the bugle sounded and the wagons started rolling many of the children . . . waved their little hands good-bye to their mountain homes."

The Cherokees had twelve hundred miles to go before they reached eastern Oklahoma at the end of the trek they would forever after remember as the Trail of Tears. As their homeland disappeared behind them the cold autumn rains continued to fall, bringing disease and death. Four thousand shallow graves marked the trail. Marauding parties of white men appeared, seized Cherokee horses in payment for imaginary debts, and rode off. The Indians pressed on, the sullen troopers riding beside them.

They came at last to the Mississippi, gray and swollen under the huge, unfamiliar sky. The ragged Indians stared across the river at the lands they had never seen and never wished to see. Behind them lay the East, the graves of their ancestors, the places of their birth, the land that they—and all the other tribes—had loved well, and had struggled to hold, and had lost forever.

Robert Lindneux, a twentieth-century artist, painted this scene of the Trail of Tears; oddly enough, there are no known contemporary views of the Cherokees on their forced march.

153

Visiting the Great White Father

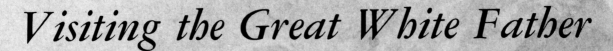

As more and more eastern Indians were forced to move west,
the federal government invited delegations of the migrants
to Washington (below, a deputation from Wisconsin sets off
for the capital) to impress them with the power of the white
man's world—and thereby encourage the peaceful surrender of
their lands. Some Indians despised the ritual, but others
reveled in its luxuries. The Assiniboin chief at the right
went so far as to dress up like a white man and even called
himself Jackson after his new hero, President Andrew Jackson.

Visiting delegations were housed luxuriously—at such choice spots as the Indian Queen Hotel (below)—and were royally wined and dined at government expense. Indians asked for and received presents; their favorites were whiskey, rifles, and peace medals. In 1824 Thomas L. McKenney, head of the newly created Bureau of Indian Affairs, realized that the visits to Washington presented a rare opportunity to gather archival material on North America's natives. As part of that project, he hired Charles Bird King to paint portraits of delegation members. A nine-man Choctaw group from Mississippi was one of the first to visit Washington under McKenney's regime. Seventy-two-year-old Pushmataha, who had fought the British in the War of 1812 and held a commission in the U.S. Army, led his tribe. The negotiations over Pushmataha's lands dragged on for more than three months, and the chief himself died during them—on Christmas Eve in his room at the Indian Queen. The Choctaws blamed the death on a persistent cold, but the Indian agent—appalled by the hotel bar bill—charged that he had drunk himself to death. The beautiful portrait of Pushmataha at right was one of Charles Bird King's first. Other examples from the more than one hundred forty that he completed over a twenty-year period appear on the following pages.

Visiting delegations ran up bills, such as the one above, that far exceeded the $1.25 per diem rate at Jessie Brown's Indian Queen Hotel (below). Additional fringe benefits for visitors included such presents as the engraved silver pipe bowl and specially decorated flag at the left.

157

After a Pawnee delegation visited James Monroe at the White House, King painted the unusual group portrait below, considered one of his best. King himself was especially proud of his painting above of Kansa chief Monchousia.

King painted Petalesharro, a twenty-four-year-old warrior hero of the Pawnees, in full war bonnet with eagle feathers.

After 1840 the development of daguerreotypes and then
photography presented a cheap and quick alternative
to portrait painting for creating a visual record
of the native visitors. But the Indians, who had been
deeply impressed with King's work, still wanted to
have their images reproduced in oil. Portraits were
painted until 1858, when the government made a final
decision to switch to photographs. Here a large
group is welcomed to the White House by Andrew Johnson.

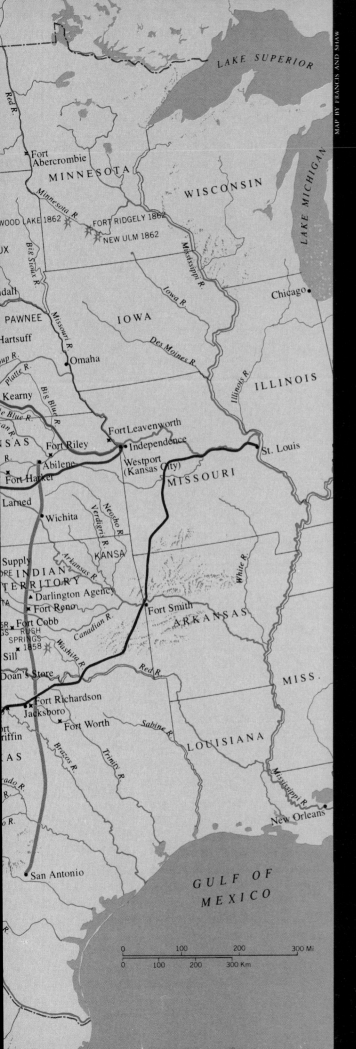

MAP BY FRANCIS AND SHAW

PART II

The WEST

1850–1890

By 1850 gold had been discovered in California, and white settlers were heading west to lay claim to the entire continent. As they moved into Indian hunting grounds, new violence erupted. Although the western tribes already had rifles to add to traditional weapons such as the shield and lance drawn by Frederic Remington (below, top), they never got their hands on sophisticated weapons such as the U.S. Army's Gatling gun (below, bottom), capable of firing two hundred rounds per minute. The battles, forts, and Indian tribes that figured in the Indian-white conflict west of the Mississippi are shown on the map at left. At the Battle of Wounded Knee in 1890, the last of the Sioux nation succumbed to the whites' clear-cut military and technological superiority.

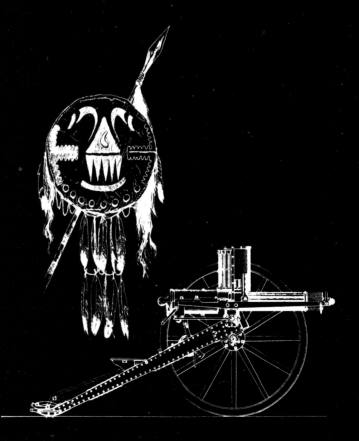

Pawnees sight a caravan in this 1837 water color by A. J. Miller.

6: Before the Deluge

On a late June day in 1846 a frail youth accompanied by a pipe-smoking French mountain man rode a horse up the Oregon Trail toward the trading post of Fort Laramie. New England Puritan and Harvard graduate, twenty-three years old, he aspired to be a historian. His name was Francis Parkman.

Young Parkman wanted to write the history of France in North America. Despite chronic bad health, he resolved to prepare himself for the task by experiencing firsthand the land and the people he intended to re-create in prose. By Parkman's time, however, the Indians as the French *voyageurs* knew them in the Mississippi and tributary valleys no longer existed as a proper laboratory study. In quest of real Indians, therefore, he headed west in that momentous year of 1846. His observations, recorded in a book that has become a classic, capture much of the essence of the Indian West as the final chapter of the frontier drama opened.

Parkman met his first real Indian as he approached the fort. A copper-skinned youth rode boldly forth on his pony and dismounted. Parkman saw before him "a young fellow, of no note in his nation," but lithe, graceful, and well proportioned, his thick black hair gathered behind his head and ornamented with an eagle-bone whistle and a pendant of brass plates, resembling coins, tapering to the size of a dime. "His chest and arms were naked; the buffalo robe, worn over them when at rest, had fallen about his waist, and was confined there by a belt. This, with the gay moccasins on his feet, completed his attire. For arms he carried a quiver of dog-skin at his back, and a rude but powerful bow in his hand."

Parkman confronted a warrior of the Oglala tribe, one of seven tribes of the Teton Dakota, or Sioux. In the next few weeks, living with the Oglala followers of Chiefs Old Smoke and Whirlwind, the young historian learned all he could about how these people lived and behaved and thought. Despite excruciating dysentery, it was an exhilarating experience, a peak of his life that he savored in memory until death.

The people of Old Smoke and Whirlwind drew upon nature for their basic wants; central to their scheme of life was nature's most bounteous creation of the plains—the buffalo. Millions darkened the plains at mid-century. The highlight of Parkman's stay in the tepee of an Indian named Big Crow was a buffalo hunt. With a swarm of horsemen he charged into the midst of a herd. "Amid the trampling and the yells I could see their dark figures running hither and thither through clouds of dust, and the horsemen darting in pursuit. . . . The uproar and confusion lasted but a moment. The dust cleared away, and the buffalo could be seen scattering as from a common centre, flying over the plain singly, or in long files and small compact bodies, while behind them followed the Indians riding at furious speed, and yelling as they launched arrow after arrow into their sides. The carcasses were strewn thickly over the ground. Here and there stood wounded buffalo, their bleeding sides feathered with arrows; and as I rode by them their eyes would glare, they would bristle like gigantic cats, and feebly attempt to rush up and gore my horse."

The buffalo supplied an incredible variety of needs. Buffalo meat was the principal Indian food. From the hide came robes for warmth and trade and skins for the distinctive conical tepee that sheltered the family. Hides, stomach, and intestines were fashioned into containers for cooking, storage, and transport, bones into tools. Even the dried droppings, buffalo chips, made fuel when wood was scarce. The Sioux also hunted deer, elk, and antelope, pheasants, grouse, sage hens, and rabbits and put them, like the buffalo, to uses beyond the camp kettle. But it was the buffalo that under-girt the economy and mightily influenced society, religion, and warfare.

Warfare dominated Sioux life, especially the man's. "War is the breath of their nostrils," observed Parkman. "Against most of the neighboring tribes they cherish a rancorous hatred, transmitted from father to son, and inflamed by constant aggression and retaliation." The hunt was a necessary chore albeit a glamorous one. But war was the path to wealth, prestige, and high rank. The enemies were the Crows, Shoshones, and Pawnees. Their pony herds yielded the principal measure of wealth and medium of ex-change, their scalps the emblems of bravery, skill, and daring. Besides plunder and war honors, the Sioux fought for possession of hunting grounds, in defense against the forays of equally aggressive enemies, and in reprisal when an enemy scored a success.

At times the Sioux warriors raided against the few white people who had filtered out onto the plains or bartered with them at Fort Laramie or another of the Platte or Missouri River trading posts. But in 1846, though Parkman recognized the portent of these early white intrusions, to the Indians they were cause for rising concern but not yet alarm. Although white men cut timber, shot or frightened off game, and permitted stock to eat grass, in truth they did not intrude much on the everyday life of the

Although some Indians hunted buffalo with close-range shotguns, the most common weapon remained the bow and arrow (above). Carl Bodmer's Mandan Indian (below) wears the costume of his buffalo society, whose rituals made "the buffalo come."

Sioux warrior. His world remained circumscribed by his lodge, his family, his band, his tribe, his hunting territory, and his enemies.

However lightly the white people trod the world of the Sioux warrior in 1846, he already owed them a profound debt of which he was only dimly aware. But for the whites he would still be stalking deer on foot among the forests of the upper Mississippi River, transporting his belongings on travois pulled by dogs, and depending entirely on his own stone-age manufactures for war and the hunt. His forebears but several generations removed had lived precisely this life, and his present nomadic buffalo-hunting existence in the plains country west of the Missouri River had evolved only in the past century.

Some of the new things the Sioux received from the whites were purely beneficial workaday goods, such as camp kettles, metal skinning knives, axes, and other tools and utensils more efficient and durable than any the Indian had previously been able to fashion for himself. Some were distinctly bad, disastrously so, such as whiskey. But of all the innovations two proved of revolutionary significance—the horse and the gun.

Spaniards brought the horse to the New World. As the Spanish frontier advanced northward in Mexico and crossed into the present boundaries of the southwest United States, horses inevitably fell into the hands of Indians there. Throughout the eighteenth century, by barter and theft, the horse spread northward from tribe to tribe. By mid-century the Sioux, who had already been shouldered westward to the plains by the more powerful Crees, had substituted the horse for the dog as the main beast of burden. The horse ranged farther, pulled larger and more heavily loaded travois,

This Comanche village, painted by George Catlin in 1834, contained some six hundred transportable lodges made from buffalo hides like the one below. The village, in Cache Creek valley in Texas, was a rendezvous for hunters and warriors.

and most remarkable bore a rider. Truly the horse was Wakan, powerful medicine. The Sioux called it sacred dog.

The gun came from the east and north, from French trappers and traders working the Great Lakes country. Guns gave the Crees the advantage that forced the Sioux to retreat westward. Then the Sioux acquired guns too. As experience with the Crees had shown, while bow and arrow sufficed for the hunt, guns were essential to fight tribes likewise equipped.

With horse and gun the Sioux warrior could range over vast distances, following the buffalo and vanquishing other tribes that stood in the way. As individuals, bands, and tribes, the Sioux were proud, arrogant, fiercely independent, and now amply provided with the means of a rich and satisfying life. By early in the nineteenth century the Sioux had reduced to impotence the Arikaras, Mandans, and other groups on the Missouri River. The white man's smallpox helped. An 1837 epidemic scourged the upper Missouri, and almost overnight the ranks of the Mandans, for example, dropped from some sixteen hundred to about thirty. "The destroying angel has visited the unfortunate sons of the wilderness with terrors never before known," wrote a visiting European, "and has converted the extensive hunting grounds, as well as the peaceful settlements of these tribes, into desolate and boundless cemeteries."

With these tribes wiped out, the Sioux thrust westward to rout the Kiowas from the Black Hills and the Crows from the Powder River basin. By Parkman's time they dominated the northern plains from the Minnesota River to the Bighorn Mountains and from the upper Missouri to the Platte and Republican. The future would bring bitter wars with the whites,

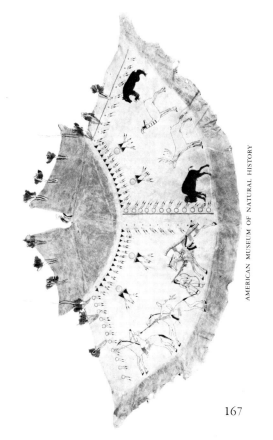

167

in which the Sioux would fight longer and harder than any other plains tribe and finally succumb only on the bloody field of Wounded Knee in the year the frontier officially vanished. During those decades of warfare, Francis Parkman labored in his darkened Boston study on the procession of soaring narratives that made him America's greatest historian of the nineteenth century. In those years of pain, debility, prostration, and blindness, as historian Bernard De Voto has so graphically recorded, Parkman's mind often leaped back to his western adventure, and he would grope for its mementoes fastened to the wall—lance, pipe, feathers, bow and arrows, medicine pouch. "On such days," De Voto wrote, "Francis Parkman could touch the bucksin or the feathers with his fingers, smell sagebrush, taste alkali, and remember a young man's courage and exaltation among the Sioux." He died in 1893, three years after the Sioux nation died at Wounded Knee.

In the perception of today's Americans, the Sioux warrior Parkman met as he neared Fort Laramie is the archetype of the Plains Indian and, indeed, of all American Indians. However erroneous the latter image, the former is close to the truth. Sioux culture did not differ importantly from that of other plains tribes. From Canada to Mexico the plains nomads followed the buffalo and warred with one another. Sharing the northern plains with the Sioux were not only their enemies the Pawnees, Crows, and Shoshones but also friends and allies such as the Northern Cheyennes and Northern Arapahos and other tribes, among them the Blackfeet and Assiniboins. On the central and southern plains the allied Southern Cheyennes and Southern Arapahos roamed between the Platte and the Arkansas and west to the Rocky Mountains, while Kiowas and Comanches, likewise allies, lived south of the Arkansas but rode farther south into Texas and Mexico and west as far as the Rio Grande. Perhaps even more than the Sioux, the Comanches succeeded in fusing horse and rider and in carrying the distinctive features of the horse-and-buffalo culture to the peak of refinement. Not inaccurately did white observers, in a mixture of fear and admiration, label them "Lords of the South Plains." As early as 1834 the pioneering western artist George Catlin pronounced the Comanches "the most extraordinary horsemen that I have yet seen in all my travels, and I doubt . . . whether any people in the world can surpass them."

The plains culture required a vast territory for a sparse population. Altogether the plains tribes counted no more than seventy-five thousand people. In contrast, the so-called Five Civilized Tribes—Cherokee, Creek, Choctaw, Chickasaw, Seminole—moved by the United States government from eastern homes to but one portion of present-day Oklahoma, numbered eighty-four thousand. All seven tribes of Teton Sioux scarcely exceeded sixteen thousand, a population that yielded about four thousand fighting men. Given the wide dispersion of these tribes, such figures belie today's set-piece motion picture and television scenes depicting hordes of charging warriors from which the popular image of the Indian wars is drawn.

Although they dominate the modern concept of the nineteenth-century western Indians, actually the plains tribes formed little more than one fifth of the 360,000 Indians of the trans-Mississippi West and in many ways differed from them. The mountains, the deserts, and the meadow and timberland of the Pacific Northwest imposed demands upon their inhabitants very different from those of the plains. And this, in turn, molded different peoples. Although most whites tended to see them all as Indians, they saw themselves as Ute or Apache or Nez Perce or Modoc, and like the plains tribes they usually warred more violently among themselves than with the white newcomers.

Despite their great diversity, however, many of the western tribes shared certain fundamental characteristics. Whatever their environment, they lived close to it, finely tuned to its vagaries, able to exploit such food and other resources as it contained, adept at making favorable use of its features, however harsh. They worshiped deities and performed sacred rituals that related primarily to nature. They governed themselves by highly democratic political systems in which leaders carried out the will of the people. They cherished the freedom, independence, and dignity of the individual, the family, and the group. With some notable exceptions, they exalted war and bestowed great prestige on the successful warrior.

Like the Plains Indians, the tribes of desert, mountain, and basin at the midpoint of the nineteenth century lived in a world still basically Indian. The white intrusions along the coast or up the river valleys and other trade routes had not disrupted the main patterns of Indian life or altered the main Indian relationships with one another. Even so, again like the Plains Indians, few remained untouched by white influences. Many had incorporated the horse and gun into their scheme of life, along with a variety of other useful innovations. Many were occasionally demoralized by the white man's whiskey and devastated by the white man's diseases. Some had been displaced from traditional ranges by the pressures, direct or indirect, of the white advance.

Of all the regions of the United States, the Southwest contained the most demanding environment. For Indian and white alike, life in most parts of this region — the sterile table of the Colorado Plateau, the maze of slopes falling off from the Mogollon Rim, the deserts spotted with barren mountains extending from the Pecos to the Colorado and deep into Mexico—was difficult and uncertain. Only the valley of the upper Rio Grande, well watered and shadowed by the Sangre de Cristo peaks, offered a comparatively congenial place to live.

The Southwest supported a bewildering variety of Indians (see map on page 162). The gentle Pueblos resided in fixed adobe villages along the Rio Grande, while the equally gentle Pimas and Papagos also led sedentary lives in the deserts of southern Arizona. Other southwesterners included Hopis, Yavapais, Mohaves, and Yumas. But the most populous, formidable, and warlike, those who most tenaciously contested white rule, were the Navahos and Apaches.

The Navahos, an early United States Indian agent declared, "are hardy and intelligent, and it is as natural for them to war against all men, and to take the property of others as it is for the sun to give light by day." Allowing for a certain bias, he was not too wide of the mark. Proud and powerful in their population of twelve thousand, the Navahos occupied the Colorado Plateau west of the Rio Grande. They lived in semipermanent log-and-brush dwellings called hogans, raised corn and fruit, and kept flocks of sheep. Like the plains warriors, they waged vigorous war on horseback.

General George Crook, considered by many of his contemporaries to be the army's most skilled Indian fighter, called the Apaches "the tigers of the human species." Ranging from western Texas across New Mexico to Arizona and south into Mexico, they were man for man probably the fiercest and most effective fighters of the western Indians. They were so feared in northern Mexico that the provinces there were on occasion willing to pay a bounty for Apache scalps. The Apaches numbered about eight thousand, divided into tribes such as Jicarilla, Mescalero, White Mountain, and Chiricahua. They lived in brush dwellings that could be erected as easily as abandoned. They practiced a rudimentary agriculture but for food relied mainly on game, desert plants, and the booty from raids. Although possessing horses and mules, the typical Apache preferred to walk—or better yet run, at which he excelled—and used his stock for food as readily as for locomotion. A hard people forged by a hard land, the Apaches knew perfectly how to turn its every feature to their advantage and to their enemy's disadvantage. During the summer of 1881 an aged, infirm leader named Nana led a two-month-long, thousand-mile raid in which his forty warriors killed forty whites and wounded many more. He won eight pitched battles, captured two hundred horses, eluded fourteen hundred army troops and armed civilians, and withdrew to his Mexican hideaway without losing a man.

The southwestern Indians counted a longer experience with whites than any others. They traced its beginnings to a July day in 1540 when an army of bearded men armored in bright metal, some astride unfamiliar beasts, drew up in front of the Zuñi town of Hawikuh, a pueblo of mud and stone nestled on a brown plain bordered by red, piñon-dappled mesas. The Indians, confident in superior numbers, sallied forth behind a volley of arrows to give battle. But, shouting "Santiago," the strangers charged with slashing long knives and mysterious sticks that spurted fire and smoke—and death. In the town the enemy leader was wounded by a rock dropped on him from a rooftop and an arrow lodged in his foot, but his men easily carried the defenses and forced the natives to surrender.

Unknown to its people, Hawikuh had been named by the whites as one of the "Seven Cities of Cibola," fabled in the lore of New Spain for supposedly untapped riches, and the wounded captain of the invaders was Francisco Vásquez de Coronado, nobleman of Spain. He found no riches at any of the seven cities, or at the pueblos that dotted the Rio Grande valley two hundred miles to the east—or, for that matter, at the elusive, ultimately illusory Quivira, on the plains far to the east, where he was directed by Indians who wanted only to be rid of him and his arrogant and brutal followers. The Spaniards never found wealth in New Mexico. But early in the seventeenth century, still drawn by the lure of rumored gold and by heathens awaiting salvation, they fastened their colonizing triad of pueblo, mission, and presidio, or fort, on the upper Rio Grande.

In the smoky adobe pueblos of the Rio Grande Indians, resentments smoldered under the oppression of Spanish officers and the efforts of Spanish priests to stamp out the old religious practices and substitute those of Catholic Spain. Popé, an Indian leader of great spiritual and patriotic power, secretly conspired with like-minded malcontents to throw off the yoke. At his direction runners bore knotted cords to all the upper river pueblos. The cords were designed so that the last knot would be untied in each pueblo on the day of the revolt—August 13, 1680. Popé was so intent on keeping the secret that he killed his own son-in-law on suspicion of treachery. Still, word leaked out and the revolt had to be launched three days early. At Taos, Acoma, Pecos, and other pueblos

In this painting by William Gary, curious Indians gather to await the arrival of the annual supply boat—the "fire canoe"—as it steams toward Fort Berthold on the upper Missouri River.

MC CRACKEN, *The Charles M. Russell Book*,
DOUBLEDAY AND COMPANY, 1957

*As early as the 1830's Jim Bridger's skill as
a mountain man and trapper had become legendary. His understanding attitude toward Indians,
described by a contemporary, was typical of the
western trapper: he "was utterly scandalized if
even the most childish of the superstitions of the Indians were treated with anything like contempt
or disrespect." In this pen-and-ink sketch by
Charles M. Russell, Bridger and his party approach Fort Benton, a fur-trading post on the
upper Missouri River in present-day Montana.*

throughout the province, the Indians murdered their priests, burned the
missions, and then converged on the Spanish capital of Santa Fe. It fell
before the onslaught, and the triumphant Popé established himself in the
adobe palace recently vacated by Governor Antonio de Otermín. More
than four hundred Spaniards perished in the uprising, and the rest fled.

Popé proved to be a far more oppressive ruler than his Spanish prede-
cessors: he demanded excessively high tribute to his central government;
he took the most beautiful women for himself and his captains; those who
refused to obey his orders were summarily executed. Civil war, drought,
and famine devastated the province throughout Popé's eight-year rule.
Four years after his death sixty soldiers and a hundred Indian allies under
Governor Don Diego de Vargas retook Santa Fe by cutting off the water
supply and all communication. Not a shot was fired, and soon thereafter
all the pueblos submitted to Spanish rule.

In the century and a half after the Spanish reconquest Apaches and
Navahos emerged as the native forces to be reckoned with in the Southwest. First under Spain, then under Mexico after the 1821 revolution,
patterns took shape that locked settlers and Indians in a complex and
deadly relationship. Apaches and Navahos raided Mexican settlers, both
in New Mexico and Old Mexico, for sheep, cattle, horses, plunder, and
for captives to be assimilated into the tribes. Mexicans banded together
for similar forays against Apaches and Navahos in which the object was
not only plunder but Indian captives wanted as slaves in Mexican house-
holds. The system fed on itself: a raid inevitably provoked retaliation,
which in turn set off still another raid. Further encouraging the raids
were Mexican traders who supplied the Indians with arms and ammunition in exchange for booty and prisoners seized in attacks on their own
countrymen. The pattern had been fixed by some 150 years of practice
when the United States declared war on Mexico in 1846, and it formed
the backdrop against which the Southwest Indian wars of the next four
decades were fought.

Unlike the Southwest, parts of California and the Oregon country
favored their native inhabitants with a benign and bounteous environment.
Deer, elk, antelope, rabbits, fowl, and other game abounded. Well-watered
streams draining the two great mountain systems, the Coast Ranges on the
west and the Sierra Nevada—Cascades on the east, offered a plenitude of
fish. Acorns, pine nuts, berries, and roots of many kinds varied the diet.
The forests yielded building materials for homes—logs and planks in some
places, brush in others.

The Indians nearest the coast had only weak social and political organization. Fragmented into tribelets occupying small and well-defined territories, poorly led, unaggressive, they indulged in a comfortable and placid
lifestyle. But they were perilously vulnerable, both geographically and
culturally, to aggressions from outside their little world.

These coastal peoples fell fatal prey to the divinely ordained purposes
of Spain. From 1542 on, tall galleons from New Spain periodically probed
the Pacific coast, objects of curiosity rather than menace to the natives.
After some two hundred years the Spaniards founded their first mission, at

San Diego. As in the Southwest, the friars erected other missions and gathered the Indians to Christianize them and teach them proper use — that is, the white man's use — of the land that would someday, through the beneficence of His Most Catholic Majesty, be theirs again. Instead, by the thousands the neophytes died of smallpox, malaria, and other diseases. When Mexico began secularization of the old Spanish missions in 1834 the survivors received half the land. But most Indians had no idea what to do with their holdings and sold their parcels for a pittance or simply walked away.

Among those who stayed, many became virtual slaves on the cattle ranches that were formed from mission lands. In fact, the very first American cowboys, originally called *vaqueros*, were California mission Indians who had been trained by the friars to ride and tend livestock. Eventually they fled to the hills and attempted to resume their former fruit-gathering, sedentary way of life. No longer members of identifiable groups, by mid-century nearly all thirty-one thousand of the former mission Indians existed in a state of hopeless poverty.

The coastal tribes of the Oregon country escaped the Spanish mission system, but they nevertheless met some Spaniards — as well as Englishmen and Russians — who touched lightly on their shores to explore and to trade. In 1778, searching for the legendary Northwest Passage, Britain's Captain James Cook discovered instead the enormous profit potential in the fur-bearing animals that flourished in the area. Soon the sailing ships of his countrymen were swarming along the coast, their masters exchanging beads, cloth, tools, and guns for sea-otter, beaver, and other furs. Other whites began competing for the trade, most notably adventurous seafarers out of New England ports; the Indians called them Bostons.

As the British and the Bostons jostled each other for the Pacific coastal fur trade, they also began to clash over the fur resources of the mountain, plateau, and basin land stretching eastward from the coast toward the Great Plains. There the quest was mainly for beaver, greatly prized for top hats by Europeans and easterners. With curiosity at first, the Indians watched the rival American and British mountain men trap the streams of their homeland. Then quickly they entered the business themselves by bartering furs for white men's goods at the trading posts planted at dozens of strategic locations, principally along the major western rivers.

Fort Union was a fair sample of one of these posts. Located at the junction of the Missouri and Yellowstone rivers, it was a bastioned, palisaded fort erected in 1828 by Kenneth McKenzie, hard-driving chief of the American Fur Company's Upper Missouri Outfit. From Fort Union the so-called King of the Missouri presided over a far-flung trading network that did business with the Blackfeet, Assiniboins, Crows, Crees, and other northern plains tribes. McKenzie's imperious carriage reflected distinguished Scottish ancestry; visitors to Fort Union marveled at his social graces, elegant lifestyle, and comfortable, tastefully appointed quarters. "His table," recorded George Catlin, "groans under the luxuries of the country," such as buffalo tongue and beaver tail, but also featured Madeira and "excellent Port" that accompanied after-dinner talk of art and literature.

Both McKenzie and his lieutenants combined bold yet astute executive talents with a readiness to make use of any stratagem to achieve their purposes. They all took Indian wives, thus cementing alliances that aided

Rudolph Kurz spent eight months at this large Fort Union trading post.

A LOVING EYE FOR THE WEST

As late as the fifth decade of the nineteenth century the only white men who had spent substantial time in the lands west of the Missouri River were the merest handful of trappers, soldiers, settlers, and — the unlikeliest group of all — artists. Armed with pencil, palette, and paintbrush, and lured by a sense of high adventure, illustrators, portraitists, draftsmen, and crude "sketchists" flocked to the wild and lonely frontier.

Among the most fascinating of these artist-adventurers was Swiss-born Rudolph Friedrich Kurz. He was something of an oddity even in this odd-fellow gathering. Unlike most frontier artists, Kurz had received classical training in Europe. For three years he studied art in Paris, and for a time he drew six days a week, from seven in the morning to ten at night. Exhausted, at one point, after eight months of intense work, Kurz was so despondent that he threw all his drawings into the Seine.

Out of this despair rose a new purpose in Kurz's mind: "The portrayal of the aboriginal forests, the wild animals that inhabited them, and the Indians" of North America.

In 1847 Kurz scraped up enough money to book passage from Le Havre to New Orleans; from there he planned to travel the Southwest and record the life of the Comanches. But the United States war with Mexico scuttled that plan. So the indomitable young artist instead went up the Mississippi River to St. Louis, and then west on the Missouri River to trappers' outposts, where he saw and sketched his first Indians.

His first American drawings and color washes displayed a careful draftsman's hand and an almost photographic rendering of detail that showed him to be both a fine artist and a reliable historian. Subsequently he observed and drew

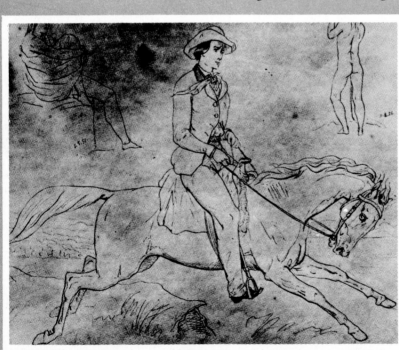

To conserve paper, Kurz sketched around his self-portrait.

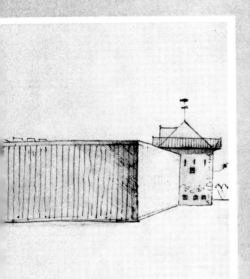

site). In May, 1851, he moved far up the Missouri to Fort Berthold, becoming the first artist to visit the region since George Catlin and Carl Bodmer had traveled the upper Missouri twenty years earlier.

What Kurz saw at the fort was disheartening: the powerful Mandan Indians that Catlin had painted in the 1820's had been decimated by smallpox. Worse yet, a cholera epidemic broke out shortly after Kurz's arrival, and the Indians, remembering the smallpox epidemic that had followed Catlin's visit, came to view Kurz's drawings of them as "bad medicine." As a result, Kurz

in his diary, which casually noted: "Constant danger from lurking enemies, the vast prairie, bounded only by sky and sea; buffaloes and bears in prospect; perhaps a violent storm by way of variety . . . what more could I desire?"

Fort Union (left) proved to be an artist's paradise. Crow, Blackfoot, Cree, Assiniboin, and Chippewa Indians converged on the fort to barter with traders. Among scores of sketches by Kurz is one depicting the Cree chief Le Tout Pique meeting with the artist and a white trader (below). Kurz also made sketches of Ours Fou (Crazy Bear),

Indians fashioning tub-shaped buffalo-hide boats to ferry their belongings across streams and made painstaking drawings of Indian burial and dance rituals.

Of the Indians encamped around the new town of St. Joseph, Missouri, Kurz noted in his diary: "The men wear very little clothing; in mid-summer, with the exception of the breechcloth and blanket, they wear no clothes at all."

With the enthusiasm of a convert to a new religion, Kurz wrote that "these beautifully formed savages riding barebacked . . . I thought as fine a sight as the Grecian horsemen at the Parthenon." An equally fine sight was fourteen-year-old Witthae, daughter of an Iowa chief. In 1850 Kurz married Witthae, and although barely able to support himself, he bought his bride "the usual short shirt or blouse of red calico, a red blanket, a choice of large pearl beads for necklaces, and many colored bands for her hair and for her costume."

Apparently this largesse was not enough, for within a week Witthae returned to her tribe. "That was the end of my romantic dream of love and marriage with an Indian," Kurz scrawled in his diary. "Brief joy!"

After his misfortune with Witthae, Kurz traveled farther upriver to Savannah, Missouri, where he purchased a mare—and audaciously sketched himself on its back (oppo-

Kurz attended this trade parley inside Fort Union.

had to sketch his subjects from a distance with the aid of a telescope. One drawing produced in this manner showed Hidatsa Indians attempting to sweat away the pestilence in steam rooms made of buffalo robes and willow branches.

Finally the Indians threatened to kill Kurz—who was one of the few healthy inhabitants in the area. A friend hurriedly got Kurz and a guide horses and pointed them upriver to the next post at Fort Union. If the artist felt any discomfiture over his situation he did not show it

a chief of the Assiniboins, who was so fascinated by Kurz's artistry that he insisted on sleeping in Kurz's room until the work was completed.

Finally in 1852 dwindling funds forced Kurz to return to Switzerland. He died there, at age fifty-three, in 1871, without realizing his dream of turning the voluminous collection of field sketches into full-fledged paintings. Even so, he left behind an important legacy: a precise documentation of a way of life along the Missouri that was to vanish by the turn of the century.

Perhaps because Father Pierre Jean De Smet and his Jesuit colleagues were far more tolerant of Indian culture than their Protestant competitors, they met with great success (above, Father De Smet's welcome by converts) in the Pacific Northwest. During his thirty-two years of missionary service De Smet published numerous detailed accounts of his work (below, the 1847 title page).

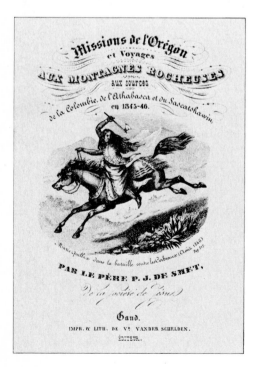

their business interests and siring offspring who in turn would influence tribal policy. These alliances were not wholly casual or cynical; many of the fort's leaders were proudly affectionate toward their Indian wives, clothing them in the latest St. Louis fashions to be displayed prominently about the posts.

Steady streams of Indian trappers and hunters arrived at such forts. In exchange for beaver fur and buffalo robes, tribesmen obtained the knives, hatchets, cooking pots, cloth, and muskets, powder, and ball that became integral features of their material culture. Of importance, too, the process afforded a chance to observe the white man's ways of behaving and thinking, although these were so alien as to be beyond comprehension, matters for endless speculation and bewilderment. Why, for example, did the whites bury a dead man beneath the ground, imprisoned by soil, when the proper place for a corpse was obviously on a raised platform or tree branch from which its soul could soar? And how could one white man sell or buy land as his very own, when every sensible Indian knew that the land was like the sea—to be used by all or at most to be divided by areas of tribal dominance, but never to be held by one person.

Two other aspects of white civilization reached the Indians through posts such as Fort Union. Whiskey was an indispensable tool in the competition of the fur trade, and McKenzie and others made free use of it. Although greatly diluted with water, it still impoverished and debauched those addicted. The ingenious McKenzie made it in his own still at the fort. This blatant violation of federal law eventually caused embarrassed company officials to disavow his action and retire him temporarily from his post. Even so, whiskey continued to run freely in tribal villages.

The other gift was disease, such as the smallpox that came on the annual supply boat that docked at Fort Union in June, 1837. This epidemic alone wiped out some fifteen thousand upper Missouri Indians.

Except for the horrors of alcohol and disease suffered by scattered tribes, however, the interaction of fur men such as McKenzie and Indians all over the West in the first five decades of the nineteenth century was essentially benign. There were occasional minor clashes, usually over business or whiskey, but generally the two got along quite well. Neither tried to dispossess or remake the other. The relationship significantly modified the Indian's material culture but not his basic institutions, beliefs, and customs. These latter, instead, were the target of a breed very different from the rough-hewn, easygoing mountain men and their shrewd business overlords. These whites were the missionaries.

The Whitmans and Spaldings, Presbyterians, exemplified those who sought to lead, or push, the Indians down the path of divine grace. Marcus Whitman, handsome and well built, dedicated, hard-working, was a medical doctor turned missionary. On the eve of facing west from New York in the service of the American Board of Commissioners for Foreign Missions, he married Narcissa Prentiss, an attractive, lively, likable schoolteacher of good intellect. In the same small group with the Whitmans came Henry and Eliza Spalding, he a hypersensitive, embittered complainer, she a severe, colorless soul. They traveled in the American Fur Company caravan of 1836 up the Platte and through the Rockies at South Pass; then they continued down the Snake and Columbia. In so doing they traced what would soon become the Oregon Trail, and Narcissa and Eliza compelled the curiosity and admiration of mountain men and Indians alike as the first white women to cross the Rockies.

The Whitmans and Spaldings decided to settle along the fertile meadows and forest lands of the Columbia and Snake River basins, the home grounds of prosperous, seminomadic Indians who traveled by horse and subsisted on fish and roots as well as game. These tribes, the Yakimas, Wallawallas, Nez Perces, Cayuses, and Flatheads, among others, tended to be well knit politically and had a strong warrior tradition — not people to be pushed around casually. The Spaldings established their mission at Lapwai, near the mouth of the Clearwater River, among the Nez Perces. The Whitmans erected theirs among the Cayuses, a small tribe of the upper Walla Walla River, at Waiilatpu, "the place of the rye grass."

Though the Spaldings' personal problems suggested an uncertain future for their ministry, Marcus and Narcissa at least superficially seemed an ideal pair to carry out a successful mission to the heathens. "Perfectly fearless and independent," in the commentary of a coworker, Whitman set about his work with single-minded devotion. But with Whitman "it was always *yes* or *no*." He never had time to discuss matters. "What would such a man have in common with an Indian? How could they sympathize with each other?" The answer was, not much, in large ways as well as small. Narcissa insulted the impulsive, hot-tempered Tilokaikt, head chief of the very Cayuse band the missionaries hoped to proselytize, by brusquely rejecting a pair of coyote paws offered as a gift for her newborn daughter. On another occasion, observing that among the Indians the women did all the heavy labor, the missionaries put pressure on a chief to change his bad ways. Their efforts were rewarded, and before long the chief, according to a triumphant diary notation, "did his part of the labor." But in Indian culture labor was the role of women. By taking that role, the chief had been publicly humiliated — bad business when dealing with an important warrior on his own home ground.

About this time other missionaries, most notably Jesuits, were arriving in various corners of Oregon country. The greatest of the Jesuits was the Belgian Father Pierre Jean De Smet, who in more than three decades touched most of the tribes of the plains and mountains and is said to have traveled 180,000 miles. The Jesuits were more tolerant of Indian ways than the Protestants. Nevertheless, their basic purpose was to make Christians of the Indians, which meant fundamentally changing the institutions, customs, and beliefs the fur men had left intact. Indian ways proved durable but not totally resistant.

What the missionaries mainly accomplished — most notably the Spaldings among the Nez Perces — was to create "Christian" and "heathen" factions. These divisions later took on the additional connotations of "treaty" and "nontreaty" and "progressive" and "nonprogressive." And they contributed importantly to the origins and outcomes of nearly every war between Indians and whites. Thus the well-intended tampering with another people's culture turned out to be a deadly process — as Marcus and Narcissa Whitman ultimately would discover.

For a decade after their arrival, however, the Whitmans and Spaldings, the Jesuits, and other zealots went about their work in relative peace, inflicting on the Indians minor irritations and inconveniences that no doubt accumulated and rankled but brought no notable explosions. Meanwhile, however, far off, forces were building that would loose waves of whites on the West and bring the two cultures into massive confrontation.

James K. Polk was elected to the White House in 1844 on a platform of territorial expansion, in which he promised to fulfill the nation's "manifest destiny" to overspread the continent. He began, in 1845, with the annexation of Texas. Then a year later, rattling sabers and twisting the British lion's tail, Polk forced a settlement of a long-festering boundary dispute in the Northwest and raised the American flag over the Oregon country. Finally, he fought a war with Mexico that ended with United States sovereignty not only over Texas but also the vast Mexican provinces of New Mexico and California. By 1848 Polk's crusade had added one million square miles to the national domain, planted the western boundary on the shores of the Pacific — and given the United States the ultimate responsibility for dealing with every single Indian west of the Mississippi.

In that same year of 1848, scarcely two weeks before diplomats in Mexico concluded the treaty ending the Mexican War, a sawmill hand named James Marshall caught a glint of yellow in a newly built millrace among the western foothills of California's Sierra Nevada. Shouted in the streets of San Franciso, the cry of "Gold! Gold from the American River!" reverberated across the continent and electrified a people already looking west. First by ship, and then overland, forty-niners by the thousands raced to California. They were the vanguard of eight million Americans who in the next four decades would seek adventure and opportunity in the West — and in the process destroy the Indian way of life.

The first to go were California's Diggers — Indians so called because they subsisted largely on roots and berries — who had the misfortune to be standing squarely in the way when the forty-niners burst into their fragile

little societies in the gold country of Sierra Nevada. The effect was sudden and catastrophic. Those who did not scatter were simply annihilated. "That a war of extermination will continue to be waged until the Indian race becomes extinct, must be expected," declared the state's governor in 1851. And indeed it was. Ten per cent of the Diggers met death violently. The rest fell to disease, malnutrition, and starvation. From almost one hundred thousand comfortable tribesmen in 1846, California's Indian population dropped to thirty thousand impoverished and thoroughly subjugated souls.

Oregon Indians proved far more formidable adversaries than those in California. The first hostilities burst from resentments built up among the Indians by the Whitmans and Spaldings. By 1847 the Cayuses near Waiilatpu nourished a deep hatred of the dogmatic doctor and his unbending wife. Neither had ever established rapport with their intended neophytes, and both had continued to offend them with intolerant or patronizing treatment. Also, competition from Catholic missionaries confused the Cayuses and helped turn them against the Presbyterians. Most serious, the Indians believed the Whitmans responsible for the procession of covered wagons that early in the 1840's began to pass their mission bearing settlers. The Cayuses feared that these Bostons would steal the Indians' land as they had in the East. In 1847 a passing immigrant train set off an epidemic of measles that killed perhaps half the Cayuse tribe. Whitman tried to treat the stricken, but the Indians, watching him fuss over their sick friends and families, came to suspect him of poisoning them as part of a plot to seize their land. That suspicion sealed the fate of the missionaries.

On November 29, 1847, Chief Tilokaikt and a companion named Tomahas appeared at the Waiilatpu mission to ask for medicine. As Whitman turned to get it, Tomahas felled him with a tomahawk, then beat him repeatedly. Other Indians swarmed over the mission complex, which contained seventy-two people, mostly transients. A bullet wounded Narcissa in the arm; later the Indians carried her from the house and shot her full of bullets. Tilokaikt, Tomahas, and other Cayuses killed twelve more men and took five men, eight women, and thirty-four children as captives.

Two days later Catholic missionary Father John Baptiste Brouillet rode into the mission grounds. The Indians supposed him sympathetic to their

Marcus Whitman and his more zealous associate, Henry Spalding (above), hoped that their Presbyterian missions (top, a contemporary drawing of Whitman's at Waiilatpu by Paul Kane) would not only convert Indians but also encourage white immigration. "It is now decided that Oregon will be occupied by American citizens," Whitman wrote in 1843. "Those who go only open the way for more another year." Neither man accurately judged the impact on the natives of more settlers or of Protestant rivalry with Catholic missionaries. Spalding did note, in 1847, that "perhaps one fourth of this tribe [the Nez Perce] have turned Papists, and are very bitter against the Protestant religion."

deed, and for sheer self-preservation he had to steel himself against the entreaties of the prisoners and the horror of the massacre scene. "What a sight did I then behold!" he wrote. "Ten bodies lying here and there, covered with blood, and bearing the marks of the most atrocious cruelty—some pierced with balls, others more or less gashed by the hatchet. Dr. Whitman had received three gashes on the face. Three others had their skulls crushed so that their brains were oozing out." Brouillet was able to disengage from the Cayuses long enough to warn the Spaldings, also marked for massacre, and they fled their Lapwai mission.

Oregonians reacted with shock and outrage. The provisional legislature voted a force of 550 citizen soldiers to march against the Cayuses, and a three-man peace commission to try to calm neighboring tribes. To head the commission the governor appointed Joel Palmer, a man of ability, integrity, and tolerance. But heading the militia as colonel was Cornelius Gilliam, a bigoted fundamentalist clergyman who had fought Indians back east and regarded extermination as the proper policy for Oregon.

At the same time the British Hudson's Bay Company, still influential and anxious to prevent a general uprising that would destroy profits, dispatched veteran fur man Peter Skene Ogden to negotiate the release of the hostages. Fearful that the Bostons and the British might unite against the tribes, the Indians accepted Ogden's proposed ransom: 62 blankets, 63 cotton shirts, 12 guns, 600 rounds of ammunition, 37 pounds of tobacco, and 12 flints. By January, 1848, therefore, Gilliam was free to advance his army up the Columbia without concern about endangering the captives.

Unfortunately, neither was he concerned about distinguishing between guilty and innocent Indians. By no means all the Cayuse tribe condoned the course of Chief Tilokaikt and his lieutenants. In fact, bubbling fac-

The fanciful engraving at left depicts the brutal murder of Marcus Whitman. In fact, two Cayuses killed him, and although Narcissa was slain too, she did not see her husband die. The chief culprits, Tomahas and Tilokaikt, were drawn by Paul Kane, who said Tomahas's face was "the most savage I have ever beheld."

Tomahas

Tilokaikt

tionalism, a recurrent theme in Indian history, now raised the prospect of a peaceful resolution of the issue. But instead of pausing to negotiate, Gilliam blundered ahead in a belligerent advance that united the squabbling villagers in an alliance to fend off invasion of their homeland.

Early in February Gilliam attacked and nearly destroyed a camp of innocent Indians, killing twenty or thirty of them. The survivors turned on Gilliam's troops, killing three and wounding two others. Palmer and the other peace commissioners, aware that Gilliam's intemperate actions threatened their mission, vainly sought a softening of the colonel's stance. Gilliam even refused to provide a small armed escort for the peace emissaries and instead insisted upon accompanying them with his full force, causing the Indians to doubt the sincerity of the peace mission. After an inconclusive talk with members of the powerful Nez Perce tribe, one of the peace commissioners wrote that "Col Gilliam left the council in a huff and declared he has come to fight and fight he will." By March even the persistent Palmer had become so disgusted with Gilliam's blustering interference that he resigned, leaving the field entirely to Gilliam.

Within the next week 250 Palouse warriors attacked Gilliam's men as they rounded up a few head of cattle they thought belonged to the Cayuses. In an all-day running battle, the troops retreated to Waiilatpu. Ten white men had been wounded, and, more important, another Columbia Basin tribe had been turned against the whites. Four days later, however, fate removed Gilliam from the field. While pulling a rope to tether his horse, he caught the rope on the trigger of his gun and was killed instantly.

Under Gilliam's second-in-command the militia continued to march about the Cayuse country, but their quarry had largely faded into the Nez Perce territory. Besides exhausting themselves, the Oregon soldiers succeeded mainly in exasperating the Wallawallas, Umatillas, Palouses, and Nez Perces. Finally it occurred to the whites that they were on the verge of uniting all the Columbia Basin tribes in war, and in June, 1848, showing rare common sense, the troops went home.

For reasons still unclear the ringleaders in the Whitman massacre, Tilokaikt, Tomahas, and three others, gave themselves up early in 1850. If they supposed the Bostons would be forgiving, or even grant an unbiased hearing, they miscalculated badly. Tried for murder and convicted, they went to the scaffold on June 3, 1850. The Reverend Henry Spalding offered them Presbyterian comforts, but they rebuffed him in favor of Catholic rites.

The legacy of the Cayuse skirmishes proved more significant in the Northwest than the war itself. Gilliam's uncompromising course exposed to all the northwestern tribes a side of the white man they had not observed in the firm but reasonable agents of the Hudson's Bay Company. Worse yet, frustrated at repeated failures to run down Whitman's murderers, Oregon officials declared Cayuse lands forfeit, thus seeming to confirm the fear of the perpetrators of the massacre that all those white-topped wagons bore people bent upon seizing their lands. If further notice were needed, the Oregon Donation Land Law enacted by Congress in 1850 opened all land to homesteading without regard to Indian title. In future troubles the distrust of Bostons planted in Indian minds by the Cayuse affair figured importantly, and in those crises, too, citizens responded more often in the spirit of Cornelius Gilliam than of Joel Palmer.

Visions of a Proud People

No other native American culture quite matched that of the western
Indian warrior for a combination of dignity and spirit. Late
in the nineteenth century photographer Edward Curtis set out to
record that unique lifestyle before it disappeared forever.
The project took Curtis—and a staff that at times numbered
sixty—more than thirty years to complete. In some forty
thousand photographs—this one is a war party of Atsinas—
Curtis captured the pride and strength of those nomadic peoples.

Little Plume, a Piegan Blackfoot, and his son Yellow Kidney rest inside their tepee.

Two Crows, also called Absarokes or "bird people," stand outside a medicine tepee.

Unlike most Plains Indians, Absarokes raided and hunted through-out the winter—and dressed accordingly. The man on the left is wearing a hooded overcoat of a heavy blanket material, used by the Absarokes after their first contacts with white traders.

A Nez Perce warrior

Two Leggings, an Absaroke

Raven Blanket, a Nez Perce

A young Piegan

Old Eagle, an Oto Sioux

In full war bonnet, Red Hawk, a Sioux who fought with Crazy Horse against Custer at
the Battle of the Little Bighorn, pauses to water his horse in the Dakota Badlands

Indian traders camp peaceably at Fort Laramie in this 1837 painting by A. J. Miller.

7: The Whites Move In

No one else in 1851 knew the West or its Indians better than Tom Fitzpatrick. Perhaps the greatest of the mountain men, companion of Jed Smith, Kit Carson, and Jim Bridger, he had trapped most of the beaver streams of the plains and Rockies, piloted the first Oregon-bound immigrants as far as the Snake River, and served as guide for John C. Frémont and other military explorers. A master of wilderness skills, Fitzpatrick was also a literate man, possessed of an uncommon intellect and a depth of character not often associated with the boisterous trapping fraternity. He looked upon Indians sympathetically but not sentimentally and accorded them the wary respect of a man who had survived almost three decades in the Indian country. In return they viewed him as a fair and honorable man and a worthy adversary. They had two names for him: "Broken Hand," because a bursting rifle had carried away three fingers; and "White Hair," because of premature graying induced by a harrowing experience eluding a pursuing band of Gros Ventres.

In October, 1846, returning from guiding General Stephen Watts Kearny's army of conquest to New Mexico, Fitzpatrick learned that he had been appointed United States Indian Agent for the Upper Platte and Arkansas Agency. In a rare act of statesmanship the government had selected a thoroughly qualified man for the post of Indian agent. By 1851 Fitzpatrick had served conscientiously and wisely for five years as the first emissary of the United States to the tribes of the High Plains. Fourteen years later the Arapaho chief Little Raven would remember him as "the one fair agent" the government had sent to his people.

In September, 1851, at the government's invitation, ten thousand tribesmen of Fitzpatrick's agency raised their tepees in a grassy valley near Fort Laramie. Fitzpatrick's chief, Superintendent David D. Mitchell, hoped to negotiate a treaty that would restrain the Indians from molesting immigrants on the Oregon and Santa Fe trails. Actually, his main concern was the intertribal warfare that imperiled white travelers simply by keeping the plains country in constant turmoil. Father De Smet, also on hand, worried about this problem too; he foresaw the diminishing buffalo herds causing intensified fighting, until the Indians "become themselves extinct over the last buffalo steak." Mitchell's solution was to persuade each tribe to agree to a particular defined territory and then remain within it.

Sioux, Cheyennes, Arapahos, Crows, Gros Ventres, Assiniboins, Arikaras, and Shoshones had come for the big council. The Pawnees, bitter enemies of the Sioux, refused. So did the Kiowas and Comanches, who told Broken Hand that they had "too many horses and mules to risk . . . among such notorious horse thieves as the Sioux and Crows." The Shoshones, accompanied by their old friend Jim Bridger, approached warily with muskets primed even though assured that the 270 soldiers standing by would keep their enemies in check.

The apprehension was justified, for a Sioux warrior with an old score to settle rushed out to gun down a Shoshone chief. An interpreter intervened and narrowly averted a collision. As "Old Gabe" Bridger explained to a dragoon, the interpreter "saved that [Sioux] fellow from hell; my chief would 'er killed him quick, and then the fool Sioux would 'er got their backs up, and there wouldn't have been room to camp 'round here for dead Sioux. You dragoons acted nice, but you wouldn't have had no show if the fight had commenced — no making peace then."

The incident dramatized the obstacles to making peace among the tribes. Even so, after many tense sessions, an impressive array of chiefs signed the treaty. They promised to dwell forever in peace with the white man and with one another, agreed that the white man could build roads and forts in their land (he already had), and even accepted boundaries around their respective territories. Mitchell and Fitzpatrick distributed great piles of presents, and more were promised in the treaty. More portentous of the future than the stilted language of the treaty, however, was the remark of an Oglala chief, Black Hawk, that revealed in stark simplicity the true nature of relationships among tribes and between tribes and whites. "You have split my land and I don't like it," he said. "These lands once belonged to the Kiowas and the Crows, but we whipped these nations out of them, and in this we did what the white men do when they want the lands of the Indians."

More realistic than Mitchell, Tom Fitzpatrick did not expect great things of the Fort Laramie treaty. Even so, he loyally assisted Mitchell in the treaty negotiations, and in 1853 he concluded a similar one at Fort Atkinson, on the Arkansas River, with the southern tribes that had refused to come to Fort Laramie.

The Fitzpatrick treaties expressed a new policy rising from the wreckage of the Permanent Indian Frontier, that simplistic abstraction demolished by the territorial acquisitions of the Mexican War and the rush west set off by the California gold discovery. The objective was no longer to separate whites and Indians by one artificial barrier. Now the government intended not only to clear the Indians away from white travel routes and keep them off white settlements, but to restrict them to specified areas. The Fort Laramie and Fort Atkinson treaties called these areas "territories." Already, in treaties with lesser tribes, the label was "reservation." And already policy makers looked to the time when the reservation would serve not only to control the Indians but to "civilize" them as well.

The Fitzpatrick treaties illustrated some of the pitfalls of the treaty system. The chiefs who signed could not, in the loose political democracy of the Plains Indians, speak for or bind all their people to the treaty promises. To compound the problem the Fort Laramie treaty engaged each signatory Indian "nation" to appoint a head chief with whom the government might thenceforth deal. Thus, in the white view, several sovereignties represented by duly authorized emissaries were working out their relationships in the way sovereignties had done for centuries.

Yet the Sioux and Comanches were not truly sovereign and would become less so in time. Chief Justice John Marshall had long since defined tribal status as that of "domestic dependent nations." This ingenious concept mainly satisfied the white man's sense of legal propriety by "extinguishing Indian title" to tribal lands that had been, or were about to be, seized by more direct means. For even though Mitchell and Fitzpatrick represented the United States in ways that Brave Bear and Little Mountain did not represent the Sioux and the Kiowas, white leaders were just as powerless to compel their own countrymen to respect the treaties.

In the final analysis the chiefs signed not so much because they under-

Comanche chiefs confer with white settlers at an 1847 treaty council in Texas, painted by the daughter of one of the whites present. The spokesman for the whites, in the center of the circle, reportedly won the confidence of the Comanches by openly emptying his rifle of ammunition when he rode into camp. In exchange for several thousand dollars worth of presents, the Indians gave the settlers what they wanted—the right of passage through Comanche lands.

stood the contents—cultural and language barriers intruded when deliberate misrepresentation did not—but because a great stock of presents stood nearby awaiting distribution. It is doubtful whether either party seriously intended to abide by the compact. Even the purest intentions tended to give way in an atmosphere of suspicion, distrust, and tension.

Tom Fitzpatrick's skepticism about treaty councils sprang from a conviction that any "big talks" were premature until the Indians had been whipped and made to feel the power of the government. However unacknowledged as an instrument of Indian policy, war or the threat of war buttressed every treaty. "It must certainly appear evident that something must be done to keep those Indians quiet," Fitzpatrick warned, "and nothing short of an efficient military force stationed in their country will do this."

The United States did not possess such a force. Even though the national boundaries had leaped to the Pacific, embracing an additional million square miles of territory and two hundred thousand Indians, President Polk had informed a receptive Congress in 1848 that "the old army, as it existed before the war with Mexico," would be adequate for all purposes. This force numbered slightly more than ten thousand officers and enlisted men, enlarged to eighteen thousand by 1860. The regular army contained some able and dedicated soldiers, but in sum they barely achieved a rating of mediocre. The enlisted soldiers were not the well-motivated youngsters of the Mexican War but too often criminals, toughs, drunkards, and fugitives swept up from the streets of the big eastern cities by industrious recruiting officers.

"The greater part of the army," a young infantryman wrote to his parents, "consists of men who either do not care to work, or who, being addicted to drink, cannot find employment." And for the officers, whether West Pointers or not, slow promotion, isolation, boredom, and whiskey dulled ambition. Even for the ambitious, professional horizons remained oppressively constricted. As Confederate General Richard S. Ewell re-

called his frontier years, an officer "learned all there was to know about commanding forty dragoons, and forgot everything else."

Awesome new challenges confronted this weak little army as it moved from the eastern woodlands into the trans-Mississippi West. Plains, mountains, and deserts presented extremes of topography, climate, and distance unknown in the East. There were few navigable rivers on which to move heavy consignments of men and materials. The scarcity of water, fuel, and natural foods made living off the land precarious for the soldier. Peopling this unfamiliar land were unfamiliar Indians, nomadic or seminomadic in contrast to their eastern kinsmen and boasting fighting skills that in combination with the hostile environment made them the most formidable of adversaries.

Even though the regular army found its principal sanction in the frontier, its leaders, from the dropsical general in chief Winfield Scott—"Old Fuss and Feathers"—on down, steadfastly refused to face up to the realities of the frontier mission They seemed to have learned nothing from earlier experiences with eastern Indians. They regarded Indian hostilities as too transitory to justify special measures, and they persisted in using tactics and organization adapted from European textbooks that contained no useful hint on how to employ troops against Indians. Again, Broken Hand Fitzpatrick saw the situation and sounded repeated warnings against the weak little outposts that were multiplying across the West: "Instead of serving to intimidate the red man, they rather create a belief in the feebleness of the white man. In fact, it must be at once apparent that a skeleton company of infantry or dragoons can add but little to the security of five hundred miles square of territory; nor can the great highways to Utah and New Mexico be properly protected by a wandering squadron that parades them once a year." Half measures would never work. "The policy must be either an army or an annuity. Either an inducement must be offered to them greater than the gains of plunder, or a force must be at hand able to restrain and check their depredations. Any compromise between the two systems will be only productive of mischief, and liable to all the miseries of failure."

Tom Fitzpatrick had seen it all happen before, and not very long before. As guide for the Army of the West, he almost certainly had stood among the people who gathered in the plaza of Las Vegas, New Mexico, on August 15, 1846, to hear the conquering general tell them that their allegiance now belonged to the United States. Standing on a flat-roofed building facing the dusty plaza, General Stephen Watts Kearny uttered predictable assurances. Among them were words to stir joy in the hearts of his long-suffering listeners: "From the Mexican Government you have never received protection. The Apaches and Navahos come down from the mountains and carry off your sheep, and even your women, whenever they please. My government will correct all this. It will keep off the Indians."

American military officials tried manfully to carry out Kearny's promise. They built a chain of forts along the Rio Grande and planted others at key locations both east and west—to guard the New Mexico end of the Santa Fe Trail, to menace Navahos from the heart of their homeland, and to watch over the immigrant road from San Antonio to El Paso and on to California. Civil authorities tried too. Successive territorial governors, holding the concurrent post of Superintendent of Indian Affairs, negotiated

treaties with the Navahos and Apaches and sent agents among them to distribute rations and encourage farming.

But the combined military and civil efforts failed to make good the promise of General Kearny. The old pattern of raid and counterraid, with slavery a principal motivation, proved too firmly fixed to break. There were interludes of comparative peace, when able agents such as Henry Dodge or Michael Steck calmed passions or when fighting had been subdued by vigorous campaigns of unusually aggressive army officers such as Philip St. George Cooke or "Baldy" Ewell. But there were years of bloody fighting too, when Navaho and Apache raiding parties swooped down on Rio Grande settlements or waylaid travelers on the long desolate roads, and when military expeditions drove deep into the Indian country to hound tribesmen and occasionally meet them in armed encounter.

Among the Apaches of this period two stood forth as commanding figures. One was Mangas Coloradas (Red Sleeves), chief of the Warm Springs tribe. A trapper who subsequently observed this chief described him as "a large athletic man considerably over six feet in height, with a large broad head covered with a tremendously heavy growth of long hair that reached to his waist. His shoulders were broad and his chest full, and muscular. He stood erect and his step was proud and altogether he presented quite a model of physical manhood." About fifty years old at mid-century, Mangas had succeeded to the leadership of his band in 1838, and by astute diplomacy, including the marriage of three daughters to other chiefs, he had come to exercise great influence over all Apaches.

Indian agent William Bent, shown above with Arapaho chief Little Raven and his three children, was one of the few honorable men to hold the post. Bent had lived among the Cheyennes and Arapahos, spoke their language, and married a Cheyenne woman. In spite of his efforts to mediate fairly between Indians and whites, treaties continued to relegate Indians to smaller and poorer plots of land in exchange for supplies that came too late or not at all. After a few years in the frustrating job, Bent resigned.

The other chief was Cochise of the Chiricahuas, neighbors and allies of Mangas Coloradas on the west. Cochise too was bigger than the typical Apache, as recalled by the attendant of the Apache Pass stagecoach station: "Cochise was as fine a looking Indian as one ever saw. He was about six feet tall and as straight as an arrow, built, from the ground up, as perfect as any man could be. . . . I don't suppose that Cochise ever met his equal with a lance. I always recall the handsome picture he made as he stood out in front of the station with folded arms until after the coach left." About twenty-five years younger than Mangas, Cochise had risen to eminence through his leadership abilities and war skills.

Neither Mangas Coloradas nor Cochise displayed hostility toward Americans during the 1850's. On occasion their warriors doubtless ran off stock belonging to whites and may even have killed a settler now and then. But in general their aggressions fell on Mexico. Against all Mexicans these chiefs and their followers nursed the most rancorous and unremitting hatred, and their raids south of the border devastated ranches and hamlets and subjected Sonora and Chihuahua to constant terror. It remained for a young army officer with more bravery than good sense to bring about similar desolation north of the border.

Late in January, 1861, the commanding officer at Fort Buchanan, a lonely outpost forty miles south of Tucson, dispatched Second Lieutenant George N. Bascom and fifty-four mule-mounted infantrymen to Apache Pass, the tortuous defile that carried the California road over the Chiricahua Mountains. The pass was the heart of Cochise's homeland and also a key stop on the Butterfield Overland Mail line. Although the White Mountain Apaches to the north were of uncertain disposition, Cochise and his Chiricahuas were still getting on well with the Butterfield employees. Never in three years of operation had the company's lumbering Concord coaches, carrying passengers between St. Louis and San Francisco in twenty-five days of jolting, sleepless agony, been threatened by Chiricahua warriors. Bascom's orders were to hunt up Cochise and demand restoration of some stock and a young boy seized in an Apache raid on the ranch of John Ward near Fort Buchanan. The boy was the son of Ward's Mexican wife, sired by an Apache during a captivity from which she had escaped. With such certainty had Ward branded Cochise the culprit that Bascom's orders were to use force if necessary to compel restitution.

On February 4 Bascom and Cochise faced each other in the lieutenant's tent, pitched about three fourths of a mile from the stage station. Cochise vehemently denied Ward's charge, correctly blaming the White Mountains instead and offering to help obtain the return of the boy and the stock. Bascom persisted and at length informed the chief that he and his small party would be held hostage until he complied. When the interpreter translated this declaration, Cochise suddenly drew his knife, slashed the tent wall, and sprang through. Amid a fusillade of shots he bounded up the canyon slope to safety. His companions—a brother, two nephews, and a woman with two children—were quickly taken prisoner.

Cochise lost no time acquiring his own hostages. In fact, he seems already to have held three white men That night he seized two more from a small wagon train at the summit of Apache Pass, then bound the eight Mexican teamsters to wagon wheels and set fire to the wagons. The next day, joined by some White Mountain warriors, Cochise appeared near the

In this George Simons painting, Indians descend on a lone stagecoach—and find an army escort riding on the roof. Since overland routes advertised by Butterfield, Wells Fargo, Overland Express (below) and other companies ran through hostile Indian territory, attacks on coaches and relay stations were frequent. During the summer of 1864 Indians burned all but one of the Overland Express stations along a 500-mile stretch.

mail station under a white flag. Bascom suspected treachery and hesitated, but three Butterfield employees, secure in their past harmony with Cochise, went out to talk. The Apaches suddenly threw down their flag and seized one of them, James F. Wallace. Both sides opened fire as the other two men raced for safety. Neither reached the station without being hit, and one died from his wounds.

Now Cochise held ample bargaining power too, and on February 6, shouting from a hilltop, he offered his hostages in exchange for Bascom's. The lieutenant agreed—but only if Ward's boy and the stock were included. That night Cochise repeated his offer in a note written by Wallace and affixed to a stake driven in the ground within sight of the station.

At this point Cochise, now apparently further reinforced by Mangas Coloradas and his followers, probably despaired of further attempts to reason with the stubborn young soldier chief. Piling stacks of dry grass in the canyon north of the stage station, he prepared to ambush the westbound stage by raising a curtain of flame and smoke that would halt the coach while his men finished it off, but its arrival ahead of schedule thwarted the plan. The eastbound coach fared less happily. Near the top of the pass warriors opened fire, dropping the lead mule and wounding the driver. The passengers cut out the dead mule and, firing back, urged on the remaining mules. The coach lurched down the winding trail toward a deep gulch. The Apaches had wrecked the bridge, leaving only stringers and abutments, but the coach was going too fast to stop. The mules leaped the chasm, the coach slid dizzyingly across on its axles, and the wheels took hold on the opposite side. A shaken group of passengers found haven at the station.

WALLA WALLA VALLEY DIPLOMACY

Isaac Stevens, the aggressive governor of Washington Territory, invited five thousand Indians living in the area to a great council in the Walla Walla valley in May, 1855. His purpose was to persuade the Indians to give up their lands and move to reservations—peacefully if they chose to go, forcefully if they did not.

The Nez Perces arrived at the meeting area on May 24, 1855. In a bellicose show of power, a thousand warriors thundered past Stevens "naked to the breech-clout, their faces covered with white, red, and yellow paint in fanciful designs, and decked with plumes and feathers and trinkets fluttering in the sunshine." Then they charged the whites at full gallop "firing their guns, brandishing their shields, beating their drums, and yelling their war-whoops," before filing off to their camp a half mile away.

If anything the Cayuses, Umatillas, and Wallawallas who arrived later were even more anxious to impress upon Stevens that they were proud and unafraid. Wallawalla Chief Peo-peo-mox-mox curtly informed Stevens that since his people had brought provisions with them, they would not be eating with whites in the grand hall Stevens had ordered built "so that, as in civilized lands, gastronomy might aid diplomacy."

Unperturbed, Stevens formally opened the council on May 29. As he spoke, interpreters translated his words to Indian criers, who in turn shouted to the assembled chiefs and their followers. At first Stevens's words seemed reassuring: "I went back to the Great Father last year to say that you had been good, you have been kind, he must do something for you."

After a lengthy preamble, Stevens got around to just what that "something" was. "We want you and ourselves to agree upon tracts of lands where you shall live," he said. In return for giving up ancestral lands, the government would provide the Indians with new homes, schools, horses, and cattle, and for chiefs, salaries of $500 a year.

When the chiefs seemed unsatisfied with these offers, the whites dropped all pretense and asserted that the chiefs would be wise to take the lands offered them before the settlers took everything.

The chiefs wavered, and Stevens thought he had carried the day. Then suddenly an elderly Nez Perce chief named Looking Glass and twenty braves in full war paint galloped into the council grounds. "My people, what have you done?" demanded Looking Glass. "While I was gone you have sold my country. Go home to your lodges. I will talk to you." The next day he demanded of Stevens a much larger piece of land than was included in the treaty. "It was my children that spoke yesterday," he informed Stevens. "And now I come."

But Looking Glass did not speak for the others, who reluctantly concluded that Stevens's offer was the best they were going to get from the white man.

"Thus ended in most satisfactory manner this great council," Stevens wrote in his diary. He had assured the Indians that they would be secure in their homelands until the treaty was ratified—perhaps for two or three years. Yet twelve days after the treaty signings a newspaper article with Stevens's signature declared the lands open for settlement. His premature announcement practically guaranteed the war that erupted a few months later.

Gustavus Sohon painted these Indians galloping into the Walla Walla peace council.

In the next two weeks Lieutenant Bascom and Cochise cast Apache-white relations for the next decade in the pattern of an eye for an eye. Warriors ran off Bascom's mules, but at the cost of five or ten hit by rifle balls. Bascom slipped out a courier, and two forces came to his aid. One, a medical team from Fort Buchanan, fell on a small White Mountain raiding party and brought in three more prisoners to add to Bascom's stock of hostages. The other was a command of two dragoon companies out of Fort Breckinridge. When the latter arrived, the troops scoured the mountains but found only abandoned camps: the Apaches had pulled out. The troops also found the burned wagon train, charred corpses bound to the wagon wheels. And they found the grisly remains of Cochise's six hostages, perforated by countless lance holes and so horribly cut up that Wallace could be identified only by the gold fillings in his teeth. Counting out the woman and two children, Bascom took his own six hostages to the scene and, with the hearty endorsement of the other officers, hanged them from the limbs of scrub oak trees. And there, beside the mail road, they hung for months afterward, grisly harbingers of a vicious warfare that would ravage the Southwest for years to come.

While the Indian wars of the Southwest smoldered, farmers and gold seekers continued to flow into the Pacific Northwest. As settlers pushed up the valleys between the Columbia River and Puget Sound and into the mountains at the head of the Willamette, the resistance of the natives stiffened and the attitude of the immigrants toward Indians coalesced into enmity. "The feeling of hostility displayed by each party," reported an Indian agent in 1854, "would be almost impossible to realize, except from personal observation." Each side, he said, had become so accustomed to shooting at the other on sight that neither seemed able, or even wanted, to break the habit.

Many of the regular soldiers sent to the Northwest to try to maintain peace between Indians and whites viewed the Indians more compassionately. They found themselves torn between a duty to protect threatened settlers and a duty to protect innocent Indians. Thus, to the dismay and fury of the local whites, the army pursued an ambiguous course, sometimes helping parties of citizens to run down offending Indians, but also sometimes standing between such parties and their intended victims. More and more the settlers responded by forming the kind of volunteer force that Colonel Gilliam had led against the Cayuses in 1848.

Embodying the conflicting viewpoints were Isaac I. Stevens and John E. Wool. Stevens was a brash young man of great ambition and enthusiasm. In 1853 he resigned an army commission to accept appointment as governor of Washington Territory, which had been carved out of Oregon north of the Columbia River. En route west Stevens headed one of the War Department's Pacific railway surveys, marking out a northern route for a transcontinental railroad. As governor he set himself the task of clearing all his territory of Indian land titles, restricting the natives to reservations, and promoting settlement. His methods featured the fast talk, bluster, and intimidation that so helped to discredit the treaty system.

John E. Wool was the opinionated and combative little general who headed the army's Pacific department, with headquarters in San Francisco. A stiff professional with forty-two years service and a bright Mexican War reputation, Wool openly sympathized with the Indians. He directed his

LIBRARY OF CONGRESS

Isaac I. Stevens was only thirty-five when he became governor of Washington Territory, a title that simultaneously made him Superintendent of Indian Affairs. Within two years of taking office, he had induced virtually every chief under his jurisdiction to sign away his lands.

Joseph Tuuwətak-kes
Chief of the Nezperré Indians

Lawyer
Hahhal-loistsot
Head Chief of the Nezperce Tribe

Friendly chiefs Old Joseph (top) and Lawyer supported treaty negotiations at an 1855 peace council at Walla Walla. Old Joseph examined the terms of the pact, concluded that he would lose little of his ancestral land under the agreement, and hoped signing would cause the whites to leave him alone. Lawyer seems to have been persuaded more by promises of a house, ten acres of cleared land, and $500 a year in salary.

field officers not to fight Indians unless forced to do so, and at all other times to persuade the tribes to become peaceful. Wool condemned the citizens for their exterminatory attitudes. Their readiness to fight their own battles in territorial volunteer units, he felt, sprang less from genuine impulses of self-defense than from a cynical intent to plunder the Indians of stock and other property while also billing the federal government for pay, equipment, and supplies. Wool considered Stevens a scoundrel and Oregon's Governor George Curry little better, and he did not shrink from feuding with them publicly and vitriolically.

In the autumn of 1855 the Northwest erupted into open hostilities on two fronts. In the mountainous Rogue River country of southern Oregon Captain Andrew Jackson Smith, the tough, fair-minded commander of Fort Lane, had long labored to keep the peace, not hesitating to interpose his dragoon company between frightened Indians and wrathful settlers. Early in October, fearful of the citizens' vengeful attitude, Smith moved Indian men to the security of the fort. Women and children were to follow shortly. Before they could, however, a volunteer unit stormed their camp and murdered twenty-three old men, women, and children. The next day a war party swept the valley killing twenty-seven settlers. Newspapers called for extermination of "these inhuman butchers and bloody fiends," and throughout the winter, while peaceful Indians gathered at Fort Lane, volunteer units combed the cold, damp mountains, ferreting out and smashing the hostile camps. "It has become a contest of extermination by both whites and Indians," declared General Wool.

Preoccupied with the Yakima War east of the Cascade Mountains, Wool could not send reinforcements to the Rogue River until the spring of 1856. When they arrived the major Rogue River chiefs, known by their white nicknames of Old John, George, and Limpy, promised to surrender to Captain Smith at Big Meadows. Instead, confused and angry about the identity of their real enemies, they gathered two hundred warriors and laid plans to attack Smith's force of fifty dragoons and thirty infantrymen.

The Battle of Big Meadows was replete with dramatic clichés that today's mythology associates with Indian fighting. Smith had been warned by two Indian women and had taken a strong hilltop position between two creeks flowing into the Rogue River. On the morning of May 27, 1856, the Indians attacked. Some fired from nearby hills while others crept up the slopes on two sides and tried to breach the defenses. A howitzer and the rifles of the infantry kept them at bay. The short-range musketoons of the dragoons proved useful only in parrying sudden thrusts at the lines. At night the soldiers dug in and threw up breastworks, but by the second day Smith's situation was grim: a third of the force dead or wounded, water supply exhausted, ammunition reserves perilously low.

That afternoon the warriors massed for a final assault. Old John shouted curses and threats, translated for Smith by the two Indian women, while his men brandished ropes to give notice of the fate awaiting any survivors. At this critical moment Smith glimpsed a welcome sight—Captain Christopher C. Augur's company of regulars coming on at double time. Rousing his men to their feet, Smith led them in a dashing counterattack down the hillside. Augur's infantry charged in from the rear. Caught between two fires, the Indians fled, dragging their dead and wounded with them.

Augur's timely arrival turned Big Meadows, so nearly an Indian triumph, into a reverse of such proportions that the hostile leaders saw the futility of further resistance. Within a month all the Indians had surrendered. Herded to the coast, they began a new life on a reservation.

The simultaneous war on a second front sprang from some of Stevens's treaties even as the governor pushed deep into the northern Rockies to conclude still more. The first treaties bound the tribes of the Columbia Basin to exchange their lands for reservations. This prospect, coupled with a gold rush across their domain to Colville, alarmed the wise and forceful Yakima chief Kamiakin, long the most powerful native leader of the Columbia Basin. Kamiakin forged an alliance of tribes aimed at containing the whites on the west side of the Cascades. In September, 1855, a group of young braves that included Qualchin, Kamiakin's nephew, murdered six whites; Kamiakin, while not condoning the killings, sent word that a like fate awaited all Bostons who crossed the mountains. When a military reconnaissance tested the ultimatum in October, five hundred warriors chased it back to Fort Dalles in disorder.

Like the Rogue River conflict, the Yakima War quickly became the province of volunteers. Advancing up the Columbia, the Oregon militia pushed the Wallawallas into hostility. The Oregonians seized the respected Chief Peo-Peo-Mox-Mox at a truce parley, shot and killed him, and sent his ears and scalp home for display. The militia also rescued Governor Stevens, returning from his treaty-making sojourn. Stevens excoriated Wool for keeping the regulars in their forts and demanded his removal for "utter and signal incapacity" and "criminal neglect of my safety." Wool in turn scored "the two war governors" for provoking a needless war solely in the interest "of plunder of the Indians and the treasury of the United States."

Not until the spring of 1856, much to Stevens's annoyance, did General Wool mount a regular army offensive. Colonel George Wright, a veteran of thirty-four years in the army, commanded the five-hundred-man infantry column. After some initial skirmishing at the Cascades of the Columbia, the troops passed almost two months trying to bridge the swollen Naches River. When they finally got across in mid-June, they found no one to fight. Kamiakin and other war leaders had fled eastward, to other tribes beyond the Columbia. Wherever Wright marched, he found Indians placidly harvesting the spring salmon crop.

Although Stevens's volunteers routed a group of Wallawallas in July, killing forty, the Yakima War ended inconclusively. The Indians continued to roam their homeland, unconquered and unconfined by reservations. Stevens complained that the Indians "scorn our people and our flag and denominate us as a nation of old women." The people of Oregon and Washington were dissatisfied with the vague nature of the "peace," scandalized at the army's apparent sympathy with the Indians, and outraged over Wool's attacks on Stevens and the militia. Largely because of this negative public opinion, well coordinated by the two governors, Wool was relieved of duty in May, 1857, and replaced by Newman S. Clarke.

The only visible consequences of the Yakima War were the building of two forts: Simcoe and Walla Walla. They would provide bases from which to prosecute the next war—which would not end so inconclusively. To Kamiakin and other chiefs, the Yakima War left a legacy of rancor that would contribute to future trouble.

Still bristling with war fervor, Kamiakin sounded the alarm among the

Kamayakhen
Head Chief of the Yakimas

Peopeo mox-mox.
Head Chief of the Walla-Walla Indians

Militant chiefs Peo-peo-mox-mox of the Wallawallas and Kamiakin of the Yakimas were among the last to yield to pressure to sign the treaty. When they saw whites moving into their lands— apparently with Governor Stevens's approval— long before the treaty was to take effect, they led their tribes on the warpath. All the chiefs on these pages were sketched at Walla Walla by army private Gustavus Sohon.

Old soldiers John Smith (left) and Thomas Buell fought under Colonel Edward J. Steptoe when his regiment narrowly escaped annihilation on May 17, 1858. Here, the two veterans revisit the battle site some fifty years later.

tribes east of the Columbia River: there must be a general uprising or else the white people would seize their land and enslave their women. Violence between Indians and gold seekers headed for Colville, together with continuing apprehension about the Stevens treaties, gave force to his words. By 1858 almost any provocation could have brought about the alliance he urged. In May of that year the Indians discovered that a column of white soldiers had crossed the Snake River and was advancing boldly into the heart of their country.

The military command, out of Fort Walla Walla, consisted of three companies of dragoons, a detachment of infantry, and two howitzers, 164 men in all. The commander, Lieutenant Colonel Edward J. Steptoe, intended to march to Colville to reassure the miners, showing the flag en route to the increasingly aggressive Palouses, Spokanes, and Coeur d'Alênes. As he proceeded, hundreds of warriors, mounted and painted for a fight, swarmed on his flanks. And one evening their chiefs, presenting themselves at Steptoe's bivouac, bluntly ordered him out of their country.

Badly outnumbered, Steptoe prudently submitted to the demand. On May 17 he turned back. But the warriors, inflamed by the tensions of the confrontation, attacked anyway. All day they stabbed at the retreating column. The dragoons fanned out to screen the flanks and rear, and close combat flared on all sides. Mortal wounds felled two officers. The short musketoons of the horse soldiers barely held back the Indian forays.

Finally, at noon, Steptoe halted on a hilltop in order to use his artillery. The howitzers and the rifles of the infantry kept the assailants at a distance, but they surrounded the hill. That night, with ammunition down to three rounds per man, the officers discussed their predicament. Annihilation seemed inescapable. Steptoe argued for a fight to the last man on the hill. His officers urged an escape plan, and at length they prevailed. Burying the dead and leaving the howitzers and other equipment behind, the troops shouldered the wounded and groped their way quietly down the dark slopes, successfully circled the Indian camps without rousing the warriors, and by daybreak were safely on the way to Fort Walla Walla.

Steptoe's dazzling escape scarcely offset the humiliation. Army leaders reacted with outrage. "You will attack all hostile Indians with vigor," General Clarke instructed Colonel Wright. "Make their punishment severe, and persevere until the submission of all is complete." Especially to be sought were Kamiakin, his brother-in-law Owhi, and Owhi's militant son Qualchin, who had helped precipitate the Yakima War three years earlier.

Colonel Wright's campaign fulfilled the most optimistic hopes. Some officers had predicted the usual futile and exhausting march in search of Indians who would not stand and fight. But the rout of Steptoe had elated the foe and left them spoiling for another fight. Late in August some six hundred gathered on the Great Spokane Plain, southwest of present-day Spokane, Washington, to contest Wright's advance. It was a foolish move, for thereby they fought on his terms. New long-range infantry rifles, backed by artillery, easily outgunned the short trade muskets and bows and arrows of the Indians. In the Battles of Spokane Plain and Four Lakes, September 1 and 5, 1858, he showed the tribesmen the dangers of challenging the white man in open battle where superior firepower, discipline, and organization could prevail.

Chastened, the Indians returned to their homes. But Colonel Wright was not ready to let them shed the label of "hostile" so easily. Grimly he marched from tribe to tribe exacting submission and seizing Indians accused of depredations or of complicity in the attack on Steptoe. Fifteen he summarily hanged, and others he put in irons. Kamiakin, severely injured in the Battle of Spokane Plain when a bursting artillery shell dropped a tree limb on him, sought safety in the British possessions to the north. When Owhi came to make peace with Wright, he was seized and forced upon penalty of death to summon Qualchin. When Qualchin appeared he was hanged almost immediately. Owhi, grieving over his son's death, was shot and killed while trying to escape.

Wright's harsh measures, however dubious their humanity or even their legality, decisively and permanently smothered the spirit of resistance among the Indians of the Columbia Basin. In 1859 Congress at last approved all the Stevens treaties. Even before Congress acted, two thousand settlers had taken up claims in the Walla Walla valley, the vanguard of an immigration that would overspread the entire basin. Resignedly the dispossessed Indians accepted the fate spelled out in the Stevens treaties and went to the reservations assigned them. Ultimately Kamiakin returned to live out his life quietly on the reservation, a defeated and embittered man, a personification of the tragedy that had overtaken his people.

Broken Hand Fitzpatrick did not live to see his warnings about the need for a strong military force to back up "big talks" confirmed. Having survived thirty years of wilderness hazards, he died of pneumonia during a visit to Washington, D.C., in February, 1854. Six months later the first of the plains wars broke out—almost within sight of the grounds where he and Mitchell had negotiated the Treaty of 1851, whose fine words, it now turned out, could not resolve so prosaic a matter as the killing of an ox.

On August 18, 1854, a Sioux warrior named High Forehead shot an arrow into the ox as it ambled behind a wagon train passing the tepees of Chief Brave Bear's people in the North Platte valley near Fort Laramie. The owner, a Mormon immigrant, complained of the deed at the fort, and the next day a hotheaded young lieutenant, John L. Grattan, appeared at the Indian camp with thirty infantrymen and two small cannon. When High Forehead refused to give up, Grattan opened fire on the village. Brave Bear—head chief of the Brûlé Sioux by authority of the treaty—fell with mortal wounds. Infuriated, his warriors burst on Grattan's little company and, aided by other Sioux from nearby, killed all but one soldier, who reached Fort Laramie only to die of his wounds.

Secretary of War Jefferson Davis branded the Grattan massacre "the result of a deliberately formed plan" of the Sioux to help themselves to trade and annuity goods stored nearby, and he called upon General William S. Harney to organize a retaliatory expedition. More than six feet tall, white-bearded, with an erect, powerful physique, Harney was a profane, terrible-tempered, no-nonsense field soldier. The Sioux would call him the Butcher, a term that accurately described his notion of how to deal with Indians. "By God, I'm for battle—no peace," he declared as he led his six hundred men out of Fort Kearny, Nebraska, on August 24, 1855.

As Harney's army marched up the Oregon Trail Chief Little Thunder, successor to Brave Bear, inexplicably sat in his tepee and waited. He knew the general was intent on revenge for the Grattan massacre, and his band of 250 people had been the very perpetrators of it. Little Thunder's village lay along Blue Water Creek within view of the immigrant road at Ash Hollow, and he made no effort to move it until Harney's troops had taken positions on two sides. By then it was too late. On September 3, 1855, infantry advanced up the valley from the south and dragoons swept down from the north. The Indians scattered in helpless rout as the troops cut them down with rifles and sabers. Eighty-five died, and seventy women and children fell captive to the soldiers.

After Blue Water Harney led his command in a defiant trek through the heart of Sioux territory. Around the Black Hills and down the White River he marched, daring other Sioux to fight. None did. Wintering on the Missouri River at the old fur post of Fort Pierre, he summoned chiefs of all the Teton Sioux tribes to a great council in March, 1856, and there dictated a peace. Fitzpatrick would have approved, for Harney had given them a new respect for the government. He had struck them a heavy blow that warned of more to come. At Fort Laramie he had compelled the surrender of warriors who had waylaid a mail coach; at Fort Kearny he held as hostages the prisoners taken at Blue Water; he had suspended trade; and now he made it clear that he would continue the war unless they did as he commanded. Meekly the chiefs signed the treaty that he placed in front of them, then withdrew to their lodges to ponder the penalties of arousing the wrath of such a powerful soldier chief as the Butcher.

The Cheyennes had yet to test the bluecoats' prowess, and the tensions of the Sioux troubles drew them into scattered depredations along the Platte road in Nebraska. To chastize the Cheyennes the army turned to an officer as colorful as Harney, Colonel Edwin V. Sumner. With a physique as powerful, beard and hair as white and flowing, and vocabulary as richly profane, he enjoyed almost the stature of Harney. "Bull" Sumner, his men called him, in recognition of a skull so thick that it had withstood a glancing musket ball at Cerro Gordo in the Mexican War.

Sumner's campaign reached a climax on the Solomon River in western Kansas, on another of those rare occasions when Indians stood in an open encounter with soldiers. On July 29, 1857, three hundred mounted warriors drew up in line of battle to oppose Sumner. They had washed their hands in a magic lake, and the medicine men gave assurance that the soldiers' bullets could not harm them. Sumner's three hundred cavalrymen, carbines at the ready, formed for the attack. But surprisingly, as a soldier recalled, the colonel shouted: "Sling—carbine. Draw—saber. . . . Now," continued the trooper, "came the command in the well-known roar of 'Old Bull,' 'Gallop—march!' and then immediately 'CHARGE!' and with a wild yell we brought our sabers to a 'tierce point' and dashed at them."

The magic waters worked on bullets, not sabers, and the Cheyennes gave way in chagrin. For seven miles the troopers galloped after them, sabering those who fell behind and leaving the rest so shaken that their agent later reported: "They said they had learned a lesson last summer in their fight with Colonel Sumner; that it was useless to contend against the white men."

Harney and Sumner had scarcely inflicted lasting defeat on their adversaries. However, their campaigns had shown the Sioux and Cheyennes that the white soldiers were not to be dismissed with complete contempt. And for several years these tribes remained warily withdrawn in the face of provocations, such as the Pikes Peak gold rush of 1858, that earlier might

Three contemporary views of Comanche atrocities: right, Texas settler Mrs. Caroline Harris is abducted by a chief in an illustration from her memoirs. After a two-year captivity, Mrs. Harris was ransomed and returned.

Above, a mounted Comanche drags a baby to death in full view of the child's mother. The woodcut appeared in an 1889 book, Indian Depredations in Texas, a work frontiersman-author John Wilbarger intended to counter "writers who are forever bewailing the rapid disappearance of Indian tribes from the American continent." At right, in another illustration from Indian Depredations, Comanches brand the feet of thirteen-year-old captive Matilda Lockhart to keep her from running away.

207

have stirred conflict. But worse provocations lay ahead.

While the Sioux and Cheyennes had been temporarily set back, the Kiowas and Comanches, whose depredations against whites far overshadowed those of their northern neighbors, had yet to suffer a damaging blow. For generations these tribes had ravaged Texas and Mexico for stock, captives, and plunder. The shift in national allegiance of their victims, from Spain to Mexico, and for Texans, to independent republic and finally the United States, had not changed the raiding pattern. Not surprisingly, the Fort Atkinson treaty wrought no change either. The raiders continued to stab destructively at the expanding frontier of settlement in Texas and farther west to ride the pathway that came to be known as the Great Comanche War Trail across the Rio Grande and deep into Mexico.

Although these tribesmen occasionally struck at trains on the Cimarron Cutoff of the Santa Fe Trail, their one concession to the treaty was a general keeping of the peace along the Arkansas River. Their reward was an annual giveaway at some point on the Arkansas at which an agent of the Great Father issued presents, including arms and ammunition that were later used in the raids to the south. Texans thought this a strange practice.

Military authorities had striven in vain to protect Texas and head off the raids into Mexico. In 1849 they had erected a line of seven forts along the frontier from the Red River to the Rio Grande. The frontier promptly jumped the line, and in 1852 they planted another six forts still farther west. But the regulars were too few—fewer than three thousand in 1854, for example—to guard a frontier four hundred miles long while also garrisoning the international border and protecting the long road from San Antonio to El Paso. Like Oregonians, Texans formed their own volunteer units, the famed Texas Rangers among them.

Texans complained bitterly as year after year the toll mounted: horses and cattle stealthily run off, men killed while at work in the fields, women dragged from their homes into captivity, even children cut down by a sudden arrow while at play. As a constituent summed up in a desperate attempt to communicate with the state's governor in 1858, "Now the woods is full of indian sine in one mile of my house I dare not to leave my house to go one mile on aney business for fear my familey is murde[r] before I can get back I pay my taxes as other citisons for protection and has failed to get it."

To many, the true solution lay in scraping together enough men, even at the expense of frontier defense, to strike at the marauders in their homes north of the Red River. Late in the 1850's General David E. Twiggs and Governor Hardin R. Runnels joined to carry out this strategy. Twiggs turned to a fresh and aggressive new regiment recently assigned to Texas, the 2nd Cavalry. Runnels called up five companies of tough Texas Rangers under the veteran Indian fighter Captain John S. "Rip" Ford.

The rangers struck first. On May 11, 1858, Ford and one hundred men swept down on a Comanche village in the Canadian River valley near the Antelope Hills. The village contained about three hundred fighting men, and for seven hours they battled with the rangers before giving way and fleeing. Ford burned the village and returned to Texas. For the first time whites had inflicted serious damage on the Comanches—seventy-six were dead.

Dragoons show off their elegance in this page from the 1851 regulations manual.

Dragoons.

FANCY DRESS WARFARE

In the pre-Civil War army, dress and field uniforms were remarkably similar. Often the soldiers fighting Indians in the rugged western terrain looked more prepared for a formal parade than a tough battle. Specifying everything from the size of a soldier's buttons to the equipment for his horse (right), the 1851 uniform regulations made the Indian fighter at once handsome, uncomfortable — and an easy target. The dragoons, as well as other branches of the army, had to wear the color pompon on their hats "on all duty under arms." The sword was to be "worn upon all occasions of duty, without exception." Furthermore, no "officers or men on any pretence whatever" — except dragoons — were permitted to wear mustaches. Not until early in the 1870's did the army begin to switch to practical field uniforms.

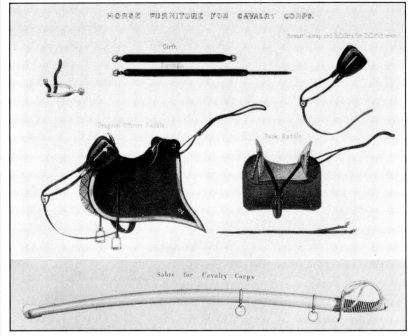

HORSE FURNITURE FOR CAVALRY CORPS.

Girth

Breast-strap and holders for dismounted men

Surcingle

Dragoon Officers Saddle.

Pack Saddle

Sabre for Cavalry Corps.

FIGHTING INDIANS, TEXAS-STYLE

Americans tend to think of Texas Rangers as big, bold, and fearless—men who made the frontier safe from cattle thieves, bank robbers, Mexican bandits, and marauding Indians. The legend was fed by tall stories, mostly apocryphal, such as one about a town being terrorized by a mob. The desperate townspeople send for the Rangers, and before long a lone horseman rides in. "Where are your men?" demands the besieged mayor. "We need a company of Rangers!"

"You've only got one mob, haven't you?" replies the Ranger.

Not surprisingly, most Rangers did not live up to this larger-than-life image. In fact, their early history is composed of one mishap and outright blunder after another.

When the regular army of the Texas republic was disbanded for lack of funds in 1835, a mix of rough frontier ranchers and farmers were organized into three 56-man companies. They were paid $1.25 a day by the Republic, and their mandate was to "range" Texas, keeping it free of outlaws, Mexican troops, and particularly Comanches, who raided at will between Texas and Mexico killing settlers and stealing horses.

The Rangers proved to be more reckless than brave, and often more drunk than sober. During a foray against Mexican troops, a Ranger company carelessly left a drunken comrade on guard. To make him move so that a sober man could take over, one Ranger excitedly yelled: "The Mexicans may swim the river and be after us any moment!" Replied the Ranger: "Let's drink to this confusion."

Remedies for this sort of drunkenness were various and sometimes fatal, as when a sodden Ranger tied to a tree to sober up choked to death instead. Settlers who had previously complained of Comanches killing their children began to protest that inebriated Rangers were killing their livestock. The Rangers' ineptitude against the Comanches served to increase the complaints.

Rangers pursuing Comanches in 1837 suddenly found themselves the pursued. They were surrounded and escaped only after more than half their force had been killed.

A Ranger scheme to detain Comanche chiefs during a treaty parley in 1840 ended disastrously when a number of the chiefs bolted and were shot dead. In retaliation, the Comanches launched their most impressive Texas raid. Some five hundred warriors destroyed the town of Victoria and burned Linnville, killing twenty-four settlers.

The Rangers' lot improved dramatically when a former surveyor named John Coffee Hays joined their ranks in 1840. He was a stickler for discipline and detail and insisted that his men have the best horses, and most importantly, the finest weapons.

Rangers had been using slow-loading long rifles and single-shot revolvers. Not only did Rangers have to dismount before using them, but a Comanche could get off a dozen arrows before a Ranger could load and fire his rifle.

Hays sent Ranger Samuel H. Walker to help Samuel Colt modify his new handgun. Together they fashioned the Walker Colt, a durable, quick-firing, easy-to-load six-shooter. Adopted by the Rangers, and shortly afterward by the army, it revolutionized mounted warfare—in favor of the Texans.

In the next twenty years mobile seek-and-destroy Ranger assault forces were the most effective fighting units against the Comanches. With some truth it was said that to be a Texas Ranger a man had to "ride like a Mexican, track like a Comanche, shoot like a Kentuckian, and fight like the devil."

In this rare old photograph of Texas Rangers Colonel Hays stands in front in white shirt sleeves.

Not until autumn did the regulars get organized. Command of the "Wichita Expedition" went to Major Earl Van Dorn, a lively little fighter considered by contemporaries to be "the very embodiment of all that was chivalrous, brave, kind, and gentle," and also, in reference to the recent Secretary of War and future Confederate president, "one of Davis's special pets." Van Dorn led his column, augmented by 135 Indians recruited from a reservation along the Brazos River, north of the Red River, established a stockaded supply base, and sent out scouts.

They found a Comanche village of 120 lodges in the valley of Rush Creek. It belonged to the powerful and ill-tempered old chief Buffalo Hump, one of the most daring and resourceful of frontier raiders. He had recently come from the Arkansas, where in receiving his annual presents he had vowed vengeance against the "white men of the south" for their attack on his kinsmen at Antelope Hills. But he had also just visited nearby Fort Arbuckle, where he and the post commander had exchanged pledges of peace and friendship. Of this Van Dorn knew nothing, nor did the Arbuckle garrison know of his proximity.

As the sun rose over Rush Creek on October 1, 1858, reflecting off a fog lying low on the Comanche tepees, Van Dorn formed his four troops of cavalry and Indian allies, about 350 men, in line of-battle. The bugler sounded the charge, and the shouting formation galloped into the village with carbines banging. Their women and children in peril, the surprised warriors stood and fought in savage contests at close quarters, with pistol against bow and arrow and saber against tomahawk. Sul Ross, a vacationing college student who led the Indian auxiliaries, went down with a bullet in his side. A Comanche leaned over him with a scalping knife just as a lieutenant put a load of buckshot into the Indian's back and saved the young man, who would become a governor of Texas. An arrow in the stomach and one in the wrist dropped Van Dorn, and another in the heart killed Lieutenant Cornelius Van Camp. After an hour and a half of ferocious combat the Indians broke and fled. They left behind the corpses of fifty-six warriors and two women, a herd of three hundred ponies, and their lodges, which the troops burned.

However darkened by the recent peace talks at Fort Arbuckle, the Battle of Rush Springs was a stunning blow to some of the most notorious of the Comanche raiders. Miraculously, Van Dorn recovered from a wound supposed to be fatal and led his men in a year of vigorous campaigning through the Comanche country between the Red and Arkansas rivers. The following spring, in the Battle of Crooked Creek, he all but annihilated a Comanche band trapped in a ravine. They "fought without giving or asking quarter until there was not one left to bend a bow," wrote Van Dorn. Indeed, not one Comanche escaped. Forty-nine warriors were killed and five wounded; thirty-two women and five men fell prisoner to the troopers.

But despite Van Dorn's victories and a comprehensive operation involving several columns in the summer of 1860, the Twiggs-Runnels strategy failed. Texans and Mexicans still lived in terror of the scourge from the north. In truth, the raids had become so firmly embedded in the culture of the Kiowas and Comanches that more decisive measures than an occasional defeat on the battlefield would be necessary to stop them. Antelope Hills and Rush Springs were but opening guns in almost two decades of warfare with the Kiowas and Comanches.

The Cult of the Warrior

To such western warriors as those in this George Catlin painting—and the ones on the following pages—one thing mattered above all else: success in battle. A man could gain some prestige as a hunter, but true glory came only through fighting, and from earliest childhood boys were taught that warfare would be their principal occupation. Indians celebrated combat in every aspect of their lives—as in the painted Cheyenne buffalo hide at right, which shows mounted warriors—and whether they warred for tangible reasons, such as encroachments on hunting lands, or for imaginary slights, the warriors fought primarily for personal glory. Perhaps the most dramatic expression of their love for battle is contained in a Blackfoot song that, in various forms, was known to virtually every warrior tribe: "It is bad to live to be old / Better to die young / Fighting bravely in battle."
KENNEDY GALLERIES

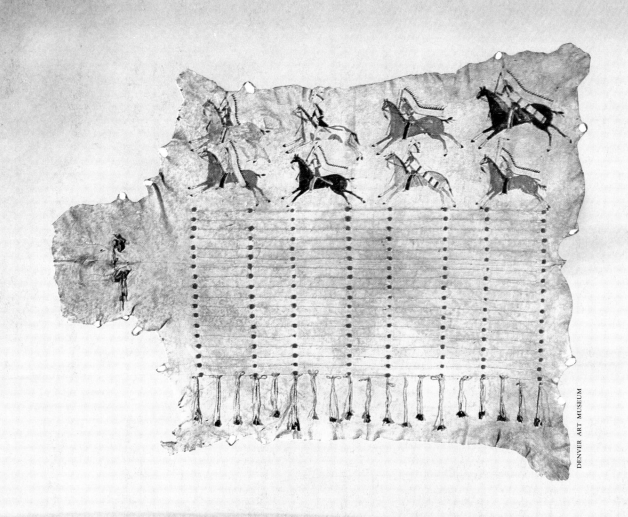

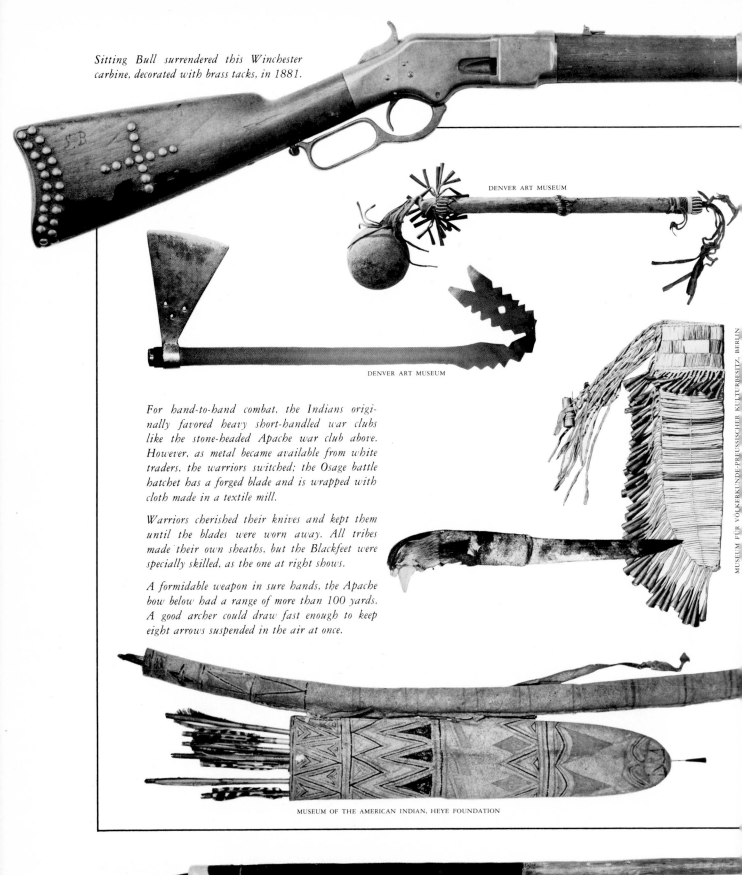

Sitting Bull surrendered this Winchester carbine, decorated with brass tacks, in 1881.

For hand-to-hand combat, the Indians originally favored heavy short-handled war clubs
like the stone-headed Apache war club above.
However, as metal became available from white
traders, the warriors switched; the Osage battle
hatchet has a forged blade and is wrapped with
cloth made in a textile mill.

Warriors cherished their knives and kept them
until the blades were worn away. All tribes
made their own sheaths, but the Blackfeet were
specially skilled, as the one at right shows.

A formidable weapon in sure hands, the Apache
bow below had a range of more than 100 yards.
A good archer could draw fast enough to keep
eight arrows suspended in the air at once.

*This nine-foot Apache war lance is
longer than most by a couple of feet.
Most Indians felt the shorter the
lance, the more courageous the user.*

NATIONAL COLLECTION OF FINE ARTS

Of all the weapons shown here, the Indians considered the gun the least honorable to use. Catlin's magnificent Comanche warrior above, whose name was Little Spaniard, gained far more glory by stabbing an enemy with his lance than by dropping him from afar with the white man's musket. On the other hand, taking a gun from an enemy was thought so courageous that the Blackfeet had a special word for it — *namachkani.* The implication was clear: the bravest deeds took place in hand-to-hand combat.

Sioux chief Charger in full robe and headdress, painted by Catlin

The Apache owner of the sturdily made horned and hair-fringed headdress above wore it both in combat and ceremony.

Each feather in Sioux chief Iron Tail's superb war bonnet (above, right) represented a brave deed of the chief, who stored his bonnet in a rawhide case such as the Kiowa one at right.

As he studied the Indians, Catlin became increasingly fascinated by the splendid war regalia they donned for ceremonies (they went into battle practically naked, wearing at most a war shirt) and gave this excellent description of a Sioux warrior who must have rivaled the chieftain above in splendor: "His dress . . . was classic and extremely beautiful; his leggings and shirt were . . . richly garnished with the quills of the porcupine and fringed with the locks of scalps . . . his head was decked with the war eagles' plumes, his robe was the skin of a young buffalo bull, decorated with scenes of the battles of his life."

A painted Apache war shirt

A Sioux war shirt, hung with scalp locks

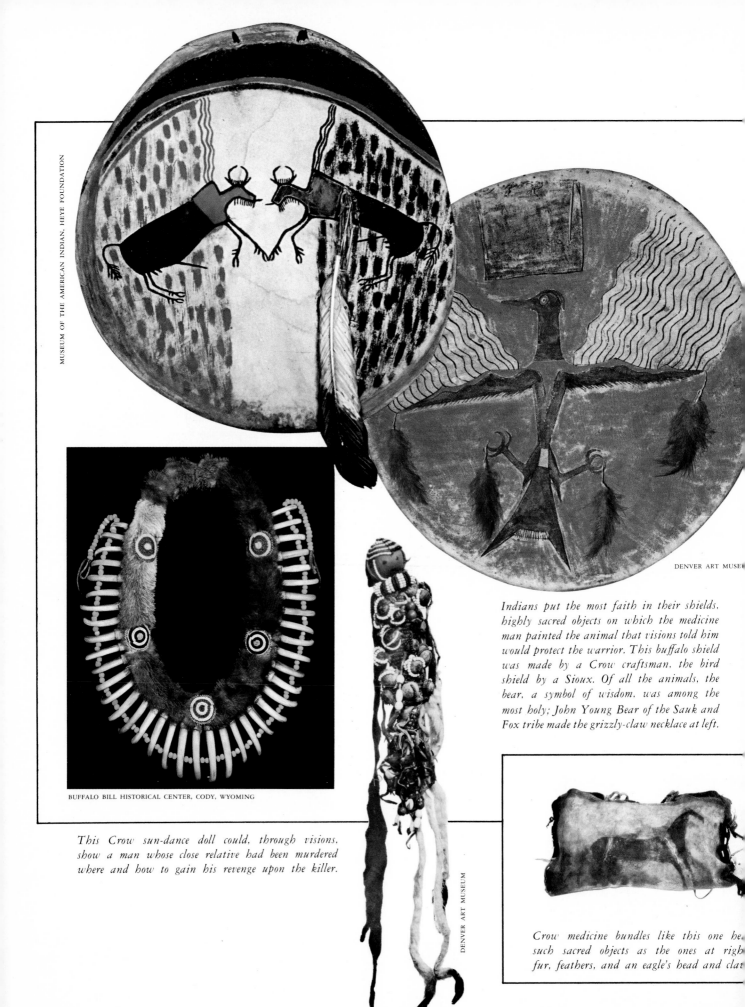

Indians put the most faith in their shields, highly sacred objects on which the medicine man painted the animal that visions told him would protect the warrior. This buffalo shield was made by a Crow craftsman, the bird shield by a Sioux. Of all the animals, the bear, a symbol of wisdom, was among the most holy; John Young Bear of the Sauk and Fox tribe made the grizzly-claw necklace at left.

This Crow sun-dance doll could, through visions, show a man whose close relative had been murdered where and how to gain his revenge upon the killer.

Crow medicine bundles like this one he such sacred objects as the ones at righ fur, feathers, and an eagle's head and clau

218

Every warrior went into battle with invisible allies at his side. These were the spirits that controlled the Indian's world; for the warrior, they held the key to his fortunes in battle. The tribesmen gave many names to these supernatural powers; the whites termed them all "medicine." Good medicine protected the warrior from harm. He invoked it in many forms before going to fight and carried magic accouterments with him into combat. His shield, for example, bore symbolic paintings of supernatural visions that had come to him—or his tribe's medicine man—in dreams. He had daubed himself with war paint to give him strength, and he carried a medicine bundle whose contents gave him magic power. Indians thought these talismans no less sacred if they failed to ward off a fatal blow, for that merely meant that the victim had violated some taboo and thereby forfeited the protection of the spirits. Even when they lost battle after battle to the powerful medicine of the white man, the warrior tribes kept their faith in the strength of their supernatural protectors.

Iowa warrior Little Wolf posed for Catlin in full war paint.

A Blackfoot warrior carried this coup stick into combat.

A Chippewa brave took this Sioux scalp.

The Indians held their most vigorous and exultant ceremonial dances after they had won a battle. In celebrations that could last for days, the warriors, faces painted black (the color for triumph), danced to the beat of drums while they shook rattles, waved the scalps they had taken, and boasted of their strength and valor. Each re-enacted the coups he had counted against the enemy—that is, the number of times he had touched a foe with a weapon or coup stick. There was honor in taking scalps, and honor in killing with a bow, but the greatest honor of all came to the man who had put himself closest to danger.

MUSEUM OF THE AMERICAN INDIAN, HEYE FOUNDATION

A tribe of Sioux Indians celebrate battle in Catlin's moody war dance scene above. The warriors danced to the music of instruments such as those at right: an Arapaho drum bearing the sacred image of the bear, and a Shoshone rattle made of rawhide and decorated with beadwork.

8: Bloody Roundup

Secession and Civil War did not slow the westward advance. On the contrary, despite the great ordeal that absorbed the energies of North and South, mineral strikes throughout the West continued to lure whites into areas of previously undisturbed Indian possession. The quickening pace of white settlement gave renewed force — and clear definition — to the Indian policy that had been pursued since the close of the Mexican War. In official language, the policy came to be known as concentration.

For whites, concentration offered a happy coincidence of self-interest and noble philanthropy. On the one hand, Indians would be cleared from lands whites wanted or already possessed, confined to lesser lands unwanted or not yet wanted, and prevented from causing any further annoyance. On the other hand, in their reservation homes the Indians could be insulated from the contaminating influence of the white man and made the beneficiaries not only of large annuities of tools and stores but of the most precious gift at the white man's command — his culture.

Before these blessings could be bestowed, however, the Indians had to be concentrated. More often than not, this meant war. The Stevens treaties had ignited wars of concentration in the Pacific Northwest in

Warriors flee before hard-charging U.S. cavalrymen in this detail from a painting by Charles Schreyvogel, a turn-of-the-century artist with a "fanatical passion" for historical accuracy.

1855–58, and the Civil War years saw their spread to most of the West. As in the Pacific region, the early wars of concentration on the plains and in the Southwest were not fought by the regular army.

The outbreak of the Civil War in 1861 stripped the frontier of regulars. But regiments of volunteer troops, raised to help save the Union, found themselves instead filling in behind the regulars at frontier stations. These volunteers enlisted in state or territorial units, organized under local authority and then sworn into the federal service to be employed where and how federal commanders decreed. By 1862 there were about fifteen thousand on Indian duty, four thousand more than in 1860, and by 1865 they numbered almost twenty thousand. Because of the patriotic motivation of the Civil War, moreover, the units tended to draw men of higher caliber than the prewar regulars. For the most part the volunteers were well officered, often by former regulars, and a fair number of the men had fought Indians before. Thus the tribes were confronted by more and better soldiers than ever before.

James Henry Carleton and Patrick Edward Connor expressed the aggressive spirit of this new frontier army. Carleton, a twenty-year veteran of the regular army, had fought Mexicans and Apaches and attained the rank of major of dragoons when the governor of California appointed him colonel of the 1st California Infantry in 1861. An imperious, flint-eyed martinet with rocklike fixity of purpose, Carleton set off early in 1862 to lead his unit, which came to be known as the California Column, across the southwestern deserts to confront a Confederate force that was marching on New Mexico from Texas. The judgment of a fellow officer, that Carleton's "unscrupulous ambition and exclusive selfishness had passed into a proverb, despite his acknowledged ability and apparent zeal," is not seriously exaggerated.

As for Connor, after an enlisted hitch in the regular army and Mexican War service as a captain of volunteers, he had settled in California. There he was successful in business and politics and attained prominence in the state militia. In the summer of 1861 the governor appointed him colonel of the 3rd California Infantry, and under federal orders Connor marched off across the Sierra Nevada to patrol the mail road between Salt Lake City and California. A fiery Irishman, he soon fell to quarreling with Mormon leaders, but he also impressed his superior as "a man of observation, undaunted firmness, and self-possession under all circumstances."

Connor earned this encomium after launching one of the most daring operations—and fighting one of the most ferocious battles—of the Indian wars. The spread of Mormon settlement northward from Salt Lake City and a gold rush to Montana in 1862 had upset Chief Bear Hunter's Shoshones, provoking scattered incidents of violence. Early in 1863 Connor conceived a bold plan for a midwinter thrust at the offending chief, known to be camped on the Bear River about 140 miles north of the lake. At the head of three hundred Californians he pushed through snow and temperatures that in a week left a fourth of his men with frozen feet.

Bear Hunter knew of Connor's approach but resolved to stand and fight. He counted about three hundred confident, well-armed warriors. His village occupied a strong defensive position in a steep-sided ravine, which the Indians had further strengthened with rock and earthen parapets. As the troops deployed for the attack on January 27, "one of the chiefs," reported a participant, "rode up and down in front of the ravine, brandishing his spear in the face of the volunteers, [and] the warriors in front sang out: 'Fours right, fours left; come on you California sons of bitches!'"

Elements of the attacking force succeeded in flanking the Indian position, and the two sides struggled desperately in the village. The Indians, Connor wrote, "continued fighting with unyielding obstinacy, frequently engaging hand to hand with the troops until killed in their hiding places." Bear Hunter fell while preparing fresh ammunition. After four hours of bitter fighting, the surviving Indians broke and fled. The casualties were heavy, heavier by far than in typical Indian combats: 21 soldiers dead and 46 wounded, 224 Indians dead and 164 women and children prisoners. "Never will I forget the scene," recalled a soldier, "dead bodies everywhere." But another remembered mainly the terrible cold: "2 feet of snow on the ground nothing for fire but green willows which would burn about as well as the snow oh! the groands of the frozen it seems to ring in my ears yet the poor feelows some lost their toes some a portion of their feet."

The Battle of Bear River earned Connor a general's star, and he followed up the victory with characteristic energy. By the autumn of 1863 he could report that "all routes of travel through Utah Territory to Nevada and California, and to the Beaver Head and Boise river gold mines, may now be used with safety."

Carleton reached New Mexico too late to join in driving the Confederate invaders back to Texas. Promoted to brigadier general en route, Carleton and his Californians, strengthened by New Mexico volunteers, turned to fighting Apaches and Navahos. Indeed, they had got a foretaste of this duty on the way to New Mexico, as advance elements of the California Column entered what one of Carleton's officers called "that most formidable of gorges"—Apache Pass.

In the year and a half since Lieutenant Bascom had hanged Cochise's relatives, settlements and travel routes from El Paso to Tucson had suffered his vengeance. Mangas Coloradas, leader of the Warm Springs Apaches, joined in the bloodletting, for a gold strike at Pinos Altos had flooded his homeland with prospectors. The chiefs thought the recent and hasty abandonment of Forts Buchanan, Breckinridge, and Fillmore, precipitated by the Confederate advance from Texas, had been prompted instead by fear of Apaches. Now, as other soldiers approached from the west in July, 1862, they posted their warriors behind rocks on the slopes of Apache Pass and waited.

On July 15, 1862, Captain Thomas L. Roberts with a company of infantry, seven cavalrymen, and two howitzers marched into Apache Pass, his objective the vital springs near the old stage station, vacant since the Butterfield line had moved northward. A sudden crash of musketry stopped the advance. Roberts deployed in skirmish formation and cut his way through to the stage station. There the Indians had thrown up rock breastworks commanding the springs, and as the captain reported, "they seemed very loath to let me have water." But they had reckoned without the artillery. Bursting shells tore at the ramparts and sent the Apaches fleeing over the ridges to safety. "We would have done well enough," one of them later explained, "if you had not fired wagons at us."

Roberts had sent six mounted men back on the trail to warn his wagon train and its cavalry escort. They had no sooner left the pass than a party

In the course of his ruthless pursuit of Navahos and Apaches, General James Carleton became the virtual military dictator of New Mexico.

When General Carleton first ordered Kit Carson (above) to war against the Mescaleros and the Navahos, the former mountain man objected to fighting his long-time friends among the Navahos. Within a few months, however, Carson had reconsidered and became Carleton's principal lieutenant in a vicious scorched-earth campaign.

of Apaches took up the chase. Private John Teal fell behind and was cut off. A bullet dropped his horse. Using it as a breastwork, he fired rapidly with his breech-loading carbine. "This repeated fire seemed to confuse the savages," he told his captain later, "and instead of advancing with a rush, they commenced to circle round me, firing occasional shots in my direction. They knew that I also had a six-shooter and a saber, and seemed unwilling to try close quarters. In this way the fight continued for over an hour, when I got a good chance at a prominent Indian and slipped a carbine ball into his breast." After that the attackers drew off, and Teal, shouldering his saddle, hiked the rest of the way back to the train.

Ten days later Carleton and the main column reached the Apache Pass mail station. Recognizing the significance of the pass to his line of communication with California, he directed his adjutant general to write out an order establishing a new stronghold, Fort Bowie, overlooking the springs.

Private Teal's carbine bullet had struck Mangas Coloradas himself. His men bore him south, to Janos in Chihuahua, and there forced a Mexican doctor to dig it out. The operation succeeded, and soon the giant chieftain was back in his home country terrorizing the miners and skirmishing again with Carleton's California troops.

In September, 1862, Carleton assumed command of the Department of New Mexico, and Brigadier General Joseph R. West took command in the southern part of the department. On January 17, 1863, for reasons still unclear, Mangas Coloradas agreed to meet with one of West's officers, Captain E. D. Shirland, under a flag of truce. He was seized immediately, and the next day delivered to West.

That night the general strongly hinted to the camp sentries that Mangas should not awake to another day. A prospector with the troops saw what happened. Repeatedly, as the old chief lay wrapped in his blanket next to a campfire, the guards heated their bayonets and applied them to his feet and legs. When he finally rose in protest, they fired their muskets into him pointblank, then put four pistol balls into his head. Reporting his investigation of the incident, General West explained that Mangas had "made three efforts to escape and was shot on the third attempt. . . . I have thus dwelt at length on this matter," he added, "in order to show that even with a murderous Indian, whose life was clearly forfeited by all laws either human or divine, wherever found, the good faith of the U.S. Military Authorities was in no way compromised."

In Santa Fe Carleton found an old friend to help fight other Indians. This was Kit Carson, who had scouted for Carleton in the earlier Apache campaigns and after a tour as an Indian agent had risen to the colonelcy of the 1st New Mexico Cavalry. Carson came to venerate the autocratic Carleton as he had an earlier chief, explorer John C. Frémont, and the general supplied the drive that kept his easygoing lieutenant at his task.

Carleton made war ruthlessly. "There is to be no council held with the Indians, nor any talks," he said in dispatching Carson to round up the troublesome Mescalero Apaches. "The men are to be slain whenever and wherever they can be found. The women and children may be taken as prisoners, but, of course, they are not to be killed." Thus prodded, Carson pounced on the Mescaleros and in less than three months conducted some four hundred of them to the reservation Carleton had marked out one hundred miles away. It was in the Pecos River valley at a place where a

Chiefs Barboncito (left) and Manuelito — the last Navaho holdouts — surrendered late in 1866 and were sent to the sterile flats of Bosque Redondo in southeast New Mexico.

circular grove of cottonwood trees supplied the name, Bosque Redondo. Intermittently over the next three years, other Apache groups were targets for Carleton and Carson, but increasingly their principal attention turned to the Navahos.

For the Navahos, Carleton had in mind a fate similar to that of the Mescaleros. Several years earlier, after a succession of futile campaigns, Colonel Edward R. S. Canby had concluded that the Navahos would have to be removed from their country altogether and re-established "at points so remote from the settlements as to isolate them entirely from the inhabitants of the territory." Bosque Redondo provided an ideal place to carry out such a plan, Carleton thought. There, guarded by soldiers at Fort Sumner, the Navahos could be converted into self-sufficient farmers.

The scheme seemed preposterous. The Navahos, who inhabited the Colorado Plateau area, could scarcely be expected to go of their own accord. Manuelito, the tall, muscular leader of the tribe's hard-liners, ignored the first overtures; and even such peace chiefs as Delgadito and Barboncito, dedicated though they were to relaxing tensions, instantly balked at the idea of exchanging their homeland of centuries for the sterile Pecos bottoms three hundred miles to the east.

Undeterred, Carleton laid down a blunt ultimatum. "Tell them," he instructed the commander of Fort Wingate on June 23, 1863, "they can

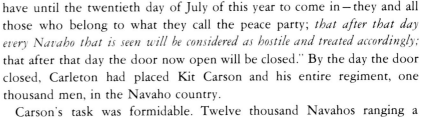

Before Kit Carson drove them out, generations of Navahos had found security and a good living on the floor of Arizona's Canyon de Chelly (here, a Curtis photograph). After a few years white officials declared Bosque Redondo a disaster and sent the Navahos to a new reservation that included Canyon de Chelly.

have until the twentieth day of July of this year to come in — they and all those who belong to what they call the peace party; *that after that day every Navaho that is seen will be considered as hostile and treated accordingly;* that after that day the door now open will be closed." By the day the door closed, Carleton had placed Kit Carson and his entire regiment, one thousand men, in the Navaho country.

Carson's task was formidable. Twelve thousand Navahos ranging a plateau expanse stretching westward from the Continental Divide to the great gorges of the Colorado River hardly compared to five hundred Mescaleros in a relatively constricted mountain domain. But Carson, under Carleton's close oversight, waged a war aimed at crops and flocks and the people's will to resist. His columns laced the Navaho country north to the San Juan, west to the Grand Canyon, and south to the Little Colorado. For six months, in summer and winter, they marched ceaselessly, destroying orchards and cornfields, seizing flocks of sheep, burning hogans, killing Navahos where they could but always keeping them on the run. Seventy-eight were reported slain, but the true cost to the Indians was reckoned in a rising sense of futility. The crucial psychological blow fell in January, 1864, when Carson and his men swept almost effortlessly through the ancient Navaho stronghold of Canyon de Chelly.

The violation of this sheer-walled bastion clinched the conquest of the Navahos. In despair hundreds of them converged on Forts Wingate and Canby to surrender. By mid-March, 1864, six thousand were camped at the two posts. Escorted by soldiers, twenty-four hundred trekked across New Mexico to Bosque Redondo in a "Long Walk" of suffering and, for almost two hundred, death. By the end of 1864 eight thousand Navahos had given up and submitted themselves to the Bosque Redondo experiment. The other four thousand, led by the unreconciled Manuelito, withdrew to the remote western reaches of the Navaho country. In the autumn of 1866, short of food and despondent over the fate of his people, even Manuelito gave up hope and surrendered.

The second stage of Carleton's plan for the Navahos — colonization at Bosque Redondo — was a disaster. The reservation did not contain enough tillable land, even with primitive irrigation, to support so many Indians, and such pitiful crops as were nursed to maturity succumbed to flood, drought, hail, and visitations of insects. The herds of sheep and goats could not find enough grass, and they also furnished tempting targets for raiding Kiowas and Comanches. Government rations barely held off starvation, and government clothing was ineffectual against the icy winters. Weakened by malnutrition and exposure, the Indians fell prey to pneumonia, measles, and other epidemics. Venereal disease spread from the fort's garrison. Mescaleros and Navahos, traditional enemies, quarreled endlessly, until in November, 1865, the Mescaleros bolted the reservation and fled back to their mountain homeland. Carleton's bright boast of transforming the Navahos into "the happiest and most delightfully located pueblo of Indians in New Mexico — perhaps in the United States" foundered on these grim realities and on repeated revelations of fraud and scandal in the administration of the reservation.

Although Carleton stubbornly refused to admit failure, his transfer to the regular army in 1866 and the reorganization of the Department of New Mexico opened the way for more objective appraisals. In the spring

229

of 1868 Manuelito, Barboncito, and other headmen were allowed to journey to Washington to tell President Andrew Johnson of their condition and ask him to let them go home. A month later peace commissioners visited Bosque Redondo and saw that in truth the Navahos "had sunk into a condition of absolute poverty and despair." The new Bosque Redondo superintendent, A. B. Norton, added his voice to the findings. A treaty concluded on June 1, 1868, conceded failure. The Navaho people could return to their homes. Before the end of July the vanguard had reached the land where the tragic Long Walk had begun four years earlier. There the government marked out a new reservation for them.

Carleton's Bosque Redondo program failed dramatically in every way but one: it ended for all time warfare with the Navahos. They never forgot the suffering, tribulation, and death of those awful years on the Pecos. *Nahondzod,* they called them, "the Fearing Time." Despite many provocations in later years, they submitted to government authority on the new reservation and never again took up arms against the white people.

Unlike the Navahos, the Eastern or Santee Sioux of Minnesota had at first accepted concentration without major hostilities. But a tiny spark, one of those mindless, almost accidental incidents that set off so many Indian conflicts, lighted a powder train that flashed the length and breadth of the Great Plains and drew the Santee and most of the big tribes into war.

On August 17, 1862, four young Santee hunters were journeying homeward. They had found no game, which added to deeper frustrations that festered in them as in all their people. An early treaty had confined them to a narrow belt of land along the upper Minnesota River. Scandinavian and German settlers had closed in around the reservation, predatory traders regularly diverted most of the annuities promised by the treaty into their own pockets, and missionaries were forever intruding upon the villagers seeking converts. Under this constant harassment and pressure, the Santee tribes split into factions, one urging resistance to government programs, the other accommodation.

Among the four young hunters one dared another to prove his courage by killing a white man, and before the dare had run its course they had shot down five settlers. For the Santees the act catalyzed the discontent of a decade. In stormy council the militants demanded that the murders be sanctioned and that Little Crow, a peace advocate, lead the people in a war against the whites. Reluctantly the chief submitted to the demand.

It was one of the most savage and bloody Indian uprisings in history. On the first day alone, August 18, a nightmare of fire and death took the lives of four hundred citizens and left their charred or brutalized bodies testimony to the depth of Sioux grievances. A contingent of Minnesota volunteer infantry strayed into rampaging warriors, and only half the forty-six men escaped back to Fort Ridgely. Three hundred refugees crowded into the fort as its shaken garrison of 155 volunteer infantrymen steeled themselves for an assault.

On August 20 and again two days later Little Crow led eight hundred warriors against Fort Ridgely. Wave after wave of shouting painted Indians dashed against the post's outbuildings only to be battered and turned back by musketry and artillery fire. Three howitzers, supervised by a regular army ordnance sergeant, spewed bursting canister shot into the massed attackers as a big 24-pounder dropped its lethal loads into the

Baltimore artist Frank Blackwell Mayer sketched this 1851 treaty conference at which Minnesota's Santee Sioux sold their hunting grounds for $3 million, payable in fifty yearly installments.

ravines where they gathered. A hundred Sioux fell in the effort to take the fort, and Little Crow would give up no more. The cannon had saved the day. "That gun the soldiers used at the end was terrible," said one of the Indians. "With a few guns like that," replied another, "the Dakotas could rule the earth."

Across the river on August 23 another 350 Sioux, more intent on plunder than conquest, stormed into the streets of New Ulm. But reinforced by men from other towns, the citizens were ready. All day fighting raged in the streets and among the buildings as the townspeople defended their homes, and at nightfall the Indians drew off, thwarted.

In a week of bloody horror, fully eight hundred whites died violently in atonement for the wrongs done the Santees, and but for the successful defense of Fort Ridgely and New Ulm, many more might have perished. For as Chief Big Eagle observed, Fort Ridgely was the door to the Minnesota River valley all the way to St. Paul, "and if we got through the door nothing could stop us this side of the Mississippi." By August 28 advance elements of a relief expedition had reached Fort Ridgely. The lower valley was safe and a foothold had been gained for a counteroffensive.

The governor had named Henry Hastings Sibley, veteran fur trader and first governor of Minnesota, to lead the expedition. On September 19, with sixteen hundred soldiers, he marched up the valley. Disputes now divided the Sioux leadership. Some favored flight to the west, some prompt surrender to Sibley, some execution of their prisoners, and some a pitched battle. The latter faction prevailed and on September 23 sent

The most brutal Indian uprising west of the Mississippi occurred in Minnesota in 1862, when the Santee Sioux swept through a region 50 miles by 250 miles, forcing some 30,000 people to flee their homes. Hundreds were killed and tortured. The scenes above, from a contemporary panorama, show a little girl's legs being methodically slashed (left) and the murder of two captives. The revolt was finally put down by forces under the command of Henry Hastings Sibley, who convened a military court to try some 400 warriors. Hastily—some decisions took five minutes—303 were sentenced to death. President Abraham Lincoln intervened, found many convictions based on flimsy evidence, and commuted the sentences of all but 38, who were hanged simultaneously (right, from the same panorama) December 26, 1862.

seven hundred warriors against Sibley at Wood Lake. His regiments, backed by artillery, swept them from the field. Three days later four hundred captive whites were yielded, and during ensuing weeks Sioux to the number of two thousand straggled in to surrender. Sibley formed a military commission to try individuals accused of specific crimes, and 303 were sentenced to be hanged. President Abraham Lincoln, skeptical of the justice of the proceedings, examined the records and set aside the sentences of all but thirty-eight. In the largest mass execution in American history these Indians were hanged at Mankato in December.

The Santee outbreak was the beginning of a Sioux war that kept the plains in turmoil for eight years. The hangings at Mankato ended only the Minnesota phase. The most prominent of the hostile Santees, including the four who had started the war, had not surrendered but had fled to Dakota, where they recounted their grievances to the prairie Sioux. Little Crow would die the following June, shot down by a settler while picking berries. But other Sioux chiefs, already unsettled by a growing traffic up the Missouri River to gold mines recently discovered in Montana, took on a new belligerence. Military expeditions in 1863 and 1864 further provoked them and shifted the focus of Sioux warfare to the Dakota country.

These expeditions were led by Sibley, commissioned brigadier general as a reward for Wood Lake, and another brigadier, Alfred Sully. A gruff, eccentric veteran of the regular army and the son of artist Thomas Sully, the latter in particular stirred up both the refugee Santees and the proud Tetons. His regiments of Iowa, Nebraska, and Dakota volunteers campaigned against the Sioux from Devils Lake on the east to the Yellowstone River on the west. And with the establishment of Fort Rice they planted the military frontier firmly and permanently on the upper Missouri. By 1865 all the Tetons and their Cheyenne and Arapaho friends were at war.

By 1865 warfare had also spread to the central and southern plains.

ATTENTION!
INDIAN
FIGHTERS

Having been authorized by the Governor to raise a
Company of 100 day

U. S. VOL CAVALRY!

For immediate service against hostile Indians. I call upon all who wish to engage in such
service to call at my office and enroll their names immediately.

Pay and Rations the same as other U. S.
Volunteer Cavalry.

Parties furnishing their own horses will receive 40c per day, and rations for the same,
while in the service.
The Company will also be entitled to all horses and other plunder taken from the Indians.

Office first door East of Recorder's Office.
HAL SAYR.

Central City, Aug. 13, '64.

Posters such as this one promising plunder helped recruit a force of 700 men, under Colonel John M. Chivington, committed to wiping out Colorado's Indians. Chivington further stirred frontier passions with such demagogic speeches as the one that drew cheers from a Denver crowd when he advocated the killing and scalping of all Indians, even infants: "Nits make lice!"

Although the Minnesota horror had badly frightened whites in Kansas and in the new mining settlements of Colorado, the Plains Indians remained generally peaceful until provoked by local authorities. Governor John Evans, rebuffed in efforts to persuade the Cheyennes and Arapahos to exchange their hunting ranges for a reservation, sensed that what could not be gained by diplomacy might fall as a prize of war. The territorial military commander, Colonel John M. Chivington, cooperated wholeheartedly. A former Methodist clergyman in zealous and unscrupulous pursuit of political ambition, the "Fighting Parson" wasted no sentiment on Indians.

In the spring of 1864 Evans and Chivington seized upon a few scattered incidents to declare the Cheyennes at war; Chivington sent out detachments charged, as one of his officers put it, to "burn villages and kill Cheyennes wherever and whenever found." Beginning in July, 1864, Cheyenne war parties struck back, and they were soon joined by Arapahos, Sioux, Kiowas, and Comanches.

To help meet the emergency, Evans and Chivington organized a short-term volunteer regiment, the 3rd Colorado Cavalry. These "Hundred Dazers" included a large number of rowdies and toughs recruited from the mining camps and Denver saloons, and they sought action and the notoriety they would gain if they smashed the Indians before their hundred-day enlistment period expired.

Colonel Chivington was of much the same mind; but disconcertingly for him, as winter approached, some of the Indians sued for peace. In the forefront of the peace movement was Black Kettle, a wise and gentle man long known as the leading peace chief of the Southern Cheyennes. On September 28, 1864, he and other Cheyenne and Arapaho leaders met with Evans and Chivington at Camp Weld, near Denver. The chiefs came away from the talks somewhat confused, but they were convinced that those Indians who wanted peace could have it by moving to the vicinity of one of the local forts and there submitting to military authority. Early in November Black Kettle and his people, about six hundred in all, laid out their camp in the broad, barren valley of Sand Creek, a tributary of the Arkansas River in southeastern Colorado about forty miles from Fort Lyon. As at Camp Weld, talks with the commander at the fort were ambiguous, but Black Kettle and his fellow chiefs departed believing they had counted themselves out of the war.

Chivington conceded no such interpretation. Late in November he suddenly appeared at Fort Lyon with the 3rd Colorado and other units and announced his intention to attack Black Kettle. Several officers remonstrated, declaring that the Cheyennes had been led to understand that they were prisoners of war. Chivington responded, as one of the protesters recalled, that "he believed it to be right and honorable to use any means under God's heaven to kill Indians that would kill women and children, and 'damn any man that was in sympathy with Indians.'"

On November 29, 1864, Chivington methodically deployed his command, about seven hundred strong with four howitzers, around Black Kettle's village. The chief, shouting reassurances to his alarmed people, ran up an American flag and a white flag over his tepee. Then the troops opened fire and charged. The Indians fled in panic in all directions. Only one pocket of resistance formed, and that was speedily eliminated.

Chivington had made clear his wish that prisoners not be taken, and a massacre followed as the soldiers indiscriminately shot down men, women, and children. Interpreter John Smith later testified: "They were scalped, their brains knocked out; the men used their knives, ripped open women, clubbed little children, knocked them in the head with their guns, beat their brains out, mutilated their bodies in every sense of the word." Two hundred Cheyennes, two thirds of them women and children, perished. Nine chiefs died, but Black Kettle made good his escape.

As the newly styled "Bloody Thirdsters" paraded in triumph through the streets of Denver and exhibited a hundred scalps on the stage of a theater, the Cheyenne survivors of Sand Creek spread word of the massacre across the plains. In a great council near the head of the Republican River, Cheyenne, Arapaho, and Sioux chiefs smoked the war pipe. "We have now raised the battle-axe until death," declared one. For more than a month, in January and February, 1865, the Indians ravaged the South Platte valley, killing fifty whites, burning stage stations and ranches, destroying telegraph lines, twice sacking the hamlet of Julesburg, Colorado, and even attacking nearby Fort Rankin. Late in February they headed northward—all, that is, but Black Kettle, who, still hoping for peace, led about eighty families to retreats south of the Arkansas. On the Powder, Tongue, and Yellowstone rivers the Cheyenne refugees told their story to Teton Sioux and Northern Cheyennes already smarting over their treatment at the hands of Generals Sibley and Sully in 1863 and 1864.

On July 26, 1865, between one and three thousand warriors fell on the weakly held military station at Upper Platte Bridge, where the Oregon-California road crossed the North Platte River. They drove in a cavalry detachment and wiped out a military supply train, then scattered for the fall buffalo hunt, satisfied that the soldiers had been properly chastised.

For the army, however, the war was not over. The pugnacious General Patrick E. Connor had been placed in command of the northern plains. In August and September he sent three thousand men in three columns into the Powder River country while General Sully and another thousand campaigned in Dakota. Sully found no Indians, but Connor carried the war into the Teton heartland. His columns destroyed an Arapaho village and skirmished with Sioux but in the end succumbed to weather, distance, and an inhospitable country. Early September storms pounded two of his columns, already exhausted and short on rations, with rain, sleet, snow, and wildly fluctuating temperatures. Nearly a thousand horses and mules perished, and as they fell the men stripped the flesh from the bones and devoured it raw. The operation showed dramatically at what peril heavy columns ventured so far from their supply sources in a hostile land.

The disastrous campaign had cost an estimated $20 million, and from Washington came orders to reduce the troops on the plains and confine military activities to defense of travel routes. Moreover, the Civil War had ended, and the volunteer regiments demanded their discharge. Six regiments of "Galvanized Yankees"—captured Confederates who preferred fighting Indians to rotting in prisoner-of-war camps—had to be released too. Having little choice, therefore, the generals went along with peace efforts that in the autumn of 1865 produced treaties with the tribes of both the northern and southern plains. But these treaties bought no more than a short breathing time, for fighting would return to the plains with the spring grass of 1866. Now, though, the volunteers had gone home, and a new regular army was forming to replace them.

The postwar army bore indelibly the stamp of William Tecumseh Sherman, hero of the Union army's march through Georgia to the sea. Until 1869 he commanded the plains division, then after the election of Ulysses S. Grant to the presidency he took over the top command. Grim-visaged, with scraggly red beard and unruly hair turning gray, he spoke his mind forthrightly and not always tactfully. Politicians and newsmen often found him insufferable, but his soldiers out west, to whose welfare he was passionately devoted, accorded him veneration bordering on worship. Sherman's chief lieutenant in the West, who succeeded him in the plains command, was also a war hero: scrappy, profane little Philip Henry Sheridan. The army knew Sheridan as a first-rate combat leader, bold, energetic, audacious, unswerving in pursuit of victory at almost any cost, and making scant concession to chivalrous or humane conventions of "civilized" war.

Both Sherman and Sheridan believed in total war against the entire enemy population—war such as they themselves had visited on the South in 1864–65. They believed in prosecuting it with several columns converging on the enemy, searching out and smashing his settlements, casting him adrift without food or shelter, remorselessly hounding him until his will to resist collapsed. And they planned to go after the Indians in the winter, a time of special vulnerability for the tribes, when with their weakened ponies and stores of meat they retired to some protected valley to await the coming of spring.

The Sherman-Sheridan strategy required heavy columns of cavalry and infantry trailing long supply trains in quest of an elusive quarry that could vanish at will and rarely had trouble staying out of the way. If the Indians grew careless, or the probing columns happened to nose out their winter hiding places, the strategy worked. More often the soldiers simply exhausted themselves and their animals, and used up their provisions, in long and fruitless marches.

Thus the postwar army was hardly more adequate for its frontier mission than the ante-bellum version had been. As Reconstruction duties in the South diminished, Congress imposed a ceiling of twenty-five thousand enlisted men. Scattered among scores of little outposts, they presented a show of weakness such as Tom Fitzpatrick had warned against as early as 1851. Many of the regiments, however, contained ambitious young field officers, majors and colonels, who had been generals during the war and wanted to be generals again. They were addressed as general in recognition of temporary, or brevet, ranks won for wartime heroism. But they no longer commanded brigades and divisions, and they were spoiling for action—of the kind that would bring fame and, more important, permanent promotion to general. The roster of aspiring Indian fighters bore such names as Benjamin H. Grierson, Wesley Merritt, George Crook, Eugene A. Carr, Ranald S. Mackenzie, Nelson A. Miles, and George A. Custer.

In 1866 this little regular army flowed westward with national energies liberated at Appomattox Court House. Drawn not only by gold but by homesteads or simply vague hopes of adventure and wealth, both northerners and southerners headed west. The overland trails carried mounting traffic in immigrant wagons, freight caravans, and stagecoaches. Steamboats plied the Missouri River. The rails of the Union Pacific and Kansas

EXILE TO THE EAST

Early in 1875 the government decided upon a tough new tactic to break the resistance of the Plains Indians. The most dangerous and incorrigible warriors would be sent —without benefit of trial—to a prison called Fort Marion, built by the Spanish in St. Augustine, Florida. To determine whom to send, officers at Fort Sill, Oklahoma (below), offered immunity to certain defeated Kiowa, Cheyenne, Comanche, and Arapaho chiefs—if they would name their most hostile fighters. On this basis seventy-two were selected for deportation— some of whom were later found to be Mexican captives.

Chained to wagons, they left Fort Sill under the supervision of Lieutenant Richard Henry Pratt, who was assigned the brutal task in spite of his relatively sympathetic attitude toward the Indians. (Four years later he would found the Carlisle Indian School.) ·

At Fort Sill. authorities ask Indians to identify their war leaders, who were then manacled and imprisoned in the ice house.

Chained to wagons for part of the trip, the prisoners were released at night to bathe as well as they could in their body shackles.

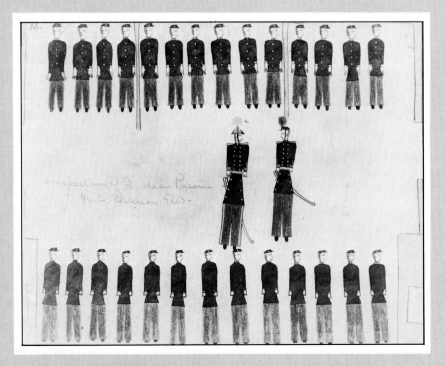

Neat uniforms and polished buttons were required to pass the daily inspections.

On the twenty-four-day journey, by wagon, railroad, steamboat, and finally horse-drawn cart, Pratt made some effort to win over the prisoners. On one such occasion a Cheyenne chief named Grey Beard asked Pratt how he would feel being taken thousands of miles from his home and family in chains. Pratt was speechless, and he admitted in his memoirs that "it was a hard question." As the train neared the Florida border the inconsolable Grey Beard managed to leap off and was shot and killed by guards.

Upon arrival at Fort Marion the prisoners were crowded into humid seventeenth-century dungeons. Several died of malaria, and one starved himself to death. Pratt set out to change the offensive conditions. He had the Indians build a barracks to live in, outfitted them in army uniforms, and held inspection every

Shortly after their arrival at Fort Marion, prisoners were led to the parapet for their first view of the Atlantic Ocean.

day (left, bottom). Job training programs slowly turned former warriors into bakers, fishermen, and field laborers.

Curious tourists thronged to the prison—at Pratt's invitation—to see how well the Indians were doing and to buy the pictures he had encouraged them to paint of their experiences. (All the pictures on these pages were painted at Fort Marion.) Twice Pratt permitted the prisoners, wearing native dress and even a little paint, to perform a variety of tribal dances for paying customers (right, bottom).

After three years at Fort Marion, such notes from the prisoners as "I good boy now" enabled Pratt to convince his superiors that his charges were ready for release. Most chose to rejoin their families on reservations, but a few stayed in the East to begin new lives as laborers.

Visitors paid fifty cents each for reserved seats at this "benefit" war dance.

Pacific advanced up the Platte and Smoky Hill rivers. The Texas frontier, driven back in the war years by Kiowas and Comanches, once more expanded to north and west, and enterprising plainsmen, connecting long-horned Texas steers with eastern beef markets, gave birth to an industry destined to overspread the Great Plains. From Dakota to Texas and from the Missouri to the Pacific the West pulsed with a life that foreshadowed the doom of the Indians. Spurred by the new surge in the westward movement, the wars of concentration continued at quickened pace.

One who watched the postwar developments intently was the Oglala Sioux chief Red Cloud. Not a major chief, he nevertheless possessed notable qualities of leadership, both political and military. His uncompromising attitude toward whites reflected the mood of the Teton Sioux of the Powder River country in 1866. Red Cloud did not like the idea of an immigrant road through the Teton domain. This road, the Bozeman Trail, linked the North Platte River with the Montana mines and was expected to attract heavy use. In June, 1866, Red Cloud and other chiefs rode down to Fort Laramie to talk over the matter with government commissioners.

The government hoped to negotiate a treaty providing for the security of the Bozeman Trail. In the midst of the proceedings, however, an infantry column marched into Fort Laramie. The commander, Colonel Henry B. Carrington, explained that he was en route to the Powder River country to build forts for the protection of the Bozeman Trail. "The Great Father sends us presents and wants us to sell him the road," declared Red Cloud wrathfully, "but White Chief goes with soldiers to steal the road before Indians say Yes or No." A handful of friendly chiefs signed the treaty, but Red Cloud and his associates rode north grimly determined that no white people should use the Bozeman Trail.

Actually, several immigrant parties used the trail that summer as the Indians concentrated on the soldiers, some six hundred strong. Carrington, a scholarly desk officer without combat experience, established three posts, Forts Reno and Phil Kearny in north-central Wyoming and Fort C. F. Smith beside the Bighorn River in southern Montana. Tormented by hit-and-run sorties, he and his men were hard pressed simply to defend themselves and complete the forts.

Among the more effective of Red Cloud's war leaders was a youth named Crazy Horse. Uncharacteristically introspective and modest for a Sioux warrior, slight of build, he combined skill in guerrilla tactics with a fearless personal courage. "Crazy Horse always led his men himself when they went into battle," testified another Oglala war leader named He Dog, "and he kept well in front of them. He headed many charges."

Carrington also counted some skilled combat leaders, hardened veterans of Sherman's Georgia campaigns. But they had no experience in Indian warfare and, contemptuous of the fighting prowess of their adversaries, faulted Carrington for sticking to a defensive strategy. The leader of this coterie of officers was Captain William J. Fetterman, who boasted that with eighty men he could ride through the whole Sioux nation. Equally contemptuous of the colonel was Captain Frederick H. Brown.

The brunt of the Sioux aggressions fell on Fort Phil Kearny, Carrington's headquarters, a bastioned, stockaded work still under construction in December, when the deadly north plains winter set in. Harassing wood trains transporting logs for the fort, the Indians became convinced that their favorite tactic, the decoy, might succeed. To Crazy Horse went the task of organizing it.

On December 21, 1866, a wood train came under attack. Captain Fetterman demanded command of the relief party. Carrington reluctantly acceded but admonished his headstrong subordinate not to cross Lodge Trail Ridge, where he would be out of sight. Riding boldly forth, Fetterman spotted the decoy party sent out by Crazy Horse; promptly Fetterman changed course and disappeared beyond Lodge Trail Ridge. Behind him, with rich irony, followed exactly eighty men.

Within moments the jaws of a lethal trap sprang shut. Between fifteen hundred and two thousand warriors swarmed over the little band of soldiers and took less than an hour to cut down every man. Since no one from Fetterman's command escaped, the details of the slaughter can only be surmised. A relief party, hurrying toward the sound of gunfire, found their bodies, barbarously mutilated, scattered down the reverse slope of Lodge Trail Ridge. Near the crest, side by side, lay Fetterman and Brown. Powder burns hinted that they had shot each other.

Reveling in their triumph, the Indians withdrew to their winter camps while a stunned army cried for revenge. Carrington was transferred, fresh troops took station on the Bozeman Trail, and breech-loading rifles replaced the old muzzle-loaders. Of this latter innovation the Sioux and Cheyennes knew nothing as they plotted massive strikes against the hated forts for the following summer. Their assaults fell on a small party of hay cutters near Fort C. F. Smith and a similar contingent of woodcutters near Fort Phil Kearny. In the Hayfield and Wagon Box fights, August 1 and 2, 1867, the new rifles worked a fearful execution that helped boost morale shattered by the Fetterman disaster. But they did not defeat Red Cloud nor open the Bozeman Trail, which increasingly, as the railroad advanced westward and opened Montana from Utah, seemed not worth fighting over.

Meanwhile, on the central plains the Indians remained quiet until the summer of 1867, when a military expedition set forth to intimidate them. The commander was Major General Winfield Scott Hancock, a handsome, widely admired officer who had gained great distinction on Civil War battlefields. Hancock's principal field officer also bore a proud Civil War record. At the age of only twenty-five, George Armstrong Custer had worn the stars of a major general and commanded a division of cavalry. In battle after battle he had made his mark as a dynamic, dashing, hard-hitting cavalry leader. With long yellow hair and flamboyant uniforms, he attracted wide press attention and gloried in the public adulation it brought. Some saw him as reckless—a brutal disciplinarian but himself undisciplined—and driven by ambition. Others admired or even worshiped him. Now reduced to the peacetime rank of lieutenant colonel in the 7th Cavalry, Custer was about to experience in the Hancock campaign his first taste of Indian warfare.

The campaign was a disaster. At Fort Larned, Kansas, Hancock tried to bully a delegation of chiefs, then, with professions of peace, marched toward a combined Sioux and Cheyenne village nearby. Fearing another Sand Creek, the occupants fled in the night, with Custer's cavalry in futile pursuit. When these Indians or others shot and burned their way northward across the Smoky Hill road, Hancock retaliated by destroying the captured village. All summer these Cheyennes and Sioux struck terror across Kansas, killing, burning, and stealing as Custer tried vainly to bring them to bay. He

CUSTER, GEORGE, *My Life on the Plains.* 1875

Within six months in 1866–67 bands of Sioux wiped out every man in two army detachments. In December, 1866, near Fort Kearny, Wyoming, warriors annihilated Captain William Fetterman and his eighty men (below). The following June near Fort Wallace, Kansas, circling vultures led Lieutenant Colonel Custer to eleven dead and mutilated cavalrymen. The eyewitness drawing at left inspired an unofficial warning to plains soldiers: "Save the last bullet for yourself."

Harper's Weekly, MARCH 23, 1867

Photographed at the Fort Laramie peace talks in 1868. Generals Harney and Sherman are seen above just to the right of the center pole.

fought several inconclusive skirmishes, but the pursuit had so exhausted his regiment as to unfit it for further service. Fighting Indians, the "boy general" discovered, was not the same as fighting Confederates.

The warfare on the Bozeman Trail and in Kansas, especially Hancock's unfortunate campaign, helped stimulate a peace movement that had been gathering in the East since the previous winter. Peace advocates urged a new round of treaties aimed at redressing the grievances of the plains tribes and persuading them to accept reservations north of Nebraska and south of Kansas, thus abandoning altogether the corridor containing the principal transcontinental travel routes. The army's dismal showing on the plains silenced military opposition to this approach, and in fact three generals, including Sherman, were named to the peace commission created by Congress in July, 1867.

The commissioners negotiated two sets of treaties, one at Medicine Lodge Creek, Kansas, in the autumn of 1867 and one at Fort Laramie in the spring of 1868. The Fort Laramie treaties ended the Red Cloud War on Red Cloud's terms. The Bozeman Trail forts were formally abandoned, the Powder River country designated "unceded Indian territory," and all of present-day South Dakota west of the Missouri River set aside as the Great Sioux Reservation. The Medicine Lodge treaties established two large reservations in Indian Territory (present-day Oklahoma), one designated for the Cheyennes and Arapahos, the other for the Kiowas, Comanches, and Kiowa-Apaches. On all the reservations the Indians would receive clothing and other presents while supporting themselves by agriculture. Although

The great Sioux chief Red Cloud, seen at left, proved himself as tough negotiating in peace councils as he had been fighting the U.S. Army. He refused to attend the talks at Fort Laramie until the "posts in the Powder River country are abandoned by the troops." Only after all his conditions were met did Red Cloud sign the treaty.

they were not provided by treaty, Congress recognized that rations would be needed during the time the nomadic hunters were turning themselves into sedentary farmers.

By persuasion rather than force, then, the plains tribes had been induced to accept concentration—or had they? As usual, they did not understand very clearly what they had signed, and anyway, even with the best intentions, they could not so quickly and lightly surrender the attitudes and customs of generations. As became almost instantly apparent, it was one thing to negotiate a treaty, another to carry it out.

Government authorities discovered the same truth in renewed attempts to concentrate the Apaches of the Southwest. Year after year hostilities dragged on as the Apache problem stubbornly defied either military or diplomatic solution. The escaped Mescaleros were out raiding again. Cochise's Chiricahuas had never stopped. New Mexico flared with guerilla action, and in Arizona the hard-pressed citizens viewed their Indian afflictions as curable only by extermination.

An atrocity reminiscent of Sand Creek dramatized the intensity of white hatreds. At the desert outpost of Camp Grant was established one of several feeding stations where Apaches professing peace could find safety and nourishment. Chief Eskiminzin and his people settled there and cemented a mutually trusting relationship with the post commander, Lieutenant Royal E. Whitman. Outraged Tucson citizens, sure that continuing raids originated at Camp Grant (they probably did not), resolved on direct measures. At daybreak on April 30, 1871, a force of 148 Papago Indians, Mexicans, and whites burst on the sleeping camp of 500 Apaches, butchered between 86 and 150 men, women, and children (the number is disputed), mutilated their bodies, raped surviving women, and carried 29 children into slavery. Hastening to the scene, Lieutenant Whitman found little use for his wagon-load of medicine. "The work had been too thoroughly done," he wrote. He saw the ground littered with dead women and children. "Those who had been wounded in the first instance had their brains beaten out with stones." Bodies were shockingly mutilated. "One infant of some ten months was shot twice and one leg nearly hacked off." Others wounded by gunshot had then been shot full of arrows.

The expedition's leader later called April 30, 1871, that "memorable and glorious morning . . . when swift punishment was dealt out to these red-handed butchers." But in the East a horrified public demanded that President Grant take action against such excesses. His response was to dispatch peace emissaries to Arizona to lay out a reservation system for the Apaches.

The President's agents were Vincent Colyer and General Oliver O. Howard. Colyer—"Vincent the Good," Arizona editors derisively tagged him—was a member of one of the Indian reform groups springing up throughout the East. Howard, another Civil War hero (he had lost his right arm during the Peninsular campaign), was also widely known as a worker in humanitarian causes. As head of the Freedmen's Bureau and founder of Howard University, the so-called Christian General had helped care for former slaves. Now he turned to Indians. In Arizona Howard found George Crook the new military commander, recently assigned after brilliant successes in Idaho and Oregon. Crook regarded Howard as a Bible-spouting visionary and wrote of him: "He told me he thought the Creator had placed him on earth to be the Moses of the Negro. Having accomplished that mis-

"I GOT INTERESTED"

"He knew the Indian better than the Indian did," one aide said of the officer in command of army forces in Oregon between 1866 and 1870. Indeed, George Crook could hunt, ride, or shoot as well as any Indian.

Furthermore, he had ideas about Indian warfare that set him apart from his contemporaries and made him the most successful field commander of all the army's frontier leaders. He used Indians to fight Indians, hauled his supplies on mules—rather than wagons—for mobility, and then used that mobility to pursue his foe until victory was complete. Once the fighting had ended, he treated the Indian with firm authoritarianism coupled with justice and humanity.

Crook took command of Fort Boise in December, 1866, and within the week was off fighting Paiutes. "I left with one change of underclothes, toothbrush, etc. and went to investigate matters, intending to be gone a week. But I got interested after the Indians and did not return there for over two years."

Thereafter, winter and summer, the Paiutes found nowhere in Oregon or Idaho safe from Crook's forces. In some 40 skirmishes, 329 Paiutes were killed and 225 captured. By mid-1868 the tribe had had enough and asked for peace. The surrender took place at Camp Harney, Oregon, on July 1.

Some 800 Paiutes formed a huge semicircle on the parade ground as Crook and Old Weawea, the Paiute chief, faced each other. Weawea explained that his people wanted peace. "I am sorry to hear this," replied Crook, as his aide recorded the conversation. "I was in hopes that you would continue the war,

George Crook early in the 1880's

and then, though I were to kill only one of your warriors while you killed a hundred of my men, you would have to wait for those little people [the children] to grow to fill the place of your braves, while I can get any number of soldiers the next day to fill the place of my hundred men. In this way it would not be very long before we would have you all killed off, and then the government would have no more trouble with you."

Having given this excellent reason why the Paiutes should keep the agreement, Crook of course granted peace. When the time came in the spring of 1871 to choose a new department commander to fight the Apaches in Arizona, his superiors passed over forty colonels in line for the job and gave it to Crook.

sion, he felt satisfied his next mission was with the Indian."

Despite the fulminations of citizens and Crook's scarcely concealed disgust, Colyer and Howard marked out four reservations in Arizona and one in New Mexico. Only Cochise and his Chiricahuas eluded their efforts, but Howard felt this failure keenly. Finally, in the autumn of 1872, he found a way to reach Cochise — through a canny frontiersman named Thomas J. Jeffords, who enjoyed a personal friendship with the fighting chief. Jeffords agreed to help if no soldiers went along.

Accompanied only by an aide and two Chiricahuas, Howard followed Jeffords in a search that led ultimately to a remote valley of the Dragoon Mountains. There, as Indians gathered to watch, the white general sat facing the now-legendary red general. For almost two weeks they negotiated, Howard urging a reservation on the Rio Grande, Cochise arguing that his people would never leave their Arizona homeland. "Why not give me Apache Pass?" he asked. "Give me that and I will protect all the roads. I will see that nobody's property is taken by Indians." Finding both Cochise and his headmen adamant, Howard at last acquiesced, with still another concession thrown in: Tom Jeffords would be their agent. Thus the trail of blood and destruction on which Cochise had embarked almost twelve years earlier seemed on the verge of ending, and at the very place where it had begun, Apache Pass.

The Colyer-Howard reservations did not bring peace. Cochise kept his word, but many of the five thousand Indians who drew rations at the other agencies were not so discriminating. A furious citizenry demanded that Crook be turned loose. He was, in an offensive launched in November, 1872.

It focused on the Tonto Basin, a wild tangle of mountains and canyons in the shadow of the Mogollon Rim. Into this forbidding wilderness Crook sent small, highly mobile strike forces aided by Indian auxiliaries. "No excuse was to be accepted for leaving a trail," his aide later wrote; "if horses played out, the enemy must be followed on foot." The strategy worked. Throughout the winter nine. commands swept the Tonto Basin and its neighboring mountain ranges. The officers took Crook at his word and never gave up on a trail. In twenty actions their troopers closed with the quarry every time and killed some two hundred.

For the Indians, more demoralizing than the combat was the constant insecurity. As one chief explained after surrendering, his people "could not go to sleep at night, because they feared to be surrounded before daybreak; they could not hunt — the noise of their guns would attract the troops; they could not cook mescal or anything else, because the flame and smoke would draw down the soldiers; they could not live in the valley — there were too many soldiers; they had retreated to the mountain tops, thinking to hide in the snow until the soldiers went home, but the [Indian] scouts found them out and the soldiers followed them."

Such a mountaintop action, Turret Peak, on March 27, 1873, proved climactic. Within a month Apaches had begun to surrender to the unrelenting soldier chief with the forked beard. By autumn about six thousand had been enrolled on the reservations, and Arizona enjoyed a peace unknown since the advent of the Americans. In the Southwest George Crook was the hero of the hour. Whites and Indians alike looked upon him with awe, and President Grant, passing over all the colonels in the army, promoted him from lieutenant colonel to brigadier general of regulars.

Warriors on the Dole

The decade of the sixties marked the beginning of a long trail of humiliation for the tribesmen of the plains and the Southwest. For the first time large numbers of western Indians consented to give up their home grounds and live on reservations. The mass confinement began in 1864, when 8,000 Navahos were herded onto barren bottom land at Bosque Redondo to subsist on government handouts and whatever they could scrabble from the soil. Here the first of the Navahos huddle under a guard's rifle awaiting a head count.
NATIONAL ARCHIVES

Apache women shoulder allotments of mesquite and cottonwood sticks for fuel.

Indians bring hay that they will sell to cavalrymen for a penny a bundle.

One of the most notorious reservations was San Carlos, 5,000 acres of Arizona desert. An army officer assigned there described it thus: "Dry, hot, dust-and-gravel-laden winds swept the plain. In summer a temperature of 110 in the shade was cool weather." At San Carlos eight different bands of mutually hostile Apaches had to line up for rations of virtually everything they needed to live. Worst of all, they were not permitted to go home, a fact that no warrior could understand or endure. "Why do you ask us to leave the rivers, the sun, and the wind, and live in houses?" demanded one Comanche under pressure to move his people to a similar reservation. "Do not ask us to give up the buffalo for the sheep. The young men have heard talk of this, and it has made them sad and angry." It did indeed, and thousands would pay with their lives.

No longer able to hunt wild animals for skins, Apaches receive cloth to make their garments.

A quartet of hungry warriors butchers their ration of scrawny and sun-baked horsemeat.

Weary, demoralized Sioux squat under their blankets
on ration day at Pine Ridge Reservation, South Dakota.
Theoretically, reservation Indians were to be well fed
while they made the transition from nomadic hunters
to sedentary farmers. Actually, the warriors despised
farming and subsistence chores. As for the food, an
army surgeon observing a meal related, "Some of the
Indians refused to eat it, saying it made them sick.
. . . The Indians reported several deaths from starvation."

9: Fire on the Plains

Black Kettle and Tall Bull represented the extremes of Cheyenne opinion. One perceptive observer judged Black Kettle the only Cheyenne chief who truly grasped the forces shaping the destinies of his people. Even Sand Creek no more than momentarily shook his dedication to the ways of peace. When he seemed to waver, it was as often because of pressures from the tribe's war faction as from inner conviction.

Tall Bull was a vocal spokesman for war. He, Bull Bear, and White Horse were chiefs of the Dog Soldiers, a separate band of some five hundred people renowned for producing superb warriors who performed stirring deeds in combat. All three had signed the Medicine Lodge treaty, but that act did not convert them into peace chiefs. Though Black Kettle was ready to go to the new reservation in Indian Territory, Tall Bull and his Dog Soldiers did not seriously intend to give up their free life on the rich buffalo ranges of the upper Republican and Smoky Hill rivers. Tall Bull was, as General Custer noted, "a fine, warlike looking chieftain," and nothing in his makeup fitted him for reservation life.

Both the war and peace chiefs among the Cheyennes had a nagging common grievance. The peace commissioners had promised them guns and am-

A Sioux war party attacks a passenger train out of Omaha in this engraving from an 1870 newspaper. Western Indians recognized the threat from the "big wagons that go on metal roads"; the Sioux and Cheyennes, particularly, fought hard to keep the railroads out of their lands.

munition for hunting purposes. Because Tall Bull had led a raid on a Kaw village, however, the Indian Bureau now declined to issue them. The Cheyennes blustered so threateningly that the officials hastily reversed themselves and on August 9, at Fort Larned, gave out the arms. But a party of two hundred warriors that had set out a few days earlier to raid the Pawnees knew nothing of this. In their anger at the government they forgot the Pawnees and instead struck the settlements on the Saline and Solomon rivers, killed fifteen men, raped five women, burned ranches, and ran off stock.

The raid exposed the shakiness of the Medicine Lodge treaties, polarized the war and peace elements among not only the Cheyennes but also the Arapahos — and set off another Indian war. Frightened, the peace factions hurried south of the Arkansas toward the new reservation while the Dog Soldiers and other militants, in scenes reminiscent of the previous summer, ripped through western Kansas and eastern Colorado.

In the opinion of General Sheridan, Hancock's successor as department commander, the solution to all these Indian problems was one deadly winter campaign. While preparing for it, he sent columns into the field to try to keep the hostiles away from the settlements and travel routes. One of these forces was a company of fifty experienced plainsmen specially recruited by Major George A. Forsyth, one of Sheridan's staff officers. On September 17, 1868, patrolling in western Kansas, the company ran into six to seven hundred Dog Soldiers and southern Oglala Sioux. Hastily the whites dug in on an island in the nearly dry bed of the Arikara Fork of the Republican River, just over the state line in Colorado. Twice deadly fire from their repeating carbines broke up masses of warriors charging on horseback.

Among the Indians was one of the most renowned Cheyenne war leaders, Roman Nose. He did not ride in the first two charges because he had just learned that he had recently broken his protective medicine by eating bread touched by a metal fork. But now, goaded by the taunts of a fellow Cheyenne with the ironic name of White Contrary, Roman Nose decided to enter the fight even though he was certain it meant death. Tall Bull protested, urging that he should at least take time for a purification ceremony. But Roman Nose refused, and in the next charge, the Indians' third and final one, a bullet smashed into his chest and killed him.

Abandoning direct assaults, the warriors placed the island under siege. With half the company dead or wounded, all the horses shot, food and water in short supply, and Forsyth himself badly wounded, the defenders' prospects appeared grim. For a week they were forced to eat their dead horses and dig in the sand for water. Meanwhile two messengers managed to slip through the Indian lines. They made it ninety miles to Fort Wallace, and on the eighth day, with Forsyth's men and ammunition near total exhaustion, a relief column drove off the Indians. The action had been of little consequence, but white men glorified their stand-off as the Battle of Beecher's Island — in honor of the slain Lieutenant Frederick Beecher, nephew of cleric Henry Ward Beecher. Indians always remembered it as the Fight When Roman Nose Was Killed.

Throughout the summer Sheridan refined his overall plan. It called for three columns to converge on the valleys of the Canadian and Washita rivers, in western Indian Territory, where the Indians were known to have established their winter camps. One column would march east from Fort Bascom, New Mexico, one southeast from Fort Lyon, Colorado, and the third and largest south from Fort Dodge, Kansas. Sheridan showed his faith in his Civil War lieutenant and special favorite, George A. Custer, by giving him command of the Fort Dodge column.

Custer promptly justified Sheridan's confidence. From the newly established base of Camp Supply, he pushed south in a punishing march across a frozen, snow-covered land and located a Cheyenne camp in the Washita valley. Shortly before daybreak of November 27, 1868, he deployed the 7th Cavalry on four sides of the sleeping village. Captain Albert Barnitz, advancing with one of the attack forces, recalled: "We had just reached the edge of a shallow ravine beyond which we could see the clustered tepees, situated among wide-branching cottonwood trees, when a shot was fired in the village, and instantly we heard the band on the ridge beyond it strike up the familiar air 'Garry Owen' and the answering cheers of the men, as Custer, and his legion came thundering down the long divide, while nearer at hand on our right came Benteen's squadron, crashing through the frozen snow, as the troops deployed into line at a gallop, and the Indian village rang with unearthly war-whoops, the quick discharge of fire-arms, the clamorous barking of dogs, the cries of infants and the wailing of women."

The charging troopers shot down startled Indians emerging from their tepees and quickly seized the village. It turned out to be but one of several in the Washita valley, and the troops soon found themselves under counterattack by growing numbers of warriors. Custer held his position through the day while his men slaughtered almost nine hundred captured ponies and put the tepees with all their contents to the torch. At dusk he mounted the regiment and with banners flying and band playing feinted boldly toward the downstream camps, causing his assailants to draw off in their defense. Then he slipped out of the valley as nightfall concealed his movement. Custer's casualty count showed five troopers killed (including Captain Louis M. Hamilton, grandson of Alexander Hamilton) and fourteen wounded. But he had also ridden from the field without searching for fifteen missing cavalrymen under Major Joel H. Elliott. Their bodies were later found where they had been cut off and wiped out.

It also turned out that the village had belonged to the ill-starred Black Kettle. Bullets cut down the chief and his wife as, mounted double on a pony, they tried to escape the slashing cavalry attack. Critics of the army promptly called the Washita another Sand Creek and Custer another Chivington. Army officers replied that however much Black Kettle himself wanted peace, his village yielded ample evidence of the raids of his warriors in the Kansas settlements and in fact contained four white prisoners, two of whom were killed by their captors as the cavalry attacked.

Whatever its other failures, the Battle of the Washita seemed to demonstrate the soundness of Sheridan's winter strategy. So did the Battle of Soldier Spring, in which, on Christmas Day of 1868, Major Andrew W. Evans's New Mexico column attacked a Comanche camp on the north fork of the Red River. But all three columns found the plains winter difficult to cope with. Sheridan and Custer marched to the Fort Cobb agency, then nearby erected a new post, Fort Sill, as a base for further operations. Rain and mud slowed the stockpiling of supplies and immobilized Custer for more than two months. By then Evans's column and Major Eugene A. Carr's column, out of Fort Lyon, had been driven to their bases by winter storms. Winter had been hard on the Indians too. Most of the Kiowas, Comanches,

Trapped on an island (later named Beecher) in the Republican River. Major George Forsyth and his men fend off Roman Nose's Cheyennes.

and Arapahos had gathered near Fort Sill to receive the rations promised to Indians who would declare for peace.

The Cheyennes held out, and early in March, 1869, Custer set forth against them. They had moved west almost to the foot of the Staked Plain in the Texas Panhandle. There on March 15 he found the villages of Medicine Arrows and Little Robe, some 260 lodges, laid out on Sweetwater Creek. Two white women were known to be captives of the Indians, so instead of attacking Custer parleyed. During the talks he suddenly seized four chiefs as hostages and sent one back as a messenger with his terms. After three days of mounting tension he ostentatiously prepared to hang the remaining three chiefs unless the women were set free at once. The threat worked. The captives were released. Moreover, disheartened by the success of the soldiers in running them down, the Cheyennes promised to go to their reservation and surrender. Custer could not tarry to make sure. His command was exhausted and largely afoot, since horses and mules had been dying by the hundreds from fatigue and starvation. With hostages to insure that the Cheyennes kept their word, he pushed north to Camp Supply.

The surrender on the Sweetwater had again divided the Cheyennes. Most were sincere in their promise to go to the reservation. The Dog Soldiers, however, returned to their favorite haunts in western Kansas. None remained more adamantly hostile than Tall Bull. By midsummer he had resolved to join the Northern Cheyennes in the Powder River country. En route there with eighty-four lodges he camped at Summit Springs, a watering place amid the sand hills of northeastern Colorado.

On July 11, 1869, a command of the 5th Cavalry under Major Carr found the camp. Carr had with him a contingent of Pawnee Indian scouts led by Major Frank North and one young white scout whose skill as marksman and plainsman had endeared him to the 5th. His name was William F. Cody, but already he was known as Buffalo Bill. In a surprise attack Carr's troopers and the whooping Pawnees crashed into the village and quickly routed the inhabitants. With about twenty people Tall Bull took refuge in a ravine, shot his horse at its mouth to signify that there he would die, and fought desperately to the last.

Summit Springs proved an important victory. It flushed the Dog Soldiers out of western Kansas for good and prompted the rest of the Cheyennes, who had been procrastinating since their surrender to Custer in March, to straggle into the agency established for them in Indian Territory. A major goal of the Medicine Lodge treaties had at last been attained. The belt of territory containing the Arkansas, Smoky Hill, and Platte roads and the Union Pacific and Kansas Pacific railroads had been cleared of Indians. In addition, the leading peace chief and the leading war chief of the Cheyennes were dead, slain by soldier bullets in surprise attacks on their camps, and the daredevil Custer had won acclaim as a brilliant Indian fighter.

A week before his inauguration in 1869, President-elect Grant told a newspaper reporter that the new administration planned a fresh and fair Indian policy. "All Indians disposed to peace will find the new policy a peace-policy," said Grant. For Indians undisposed to peace, he added in a caveat drowned in the public acclaim for the Peace Policy, there would be "a sharp and severe war policy." On their reservations the Indians would be educated, Christianized, taught to support themselves by farming, and given rations, clothing, and other goods to ease the transition. There too

A Mathew Brady photograph of George Armstrong Custer about 1865

A RECKLESS BOY

Young, blond, wildly energetic, George Armstrong Custer cut a dashing figure among the soldiers sent west to fight Indians at the close of the Civil War. General George B. McClellan, Custer's commanding officer early in the Civil War, described him as "a reckless, gallant boy, undeterred by fatigue, unconscious of fear . . . he always brought me clear and intelligible reports of what he saw under the heaviest fire. I became much attached to him." General Sherman found Custer "very brave, even to rashness, a good trait for a cavalry officer," but he added that the man lacked sense. Custer seems to have been hotheaded even when not acting the officer—his wife related that he often broke furniture out of irrepressible happiness at good news. And once, when Custer was enthusiastically hunting a buffalo,

he managed to shoot his own mount.

Custer's military training began at West Point, where he graduated in 1861, thirty-fourth in a class of thirty-four. Two years later, in the heat of the Civil War, the twenty-three-year-old lieutenant was promoted directly to brigadier general after a series of successful charges, most spectacularly at the Battle of Aldie in northern Virginia.

At the conclusion of the war, the boy general considered going into politics but decided instead to join the 7th Cavalry at Fort Riley in Kansas. Less than six months after his first assignment, the Civil War hero's luck began to run out.

In the spring of 1867 Custer was ordered to make war on hostile Indians near the Republican River. In his overzealous determination to get the job done, he ordered long forced marches, not even stopping for

water. Many of his men were more interested in paychecks than promotion or glory. Whenever their route passed near the road to the Colorado mines, they deserted a few at a time. One day fifteen tried to slip away during a midday break. A furious Custer ordered pursuit, demanding that none be brought back alive. Five of the fifteen were captured, and though none was dead, one later died of his wounds.

The next day Custer pushed the regiment to Fort Wallace, then set off with 100 men for Fort Hays, where he hoped to find supplies. In all, he marched the troops 150 miles in 60 hours with only 6 hours rest. Two exhausted stragglers who fell behind the column were killed by Indians. When Custer found supplies lacking at Fort Hays, he pushed on to Fort Harkner. There, leaving his men to load supplies, he jumped on a train to visit his wife.

Ten days later Custer was placed under arrest, charged with leaving his regiment without orders, shooting deserters, abandoning the two men who had been killed by Indians, and marching his troops beyond their endurance. At his court-martial, Custer attempted to justify his actions as necessary to the safety of his remaining troops. He explained his unauthorized visit to his wife by saying that General Sherman had given him permission to go anywhere he liked, "to Denver City or hell if he wanted." Custer's arguments proved unconvincing: he was convicted on all counts and suspended from duty for one year.

Custer did his best to gloss over his disgrace, writing in his memoirs, "I established my base of operations in a beautiful little town on the Western shores of Lake Erie, from which I projected various hunting, fishing, and boating expeditions." Within ten months the unrepentant soldier's continued high opinion of himself was confirmed by a telegram from General Sheridan. Sheridan wired that he could not fight Indians without him and appealed to Custer to return to the field. Elated, Custer boarded the next train—for a journey that would end eight years later at Little Bighorn.

After a dawn raid on a Cheyenne camp near the Washita River in present-day Oklahoma, Custer rounded up some fifty women and children for a forced march (above) to Camp Supply on the Canadian River, where they were welcomed with a formal review.

they would be safe from the army. But if any felt the pull of old habits and strayed off the reservation, they could expect to be treated as hostiles.

On the theory that good Christian men would make good Indian agents, the President turned to the country's religious leaders for help in carrying out the Peace Policy. This idea had been advanced by the Society of Friends, or Quakers, whose pacifism dovetailed with the basic tenet of the Peace Policy — "conquest by kindness." "Give me the names of some Friends for Indian agents," he told a Quaker delegation, "and I will appoint them. If you can make Quakers out of the Indians it will take the fight out of them. Let us have peace."

Inspired by the call for peace, a big-framed, baldheaded Iowa farmer named Lawrie Tatum went to Fort Sill, headquarters of the Kiowa-Comanche reservation in Indian Territory. Endowed with iron rectitude and staunch faith in his church, Tatum was an honest, steadfast administrator with a good measure of common sense. His agency became a major testing ground for the Peace Policy — and also for Tatum, who was to discover that controlling untamed Indians, much less transforming them into imitation whites, required more than the recitation of Christian principles.

For the Kiowas and Comanches, raids into Texas and Mexico were still a way of life, and they saw no reason to change their habits merely because they lived on a reservation. Now, in fact, they could continue the practice while also receiving the government's bounty and even its protection under Bald Head Agent, as they called Tatum. Texans branded the Fort Sill reservation a "city of refuge" and loudly protested a policy that made them repeated victims of the "bloody Quaker pets."

Foremost among the sanctuaried raiders was the Kiowa chief Satanta. Mercurial, boastful, and arrogant, with a big chest and powerful voice, he lived in a bright red tepee and reveled in the justly earned title "Orator of the Plains." "I love to roam the wide prairie," he had told the commissioners at Medicine Lodge, "and when I do it, I feel free and happy, but when we settle down, we grow pale and die." Such an autonomous personality, Tatum gradually concluded in contradiction both to the Peace Policy and his own religion, could be tamed only by force.

Across the border in Texas a new commander at Fort Richardson shared that conviction. Like Custer a war hero and brevet general of volunteers while still in his twenties, Colonel Ranald S. Mackenzie commanded the 4th Cavalry with a diligence and discipline that made it the best of all the cavalry regiments. Intense, nervous, short-tempered — his career would end in insanity — Mackenzie nevertheless won the loyalty and energetic support of his men. The troopers of the 4th vigorously patrolled and defended the Texas frontier. But their pursuit of hostiles had to end at the Red River, the boundary of the Fort Sill sanctuary.

An incident in May, 1871, momentarily invoked the force Texans demanded. Raiding in Texas, Satanta and others set up an ambush on Salt Creek Prairie, near Fort Richardson. A small train was allowed to pass in safety because the medicine man foretold a larger one to come. He was right, and later in the day a caravan of ten wagons manned by twelve teamsters fell into the trap. The party that had escaped so narrowly was a visiting military inspection team headed by none other than General William Tecumseh Sherman. When he learned of the Salt Creek massacre, Sherman put Mackenzie on the trail of the raiders with orders to enter the reservation if the Indians indeed headed that way. Then the general himself grimly set out for Fort Sill.

There Sherman found Tatum shaken by the insolence and turbulence of his charges. When less than a week after Sherman's arrival a small delegation of chiefs arrived at the fort to pick up their rations, Tatum asked them if they knew anything about the Salt Creek massacre. Satanta at once spoke up. "Yes, I led in that raid," he boasted. "If any other Indian claims the honor of leading that party he will be lying to you. I led it myself." Furthermore, he declared, he wanted arms and ammunition to conduct more raids in Texas. Old Chief Satank agreed, as did the young Big Tree, both of whom had been there too. This was too much for Tatum. However contrary to the precepts of his church, he thought that "forebearance in the case would not be a virtue but a crime," and he conspired with Sherman and the post commander, Colonel Benjamin H. Grierson, to arrest the culprits for "murder in the first degree."

The leading Kiowa chiefs assembled on the front porch of Colonel Grierson's quarters to meet the big soldier chief from Washington. Among them were Lone Wolf and Kicking Bird, chiefs respectively of the tribe's war and peace factions, Satanta, Satank, Stumbling Bear, and others. Again Satanta boasted of his deed. Curtly Sherman declared that he, Satank, and Big Tree were under arrest and would be taken to Texas to stand trial for murder. Satanta threw back his blanket and grasped his pistol. Sherman barked a command and the window shutters flew open to uncover a squad of black cavalrymen with carbines trained on the Indians. Tensely the talks proceeded. Suddenly Stumbling Bear fitted an arrow to his bow and let fly at Sherman, but a soldier deflected his aim. At the same time Lone Wolf shouldered his carbine and pointed it at Sherman. Grierson grabbed the weapon and the two sprawled on the floor.

The white general had his way, and the three Indians found themselves shackled and confined. When Colonel Mackenzie arrived after a fruitless pursuit across the reservation, he had them loaded in wagons and, under heavy escort, started down the road to Texas. As the column pulled out, Satank began to sing his death song. Under his blanket, tearing the flesh from his wrists, he stripped off his handcuffs. With a small penknife that had escaped discovery, he suddenly stabbed one of his guards in the leg. From the wagon behind, which carried Satanta and Big Tree, Corporal John B. Charlton stood up and fired two shots into Satank's chest. His body was left beside the road, to be reclaimed by a detail from Fort Sill.

Although a Texas state court convicted Satanta and Big Tree of murder and sentenced them to die, the sudden application of force did not, as it seemed, signal an abandonment of the Peace Policy. Tatum's Quaker superiors disapproved of his action and grew increasingly critical of his tendency to look to the army for help in controlling the reservation. Humanitarian groups and federal Indian officials lamented his resort to force. They induced the governor of Texas to commute the sentence of the two Kiowas to imprisonment and later, in 1873, to free them to return to their people. His position thus undermined—and to the genuine regret of many Kiowas and Comanches—Bald Head Agent resigned, to be replaced by an agent less inclined to stray from the paths of nonviolence.

The release of Satanta and Big Tree did not, as its advocates had hoped, buy security for the Texas frontier. Kiowa and Comanche raiders continued

Kiowa Chief Satanta

Kiowa Chief Satank

to drive deep into Texas and across the Rio Grande into Mexico. A chain of forts intended to enclose the Texas frontier from the Red River to the Rio Grande proved inadequate to protect the settlements.

Nor did conditions on either the Kiowa-Comanche or the neighboring Cheyenne-Arapaho reservation encourage the Indians to cooperate in the civilization programs. Rations and clothing were insufficient and not to their liking anyway. Farmers, schoolteachers, and missionaries tried to hurry them into a way of life that held no appeal. And west of the reservations white hunters slaughtered buffalo by the millions for their hides and tongues alone. If the extinction of the buffalo did not decree the extinction of the Plains Indians, it decreed the extinction of their old way of life. The buffalo hunters aroused their fury, and Cheyennes began to join with Kiowas and Comanches in the raids on white settlements.

By 1874 the southern plains verged once more on a full-scale Indian war. On June 27, at a makeshift village in the Texas Panhandle called Adobe Walls, twenty-eight buffalo hunters with high-powered rifles withstood an all-day attack by seven hundred Comanche and Cheyenne warriors, who then turned in fury and revenge on the Kansas travel routes as well as the Texas frontier. Men, women, and children were tortured, slain, or taken captive. The reservations themselves seethed with intrigue and violence. No longer could Indian Bureau officials defend the policy that stopped the army at the reservation boundaries. On July 20, 1874, General Sheridan received authority to make war on hostile Indians wherever they were to be found.

Alarmed at the obvious stiffening by the military, the war elements on both reservations pulled out and fled westward to the Texas Panhandle,

Kiowa Indian agent Lawrie Tatum, a Quaker, was a hero to these Mexican boys he rescued from reservation renegades. Although Tatum refused to pay ransom, he managed to achieve the release of 26 captives by such threats as withholding rations. After four years Tatum was thoroughly disillusioned by the unchangeable warlike nature of the Kiowas and resigned in 1873.

where they scattered in bands of varying size. Altogether there were almost four thousand people, including about twelve hundred fighting men. The roster of chiefs bore most of the big names of the southern plains—Medicine Arrows, Bull Bear, Grey Beard, Stone Calf, and Medicine Water of the Cheyennes; Lone Wolf, Satanta, Big Tree, Woman's Heart, and Mamanti of the Kiowas; Wild Horse, Mow-way, Tabananaka, Black Beard, and White Horse of the Comanches.

Sheridan and his principal subordinates, Generals John Pope and Christopher C. Augur, worked out a plan of convergence such as had been employed in the Washita campaign of 1868–69. Against the target area—the Staked Plain and the bordering breaks giving rise to the Washita and Red rivers—Sheridan launched two columns from Fort Sill and one each from Texas, New Mexico, and Kansas. The hard-driving Mackenzie headed the Texas column. The ambitious Colonel Nelson A. Miles, just embarking on a formidable Indian-fighting career, led the Kansas column.

Both soldiers and Indians suffered acutely from severe weather. Through August and early September a drought of furnace intensity punished them with temperatures as high as 110 degrees, dried the water holes, and withered grass that clouds of locusts then stripped to the roots. Drenching September storms brought plunging temperatures, roiling streams, and a prairie everywhere turned to mud. This period of storms the constantly retreating Indians remembered as the time of the "Wrinkled-Hand Chase." Winter followed with hammering northers, subzero temperatures, snow and ice, and bitter, driving winds.

Against these extremes the two sides maneuvered strenuously; neither side did much killing, but the combination of constant pressure from the army and the unrelenting adversity of the weather was disastrous for the Indians. The key action took place on September 28, when Mackenzie fell on a combined village of Kiowas, Comanches, and Cheyennes in Palo Duro Canyon. He killed only three Indians but dealt a crushing blow by destroying the camp and all its contents and seizing the herd of almost fifteen hundred ponies, most of which he killed in order to prevent their recapture.

Discouraged, destitute, and hungry, the first Indians to surrender started coming into the agencies in October. In small parties they straggled in throughout the winter. Most of the military forces returned to their bases before Christmas, but Miles stayed out, his infantrymen lustily singing "Marching through Georgia" as they tramped across the icy plains.

Their perseverance paid off. By April, 1875, the last of the Indians had surrendered. Even the proud Kwahadi Comanches, who had never signed a treaty or lived on a reservation, came in from the far reaches of the Staked Plain. With them was a young warrior of growing influence destined to be the leading Comanche chief in the difficult years ahead—Quanah Parker, son of a chief and a white wife seized in childhood in a Texas raid.

The Red River War ended hostilities on the southern plains for all time. At last the Kansas travel routes, the Texas frontier, and the remote villages of Mexico knew security from Cheyenne, Kiowa, and Comanche raiders. The Indians settled unhappily on their reservations to live as best they could with the strange system the white officials had worked out for them.

The conquest was decisive in large part because General Sheridan made certain the war leaders did not remain with their people to foment trouble again. Seventy-four so-called ringleaders were hauled off to the old Spanish fortress of Castillo de San Marcos at St. Augustine, Florida, and Satanta was returned to the Texas penitentiary. Ultimately some of the Florida prisoners were moved to Pennsylvania, where they formed the founding cadre for the famed Carlisle Indian School. By contrast, in 1878 a despairing Satanta jumped from a prison window to his death.

On the northern plains it appeared that the warrior tribes had fared much better. In the Fort Laramie treaty following Red Cloud's war, the government had agreed to abandon the Bozeman Trail and its guardian forts and to look upon the Powder River country as "unceded Indian territory" in which the Sioux might continue to roam. But there were some subtleties in the treaty that escaped the Indians. A reservation was created adjacent to the unceded territory, and the right to hunt outside the reserve existed only "so long as the buffalo may range thereon in such numbers as to justify the chase." Whether they knew it or not, the Sioux had agreed to concentration.

Some, with their Cheyenne and Arapaho friends, went at once to the Sioux reservation to accept government dole and acquiesce—though without enthusiasm—in government civilization programs. Others, scorning the reservation and all its trappings, remained in the unceded territory. Still others sampled both worlds, drawing rations on the reservation in the winter and riding with the hunting bands in the summer.

After Red Cloud "touched the pen" at Fort Laramie, he abruptly gave up the warpath and even, strangely, the free life of the hunting bands in the country for which he had so successfully fought. He and Spotted Tail of the Brûlés became the principal leaders of the reservation Sioux. But neither became a compliant tool of the government. Neither would go to one of the agencies established on the Missouri River, as the treaty negotiators intended. In 1873 the two chiefs finally accepted agencies on the upper White River, south of the reservation line in Nebraska and remote from military surveillance.

The Red Cloud and Spotted Tail agencies were wild places in the middle 1870's, with the two chiefs locked in a contest of wills with their agents, mediating the quarrels of their followers, and trying to restrain the unruly young men who came down from the unceded country. Even after the founding nearby of Camps Robinson and Sheridan in 1874, the two agencies verged constantly on anarchy and violence.

Meanwhile, shrinking in winter, swelling in summer, the hunting bands drifted about the unceded country following the buffalo as they had always done. They were largely Oglalas, Hunkpapas, Miniconjous, and Northern Cheyennes, although all the Teton tribes claimed some representation, as did the Yanktonais and Santee Sioux. There were never as many of these free spirits as white officials thought, probably no more than three thousand people in about four or five hundred lodges.

Among the Oglala hunters Crazy Horse emerged as the most powerful chief. Since his triumph in the Fetterman massacre, he had grown in stature as an uncommonly able warrior and uncompromising foe of reservations.

Towering above all the other hunting chiefs, however, was Sitting Bull of the Hunkpapas. About forty years old early in the 1870's, he was broad-shouldered and lithe of body, a skilled fighter despite a pronounced limp caused by a Crow bullet through his foot. Thin lips and steely eyes suggested the sharp, canny mind that lay behind. Thick black hair wreathed a

The tempo of the buffalo slaughter quickened in 1871, when buffalo robes, such as those advertised above, became fashionable. For the next decade hunters killed more than one million buffalo each year, prompting a Sioux chief to predict that "the red hunters must die of hunger."

Quanah Parker—who took the name of his mother, Cynthia Ann Parker, captive wife of a Comanche chief—emerged as the most daring and imaginative Comanche war chief in the 1870's. When he and his Kwahadi band refused to attend the peace talks in 1867 at Medicine Lodge, Quanah explained: "My band is not going to live on the reservation. Tell the white chiefs that Kwahadies are warriors." Quanah spent the next eight years raiding the Texas countryside and was never really defeated in battle. In 1871, on his home territory known as the Staked Plain, Quanah outsmarted and bested Ranald S. Mackenzie, whom Ulysses S. Grant had singled out as "the most promising young officer in the Army."

large swarthy face. No other Sioux boasted his attainments in war, politics, and religion, and his name, remarked a white scout, "was a 'tipi word' for all that was generous and great." Sitting Bull's influence extended far beyond his own tribe, to the other Tetons and even to the Cheyennes and Arapahos. Stubbornly wedded to the hunting life, he rejected all overtures from the government. "You are fools," he told the agency Indians, "to make yourselves slaves to a piece of fat bacon, some hard-tack, and a little sugar and coffee."

Both sides violated the Fort Laramie treaty. Indians occasionally raided white settlements in Montana, Wyoming, and Nebraska, and whites as usual pressed against the Indian lands. The first real threat to the unceded country came when surveying parties marked out a route up the Yellowstone River for the Northern Pacific Railroad. Sitting Bull gathered his warriors to contest the survey of 1873 and twice collided with the military escort—Custer's 7th Cavalry, now operating out of Fort Abraham Lincoln, on the Missouri River. But the long-range threat of the railroad paled beside a second danger, this one directed at the most treasured portion of the Sioux reservation itself. In 1874 an exploring expedition—under Custer—found gold in the Black Hills, sacred dwelling place of the Sioux gods. By the summer of 1875, despite halfhearted military attempts to stop the invasion, miners by the thousands probed the flowered valleys and forested slopes of the Black Hills.

The government faced a difficult problem. Whites had entered the Black Hills in violation of treaty guarantees, but to remove them would provoke an irresistible public outcry. The obvious solution was to buy the Hills from the Sioux, but the agency chiefs could not be persuaded to sell, largely because of the opposition of the young men of the hunting bands. Only by neutralizing these hostiles, which meant bringing them under government control, could the Black Hills be purchased and the white occupation be given legal validation. That these Indians had in the meantime been guilty of depredations cast a comforting rationalization over the government's decision. Early in December, 1875, messengers set forth bearing an ultimatum to the hunting bands: report to an agency before January 31, 1876, or be classed as hostiles subject to military action.

When, as expected, the Indians did not come in by the prescribed date, General Sheridan, ever the proponent of winter operations, tried to organize two quick strikes that would end the war before spring. One to be led by Custer westward from Fort Lincoln was repeatedly postponed because heavy snow impeded the stockpiling of supplies.

Command of the other expedition went to General George Crook, fresh from his triumph over the Apaches in Arizona. Crook's column of nine hundred men marched out of Fort Fetterman, Wyoming, on March 1, 1876, and headed up the old Bozeman Trail into the unceded territory. For almost three weeks, struggling against snow, ice, wind, and bitter cold, they searched the Powder River country for Indians. At last the scouts found a trail, and Crook sent Colonel Joseph J. Reynolds and most of the cavalry to follow it. At dawn on March 17 Reynolds charged into a village of 105 lodges in the Powder River valley. The surprised Indians, Oglalas and Cheyennes, fled to bordering bluffs, rallied, and counterattacked with such vigor that the soldiers withdrew and made their way back to rejoin Crook. Disgusted, his supplies running low, the general led the worn-out command

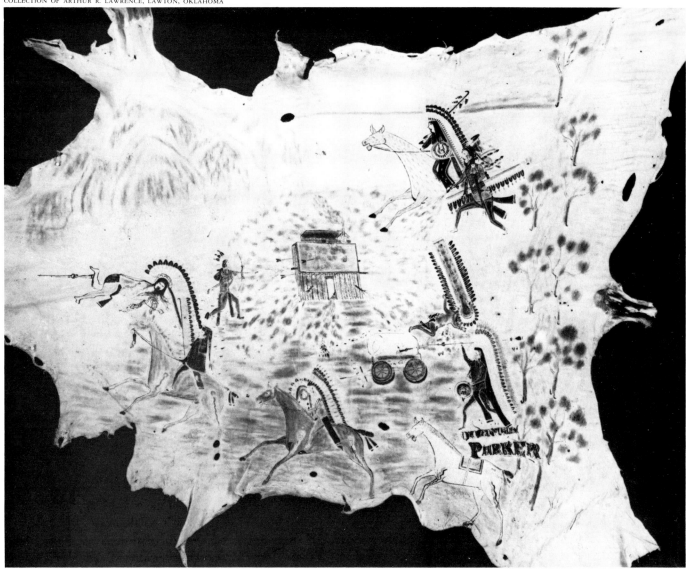

back to Fort Fetterman and promptly preferred charges against Reynolds for mismanaging both the attack and the retreat.

The Battle of Powder River alerted the hunting bands that the government meant business, and as spring began they united for self-defense into a single village of some 450 lodges. At the same time the spring exodus of agency Indians, this year swollen by the war fever and the tensions over the Black Hills, brought thousands more Sioux and Cheyennes to the unceded country to join the camp of Sitting Bull and Crazy Horse.

Sheridan now applied his favorite strategy of convergence to a summer campaign. General Crook was to come from the south, the scholarly ex-lawyer General Alfred H. Terry (with Custer and the 7th Cavalry) from the east, and Colonel John Gibbon, Civil War commander of the famed Iron Brigade, from the west. Gibbon, with 450 infantry and cavalry out of Forts Shaw and Ellis, Montana, had been on the Yellowstone River since April. Terry and Custer, 925 strong, pushed off from Fort Lincoln for the Yellowstone on May 17. And Crook, with more than a thousand men, finally marched again from Fort Fetterman on May 29, likewise pointed toward the Yellowstone.

As the agency Indians journeyed toward the Yellowstone too, Sitting Bull and Crazy Horse worked their way slowly westward, across the streams

This Comanche painting on deerskin depicts the June, 1874, assault led by Quanah Parker on 28 buffalo hunters and merchants at Adobe Walls, a deserted trading post on the South Canadian River. The hunters, armed with Sharps rifles with telescopes, held off 700 Indians for three days. At the lower right Quanah lances a hunter, one of only three whites killed. Within a year after the battle, Quanah Parker surrendered.

267

The one hundred ten wagons of Custer's Black Hills reconnaissance expedition of 1874 wind through the rough Dakota Territory.

flowing north into the Yellowstone. Early in June, on Rosebud Creek, they held a sun dance, the sacred ceremony of the Plains Indians. There Sitting Bull experienced a vision such as all participants in the sun dance sought. It foretold a grand triumph for the Sioux, with many dead soldiers "falling right into our camp." The people thrilled to the imagery and the promise. And indeed soldiers were not far away. To the next campsite, across the divide to the west, scouts brought word of a blue column approaching from the south, and several hundred warriors rode forth to do battle.

The blue column belonged to Crook, and on June 17 he signaled a mid-morning halt at the head of Rosebud Creek. On the way north he had signed up 262 Crow and Shoshone Indian auxiliaries. Scouting the bordering hills while the soldiers made coffee, they discovered the big force of Sioux and Cheyennes bearing down on the unsuspecting troops and gave enough warning to avert disaster. For six hours Crook's men fought furiously against the vigorous thrusts of confident, well-armed groups of warriors. But the general's insistence on withdrawing units to attack a village that he erroneously supposed to be nearby kept his defensive line in a precarious situation. At times it was preserved only by the tenacious combativeness of the Crow and Shoshone allies. Because the Indians finally withdrew, Crook claimed victory; but it was hardly that. He was sent limping back to his supply base at the most critical time in the campaign.

After the Battle of the Rosebud the Indians laid out their village in the valley of a stream they called the Greasy Grass. Throughout their long trek from the Powder their strength had remained comparatively stable, about 450 lodges. On the Greasy Grass, however, agency Indians suddenly began arriving in large numbers. In the week following the Rosebud fight the village doubled in size, to more than seven thousand people, eighteen hundred warriors, in five tribal circles of Sioux and one of Cheyennes.

As the Indians danced and feasted on the Greasy Grass, General Terry met Colonel Gibbon on the Yellowstone at the mouth of the Rosebud. On June 21, ignorant of Crook's reverse four days earlier, they gathered with Custer and other officers in the cabin of the steamboat *Far West* to plot how to bring the enemy to battle. A scouting expedition under Major Marcus A. Reno had tracked the Indian trail forty-five miles up the Rosebud, and the officers guessed that farther up it would turn west to the next valley. The Indians, they concluded, would be found somewhere on the stream called Greasy Grass. Terry's map labeled it Little Bighorn.

The plan Terry settled on called for Custer and the 7th Cavalry to follow the Indian trail up the Rosebud, cross to the Little Bighorn, and drive down its valley from the south. Terry and Gibbon would march up the Yellowstone and Bighorn to take up a blocking position on the north at the mouth of the Little Bighorn. The Indians, the general hoped, would be caught between the two forces.

At noon on June 22 the 7th Cavalry passed in review for Terry, Gibbon, Custer, and other officers. Six hundred strong, the regiment made a smart appearance. When the pack train straggled by looking much less efficient, the buckskin-clad Custer shook hands with his fellow officers and wheeled to depart. "Now, Custer, don't be greedy," called Gibbon, "but wait for us."

"No," came the cryptic reply, "I will not."

"Little did we think that we had seen him for the last time," recalled another of the officers, "or imagine under what circumstances we would

Crazy Horse leads Sioux warriors against George Crook's column near Rosebud Creek in Montana on June 17, 1876. Crook escaped defeat when his Shoshone and Crow allies fought off later charges. But the battle ended in a draw—and prevented Crook from rendezvousing with Custer.

next see the command, now mounting the bluffs in the distance with its guidons gayly fluttering in the breeze."

Gibbon's admonition implied a concert of action between the two columns that Custer's critics have ever since sought to reinforce. At the time, however, all understood that whichever column found the Indians first should pile into them at once. The hope was that the more mobile Custer, thrusting down the Little Bighorn valley from the south, would strike and drive them northward against Terry and Gibbon. The still popular notion that Custer rushed into battle before he was supposed to in order to win all the glory for himself was concocted after disaster had necessitated explanations.

Nor can it be truly said that Custer disobeyed Terry's orders. Those orders contemplated his continued march up the Rosebud beyond where the trail was expected to turn west. Thus he would be certain to enter the Little Bighorn valley above, or south of, the Indians and enclose them between him and Terry. But the orders were wholly discretionary, explicitly freeing him to use his judgment as unforeseen circumstances dictated.

Such circumstances materialized. At the close of the third day's march, June 24, the Indian trail turned west. That much was foreseen. But it also suddenly turned alarmingly fresh, only a few days old. A new trail—the large influx of agency Indians—had recently overlaid the older one, and it left no doubt that Indians were so near that they could not be in the upper valley of the Little Bighorn. Since the purpose of continuing up the Rosebud instead of following the trail was to cover the upper Little Bighorn, Custer now departed from the sequence suggested in his original orders from Terry. He would pause for a day while locating the village and scouting the terrain, then attack on June 26, the day Terry and Gibbon were to reach their blocking position at the mouth of the Little Bighorn.

Events conspired to spoil Custer's timetable. From a mountaintop at dawn on the twenty-fifth his scouts detected the enemy camp fifteen miles in the distance. At the same time, however, they discovered Sioux warriors lurking nearby. Instantly Custer saw that his plan would have to be changed. His quarry would soon be warned of his presence. Unless he attacked at once, there would be no Indians left to attack. As always, they would flee and scatter. He must seek out and strike the village before that happened.

It is an irony that Custer's original plan might have worked after all. The Sioux who observed him had left the big Sioux camp and were on their way back to the agencies. Their brethren on the Little Bighorn remained unaware of his approach. Furthermore, on this occasion the Indians might well have stood and fought even if alerted. Sitting Bull, Crazy Horse, and their fellow chiefs counted eighteen hundred well-armed, well-led fighting men—three times the strength of the 7th Cavalry and more than twice the number the army expected. They had just whipped Crook on the Rosebud. Rarely before had they been so strong, united, and confident, or so deeply outraged by the white man's war aims.

On this day Custer's legendary luck deserted him. Knowing neither terrain nor the exact location of the Indian camp, he had to grope toward it half blindly, allowing his battle plan to take shape as circumstances unfolded. By the time he knew enough for informed action, it was too late.

As he crossed the divide between the Rosebud and Little Bighorn, Custer sent Captain Frederick W. Benteen and three troops to the left, or south, to insure that the Indians had not, after all, strayed toward the upper valley of the Little Bighorn. Approaching the river by a more direct route, Custer flushed a party of about forty Sioux warriors. At the same time dust boiling up from behind intervening bluffs at last fixed the site of the village. He ordered Major Reno and three more troops to pursue the warriors, cross the river, and charge the Indian village, promising support from the five troops he retained under his personal control.

Shortly afterward Custer and this command turned to the north. Probably he hoped to strike the northern end of the village as Reno hit the southern end. But Custer still had not seen the village, and he did not know the character of the terrain he would have to cover to reach the other end. He soon found out. From the crest of the bluffs his situation finally revealed itself with frightening clarity. Below lay the Sioux and Cheyenne tepees scattered for three miles along the winding, tree-shaded river. Reno's squadron of 175 soldiers and Indian scouts had fallen into a desperate battle against swarms of Sioux at the camp's upper end. The lower end lay beyond the immediate reach of Custer's own squadron of 210 men, cut off by a maze of bluffs and ravines. Benteen was back on the trail somewhere, as was the pack train with the spare ammunition and escorting troop. Step by step Custer had fragmented the regiment, and now the four parts lay exposed to separate defeats before he could get them back together.

To Sitting Bull, whose Hunkpapas anchored the upper end of the Sioux village, the soldiers' situation must have seemed vivid confirmation of his sun-dance vision. But Major Reno halted his charging men before they could fall right into camp as foretold by the vision. Pressed by hundreds of warriors, he fought about ten minutes on a dismounted skirmish line, then retreated into the timber and brush along the river. That position proved untenable too, and after half an hour he headed for the bluffs east of the river. "Indians covered the flat," recalled the Cheyenne chief Two Moon. "They began to drive the soldiers all mixed up—Sioux, then soldiers, then more Sioux, and all shooting. The air was full of smoke and dust. I saw the soldiers fall back and drop into the river-bed like buffalo fleeing. They had no time to look for a crossing. The Sioux chased them up the hill."

No sooner had they driven these soldiers back across the river than the Indians discovered more approaching the other end of the village. Now fully aroused and painted and mounted for battle, all the men rushed to meet these soldiers as they rode down a broad coulee toward a river crossing. The mass of warriors, mainly Cheyennes under Lame White Man and Hunkpapas under Gall, crossed the river at this ford and crashed into

Gall, talented war chief of the Hunkpapa Sioux, routed Major Marcus Reno as the Battle of Little Bighorn began and then diverted hundreds of warriors for a frontal attack against Custer's column. At the same time, Crazy Horse and Two Moon struck the soldiers' flank and rear.

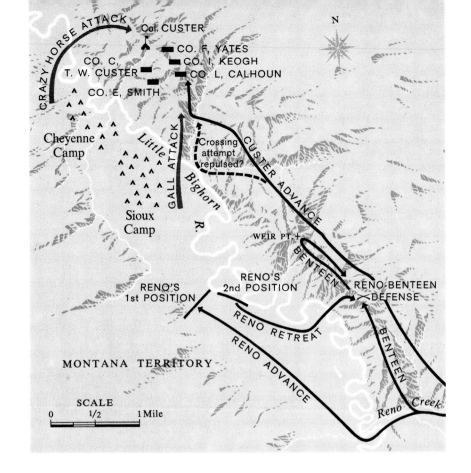

CRAZY HORSE ATTACK

Col. CUSTER

CO. F, YATES
CO. C,
T. W. CUSTER
CO. I, KEOGH
CO. L, CALHOUN

CO. E, SMITH

Cheyenne
Camp

Little Bighorn R.

Crossing
attempt
repulsed?

CUSTER ADVANCE

GALL ATTACK

N

Sioux
Camp

WEIR PT. +

BENTEEN

RENO'S
2nd POSITION

RENO-BENTEEN
DEFENSE

RENO'S
1st POSITION

RENO RETREAT

BENTEEN

MONTANA TERRITORY

RENO ADVANCE

SCALE
0   1/2   1 Mile

Reno Creek

This map details the movements of forces under Captain Frederick Benteen, Major Reno, and Colonel Custer — as well as they are known — and the attacks of Crazy Horse and Gall at the Battle of Little Bighorn on June 25, 1876.

the advancing bluecoats, forcing them back to a long high ridge to the north. Another force, largely Oglalas, followed Crazy Horse downstream and doubled back in a sweeping arc from the north. The giant pincers movement engulfed Custer's little squadron, and Indians poured in upon him from all directions.

"I called to my men," Low Dog said, "'This is a good day to die: follow me.' We massed our men, and that no man should fall back, every man whipped another man's horse and we rushed right upon them. As we rushed upon them the white warriors dismounted to fire, but they did very poor shooting. They held their horses' reins on one arm while they were shooting, but their horses were so frightened that they pulled the men all around, and a great many of their shots went up in the air and did us no harm. The white warriors stood their ground bravely, and none of them made any attempt to get away." In less than an hour Custer and all his men lay dead on the grassy heights above the Little Bighorn.

Four miles up the river Reno's men were battered and demoralized. It had been a rout, with Indians dashing among them and spilling them from their saddles with pistols, arrows, and even tomahawks. The river crossing, with steep banks slowing the rush, had cost many lives, including likable little Lieutenant Benny Hodgson. A bullet had knocked him into the water. He had grasped the stirrup of a passing horseman and made the bank only to be hit again, fatally. Reno's attack and retreat had taken half his command — forty killed, thirteen wounded, and seventeen missing (they would survive after two harrowing days hidden in the valley). Only Custer's threat to the lower end of the camp saved Reno from worse disaster.

Benteen joined Reno, and soon the pack train with its escort arrived, augmenting the ranks to 368 officers and enlisted men. Benteen had a written message, brought to him by Custer's trumpeter, urging him forward

OVERLEAF: *Long after Little Bighorn, Kicking Bear, a veteran of the fight, painted his version of the battle. In this detail, Custer is near the center in buckskin and long hair (actually, it had been cut just before the battle). The rising figures in outline at top left represent departing spirits of dead soldiers. The artist placed himself among the four Indian leaders at center, from the left: Sitting Bull, Rain-in-the-Face, Crazy Horse, and Kicking Bear — whose footsteps encircle one of the battle's victims.*

SOUTHWEST MUSEUM, LOS ANGELES

273

with the ammunition. "Be quick," Custer's adjutant had scrawled on a scrap of paper torn from his memorandum book, "Big Village." But no one knew where to find Custer, and a sortie to the north, the direction he had disappeared, encountered swarms of Sioux warriors. Now surrounded by Indians, the remnant of the 7th Cavalry dug in on the bluffs and fought off their assailants until night brought a lull in the Indian assaults.

Through another burning hot day the siege continued. A steady fire from all around the perimeter kept the soldiers in their shallow trenches or behind mule packs and ammunition boxes. Twice warriors charged the lines but were driven back, once in a cheering, tumbling counterattack down the slopes behind Captain Benteen. Relentlessly the casualty list grew, another thirteen dead and forty-seven wounded. By late afternoon the firing had subsided and most of the warriors had gone back to the valley, where they set fire to the prairie grass. From behind a billowing curtain of smoke, as dusk approached, a scene took form that the watching soldiers would never forget—a cavalcade of seven thousand Indians, men, women, and children, some mounted, others walking, ponies dragging travois laden with tepees, utensils, and infants, all crawling up the bench across the valley and wending slowly toward the snowy peaks of the Bighorn Mountains.

The Indians had learned that the soldiers of Terry and Gibbon were advancing up the valley from the north. The next morning, June 27, as Terry and Gibbon's scouts picked through the litter of the hastily abandoned village, ominous signs multiplied—a cavalry saddle, a dead army horse, a bloody and bullet-pierced buckskin shirt marked "Porter," gauntlets bearing the inscription "Yates 7th Cav," blood-stained underwear. The chief of scouts soon rode in with the chilling explanation. He had counted 197 naked, mutilated bodies scattered among the ravines and ridges across the river. A stunned General Terry rode on to the bluffs and gave the reprieved survivors of Reno Hill their first word of the fate of Custer and the five troops that had followed him down the Little Bighorn two days earlier.

A burial party found Custer at the northern end of the battle ridge, lying amid a handful of troopers who had apparently gathered around his red and blue pennant with white crossed sabers for the last stand that was to become legend. His body bore two bullet holes, but though stripped of his buckskins, he had escaped scalping and mutilation.

George Armstrong Custer had presided over one of the most complete disasters in American military annals, one that instantly set off endless controversy, debate, and speculation, and one that a century later showed no sign of losing its hold on public fascination. In shattering defeat and death, the golden-maned boy general achieved immortality.

For the Sioux and Cheyennes, the killing of the man they called Long Hair and his soldiers marked the peak of their power as free people. Custer's Last Stand shocked and outraged the American people. It moved them to flood the Indian country with soldiers. It afforded a superlative rationalization for forcing resolution of the Black Hills impasse; the following October a new commission concluded an "agreement" (the new term for treaty) with the agency chiefs that redrew the boundary of the Sioux reservation so as to exclude the Black Hills. More battles lay ahead before all the Sioux and Cheyennes acknowledged the reality, but in fact their final defeat lurked unseen in their soaring victory amid the brown hills overlooking the Greasy Grass.

Such vicious cartoons as this, printed in 1876, expressed white America's shock and outrage over Custer's defeat and fueled a rising anti-Indian sentiment. The sign refers to the fact that four of Custer's relatives died with him.

Sitting Bull—Sioux warrior, politician, and spiritual leader—was the major architect of the stunning victory at Little Bighorn.

Garrison Life

The western soldier might be out on campaign for half the year; he spent the rest of his time in one of the dozens of forts scattered along the frontier between the Canadian border and the Rio Grande. Whether he was stationed at a post like Fort Grant, Arizona (left), where, a soldier wrote, "everything that grows pricks and everything that breathes bites," or at dreary, treeless Fort Yates, North Dakota (below), his daily routine was identical—a ceaseless round of drills, hard work, bad food, and a battle with boredom.

By the 1880's target practice—a decade earlier discouraged by stingy and overconfident commanders—had become the single most important training exercise. The troopers of the 1st Cavalry, above, are practicing at Fort Grant; at top, men of the 6th Cavalry fire over their well-trained horses in a difficult exercise at Fort Bayard, New Mexico.

The soldier's twelve-hour day began as early as five o'clock with trumpeters' assembly, and from then on the bugle called him almost hourly to new duties. These included inspection, target practice, stable police, cavalry drill, and the universally loathed fatigues—nonmilitary jobs such as grading roads and stringing telegraph wire. The privates, who were paid a mere thirteen dollars a month, complained bitterly about being used as cheap labor when they were not busy fighting Indians. Three times a day mess call brought them in for food prepared by soldiers who were assigned the task on the ingenuous theory that it would help them learn to cook their own rations in the field. The routine was so bleak that some of the men actually enjoyed the minor pageantry of dress parade, when, like the Dakota troops on the preceding page, the entire garrison turned out in full uniform. Others loathed every aspect of military life. "None but a menial cur," wrote one disgusted trooper, "would stand the usage of a soldier in the Army of today. . . ."

Army cooks line up in their mess hall at Fort Leavenworth, Kansas.

On one of their detested fatigue duties, soldiers grub around in the reservoir at Fort Grant.

Winter duty on the northern posts meant perpetual misery as
simple tasks were rendered all but impossible by savage
temperatures that hovered around thirty below for weeks on end.
Here, men of the 1st Cavalry stationed at Fort Keogh turn out
for fatigue duty in a Montana snowstorm. Every spring, when
the thaw set in, men who had had enough deserted by the score.
NATIONAL ARCHIVES

CHRISTIAN BARTHELMESS COLLECTION, MILES CITY, MONTANA

Soldiers and civilians gather to socialize in the trader's store at Fort Keogh.

The army showed little interest in providing recreation, and soldiers had to make their own fun. Boxing was a popular diversion; so were foot races, in which the troops would sometimes bet most of their meager salaries on the outcome. Many companies formed their own baseball teams, outfitted with mail-order uniforms. In less active moments, soldiers loved to sing, favoring lugubrious ballads of lost love and childhood homes. An invaluable aid to such singing disappeared from the posts when liquor was outlawed in 1881. Thereafter the men had to make do with beer from the trader's store. Each post had one of these stores—franchised by the army to civilians—which also sold tobacco, canned fruit, and other small luxuries that made frontier life a little more bearable.

KANSAS STATE HISTORICAL SOCIETY

Men of the Fort Riley, Kansas, medical unit spar before a spectral onlooker.

Aided by songbooks and a conductor, troops at Fort Keogh engage in a formal sing.

Women were scarce on army bases; no soldier could
maintain a wife on his salary alone, and the army
actively discouraged marriage. Nevertheless, a
number of officers managed to raise families on the
posts; and some noncoms and even a few privates
kept wives who took in soldiers' laundry for a
couple of dollars a month. The rest of the men scoured
the countryside for female companionship—and found
bedraggled Indian women or prostitutes too old or
too ugly to work in the East. During the 1880's
eight per cent of the army contracted venereal disease.

Ensconced in rare luxury, a sergeant reads to his wife at Fort Stanton. New Mexico.

Well-armed officers picnic with their families near Fort Thomas, Arizona.

10: The Closing Circle

As the Plains Indians' resistance to the reservation process burgeoned toward a climax at Little Bighorn, a small tribe in far-off California expressed its own opposition in a sudden violent revolt. For eight months in 1872–73 the Modoc War held national attention and shook almost to collapse the foundations of President Grant's Peace Policy.

Never a large tribe — by 1870 fewer than three hundred — the Modocs were a rugged, combative people who, like kindred groups in the Great Basin, lived by a combination of hunting, fishing, digging roots, and gathering. Surrounding tribes feared them as violent neighbors, plunderers, and slave traffickers. White immigrants of the 1850's, destined for Oregon or California on the Applegate Trail, also experienced their warlike character, until Californians banded together in a bloody retaliation that all but ended the menace. The Modocs fell into a friendly trade relationship with the people at Yreka, California, began to wear white men's clothes, and even adopted the names that the whites gave them — Bogus Charley, Hooker Jim, Steamboat Frank, Shacknasty Jim.

One of the foremost Modoc leaders was a young man named Kintpuash, whom the whites called Captain Jack. His downturned mouth and heavy, sad eyes gave him a lethargic cast belied by his dynamic, ambitious, and aggressive character. He was not the principal Modoc chief, but his out-

Judge, JANUARY 3, 1891

EVER OUR INDIAN POLICY.
THE ONLY GOOD INDIAN IS THE DEAD ONE !

This Judge *cartoon, showing a fat, smug Secretary John Willock Noble heading the Interior Department, attacks anti-Indian hard-liners who dominated policy after the resignation of liberal Secretary Carl Schurz.*

spoken opposition to reservation life voiced the sentiments of most of the tribe and lifted him to a position of commanding, if fleeting, leadership.

Some years before, with great misgivings, Captain Jack had signed at Council Grove a treaty that bound Modocs, Klamaths, and Northern Paiutes to cede their lands and settle on the Klamath Reservation north and east of Upper Klamath Lake in Oregon. As expected, he found life among the arrogant Klamaths intolerable, and after a year, with a band of like-minded followers, he left the reservation and returned to his homeland—a grassy plateau country dappled by lakes and lava deposits lying at the eastern base of the Cascade Mountains along the California–Oregon boundary. Jack and his people took up residence on Lost River where it flows from the north into Tule Lake.

For the next seven years Modocs and settlers lived uneasily side by side in this country, the Modocs increasingly apprehensive as more and more whites arrived, the settlers equally apprehensive as the Indians stubbornly resisted all efforts to persuade them to go back to the Klamath Reservation. When the Council Grove Treaty finally won ratification in 1870, agitation for removal of the Modocs intensified. At last, in 1872, the Indian Bureau obtained consent to call on the army to make the Indians return. At dawn on November 29, 1872, a troop of cavalry from Fort Klamath drew up on the edge of Captain Jack's camp. After an exchange of rifle fire the Indians scattered, and the Modoc War was on.

Instead of going north to the reserve, the Modocs hurried south, leaving a trail of death and destruction among settlers around the margins of Tule Lake. On the south shore of the lake lay the lava beds, a twisted mass of black rock piled up in fantastic formations and riddled with subterranean passages. The Indians called it Land of Burnt-Out Fires. To the soldiers who began to close around it after the Modocs took refuge there it became known as Captain Jack's Stronghold. It was an almost impregnable fortress. Scarcely more than fifty fighting men manned it against a besieging force that ultimately numbered a thousand regulars and militiamen.

The army began to concentrate units at Tule Lake immediately after the Lost River encounter. The military commander in the Northwest was Brigadier General Edward R. S. Canby, a spare, beardless veteran of the Navaho campaigns of the 1850's and the bearer of a distinguished Civil War record. A compassionate man, Canby had not approved of the decision to coerce the Modocs—but he had not protested it either. He sent Lieutenant Colonel Frank Wheaton to blast the Indians out of their fortress with cannon and riflemen. On January 16, 1873, the blue lines advanced.

The Battle of the Stronghold was a disaster for the army. Heavy fog obscured the scene. The artillery dropped a few rounds in front of the advancing skirmish lines but ceased when the shells began to endanger friend more than foe. The Indians fired with an accuracy that, combined with the rugged terrain, slowed and then halted the assault. When the fog at last lifted, the troops were caught in exposed positions, and Modoc fire kept them pinned down until darkness allowed them to retreat in safety. The battle cost the attacking force nine killed and twenty-eight wounded and shattered morale as well. Not once had a soldier even seen a Modoc.

The government next resolved on diplomacy, and in February a peace commission arrived. It foundered in confusion until late in March, when General Canby was placed in charge. He adopted a twofold policy of

Kintpuash, or Captain Jack—the name whites gave him—led a rebellion by Modocs who bitterly objected to being pushed onto a reservation with their long-time enemies, the Klamaths. Before going on the warpath, Kintpuash asked for a separate Modoc reservation near the Lost River on the Oregon–California border. He was refused.

urging peace talks while bringing in reinforcements and drawing his lines in a tightening ring around the stronghold. Captain Jack consented to talk, and a tent was pitched midway between the lines. Jack demanded a reservation in his homeland. Canby offered only unconditional surrender.

The peace initiative opened a rift in the Modoc leadership. Jack argued that patience and persistence would earn favorable terms in the end, but most of the other chiefs disagreed. The white people could never be trusted, they declared; the best course was to murder the peace commissioners in hopes that this would scare the soldiers away. Jack attacked such treachery as folly that would bring death to every Modoc. The militants shouted him down, called him a woman and a coward, even roughed him up. At length they goaded him into accepting their plan and taking the lead in carrying it out.

On Good Friday morning, April 11, 1873, a fateful meeting took place at the peace tent. The commissioners had been warned of possible treachery by Toby Riddle, the Modoc wife of Canby's interpreter. Noting his array of military strength, however, the general ignored the warning. Another commissioner, the Reverend Eleasar Thomas, said that "where God called him to go *he would go,*" to which Commissioner Alfred B. Meacham replied that God had not been in the Modoc camp all winter.

The warning was tragically prophetic. The council had just begun when Jack suddenly shot Canby full in the face, then stabbed him repeatedly until he died, and finally stripped him of his dress uniform, which the Modoc chieftain later donned as a symbol of his deed and his continuing leadership. Other Indians killed Thomas and wounded Meacham. The interpreters and a fourth commissioner, L. S. Dyar, escaped unharmed.

As Captain Jack had foreseen, the brutal slaying of Canby—the only general of regulars killed in the entire history of Indian warfare—served only to enrage the whites and bring in more soldiers. In the face of another attack, on April 15, the Modocs slipped out and took up new positions in a lava formation farther south.

On April 26 the Modocs sighted a reconnoitering party of sixty-six soldiers and a dozen Indian scouts. Incredibly the troops paused for lunch in a bowl-like depression perfect for an ambush, taking no precautions against a surprise attack. Scarfaced Charley, the true military genius of the Modoc resistance, struck with only twenty-two warriors. Some of the soldiers fled in panic while the rest stood their ground in a brief but futile defense. All five officers perished along with twenty enlisted men. To the survivors, including sixteen wounded, Scarfaced Charley called out in contempt: "All you fellows that ain't dead had better go home. We don't want to kill you all in one day." He then permitted them to retreat without further assault.

Although humiliating to the army, this Modoc victory failed to quiet the dissension among the Indian leaders. In fact, some of the very militants who had forced Captain Jack to kill the peace commissioners turned on him and urged an end to resistance. By the middle of May all the Modocs had slipped out of their defenses and scattered.

Meanwhile, a new commander had infused fresh spirit into the troops. This was Colonel Jefferson C. Davis (no relation to the recent Confederate president), a fiery, profane veteran of Sherman's Georgia campaigns. Under his forceful leadership, the troops combed the countryside, scooping

When fighting broke out in November, 1872, Captain Jack led his people, including perhaps 75 warriors, to the labyrinthine lava beds near Tule Lake, California. In January some 400 soldiers attacked (right, pickets on duty), but they only forced the Modocs deeper into their stronghold—where Captain Jack held out in his rocky headquarters (below) for nearly six more months.

Harper's Weekly. JUNE 28, 1873

Toward the end of the lava-bed fight die-hard Modocs persuaded Captain Jack to shoot General Edward R. S. Canby, the head soldier, at a peace parley (left). Jack's niece Toby Riddle, the wife of Canby's interpreter (the Riddles are standing at right below), warned the general, but he ignored her.

up one party of Indians after another. By the end of May almost all the fugitives had been seized. On June 1 a cavalry patrol coaxed an exhausted Captain Jack and his family out of a cave and took them prisoner.

General Sherman demanded retribution swift and severe: the slayers of Canby to be tried for murder and all the Modocs sent to reservations far to the east, "so that the name of Modoc shall cease." Scarcely a month after his surrender, Captain Jack and five other Modocs—without benefit of a lawyer or an interpreter—were tried by a military commission and sentenced to death. President Grant commuted two of the sentences to life imprisonment. On October 3, 1873, Captain Jack, Boston Charley, Black Jim, and Schonchin John died on a scaffold erected on the Fort Klamath parade ground. In a grisly gesture to scientific inquiry, their heads were sent to the Army Medical Museum in Washington, D.C. Escorted by soldiers, 155 Modocs took up the journey to new homes in Indian Territory, far to the east. "They are a sorry, pitiful-looking set to have given so much trouble," observed an officer.

Few Indian tribes of the West could boast the internal unity needed to offer effective opposition to the white advance. Almost every tribe broke into two major factions, one favoring accommodation with the whites and the adoption of white ways, the other holding firm to the old ways and resisting the blandishments of the whites. Out of the frictions and rivalries between these two factions flowed forces that directed the internal politics of the tribe and its relations with the whites. No other tribe exemplified this tendency more clearly than the Nez Perces, that vital and appealing people inhabiting the country drained by the Snake, Clearwater, and Salmon rivers in Idaho.

The zealous Presbyterian missionaries Henry and Eliza Spalding had driven the first wedge by teaching an ever-expanding body of Nez Perces how to farm and live like white people. Ably led by Lawyer, the name given Hallalhotsoot by whites awed by his debating skill, these "Christian" Nez Perces became the dominant element of the tribe. They continued to prosper even after the departure of the Spaldings in the wake of the Whitman massacre, and by 1860 they composed about two thirds of the four thousand Nez Perces. The remaining one third, the "heathens"—Eagle from the Light, Looking Glass, White Bird, Joseph, and others—rejected the teachings of the Spaldings and clung to traditional ways.

White pressure on Nez Perce lands widened the gulf between the factions. At Walla Walla all had agreed to a reservation that included most of their homeland, but a gold rush to the Clearwater in 1863 prompted an attempted treaty revision designed to remove the mineral districts from the reservation. Lawyer and his followers, their homes safely within the new boundaries, signed. Others, their lands thrown outside, refused to sign and withdrew from the treaty council altogether.

Prominent among the "nontreaties" was the old and respected Chief Joseph. He did not consider himself bound by the treaty of 1863 because he had not signed it and had specifically repudiated Lawyer as his spokesman. Moreover, since few white settlers filtered into his territory in the high, grassy Wallowa valley across the Snake River in Oregon, his interpretation went unchallenged. President Grant even seemed to confirm it in 1873, two years after Joseph's death, by setting aside part of the Wallowa valley as a reservation for his band. But Oregon citizens were beginning to dis-

The army acclaimed Chief Joseph (above) — the proud, eloquent political leader of the Nez Perces — a military genius.

cover the worth of the valley for stock grazing, and they raised such a protest that in 1875 Grant reversed himself and opened it to settlement.

Leadership of the Wallowa band had passed to Young Joseph upon the death of his father. Already at thirty-one he was a man of great dignity, humanity, and wisdom. As a youth he had come under the Spalding influence at the Lapwai mission, but after the Whitman massacre his training had fallen to men schooled in the old Indian ways. A soft-spoken, gentle man, he gained stature as a political rather than a military or religious leader. Since the white threat focused on the Wallowa valley, Joseph emerged in the middle 1870's as the spokesman for all the nontreaty chiefs in the building confrontation with the government. The others—Eagle from the Light, White Bird, Toohoolhoolzote, and Looking Glass (the younger, who succeeded his father in 1863)—backed Joseph in his contention that his father had not sold the Wallowa valley.

With the death of Lawyer in 1876, the government lost an influential ally in its growing conflict with the nontreaty chiefs. But at the same time the whites gained a strong and equally stubborn chief of their own with the assignment of General Oliver O. Howard to the northwestern command. His reputation as a humanitarian greatly enhanced by his successful peace mission to Cochise in 1872, his public image symbolized by an empty sleeve and a Bible, the "Christian general" now brought his own distinctive blend of compassion and evangelism to bear on the Nez Perce question. Although he saw himself as the Moses to the Indians, as he had told General Crook, he was to discover that he and Chief Joseph held quite different conceptions of the Promised Land.

Howard agreed that Joseph's father had never sold the Wallowa valley, and his sympathies lay firmly with the Indians. His solution, however, was not to buy out the trespassing settlers but to buy out the Indians. As head of a negotiating commission he presented this proposition to them in two lively councils held at Lapwai, the reservation headquarters, in November, 1876, and May, 1877. Joseph spoke eloquently and lucidly, demonstrating convincingly the depth of his people's attachment to their homeland and the validity of their ownership of it. In the second conference, Old Toohoolhoolzote also spoke with clarity and force, so much so that Howard lost his temper and threw him in the guardhouse at Fort Lapwai. Persuasion had failed, and the general broke the deadlock, as one Indian phrased it, by showing the rifle. The nontreaty Nez Perces had thirty days, he declared, to move to the reservation or he would send in his soldiers.

Embittered and with heavy hearts, the chiefs complied. They knew war to be suicidal. En route, however, some of White Bird's young men, emboldened by firewater, killed four whites. Other angry warriors followed their example and killed still more whites. A hundred cavalrymen from Fort Lapwai hastened to the scene, but on June 17, 1877, in the Battle of White Bird Canyon, they were cut to pieces and driven back with one officer and thirty-three enlisted men slain.

Stung by this disaster, the army mobilized. As troops converged on Idaho, General Howard took the field with a command of more than four hundred infantry and cavalry. The combined Nez Perce bands numbered about three hundred warriors and five hundred women and children. Occasional skirmishes marked the chase, but for almost three weeks the Indians easily evaded their pursuers. Then on July 11 Howard overtook them. On an open plain above their village on the south fork of the Clear-water River, warriors and soldiers clashed in a vigorously contested action that lasted two days and ended in the rout of the Indians.

The Battle of Clearwater might have ended the Nez Perce War had Howard followed up his victory. But he allowed the Indians to escape and thus set the stage for the memorable hegira that followed. In a tense council on Weippe Prairie on July 15, the chiefs resolved on a dramatic move—a trek across the Bitterroot Mountains to the plains of Montana. For generations the Nez Perces had made that journey to hunt buffalo on the plains. Now perhaps they could find safety there with the Crow Indians or even, failing that, join Sitting Bull and the Sioux who had fled to Canada after Little Bighorn.

Joseph did not make this decision alone. It was made, rather, like all Indian decisions, by a council of chiefs. Later the white generals would fix a "Red Napoleon" myth on Joseph, partly in genuine admiration and partly in an embarrassed need to explain their own failures. In fact, the principal war leader was Joseph's younger brother Ollokot, a bold and energetic fighter; all the major tactical decisions flowed from the deliberations of the chiefs' council. Joseph participated, of course, and spoke with great authority, but he did not dictate. Even so, to award military credit to all the chiefs, indeed to all the Nez Perces, does not diminish Joseph's stature as a wise and influential leader.

General Howard continued to tarry, giving the Nez Perces a comfortable head start up the tortuous Lolo Trail. By early in August they had surmounted the Bitterroot Mountains, ascended the Bitterroot valley, and crossed the Continental Divide. On the Big Hole River Looking Glass talked the other chiefs into pausing to rest. The delay allowed Colonel John Gibbon and a column of almost two hundred infantrymen from Fort Shaw, Montana, to catch up. At daybreak on August 9 Gibbon attacked, driving the surprised Indians from their tepees and cutting down at least eighty-nine in the first sweep. Rallying, the warriors counterattacked, retook the village, and pinned down the troops for two days while the women and children made good their escape. Left with seventy-one dead and wounded, Gibbon limped back to his station.

Across the recently established Yellowstone National Park the Indians hurried, terrorizing tourists and narrowly missing a vacationing official

Ollokot (below), Joseph's younger brother, was chief strategist of the Nez Perces' retreat. They left Idaho with some 800 people, including women and children. In battling some 2,000 soldiers (bottom, a Harper's Weekly *sketch), the Nez Perces proved themselves better fighters and marksmen.*

In pursuit of Joseph.

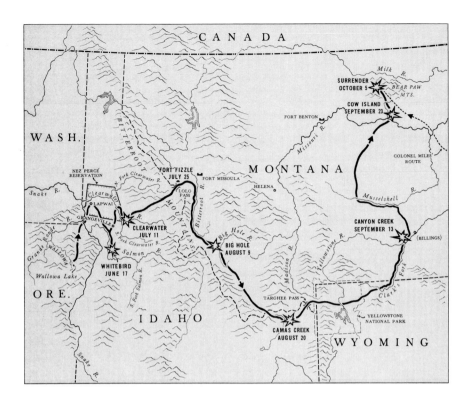

party that included General Sherman. Howard's column, seven hundred strong, followed closely, never quite able to overtake the quarry. Colonel Samuel D. Sturgis and elements of the 7th Cavalry moved to block the eastern exits of the park. Cleverly feinting southward, the Nez Perces drew Sturgis away from their intended route and slipped out of the mountains onto the Montana plains. The cavalry raced after them, only to be stopped in a clash of arms at Canyon Creek on September 13.

The Nez Perces had now reached the land of the Crow Indians, among whom the chiefs had thought to find a haven. This hope collapsed in disillusion when they discovered Crow scouts fighting against them as part of Sturgis's command. Canada, two hundred miles to the north, offered a last hope. Surely Sitting Bull would welcome the Nez Perces.

Again Looking Glass urged fatal counsel. The people were exhausted and needed rest. The soldiers had been left far behind. The pace should be slowed and the daily marches cut short. But Howard, hoping for just such a result, had slowed his own march while sending a courier down the

NATIONAL ARCHIVES

When Chief Joseph surrendered to Colonel Nelson A. Miles (left, by Frederic Remington), the victors counted just 431 Nez Perce prisoners, including 79 fighting men. The army had lost some 180 killed and 150 wounded in the campaign.

297

Yellowstone River to Fort Keogh. There the ambitious, energetic Colonel Nelson A. Miles commanded a garrison of hardened veterans of Sioux warfare. Miles swiftly organized a strike force of almost four hundred men and hurried northwestward to cut off the Nez Perces. He found them on the morning of September 30 camped beside Snake Creek, on the northern edge of the Bear Paw Mountains, less than forty miles short of the Canadian border.

The Indians discovered the soldiers in time to take positions in a cutbank south and east of their camp. A squadron of the 2nd Cavalry, circling to the west, succeeded in capturing most of the Indians' pony herd; but a squadron of the 7th, attacking frontally, ran into the well-posted Nez Perce riflemen. Their deadly fire shattered the charge and felled sixty of the horsemen. The marksmen had aimed at the leaders and had cut down six officers and seven sergeants. Such casualties prompted Miles to call off the attack and settle into a siege, which lasted through six days of snow and damp cold. Howard came up, but he generously left the command to Miles.

In the village the chiefs argued. Toohoolhoolzote was dead, as was Ollokot. Joseph urged surrender, White Bird and Looking Glass resistance. The dispute was resolved in typically democratic fashion. White Bird and some three hundred people slipped out and made a successful dash for the Canadian sanctuary. (Looking Glass was not with him; a stray bullet had buried itself in his brain.) Joseph and the rest, about four hundred people, sadly prepared to surrender. On October 5, 1877, Joseph faced Howard and Miles and, with Howard's aide writing down the words as translated by an interpreter, delivered the memorable speech that brought the war to a close: "Tell General Howard I know his heart. What he told me before, I have in my heart. I am tired of fighting. Our chiefs are killed. Looking Glass is dead. Toohoolhoolzote is dead. The old men are all dead. It is the young men who say yes or no. He who led the young men is dead [Ollokot]. It is cold and we have no blankets. The little children are freezing to death. My people, some of them, have run away to the hills, and have no blankets, no food. No one knows where they are—perhaps freezing to death. I want to have time to look for my children and see how many I can find. Maybe I shall find them among the dead. Hear me, my chiefs! I am tired. My heart is sick and sad. From where the sun now stands, I will fight no more forever."

The Nez Perce drama caught the imagination of the nation and stirred sympathy for their cause. For three months 800 Indians had made their determined way across 1,700 miles of tangled mountains and rolling plains. Their chiefs had outwitted and outgeneraled and their people had outmarched and outfought a considerable portion of the United States Army. Despite the public sympathy and the promises of Howard and Miles, however, the Nez Perces were never allowed to go home. After a time in Kansas and Indian Territory, where many of them died, about 150 were transferred to the Colville reservation in Washington. For Chief Joseph, an unflagging quest for permission to return to his beloved Wallowa valley ended only with his death at Colville in 1904.

Theodore Roosevelt would one day label Nelson A. Miles, the self-proclaimed hero of the Nez Perce chase, a "brave peacock." The term suggested the unattractive side of the young officer's personality. Vain,

BITTE[

Custer's Last Stand rekindled the national debate over what ought to be done with the Indians. Hardliners in the eastern press railed against the government's coddling of murderous savages. *Harper's Weekly* cartoonist Thomas Nast (two of his cartoons appear on these pages) led the attacks, many of which were focused on Secretary of the Interior Carl Schurz. Schurz believed that Indians, if treated with respect, would react in kind. Furthermore, he felt that Indians ought to become voting citizens, and he opposed the proposed transfer of the Indian Bureau from Interior to the War Department. Nast held that Indians could never be civilized and ought to be kept under constant military supervision. Schurz kept the Indian Bureau, but his more humanitarian ideas were never adopted. Cartoons such as the one below, right, satirized that failure.

Harper's Weekly, MARCH 13, 1880

Thomas Nast lambasts Carl Schurz and his p
to give the Indians the vote in this 1880 carte

ISPUTES OVER POLICY

Harper's Weekly. DECEMBER 28, 1878

CULVER PICTURES

The well-fed chief with Upton's book of infantry tactics on his shelf says, "White Father treat Big Injun well. Next Spring be hearty enough to wipe out mean little army."

Thomas Nast titled this swipe at Carl Schurz's liberal Indian policy "Patience Until the Indian Is Civilized—So To Speak."

Puck. JANUARY 21, 1891

This pro-Indian cartoon by Joseph Keppler was published with a poem to the Indians, supposedly from Uncle Sam. It read, in part, "If you don't like my style and my rations, / Down your throats I will cram them with steel."

Bundled against the snow and cold of a January, 1877, Montana morning, Colonel Nelson A. Miles (center, in broad-brimmed hat) and his staff prepare for a raid against Crazy Horse.

pompous, dogmatic, quarrelsome, he pursued fame and position with ruthless intensity, shamelessly ridiculing his fellow officers, extolling his own virtues, and exploiting his wife's position as niece of the powerful Sherman brothers, General William T. and Senator John. Yet Miles advanced by merit as well as influence. In four years of Civil War service this self-educated Boston crockery clerk had flowered into a first-rate combat leader, fearless, bold, imaginative, innovative, and above all tenacious. He fought in almost every major battle of the Army of the Potomac, was four times wounded, and rose to corps command with the rank of major general — all by age twenty-five. To a man of such restless and extravagant ambition, the peacetime army offered few opportunities, especially for a colonel of infantry. But he made a name for himself in the Red River War, and on August 2, 1876, having used every influence at his command to get into the Sioux War, he had disembarked his 5th Infantry from a steamer on the Yellowstone River determined to avenge the death of his friend George Custer and bring glory to the name of Nelson Miles.

With an astute reckoning of probabilities, Miles promoted for himself the independent assignment of patrolling the line of the Yellowstone to make certain the Sioux and Cheyennes did not escape northward. Meanwhile, to the south, Generals Terry and Crook pushed a "stern chase" after the slayers of Custer. Miles had found Terry and his officers suffering "the worst kind of demoralization and timidity," and Crook had been similarly afflicted, which became plain when the two generals and their commands joined on the middle Rosebud on August 10. Both had held back awaiting heavy reinforcements, and now, with some four thousand

horse and foot, they set forth against Indians already far to the east and scattering. When he asked Terry to send him back to the Yellowstone, Miles had doubtless hoped to disengage himself from an enterprise likely to fail from the sheer weight of numbers. "The more I see of movements here the more admiration I have for Custer," he wrote to his wife, "and I am satisfied his like will not be found very soon again."

Miles saw his pessimism confirmed. For three weeks the ponderous army slogged through rain and mud as the men grew weary and discouraged and relations between Terry and Crook deteriorated. "It has reached beyond a joke," Lieutenant Colonel Eugene A. Carr wrote to his wife, "that we should be kept out and exposed because two fools do not know their business." Finally Crook cut loose to pursue the Indian trail as Terry, done in by logistics, disbanded his expedition and forwarded his valuable supplies to Miles. Crook marched east into Dakota, then headed south in an epic "mud march" that turned into a grim struggle with weather and starvation. En route, on September 9, part of the command seized and destroyed a small Sioux camp at Slim Buttes. Though trumpeted as a great victory, the action had seen disaster narrowly averted, and it did nothing to dissipate the cloud of failure that hung heavily over the war the generals had so confidently declared prior to Custer's astounding defeat.

Miles's reputation remained untarnished, however, and in fact he had skirmished creditably with Sioux warriors while Terry and Crook were miring ever deeper in muddy futility and querulous bickering. Moreover, as the other troops returned to winter quarters, Miles and his hardy foot soldiers, less than five hundred strong, threw up a rude cantonment at the mouth of the Tongue River and kept after the Indians. "They expected us to hive up," he wrote to his wife, "but we are not the hiving kind." Through the fall months and into the winter the infantrymen remained in the field. Enveloped in huge coats of buffalo fur, they faced the stinging blizzards and numbing temperatures of a Montana winter. Indeed, the Battle of Wolf Mountain, January 8, 1877, was fought with Crazy Horse and some five hundred Sioux and Cheyenne warriors in a raging snowstorm and ended with the Indians swept from the field by bursting artillery shells and charging infantry. He "had taught the destroyers of Custer," Miles wrote, "that there was one small command that could whip them as long as they dared face it."

Crook also took the field briefly at the beginning of winter. He headed another of those heavy columns that had so signally and repeatedly failed in this war, and Miles made some contemptuous comparisons between the 2,200 infantry and cavalry that followed Crook up the old Bozeman Trail and his own handful of infantrymen. Nevertheless, Crook's aggressive cavalry commander, Ranald Mackenzie, succeeded in surprising Dull Knife's Cheyenne camp of 183 lodges in a canyon of the Bighorn Mountains. On November 25, 1876, he inflicted a terrible defeat that cast more than a thousand Cheyennes into the wilderness without food or shelter.

After this victory, however, Crook withdrew in the face of the fierce winter, and it was Miles, persisting through the winter and fighting several successful actions such as Wolf Mountain, who could claim (and did, loudly) the largest credit when Indian resistance began to collapse. In January, 1877, Sitting Bull and the Hunkpapas sought haven in the land of the "Great Mother," Queen Victoria, while Crazy Horse with the Oglalas and the impoverished Cheyenne refugees from the Mackenzie fight lost heart as this dogged man they called Bear's Coat kept ceaselessly after them. In the spring the Cheyennes surrendered to Bear's Coat on the Yellowstone, but in an irony that rankled Miles the rest of his life Indian emissaries from Crook persuaded the Sioux to go south and surrender at Red Cloud Agency. Throughout the spring of 1877 small parties drifted

This pictograph by a Sioux named Amos Bad Heart Bull leaves no doubt that the artist believed Crazy Horse was murdered in cold blood by a guard at Camp Robinson. The only known facts are that Crazy Horse was arrested; he fought it and was mortally stabbed in the struggle.

quietly into the agency. Then on May 6 a procession of more than a thousand people and twenty-five hundred ponies approached nearby Camp Robinson. In the van rode Crazy Horse and his principal chiefs. As Crook and his staff watched, the three hundred massed warriors proudly, almost defiantly, broke into their war songs. Throwing three Winchester rifles to the ground, Crazy Horse gave up the warpath.

Crazy Horse was almost a bigger threat to the government on the reservation than off. He had never known any but the unfettered life of the plains, and the reservation proved unfamiliar and confining. Rumors that the Sioux would have to move to the Missouri River, coupled with the army's efforts to enlist his warriors to help fight the Nez Perces, did not improve his disposition. "This incorrigible wild man," in his agent's words, grew more and more "silent, sullen, lordly, and dictatorial." The agency chiefs, fearing that he would do something rash and get them all in trouble, drew back from him. Finally, early in September, 1877, General Crook ordered him imprisoned. There was a scuffle. Whether the fatal stab wound was inflicted by his own knife or another Indian's or by a guard's bayonet is still argued, but that night the great war chief of the Oglalas died. "It is good," said one of the other chiefs, "he has looked for death, and it has come."

The death of Crazy Horse might have seemed to mark the close of the Sioux War, but it could not be over so long as the greatest and most irreconcilable chief remained at large, even in Canada. Moreover, some two thousand followers of Crazy Horse had decamped after his death and doubled the number of refugees with Sitting Bull, adding up to more Indians than had ridden with the hunting bands before the war. In Canada the Sioux got along well with the Great Mother's scarlet-coated policemen, but there was not enough game to keep hunger from their lodges, and inevitably they crossed the boundary to Montana in search of buffalo. In October, 1877, General Terry, aided by the North West Mounted Police, sought out Sitting Bull to talk him into going to the reservation, but the chief was adamant. "You come here to tell us lies," he spat at Terry. "Go home where you came from."

But famine threatened, as did war with Canadian tribes not pleased to share their diminishing game with these foreign Indians. And along the boundary Bear's Coat and his soldiers patrolled back and forth, ready to shoot any Sioux who ventured across. Steadily Sitting Bull's following eroded as small parties slipped back to the United States and gave up. For his part, declared the stubborn chief, "so long as there remains a gopher to eat, I will not go back." But at last, on July 19, 1881, with less than two hundred destitute people, he appeared at Fort Buford, Dakota Territory. He gave his Winchester to his eight-year-old son to hand to the post commander. "I wish it to be remembered that I was the last man of my tribe to surrender my rifle," he said, "and this day have given it to you."

Farther west, even as the Sioux War dragged on, the army was contending with other tribes fighting confinement on reservations. For his handling of the Nez Perce War General Howard endured the jeers of the press, the criticism of his peers, and the reproaches of his own conscience, all aggravated by a nasty public controversy with Colonel Miles (once, during the Civil War, his aide) over the division of credit for the capture of Chief Joseph. A year later, in 1878, an opportunity to refurbish his reputation

Sarah Winnemucca, the daughter of the Paiute chief with whom she is pictured above, risked her life to keep her tribe out of the war between the army and the Bannocks. At the army's request, she undertook a secret night mission to the Bannock camp, hoping to persuade the Paiutes who had joined them to leave. She escaped—barely—with just her father and a few peaceably disposed followers. "Princess Sarah" served as a scout and interpreter for the army throughout the campaign and later married a lieutenant.

presented itself, and this time Howard proved equal to the challenge.

The adversaries were the Northern Paiutes and the Bannocks. The former had fought a long and vicious guerrilla conflict against white settlers and travelers in Oregon until finally crushed by George Crook in 1868. Now, while occasionally drawing government rations at one of the four Paiute agencies, they mostly drifted about the northern margins of the Great Basin in search of game, roots, and nuts. During the 1870's, however, white newcomers began to make inroads on these food resources, especially game, and the agents could not provide enough rations to make up the deficiency. Unrest, intensified by the Nez Perce War, spread. Increasingly they heeded the incendiary talk of a powerful shaman named Oytes.

To the east similar conditions afflicted the Bannocks, who were close friends of the Paiutes and who were affiliated with two agencies on the upper Snake River in Idaho. About a thousand in number, the Bannocks looked increasingly for leadership to an energetic young chief named Buffalo Horn, who, ironically, had made a name for himself scouting for the army against the Sioux and Nez Perces.

The frustrations of the Bannocks and Paiutes erupted into violence in the spring of 1878. People from both tribes had gathered on Camas Prairie, ninety miles southeast of Boise, Idaho, to dig camas roots, a right guaranteed by treaty. Incensed at the increasing destruction of this staple by the hogs of white ranchmen, they indulged in a spate of menacing talk. After a Bannock shot and wounded two white men on May 30, 1878, Buffalo Horn gathered about 200 angry young warriors and raided westward across southern Idaho. A clash with a party of civilian volunteers on June 8 felled Buffalo Horn. His followers rode on into Oregon to Steens Mountain, where they were joined by Paiutes from the Malheur Agency under Oytes and the able and forceful Chief Egan. The combined group numbered about 700 people, including 450 fighting men. Oytes preached war, and Egan reluctantly bowed to the popular demand that he take the place of the slain Buffalo Horn.

Another full-scale uprising had burst on the Christian general. Mobilizing his troops and calling for reinforcements, Howard traveled by stagecoach to Boise, then joined a pursuing column that had already taken the field from Fort Boise. As he moved on Steens Mountain in three columns totaling some 480 cavalry and infantry, the Indians fell back, hurrying across the desert to Silver Creek, northwest of Harney Lake. Howard's aggressive cavalry commander, Captain Reuben F. Bernard, rode swiftly after them. On June 23 Bernard's squadron of the 1st Cavalry swept through the Indians' camp in a surprise attack that scattered them in disorder.

With Howard in pursuit, the Indians crossed the Strawberry Mountains to the twisted drainage of the John Day River. Pillaging ranches, they traveled northward toward the Umatilla Reservation, apparently hoping to gain recruits from that tribe. Bernard's cavalry, far in advance of the infantry, pushed them hard. On July 8 Howard's force, heavily reinforced the day before, found the Indians in rocky positions on top of steep bluffs overlooking Birch Creek. Bernard led an assault by seven troops of cavalry up the slope. Despite heavy fire, his men drove the defenders out of strong positions and gained the field.

Feinting southward, the Indians deceived Howard into thinking they were headed for the Nez Perce country, and he took Bernard's cavalry to

A CHEYENNE'S PLACE IN THE SUN

One of the heroes of Indian resistance to the reservation system was Dull Knife, chief of the Northern Cheyennes. In the spring of 1877, a few months after a ruinous defeat at Powder River, Dull Knife surrendered at Fort Robinson in Nebraska, expecting to live with the Sioux on a reservation near his homeland. But not long after the surrender General George Crook, under orders from Washington, informed Dull Knife that he and his band were to move to a reservation in Indian Territory. Crook promised Dull Knife that if he did not like the reservation he could return.

Escorted by white soldiers, 972 Cheyennes traveled 70 days to the reservation at Fort Reno. At a welcoming feast, the new arrivals were served nothing but watery soup—there was no better food.

Dull Knife and his tribe waited more than a year for permission from Washington to return home. An epidemic of malaria broke out and many died. A lieutenant sent to investigate conditions reported to his superiors, "They are not getting supplies enough to prevent starvation. The beef I saw given them . . . would not have been considered merchantable *for any use.*" Still no permission came.

Early in September of 1878 Dull Knife and some 300 Northern Cheyennes slipped away from the reservation. In a six-week flight, most of the band managed to escape the bullets of the 10,000 soldiers sent to overtake them. At the end of that time, while about half of the tribesmen continued north on their own, Dull Knife led 124 exhausted Cheyennes to Fort Robinson. Foreseeing that their arms would be confiscated, the Indians dismantled their best rifles, hiding the parts among their other belongings.

Unfortunately, the reservation at Fort Robinson had closed. Unsure whether to send the Cheyennes to join the Sioux at Pine Ridge or back to Fort Reno, the officers wired Washington for instructions.

General Philip Sheridan answered, "Unless they are sent back to where they came from, the whole reservation system will receive a shock which will endanger its stability." Dull Knife spoke for the Cheyennes, "We bowed to the will of the Great Father and went south. There we found a Cheyenne cannot live. So we came home. You may kill me here, but you cannot make me go back. We will not go."

On the night of January 9, 1879, the Indians quietly took gun barrels, triggers, and cartridges from their hiding places, shot the guards on duty, and poured out of the fort to freedom. Their triumph proved short-lived. In the first few hours after the breakout almost all the Indians were either shot (below) or captured. Only six, led by Dull Knife, made it to Pine Ridge. And by the time the government relented and set aside territory for the tribe near its homeland, fewer than eighty of his people were alive to take up residence there.

In this painting by Frederic Remington, soldiers from Fort Robinson survey the bodies of Cheyennes killed after their attempted escape.

cut them off. But they doubled back, and before Howard could return they suddenly appeared at the Umatilla Agency, near Pendleton, Oregon. Captain Evan Miles and a strong infantry column arrived there on July 12; the next day, while the Umatillas watched beneath a white flag, the troops skirmished for six hours with the hostiles and then drove them eastward into the mountains. Shrewdly predicting the winning side, a party of Umatillas followed and returned with a bloody scalp they said was Egan's. Seeking confirmation, Miles's surgeon rode forth "on an errand for the Medical Museum." He came back with Egan's head.

The repeated defeats, the death of Egan, the treachery of the Umatillas, and the growing ranks of soldiers hounding them from all directions disheartened the Bannocks and Paiutes. Once more they turned southward. Howard pursued, but he soon discovered there was nothing to pursue. The Paiutes had scattered in small groups all over southeastern Oregon, while the Bannocks had veered east and were cutting a swath of destruction across Idaho. Howard divided his army into detachments and began a systematic mopping-up operation. The surrender of Oytes on August 12 marked the close of Paiute hostilities. Other troops headed off the Bannocks, although one band, trying for a Canadian refuge, succeeded in crossing Yellowstone National Park before being intercepted.

Howard's soldiers gathered some 600 Paiute prisoners at Camp Harney, Oregon. The Paiutes' Malheur Reservation was officially abandoned, and they were at length colonized on the Yakima Reservation in Washington. The Bannock prisoners, 131 in number, were held at several military posts through the winter and permitted to return to their reservation on the upper Snake in the summer of 1879. With the successful conclusion of the Bannock-Paiute War, the one-armed general had regained some of the stature lost in the Nez Perce War.

During this same period the Ute Indians learned what the Nez Perces and many other tribes had so painfully learned: minerals on their lands were a fatal possession. The seven Ute bands, some four thousand people, lived in western Colorado and eastern Utah. In return for the government's acknowledgment of their ownership of a huge territory embracing the upper reaches of the White, Colorado, and San Juan rivers, they had relinquished all claim to territory elsewhere and affiliated with four agencies. Then came the Colorado silver strikes of the 1870's. Discovery of silver in the San Juan Mountains gave rise to pressures that forced the Utes to surrender four million acres, the entire southern quarter of their new reservation. Greedily the miners eyed the rest of the reservation, and when Colorado entered the Union in 1876, they began a steady agitation for the removal of the Utes to Indian Territory and the opening of all the reservation to white settlement.

The government provided a catalyst for this volatile situation in 1878 in the person of a wildly unqualified Indian agent. A utopian dreamer of advanced age and righteous zeal, Nathan C. Meeker set forth to make instant farmers of the Ute bands at the White River Agency in northwestern Colorado. Chiefs Jack and Douglas and their people resisted stubbornly. Throughout the summer of 1879 Meeker tried in vain to have soldiers sent to help him work his will.

The central issue was Meeker's demand that the Indians plow the meadows where their ponies grazed. On September 10, 1879, a medicine

THOMAS GILCREASE INSTITUTE OF HISTORY AND ART, TULSA

THE UTE MASSACRE!

Brave Miss Meeker's Captivity!

HER OWN ACCOUNT OF IT.

ALSO,

The Narratives of Her Mother and Mrs. Price.

TO WHICH IS ADDED

FURTHER THRILLING AND INTENSELY INTERESTING DETAILS, NOT HITHERTO PUBLISHED, OF THE BRAVERY AND FRIGHTFUL SUFFERINGS ENDURED BY MRS. MEEKER, MRS. PRICE AND HER TWO CHILDREN, AND

BY MISS JOSEPHINE MEEKER.

PUBLISHED BY

THE OLD FRANKLIN PUBLISHING HOUSE,
PHILADELPHIA, PA.

Entered, according to Act of Congress, in the year 1879, by the OLD FRANKLIN PUBLISHING HOUSE, in the office of the Librarian of Congress, at Washington, D. C.

After Ute Indians killed Nathan Meeker at his White River Agency in Colorado in 1879, they seized his wife, Arvilla, his twenty-two-year-old daughter Josephine, and an agency employee named Flora Price and her two children (above, a fanciful depiction of the capture). Released after twenty-three days, the women testified that Josephine had been raped repeatedly and that a chief had even insisted upon "having connection" with Mrs. Meeker. Although never proved, such reports boosted the sales of Josephine's own published story (above, the title page) of the ordeal.

man known as Johnson went to Meeker's home and heatedly protested the destruction of the grass on which his ponies depended. "You have too many ponies," replied Meeker curtly. "You had better kill some of them." Outraged, Johnson seized the agent and threw him out the front door. A telegram recounting this incident and declaring the lives of agency employees in danger at last caught the attention of Washington officials. Meeker would have his soldiers. At Fort Fred Steele, 175 miles to the north in Wyoming, Major Thomas T. Thornburgh received orders to march to the relief of the White River Agency.

Thornburgh's march toward the Ute reservation with a mixed force of infantry and cavalry, 175 strong, infuriated the Utes and even alarmed Meeker, who joined them in urging the major to halt his column and come to the agency for a parley. Thornburgh agreed but later decided to advance his 120 cavalrymen to a point closer to the agency. Understandably, the Utes thought themselves deceived, and on September 29, when the horsemen forded Milk Creek and entered the reservation, Chief Jack blocked the trail with 100 warriors.

Each side confronted the other warily and with evident intent to reconcile matters peacefully. But someone, Ute or soldier, mistook the adjutant's friendly wave of his hat as a signal, fired a single shot, and thus kicked off the Battle of Milk Creek. After a brief exchange of fire, the soldiers began to fall back toward Milk Creek and their wagon train. Major Thornburgh, riding among cottonwood trees yellowed by autumn frost, was struck above the ear by a heavy slug from a Sharp's rifle and killed instantly. Captain J. Scott Payne rallied the troopers at the corralled wagon train across the creek.

For almost a week the Utes held the soldiers under siege. Rifle fire killed all the horses, mules, and oxen, and occasionally knocked over one of the defenders. Food and water ran short. But Captain Payne, before collapsing from wounds, had sent out two messengers who succeeded in slipping safely through the Ute lines. A troop of black cavalrymen showed up on October 2 to bolster the shattered command—"You men of the Ninth Cavalry are the whitest black men I have ever seen," a captain

THE MEN
OUT FRONT

Yellowstone Kelly

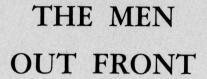

LIBRARY OF CONGRESS

Buffalo Bill Cody

"It is usual on the Plains . . . for every detachment of troops to be accompanied by one or more professional scouts or guides. . . . Who they are, whence they come or whither they go . . . are all questions which none but themselves can answer. . . . Do you know the country thoroughly, and can you speak any of the Indian languages, constitute the only examination. . . . [Then] the door to congenial employment most often leading to a terrible death, opens before him."

So wrote George Custer in *Life on the Plains.* In describing these professional army scouts, Custer did

Mickey Free

Jack Crawford

not indulge his penchant for exaggeration. They were an odd group. The army recruited them from among trappers, hunters, trail drivers, or anyone else familiar with the country, at $60 to $150 a month, far more than the soldiers earned. Even friendly Indians were recruited, but some officers tended to be uneasy about their loyalty.

William "Buffalo Bill" Cody was the most famous white scout. A former meat hunter for the railroad, he scouted with Wild Bill Hickok during the winter of 1866–67 in and around Fort Ellsworth, Kansas. He even scouted a short while for Cus-

ter. But instead of waiting around for the scout's "terrible death," he cashed in on the nation's curiosity about the West and launched his Wild West Show.

Yellowstone Kelly was as picturesque as Cody and in the opinion of many, a more able scout. Kelly, a well-educated hunter who loved the frontier, attracted the attention of Colonel Nelson Miles in 1876 by sending the paw of a bear he had just killed as a calling card. Intrigued, Miles hired him and set out in pursuit of Sitting Bull.

Poet-scout Jack Crawford led Colonel Wesley Merritt's 5th Cav-

alry against Chief Joseph and the Nez Perces in 1877. During lulls in the fighting Crawford tried to sell copies of his poetry books by autographing them and at times adding impromptu verses.

Fighting Apaches in Arizona George Crook employed a scout with a unique background and reputation as a local character who called himself Mickey Free. His left eye had been gouged out by a deer, but Free was a sharp tracker and a tough fighter. A fellow scout admiringly described him as "half Irish, half Mexican and whole son-of-a-bitch."

claimed in intended tribute. Finally, on October 5, the Indians pulled back as Colonel Wesley Merritt and a strong relief force reached the scene.

Not only had Milk Creek cost the army heavily—thirteen killed and forty-eight wounded—but it had prompted the Utes to vent their rage on Meeker. When Colonel Merritt marched into the White River Agency on October 11, he discovered the bodies of the agent and nine other employees lying among the burned-out buildings. Equally serious, the Indians had seized Mrs. Meeker, her daughter, and another woman and her two children and had fled with them to the mountains.

From north, east, and south thousands of troops converged on the Ute country, and the army readied plans for tracking the culprits down and exacting a swift and decisive retribution. Almost surely, however, such action would cost the lives of Mrs. Meeker and her fellow captives as well as spreading the war to the other Ute bands. Carl Schurz, the mercurial reformer who held the post of Secretary of the Interior, insisted that a peace effort be tried first.

While Generals Sherman and Sheridan fumed in impatience, Schurz launched his peace mission. It depended on two men of unusual ability. One was Charles Adams, a former agent to the Utes. The other was Ouray, chief of the Uncompahgre band and the wisest and most powerful of the Ute leaders. Although slowly dying of Bright's disease, Ouray commanded great respect among all the Ute bands. With a chief who could speak for the ailing Ouray, Adams approached the White River fugitives. In a stormy meeting on October 21 their chiefs, confronted with Ouray's threat to unite Ute bands against them, consented to give up their prisoners.

The skillful diplomacy of Schurz, Adams, and Ouray had averted further fighting and won the release of the captive women and children. Both Adams and Ouray sat on a commission charged with determining whether individual Indians should be marked for punishment. The commission cleared the Milk Creek combatants, but over Ouray's protests it named twelve Indians to stand trial for the murder of Meeker and his associates and for "outrages" against the captive women. None of the offenders came to trial, however, for this issue quickly became lost in a larger one.

Milk Creek and the Meeker massacre had moved Coloradans to step up their campaign to have the Ute Reservation thrown open to settlement. In Washington in the summer of 1880 Ouray and a delegation of chiefs bowed to the inevitable and accepted a proposal to part with most of their remaining land. Ouray himself did not live to see the sad spectacle of his people's expulsion; he died in August, 1880, while helping to obtain the signatures needed to give tribal sanction to the agreement. Four Ute bands, including the two from White River, moved to new homes on reservations in eastern Utah, while the three southern bands retained a small reservation in southwestern Colorado.

Doubtless the Utes would have been forced to surrender their homeland sooner or later had Meeker never ventured onto the scene. But it was Meeker who precipitated the process. Charles Adams summed up what had happened at White River in a perceptive understatement: "I don't think that Mr. Meeker understood those Indians. He was a great agriculturist, and he thought he could succeed in forcing the Indians to work and to accept the situation as farmers, but he did not take into consideration that it is almost impossible to force Indians into that sort of labor all at once."

In the Southwest the middle 1870's once more raised the specter of Apache hostilities. The iron military rule imposed by General Crook relaxed after his transfer in 1875 to the Sioux country. At the same time, the Indian Bureau launched a new concentration program calculated to unsettle Apaches everywhere. The small reservations in New Mexico and Arizona established by Vincent Colyer and General Howard in 1871–72 would be replaced by a single large reservation. All Apaches west of the Rio Grande would be required to move to the San Carlos Reservation, a hot, barren, malarial flat on the Gila River in Arizona.

Although most of the Apaches went resignedly to San Carlos, the proudly independent Chiricahuas and Warm Springs did not. The contentment with which the Chiricahuas had settled on their new reservation with Agent Tom Jeffords following General Howard's peace mission in 1872 had vanished. The Indian Bureau, never reconciled to the unconventional and uncontrollable Jeffords, had quickly found a reason to replace him. Then in 1874 the legendary Cochise died. Neither of his sons, Taza or Nachez, proved equal to the test of the chieftainship, and the tribe broke into quarreling factions. About half heeded the order, in 1876, to move to San Carlos. The rest fled to Mexico, where high in the Sierra Madre the Nednhi band of Chiricahuas under Juh had always provided a haven for disaffected kinsmen from north of the boundary.

The Warm Springs Apaches, living on the Ojo Caliente Reservation in western New Mexico, greeted San Carlos even less enthusiastically than the Chiricahuas. Ordered there in 1877, many slipped off to the mountains, and others gave their new home scarcely a four-month trial.

The history of the final decade of Apache warfare, 1876–86, is the story of the resistance of these two closely allied Apache groups, children of Mangas Coloradas and Cochise, to life at San Carlos. And it is as well the story of two of the most dynamic and resourceful war leaders any Indian tribe ever produced, worthy heirs of Mangas Coloradas and Cochise: Victorio and Geronimo.

Victorio had learned the arts of Apache warfare from the great Mangas Coloradas, whom he equaled and perhaps even surpassed in courage, stamina, cunning, and leadership. Scornful of all curbs on his independence, especially those imposed by whites, burning with outrage over the treacherous slaying of his mentor more than a decade earlier, he nonetheless seems to have wanted peace with the white people — if it did not come at an intolerable price.

San Carlos was intolerable. "That horrible summer!" recalled one of Victorio's followers. "He saw babies almost devoured by insects. He saw people suffer from malaria, and that the medicine men could not save their lives." On September 2, 1877, he led his people and some Chiricahuas, more than three hundred in all, in a break from the reservation. The flight collapsed in little more than a month as they gave up near Fort Wingate, New Mexico; but they had won a round even so, for the soldiers escorted them back to their beloved home at Ojo Caliente while the government tried to decide what to do with them. Almost a year later the decision came: go back to San Carlos. Many people did, but not Victorio, who with eighty men took to the mountains.

For another year the determined chief sought a solution that would avoid the hated San Carlos. Once more he tried, vainly, to settle at Ojo

Caliente, and early in 1879 he talked with the agent at the Mescalero Apache Reservation, east of the Rio Grande, about settling there. The agent held forth hope and even said he would try to have the rest of the Warm Springs people transferred from San Carlos. But this hope, too, turned to ashes when on September 4, 1879, Victorio and sixty warriors swept down on the herd camp of Troop E, 9th Cavalry, near Ojo Caliente, killed the eight black soldiers standing guard, and rode off with all forty-six of the unit's horses. It was the opening shot of the Victorio War.

On both sides of the boundary people paid a frightful price for the government's determination to force Victorio onto the San Carlos Reservation. Fresh warriors joined his ranks, chiefly Mescaleros from the reservation and the Sierra del Carmen bands, bringing his force to between 125 and 150 fighting men. Here and there they darted with lightning speed, cutting down isolated sheepherders and waylaying hapless travelers. In November they turned up in the Candelaria Mountains of Chihuahua, where they ambushed and wiped out a party of eighteen Mexicans. Another party, searching for the first, rode into the same ambush and saw fifteen of its number slain before breaking free. From Chihuahua through western Texas and southern New Mexico to Arizona the raiders ranged, riding even to the edges of the San Carlos Reservation, where the families of some still dwelled.

Troops of both nations converged on the afflicted area. Colonel Edward Hatch and Major A. P. Morrow campaigned tirelessly in southern New Mexico with the 9th Cavalry, while Colonel Benjamin H. Grierson and the 10th, also composed of black troopers serving white officers, covered western Texas. General Gerónimo Treviño mobilized Mexican troops to pursue the marauders in Chihuahua. American units freely entered Mexico, usually with the tacit approval of Mexican authorities.

General George Crook encouraged vigorous recruitment of Apaches at Arizona's San Carlos Agency (below) to fight those few tribesmen who had not yet surrendered. On one successful 1883 expedition, Crook's command consisted of 193 Apaches and only one small company of the 6th Cavalry. A contemporary praised Crook's controversial strategy this way: "Unless the fullest use were made of scouts to the manner born, thoroughly posted in the minutest details of the country, able to detect the slightest mark on the trail and to interpret it correctly—in short, unless savage should be pitted against savage, the white man would be outwitted, exhausted, circumvented, and possibly ambuscaded and destroyed."

For a year the troops tried in vain to crush Victorio. Time and again they closed in combat, only to see the elusive chieftain turn and slip away with scant loss. On one occasion, in May, 1880, an Indian scout company trapped the Apaches in the Black Range of western New Mexico, killed thirty, and lodged a bullet in Victorio's leg, but they ran out of ammunition and had to withdraw. In July, in western Texas, Grierson's black troopers outmaneuvered the raiders and twice turned them back to Mexico. In one encounter Grierson himself, with a small detachment, held a vital water hole against a determined Apache assault and was saved only by the timely arrival, in the best Hollywood tradition, of reinforcements charging onto the field with guidons snapping and trumpets sounding — "& golly," Grierson's teen-age son wrote exuberantly in his diary, "you ought to've seen 'em turn tail & strike for the hills."

The raiders began to tire. They were hungry, destitute, and running low on ammunition. In the autumn of 1880 they drifted eastward into the parched Chihuahuan deserts, seemingly without plan or purpose. Several hundred soldiers under Colonel George P. Buell had been organized into a formidable expedition that marched ever deeper into Chihuahua in search of the Indians. Another force had gathered too, a motley aggregation of 350 Mexican militiamen and Tarahumara Indians under a hard-bitten veteran of Apache warfare, Colonel Joaquin Terrazas. Scenting a kill and unwilling to share it with the Americans, Terrazas ordered Buell out of Mexico. Amid three low peaks that rose sharply from a vast desert plain, Terrazas encountered the object of his search.

Tres Castillos the three peaks were called, and for two days, October 15–16, 1880, Terrazas and Victorio battled among them. In the first attack the Mexicans captured the Indians' stock and drove them up the boulder-strewn slopes of one of the hills. All day and into the night the two sides exchanged fire. In the darkness the Apaches tried to break free but were held back. At midnight the Mexicans heard the chant of death songs from the heights as the Indians threw up rock fortifications for a fight to the last. At daybreak the Mexicans advanced up the slopes. "The Indians fought fiercely to the last," the colonel reported, "sustained by the very advantageous positions which they had prepared during the night and which were taken by us by assault, our force throwing itself upon theirs, fighting man against man, the combatants wrestling with each other and getting hold of each other's heads." When the smoke and dust cleared, the Mexicans counted seventy-eight dead Indians among the rocks (sixty-two men and sixteen women and children) and sixty-eight prisoners. "The indian Victorio is of the dead," concluded the commander in his report.

And so it was. Despite an abundance of imaginative accounts, no one really knows how or when Victorio died. He may even, as modern Apaches believe, have stabbed himself rather than be taken prisoner. Certain it is, though, that Victorio's remarkable career came to an end in the bloody Battle of Tres Castillos. His death closed an era in Apache warfare. It now remained for a similarly endowed leader to make the last stand of the Apaches. More than the spirit of Victorio participated, for not all his people had fallen to the Mexicans. A handful escaped the battle, and others were absent on a raid. Under the ancient and incredibly durable Nana, they returned to New Mexico and at length cast their lot with this other Apache who found San Carlos intolerable. His name was Geronimo.

Soldiering in the West

Frederic Remington's "Cavalrymen in an Arizona Sandstorm" jibes with a soldier's description: "All in one moment the whole sky seemed to rush down upon us as if it were a big pepper-box with the lid off, and instantly all was dark as night, and I felt as if forty thousand ants were eating me up at once." Artist Remington actually rode with troops on scouting forays and brought his vivid experiences to life in realistic canvases, such as this and the ones on the following pages.

AMON CARTER MUSEUM, FORT WORTH

Century, APRIL, 1889

Among the cavalry regiments Remington rode with were the 9th and 10th—both composed of black troops commanded by white officers. Although they were offered higher rank and more rapid promotion, many officers refused to serve with blacks. Many who chose to serve did so because they were dedicated to proving that black soldiers could succeed. And they did, particularly in Texas, where they fought Apaches and Comanches for more than ten years. Remington, who was there, thoroughly endorsed a veteran officer's very positive evaluation: "They follow wherever led, they will go without leading, and will stay with their leader through all danger and never desert him."

A trooper on patrol in hot country takes a quick drink.

This early Remington shows a detachment signaling the main command.

An officer watches troopers of the 10th Cavalry helping an Apache scout.

Troopers and Indian scouts watch terriers attack a badger.

Drawings by Frederic Remington. 1897

In a frontier devoid of mirrors, buddies shave each other.

Drawings by Frederic Remington. 1897

A pipe-smoking cavalry cook carries water for breakfast.

For Remington, who greatly admired the professional
soldiers he met in the West, the days passed in
the field coincided closely with his vision of the
perfect life — purposeful, spartan, vigorous,
and filled with camaraderie. "The freemasonry
of the army," he wrote, "makes strong friendships,
and soldiers are all good fellows, that being
a part of their business. . . . The cold, bloodless,
compound-interest snarler is not in the army."

Troopers cook their grub in this detail from "Cavalryman's Breakfast."

Remington had warm memories of the Christmas he spent inside this Sibley tent: "The . . . stove sighs like a furnace while the cruel wind seeks out the holes and crevices. The soldiers sit in their camp drawing-room buttoned up to the chin in their big canvas overcoats, and the muskrat caps are not removed. . . . They have met before, and memory after memory comes up with its laughter and pathos of the old campaigns."

"21" CLUB

Remington's most popular works were his impressions of combat. Though he never saw action himself, his creations, such as "Cavalry Charge on the Southern Plains," were highly touted by men who had been there.

Frederic Remington
1907

11: The Final Volleys

Geronimo—the name Mexicans gave to the Chiricahua chief Goyahkla—was the last of the great Apache war leaders. Others claimed more prestige and influence, but none struck greater terror in Mexicans or Americans. Mexicans especially feared him, for in 1858 Mexican soldiers had killed his mother, wife, and children, and for the rest of his days of freedom he exacted a frightful retribution. Short, thick, scowling, he nourished a fondness for strong drink that when indulged, as it often was, exacerbated his inherent ill temper. Lieutenant Britton Davis, an officer of Apache scouts who knew him well, branded Geronimo "a thoroughly vicious, intractable, and treacherous man," a judgment many of his own people shared. Yet his cousin, who rode with him and later gained a white man's education at Carlisle Indian School, thought that of all the Apache leaders "Geronimo seemed to be the most intelligent and resourceful as well as the most vigorous and farsighted. In times of danger he was a man to be relied upon." Even Lieutenant Davis admitted he had the "redeeming traits" of "courage and determination."

For many years Geronimo rode with Juh's Nednhi band of Chiricahua and assorted other Apache "outlaws" who lived in Mexico's Sierra Madre. They scorned reservations and were viewed by other Apaches, recalled one, "as being true wild men . . . devoted entirely to warfare and raiding the settlements." Geronimo had returned to the Nednhis in 1876 upon the abolition of the Chiricahua Reservation but appeared at the Ojo Caliente Agency in southwestern New Mexico in the spring of 1877. There the irrepressible young San Carlos agent John P. Clum, on hand to move Victorio's people, seized Geronimo and carried him off to San Carlos in irons. He stayed for a year before disappearing once more across the border and into the Sierra Madre. Then early in 1880, pressed too closely by Mex-

During the final fight at Wounded Knee, Hotchkiss gunner Paul Weinert, shown here with other artillerymen at the Pine Ridge Agency, saw his lieutenant hit, cried, "By God I'll make 'em pay for that"—and did. His fire drove the Sioux from a key position and won Weinert a Medal of Honor.

324

ican troops, Juh and 105 people, including Geronimo, presented themselves at San Carlos.

Conditions at San Carlos formed the backdrop for the final stages of Apache warfare. Besides heat, sterile soil, disease, reptiles, and insects, the reservation festered with intrigue, intertribal rivalries, incompetence and corruption in the Indian Bureau's administration, and conflict between military and civilian authorities. A growing white population raised fears of further encroachment on Indian land. Almost any incident, important or trivial, could crystallize these sources of discontent.

Trouble with the White Mountain Apaches provoked such an incident. A prophet, Nakaidoklini, preached a militant new religion that alarmed white officials and led to an order for his arrest. On August 30, 1881, Colonel Eugene A. Carr, the commandant of Fort Apache, took the medicine man into custody at his village on Cibicue Creek. Shouting swarms of the faithful surrounded the small command. Fighting erupted. The company of White Mountain scouts mutinied and killed their captain; a sergeant fired a fatal bullet into Nakaidoklini, and Carr barely extricated his force. Later warriors attacked Fort Apache itself but were turned back.

Newspapers spread wild stories of a massacre of Carr's entire command, and in response San Carlos soon swarmed with soldiers who had hastened in from all over the Southwest. On September 30, frightened by a threatening military movement, Juh, Chato, Geronimo, Nachez (son of Cochise and titular chief of the Chiricahuas), and seventy-four Indians suddenly broke out and headed for Mexico. There they united with old Nana and the remnant of Victorio's people.

The Cibicue misfortune and the inept movements that stampeded the Chiricahuas gave rise to doubts about the quality of military leadership in the Department of Arizona, commanded by Brevet Major General Orlando B. Willcox. These doubts intensified in April, 1882, when a war party from Mexico under Juh, Geronimo, and others burst on San Carlos, shot the chief of police, and forced Loco, the leader of the Warm Springs Apache band, and several hundred more people to go south with them. Then in July a band of disaffected White Mountains, remnants of Nakaidoklini's following, stormed the agency and killed the new police chief and three of his men. Although cavalry later destroyed the raiders, orders had already been issued transferring General Willcox to a new assignment and returning to Arizona the one officer who had shown that he could deal effectively with the Apache problem, General George Crook.

Crook went to work with characteristic energy. Blending justice with firmness, he reasserted military control of San Carlos. To keep the peace on the reservation and ultimately to dig the so-called "renegades" out of the Sierra Madre, he organized five companies of White Mountain Apache scouts under his brightest young officers. For these units he signed on "the wildest I could get," for despite the risk of dubious loyalty they promised the best chance of overtaking their elusive kinsmen. In another hallmark of Crook's methods, skilled packers organized efficient and sturdy mule trains. No cumbersome wagons would limit his mobility.

A daring Apache raid set Crook in motion. In March, 1883, Chato and 25 warriors slashed across Arizona and New Mexico, then faded back into Mexico. In response, on May 1 Crook crossed the border at the head of a force of 193 Apache scouts under Captain Emmet Crawford and Lieu-

tenant Charles B. Gatewood, a troop of regular cavalry, and a train of 350 mules. With mountain piled on mountain and gashed by great gorges of dizzying depth, the Sierra Madre afforded the Apaches a refuge and fortress they thought to be impenetrable. Even Mexican troops had never ventured far into this wilderness.

But Crook had a guide who knew where to look for the enemy. Called Peaches by the soldiers, he was a sleepy-eyed Indian who had defected from Chato during the March raid. Unerringly Peaches led the expedition in a tortuous and punishing climb. An attack on Chato's camp on May 15 gave notice to the Chiricahuas that their sanctuary had been breached.

One by one the Chiricahua leaders drifted in to talk with the soldier chief. A "piratical gang," in the eyes of Crook's aide, they included Chihuahua, Chato, Bonito, Loco, Nachez, Kaytennae, old Nana, and finally Geronimo himself, who had been off raiding in Chihuahua. Juh had been killed in an accident, and the captains now seemed to look to Geronimo for guidance. For a week they parleyed with Crook, Geronimo serving as the principal spokesman. At any time they could have slaughtered the whites and scattered into the mountains. But Crook's bold foray into their stronghold, coupled with their distress over his ability to mobilize other Apaches against them, gave him psychological advantages. Affecting a stern demeanor and indulging in threats he could not have carried out, he bluffed his way through.

As he later described the negotiations—with perhaps a pardonable trace of exaggeration—Crook told the Apaches that "they had been committing atrocities and depredations upon our people and the Mexicans, and that we had become tired of such a condition of affairs and intended to wipe them out; that I had not taken all this trouble for the purpose of making them prisoners; that they had been bad Indians, and that I was unwilling to return without punishing them as they deserved; that if they wanted a fight, they could have one any time they pleased. I told them that the Mexican troops were moving in from both sides, and it was only a matter of days until the last of them should be under the ground. The best thing for them to do was to fight their way out if they thought they could do it. I kept them waiting for several days, and each day they became more and more importunate. Jeronimo and all the chiefs at last fairly begged me to be taken back to San Carlos. . . . 'We give ourselves up [they said], do with us as you please.'"

"I look upon Crook as a frontier savior," declared the mayor of Chihuahua City. The accolade of Arizonans was only slightly less enthusiastic—until it became known that most of the Chiricahuas, including Geronimo, had tarried behind and had not come in with the Warm Springs followers of Nana and Loco. As month after month slipped by with no sign of the Chiricahuas, Crook's reputation plummeted. Late in 1883, however, they began to appear at San Carlos, and Geronimo's arrival in March, 1884, marked the final though belated success of Crook's Sierra Madre venture.

At San Carlos, however, tensions began building almost at once. Restive under military oversight, defiant of Crook's vexing rules against beating their wives and drinking the volatile concoction tiswin, the Chiricahuas began thinking about the Sierra Madre again. At last, in May, 1885, they openly challenged the ban on tiswin and precipitated a crisis that led to still another breakout. Forty-two men, among them Geronimo, Nachez,

During the 1880's the last Indians to present a constant threat to whites were the Apaches, whose most notorious leader was Geronimo (below, right, with a comrade). Striking from strongholds in Mexico, the Apaches raided into the U.S. for supplies and revenge against the hated whites. On one such raid they killed the parents of five-year-old Charley McComas (left) and bore him off to Mexico. By the time General George Crook's troops caught up with the Apaches, Charley was dead—either starved by neglect or murdered by one of the women.

Chihuahua, and Nana, and ninety-two women and children bolted the reservation and hurried south to Mexico.

Once again mobilizing his scout units and pack trains, Crook repeated his strategy of 1883. While regulars patrolled the border, scouts under Captain Crawford, Lieutenant Gatewood, and others combed the mountains of Chihuahua and Sonora. The fugitives stayed clear of their pursuers and twice, slipping through the border defenses, cut a path of terror across Arizona and New Mexico. General Philip H. Sheridan, now the army's commander in chief, hurried to Fort Bowie, where Crook made his headquarters, to voice doubts about such heavy reliance on Indian scouts.

Even as the two generals argued, however, the Chiricahuas were tiring of the relentless chase. Early in January, 1886, two hundred miles south of the boundary, they sent word to Captain Crawford that they wanted to talk. Before a conference could be held, a Mexican militia force, probably not so mistakenly as later contended, attacked Crawford's scout command. His Apaches put up a rousing defense, but before the fighting could be stopped Crawford went down with a bullet in his brain. Two days later Geronimo, Nachez, Chihuahua, and Nana met with Crawford's lieutenant and said they wanted to discuss surrender with General Crook in person.

The conference at Canyon de los Embudos on March 25, 1886, recalled that other conference high in the Sierra Madre two years previously. Again Crook faced Geronimo and his associates. Again Crook bluffed, demanding unconditional surrender or "I'll keep after you and kill the last one, if it takes fifty years." But he offered conditions nonetheless: the hostiles, with their families, must go to a place of confinement in the East for two years. After that they could return to Arizona—but only to San Carlos. Two days later, after long nighttime arguments among themselves, Geronimo, Nachez, Nana, and Chihuahua accepted Crook's terms.

Again Crook's triumph was fleeting. At Fort Bowie, where he had gone to telegraph the happy tidings to Washington, Crook learned that following a drinking bout Geronimo and Nachez had led twenty men and thirteen women in a sudden stampede back to the Sierra Madre. Compounding the humiliation, he received directives from General Sheridan that in effect required him to substitute unconditional surrender for the terms on which the Indians had agreed. Unable to bring himself to an act of such treachery, tired, and discouraged, Crook asked to be relieved of command. Sheridan complied at once, penning orders for Brigadier General Nelson A. Miles to hasten to Arizona and take his place.

General Miles heeded his chief's admonition to rely less on Indian scouts and more on regulars. As Geronimo's warriors raided again in Arizona, Miles formed a tightly knit strike force of cavalry, infantry, and scouts at Fort Huachuca. Tough Captain Henry W. Lawton commanded, assisted by a doctor who wanted to be a line officer and was destined to rise one day to army chief of staff—Leonard Wood. Through the brutally hot summer months of 1886 Lawton's command combed the Sierra Madre as far as two hundred miles south of the boundary. It was an ordeal as painful and exhausting as seemingly futile. Regulars might keep the fugitives on the move and tire them out, but they could not close with them in a fight.

In the end Crook's techniques, fortified by an innovation of Miles's own devising, proved crucial. Miles's measure was nothing less than the deportation to detention camps in Florida of all the Chiricahua and Warm Springs

This picture of the tense 1886 peace parley between Geronimo (seated, in bandanna) and a pith-helmeted George Crook (second from right) in the Apache's mountain lair was recorded by a daring frontier photographer named C. S. Fly, who accompanied the troops.

Apaches at San Carlos—even those who had served Crook faithfully as scouts. The measure borrowed from Crook was the dispatch of Lieutenant Gatewood, a trusted Crook protégé who enjoyed the confidence of the hostile leaders, to try to open talks with Geronimo.

Again, in part because of the operations of Lawton and Wood, Geronimo was ready to talk. On August 24, at considerable peril, Gatewood made his way into the hostile camp accompanied only by two Indian guides. In tense sessions he tried to persuade Geronimo to surrender and go to Florida until the President decided his ultimate fate. Geronimo replied that he stood ready to surrender, but only if he could return to San Carlos and live with the rest of his tribe. Then Gatewood dropped the news that no Chiricahuas would be at San Carlos: all were even then being rounded up for the move to Florida. This revelation stunned the hostiles and at last moved them to give in. He would surrender, Geronimo said, to General Miles in person. Keeping a respectable distance to avoid another stampede, Lawton and Wood escorted this last band of Chiricahua rebels northward to American territory. At Skeleton Canyon on September 4, 1886, Geronimo formally surrendered to General Miles.

There would be years of controversy over the exile of the Apaches to Florida and the proper division of the honors for bringing about their final surrender—Miles's ego was bigger than ever and he still disdained Crook as much as ever. The Indians would one day be allowed to return to the West, but only as far as Oklahoma, never to their Arizona homeland. Geronimo would live out the last years of his life at Fort Sill, Oklahoma, where he died in 1909 at the age of about eighty. But for the Southwest the long bloody history of Apache warfare ended when Geronimo, Nachez, and their handful of die-hard followers gathered on the Fort Bowie parade ground to begin the journey to Florida. As they climbed into the wagons that would take them to the railroad, the regimental band of the 4th Cavalry snapped to attention and gave forth with "Auld Lang Syne."

A trainload of Apaches rattling across the Arizona deserts toward faroff Florida signaled, at last, that the reservation system would prevail. Every big Indian conflict since 1870 had been essentially a war not of concentration but of rebellion—of Indians rebelling against reservations they had already accepted in theory if not in fact. The Red River War of 1874–75, the Sioux War of 1876–81, the Nez Perce, Paiute, and Ute wars of 1877–79, and the Victorio and Geronimo wars had all been fought in large part with reservation Indians who did not like the reservation and still, however hopelessly, retained some ability to resist. Geronimo and his people could challenge the reservation by armed force and seek an alternative life only because the wilds of Mexico offered a haven denied to most other tribes.

The regular army supposed that it had conquered the Indians. But the real conquerors were the pioneers who tramped westward by the thousands and then millions. Simply by spreading across the land and destroying the game, grass, timber, and other resources that sustained the Indian's way of life, they left him but one alternative. That was the reservation and its promise of rations, clothing, and other necessities. By 1886, with the collapse of Geronimo, all the tribes had acknowledged this reality.

Undermanned and weakly led, the regular army had struggled through to the close of the Indian wars unaware that it was more a big police force than a little army. And police force it should have been. The conditions of the Indian frontier did not call for a conventional army but rather a constabulary able to identify and take action against offending individuals rather than offending tribes—for rarely were there truly any of the latter. Such a constabulary, moreover, should have consisted in large measure of Indians, able to understand Indian thinking and customs, to anticipate trouble and take appropriate action to forestall it, and to apprehend offenders by Indian methods when trouble could not be prevented.

Perhaps the tribes could have slowed the process, or compelled a more just conclusion, had they been able to unite against the common threat. But they failed to see the white advance as truly apocalyptic until too late, and they never overcame the cultural forces that made them see other tribes as greater enemies than the white people. Moreover, as the Sioux and Cheyennes discovered in 1876, the harsh western environment treated large bodies of Indians only slightly more generously than large expeditions of soldiers: forage, game, fuel, and water did not exist in a plenitude permitting tribal coalitions to remain together for long. Even so, had the tribes been able to forge and sustain widespread alliances that simply bound them all to fight back at the same time and not make peace separately, they might have impeded the process of conquest enough to have retained more of their land, or gained more compensation for it, or obtained a reservation system that was less racially and culturally devastating.

By the middle 1880's there were 187 reservations embracing 181,000 square miles of territory and 243,000 Indians. From fewer than 300 officials in 1850, the Indian Bureau had grown to a far-flung bureaucracy

Disheartened, ragged, their moccasins in tatters, these Chiricahua Apaches cluster around a porch at Fort Bowie, Arizona, after a forced march under the guns of the scouts and soldiers who had broken into Geronimo's Sierra Madre hideout.

of more than 2,500, and it held virtually life-and-death control over all the Indians of the United States.

Few government agencies lent themselves more readily to patronage politics and corruption than the Indian Bureau, and none achieved a worse reputation. Blanketing the nation, it afforded hundreds of government jobs in which the consequences of bad appointments fell chiefly on people who had little effective means of protest. As one state governor laughingly conceded, for party hacks fit for nothing else a position could usually be found in the Indian Bureau. Thus, despite some notable exceptions, most Indian agents were deplorably unqualified. At best they were inexperienced in the difficult art of dealing with Indians — and were replaced before they could gain experience. At worst they were incompetent, corrupt, or both.

The bureau offered special opportunities for fraud. Annual appropriations of $7 million were customary. Most of this sum went for the purchase of food, clothing, and other goods for issue to the Indians. From factory to agency warehouse, corrupt alliances enriched government officials and suppliers and penalized the Indians in both quantity and quality of issues. At San Carlos, for example, inspectors found the agent selling Indian goods on the open market, diverting Indian cattle to his private herd, feeding the cattle government grain, and herding them with a government employee. As an indignant congressman observed, "No branch of the national government is so spotted with fraud, so tainted with corruption, so utterly unworthy of a free and enlightened government, as this Indian Bureau."

As the reservation system grew, the agents gained ever more varied staffs to aid them in their work — clerks, teachers, farmers, herders, blacksmiths, carpenters, and others. The farmers tried to teach Indians how to farm like white men but with indifferent success, especially since few reservations contained land suitable for agriculture. The teachers opened schoolhouses but had trouble keeping them stocked with pupils. Although not on the government payroll, missionaries and traders were enormously influential reservation figures. The missionary offered the white man's God, and He was accepted by many, though usually in addition to, not in place of, the native deities. The traders supplied a range of useful items not issued by the government — and some not so useful, notably whiskey.

The reservation system featured a concerted effort to destroy tribal organization and identity and emphasize the individual, to root out the beliefs and customs of the old life and substitute new ones from the white man's culture, and to carve up the reservations into individual homesteads, returning "surplus" lands to the public domain for white settlement. Coercion marked this program. The agent controlled rations and could cut off issues to the uncooperative. Indians working as police and judges backed his authority and sought to enforce a long list of "Indian offenses" — such "demoralizing and barbarous" customs as feasts, dances, plural marriage, and the medical and religious practices of the medicine men.

By the 1880's the reservation system had in effect deprived the Indians of the ability to hunt or make war — the two pastimes that had consumed most of their energies and, more important, shaped their social, economic, political, religious, and military institutions. And many institutions that might have been adapted to the new life had come under attack by the agent and his minions. To make matters worse, the issues of food and clothing were too little and of poor quality: the people were hungry much of the

AFTER THE FALL

As final defeat rolled over the western tribes, many of the great warriors, such as Roman Nose, died in battle. Others, such as Crazy Horse, died after a brief captivity. But four of the most famous chiefs—Joseph, Quanah Parker, Geronimo, and Sitting Bull—lived out their lives on reservations in very different ways.

Chief Joseph at Colville in 1903

Part Comanche, part white, Quanah Parker made a unique transition from warrior to wealthy businessman in the white world. When he surrendered in 1875 he spoke little English and had never lived in a house. But he soon mastered the language well enough to make deals leasing reservation lands to cattlemen, buy shares in a profitable railroad, and lobby for Indian rights in Washington. He built an elegant twelve-room home and served as chief judge on the reservation's Court of Indian Offenses. Although he adopted many white customs, Quanah did not abandon his Comanche heritage entirely. When a commissioner of Indian Affairs told him he had to choose one from among his five wives and tell the others to go away, Quanah closed the subject by responding, "You tell them." When he died in 1911, the much-married Quanah was buried in the full regalia of a Comanche chief.

After Chief Joseph surrendered in 1877 he asked to be "free to choose my own teachers, free to follow the religion of my fathers, free to think and talk and act for myself—and I will obey every law, or submit to the penalty." Instead, Joseph and other supposedly dangerous Nez Perces were sent to a reservation in Colville, Washington. Joseph's persistent entreaties were ignored, and he died—reportedly from a broken heart—in 1904.

After Geronimo turned himself in in September, 1886, government officials were in no mood to be charitable. Instead of the promised reservation in Oklahoma, they sent Geronimo and his men to Fort Pickens, on Florida's west coast, and their families to Fort Marion, on the east coast. For eight years the Apaches trekked to various prisons in Florida and Alabama before settling permanently at Fort Sill, Oklahoma. Never much interested in farming, Geronimo traveled to fairs and exhibitions, where he made some money by selling his autograph and posing for snapshots. He spent a good portion of his income on liquor. Riding back to Fort Sill after a spree in 1909, Geronimo fell off his horse, lay on the damp ground all night, caught pneumonia, and died shortly afterward.

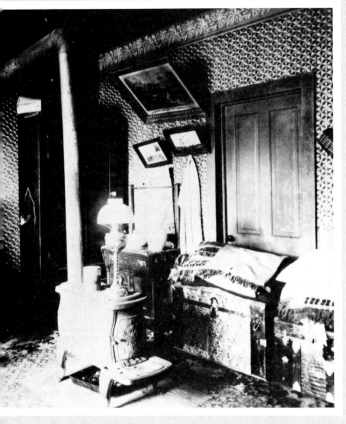

uanah Parker in his chambers beneath a picture of Custer's Last Stand

Sitting Bull and Buffalo Bill before a show in 1885

One of the Sioux masterminds behind Little Bighorn, Sitting Bull was the most publicized chief to be confined to a reservation. In 1885, four years after he had surrendered, Buffalo Bill recruited him for his Wild West Show for $50 a week plus expenses, $125 bonus for signing—and a chance to present his grievances at the White House. Sitting Bull considered Buffalo Bill one of his best friends, but he refused to join the show for a trip to Queen Victoria's Golden Jubilee in 1887. "It is bad for our cause for me to parade around. I am needed here. There is more talk of taking our lands." Indeed, the government was trying to buy 10 million acres of Sioux reservation lands at 50 cents an acre. Sitting Bull talked the other Sioux into not signing, but in 1889, against his wishes, they agreed to $1.25 an acre. "There are no Indians left but me!" lamented Sitting Bull. A year later he was gone—shot and killed on the reservation by an Indian policeman.

Geronimo and his family in a Fort Sill pumpkin patch

time. Finally, in groping for ways to adjust, the tribes divided into factions: "progressives," who tried to cooperate with the white officials and follow the path to "civilization," and "nonprogressives," who stubbornly resisted the new ways and dreamed of the old.

No other reservations more graphically exemplified the process by which a proud and free people were reduced to misery, degradation, and futility than those of the Sioux. There were now six such reservations—the result of still another land agreement that splintered the Great Sioux Reservation. On these the followers of Red Cloud, Sitting Bull, and other great chiefs tried to cope with the new order. Red Cloud and Sitting Bull represented two ways of coping.

Although never perceived as a "progressive," Red Cloud acknowledged the reality of the government's power. On the Pine Ridge Reservation he fought the system enough to retain the backing of most of his people but not so stubbornly as to provoke the whites beyond toleration. He opposed Indian police and judges, land allotment, ration issues directly to individuals rather than through the chiefs, and other innovations the whites regarded as reforms. But he also, by adroit politics and diplomacy, exerted enough influence over all factions of the Oglala tribe to remain valuable, even indispensable, to government officials as an intermediary. And he learned how to extract conditions and concessions for every enforced acquiescence. Agents might be enraged by his perversity, but they could not ignore or rid themselves of him.

Sitting Bull, on the other hand, remained uncompromisingly Indian. On the Standing Rock Reservation, where the Hunkpapas lived, he was the arch "nonprogressive," devoted to the true Indian life, fixedly intent upon having no more to do with the whites and their ways than circumstances forced. Gall, Crow King, and other heroes of the Little Bighorn might cooperate with the agent and even become Christians. Not Sitting Bull. He disdained the agent and labored diligently to rebuff all threats to old Indian ways. Not surprisingly, the agent saw him as "crafty, avaricious, mendacious, and ambitious."

A decade of intensive civilization programs had left the Sioux angry and bitter, yet also oppressed with a crushing sense of helplessness and hopelessness. Deepening the despair as the 1880's drew to a close was a series of droughts that killed their crops, hunger and even starvation resulting from a severe ration cut decreed by an economy-minded Congress, epidemics of disease, and, once again, a government commission that wanted to reduce their reservations even further. The land question especially inflamed the Indians, and that they had let themselves be talked into signing another cession agreement did not help matters. "They made us many promises," recalled an old Sioux, "more than I can remember, but they never kept but one; they promised to take our land and they took it."

To people so afflicted, the voice of a prophet is a compelling sound. Repeatedly in history temporal conditions grown too oppressive to bear have called forth spiritual solutions. By 1889 the western tribes, especially the Sioux, were ripe for the exhilarating word that came from Nevada. A messiah had appeared, stirring visions of an Indian promised land.

A shy, gentle, husky man in his early thirties, Wovoka was the son of a Paiute prophet and a shaman himself. But he had also lived with a white rancher's family. They had given him the name Jack Wilson, and from them he learned about Jesus and other great medicine men described in the white man's Bible. So the religion Wovoka preached—after he claimed to have died and visited God in heaven—was a strange mixture of Christianity and the old Indian beliefs. It was called the Ghost Dance religion.

For Indians everywhere the Ghost Dance cult painted in graphic detail a new world, inhabited only by Indians, in which the buffalo and other game would once again darken the land and previous generations of Indians would come back to life. All would dwell blissfully and eternally without want, sickness, or discomfort. To bring about the millennium, Indians must dance the Ghost Dance and practice the tenets of the faith. Above all, the doctrine was pacific. "You must not fight," Wovoka enjoined. "Do no harm to anyone. Do right always."

On most of the western reservations the Indians heeded Wovoka's injunction and danced peacefully in joyous expectation of the grand new world. But among the Sioux, beset with special misfortunes in addition to the cultural disintegration all tribes suffered, the plea for peace was transformed into a call to arms. Short Bull and Kicking Bear, the high priests of the new religion among the Sioux, prophesied that the day of deliverance would be hastened if the obliteration of the whites were not left entirely to God and Wovoka. They invented a holy "ghost shirt," said to armor its wearer against the white man's bullets, and indulged in fiery rhetoric that badly frightened reservation officials and settlers in Nebraska and Dakota.

Just how real the danger of violence was is not clear even today. By November, 1890, however, conditions approaching anarchy prevailed on the Pine Ridge and Rosebud reservations. At Pine Ridge, moreover, the agent, Daniel F. Royer, was a newly appointed mediocrity both ignorant and fearful of Indians. His only solution, repeatedly urged, was to bring in soldiers to make the Indians stop dancing. Calmer counsels warned that such a move could provoke the very violence it was intended to forestall. Left alone, they felt, the dance would run its course. But hysteria gripped the towns around the reservations, citizens appealed for protection, and Royer became altogether unnerved. "Indians are dancing in the snow and are wild and crazy," he wired his Washington superiors on November 15. "We need protection and we need it now."

The appearance of cavalry and infantry at Pine Ridge and Rosebud agencies on November 20 electrified the Sioux. Those who feared the consequences of resistance, the "friendlies," gathered at the agencies. Under Short Bull and Kicking Bear, those still committed to the Ghost Dance, the "hostiles," fled to the distant northwest corner of the Pine Ridge Reservation. At length, numbering about three thousand, they took refuge on a plateaulike elevation called the Stronghold and threw themselves with new vigor into the dances.

Army plans focused on trying to persuade the dancers to abandon the Stronghold and return peacefully to their homes. The commander at Pine Ridge was Brigadier General John R. Brooke, a mild and somewhat hesitant officer whose emissaries, nevertheless, made good progress in breaking down the defiance of the refugees. But Brooke's superior, none other than Nelson A. Miles, believed affairs would be better managed if Miles himself assumed direct command. He was now a major general and, by virtue of the sudden death of George Crook, the new commander of the Division of the Missouri. Miles brought to his task a long experience in

On reservations such as *Pine Ridge* (below) agents systematically forced the Sioux away from their traditional way of life. A commissioner of Indian affairs explained that "to domesticate and civilize wild Indians is a noble work ... to allow them to drag along ... in their old superstitions, laziness, and filth, when we have the power to elevate them in the scale of humanity, would be a lasting disgrace to our government." Plows and seed corn replaced guns for the hunt. Feasts, war dances, and other "demoralizing and barbarous" customs were forbidden. One of the few white institutions successful among the Sioux was the police, which called forth cherished personal attributes of their society.

An agency policeman stands proudly with his family. Two women are wearing Mother Hubbards. but Grandmother clings to her traditional blanket.

A quintet of "nonprogressive" reservation warriors don traditional costumes before performing a tribal dance still legal at Pine Ridge in 1890.

Two Sioux warriors, Kicking Bear (above) and Short Bull, brought the Ghost Dance religion to the demoralized Indians at Pine Ridge Agency in 1890. The zealots promised that the white man would disappear and the buffalo would return.

fighting and negotiating with Indians and an intimate acquaintance with these particular Indians: he had fought them to a standstill in 1876–77 after Terry and Crook had returned to their headquarters. For this new campaign Miles set up his headquarters in Rapid City on December 17.

Meantime, violence had already broken out, not at Pine Ridge but, surprisingly, on the Standing Rock Reservation, where the able agent James McLaughlin ruled with quiet authority. In October Kicking Bear had carried word of the Ghost Dance to the Hunkpapas and had instructed Sitting Bull in its practices. It is doubtful whether the old chief truly believed in a doctrine so firmly rooted in the white man's religion, but he probably saw in it another weapon in his long struggle with the equally stubborn agent. Whatever his motives, Sitting Bull became the apostle of the new religion among the Hunkpapas and thus reinforced a conviction that had been maturing in McLaughlin's mind for several months: Sitting Bull would have to be arrested and removed from the reservation.

General Miles agreed—one of the few matters on which the two did agree. But McLaughlin wanted the arrest made by his Indian police, not soldiers. Miles had other plans. He dispatched Buffalo Bill Cody, whose Wild West Show had catapulted him to national fame, to carry out the mission. With three cronies and a squad of newsmen, Bill appeared at Standing Rock on November 27. Appalled at the possible consequences, McLaughlin conspired with the equally appalled commandant of nearby Fort Yates, Lieutenant Colonel William F. Drum, to interest Cody in the pleasures of the post officers' club. By relays the officers kept him occupied all night while the agent telegraphed his superiors. Cody's capacity for strong drink was already legendary, however, and the next morning he started for Sitting Bull's camp in seemingly stable condition. Again he was misled by carefully coached emissaries of McLaughlin, and this delay afforded the crucial time for a reply from Washington canceling the old scout's assignment.

But just at this point McLaughlin's hand was forced by a report that Sitting Bull had been invited by Short Bull and Kicking Bear to join the dancers in the Stronghold. As the agent knew, Sitting Bull's presence there would be certain to hinder any peace efforts and unite the dancers in continued defiance. Learning that Sitting Bull intended to accept the invitation, McLaughlin and Colonel Drum moved quickly to head him off.

Shortly before dawn on December 15, forty-three of the agent's "metal breasts" quietly surrounded Sitting Bull's cabin. Lieutenant Bull Head and Sergeants Red Tomahawk and Shave Head entered the cabin while others went to saddle the chief's horse. By the time the officers emerged from the cabin with their prisoner, the people of the community had been roused by barking dogs and were crowding in a shouting, threatening throng around the entrance. "Come on now," shouted Catch-the-Bear, "let us protect our chief." As the police tried to push forward, he shouldered his Winchester and shot Bull Head in the side. Spinning, Bull Head fired his pistol pointblank into Sitting Bull's chest. At the same instant Red Tomahawk shot him in the back of the head. Sitting Bull fell to the ground dead.

In a furious melee the police and dancers fought hand to hand in front of the cabin. Sitting Bull's horse, a gray circus animal presented to him by Buffalo Bill, suddenly sat down and began to perform its old circus tricks. Cavalry from Fort Yates, assigned to help the police if needed, raced to the

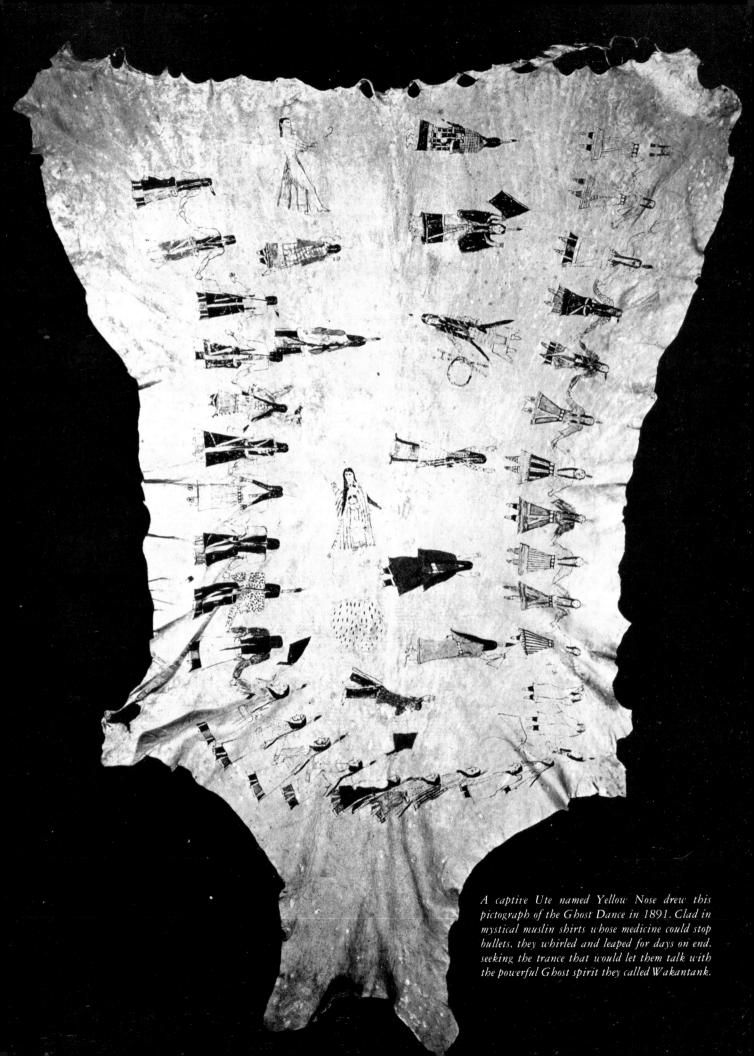

A captive Ute named Yellow Nose drew this pictograph of the Ghost Dance in 1891. Clad in mystical muslin shirts whose medicine could stop bullets, they whirled and leaped for days on end, seeking the trance that would let them talk with the powerful Ghost spirit they called Wakantank.

Red Tomahawk, a policeman from the Standing Rock Agency, shot Sitting Bull in the back of the head during an attempted arrest.

scene, but the dancers had already broken off the fight and fled. On the ground and in the cabin the officers counted Sitting Bull and seven of his followers lying dead. Four policemen had been slain and three wounded, two of whom, Bull Head and Shave Head, would die later.

And so in one of history's ironies the greatest chief of the Sioux, the architect of the mighty coalition that had wiped out Custer, the staunchest of all the "nonprogressives," met death at the hands of his own people.

But even the demise of Sitting Bull did not end the story of the Indian wars. One other chief who worried General Miles was Big Foot, whose band of Miniconjou Sioux lived in rude cabins on the Cheyenne River a few miles below its forks. Actually, though once a leading Ghost Dancer, Big Foot had lost confidence in the religion. Miles did not know that, however, and he planned to have him arrested. But like Sitting Bull, Big Foot had already received an invitation from Pine Ridge. It was not from the dancers in the Stronghold but from Red Cloud and other "friendlies" at the agency, who wanted him to bring his well-known peace-making talents to bear on the troubles with the whites. On December 23, therefore, before Miles's orders for his arrest could be carried out, Big Foot and his band abandoned their village and journeyed south toward Pine Ridge.

Miles naturally assumed that Big Foot was headed for the Stronghold, where his appearance could not be more untimely. Brooke's agents had at last persuaded many of the dancers to move to the agency; the slightest incident might stampede them back to the Stronghold. Vigorously, therefore, Miles's columns laced the prairies and badlands between the Cheyenne and White rivers looking for the Miniconjous. Not until December 28 were they found, and then scarcely thirty miles from Pine Ridge Agency. The intercepting unit was a squadron of the 7th Cavalry, Custer's old regiment. Big Foot, struck down by pneumonia, lay in his wagon, but he persuaded Major Samuel M. Whitside that he meant no harm. Together the Indians and soldiers camped for the night twenty miles east of the agency beside a pleasant stream called Wounded Knee Creek.

Although the Sioux awoke on December 29 with a sense of fear and distrust, neither they nor the troopers intended to have a fight. There were only 350 Indians, and 230 of these were women and children. Furthermore, the soldiers had been strengthened during the night by the other squadron of the regiment and now counted about 500 men. Colonel James W. Forsyth had taken command. He posted his men on all sides of the Indian camp. From a nearby hill four Hotchkiss cannon pointed at the tepees. Clearly resistance would be suicidal. For his part, pursuant to orders, Colonel Forsyth planned to disarm the Indians and escort them to the railroad, in Nebraska, to be taken out of the zone of military operations.

But as the soldiers began to search for the Indians' guns powerful emotions built up on both sides. A medicine man pranced about inciting the men to fight—their ghost shirts would protect them. The troopers grew more and more nervous. One seized a deaf man to take away his rifle. It went off. The medicine man tossed a handful of dirt in the air. A knot of warriors threw off their blankets and leveled their Winchesters at a rank of cavalrymen. Both sides fired at once, and the fight that neither side intended or expected burst upon them.

The clash at Wounded Knee was a horror of murderous fighting. Soldiers and Indians faced each other at close range and shot, stabbed, and clubbed one another. A bullet shattered Lieutenant John C. Gresham's elbow. Another carried away the top of Captain George C. Wallace's head. A warrior slashed at interpreter Philip Wells with a long knife and left his nose hanging by a shred of skin. Weakly Big Foot rose from his pallet to watch. A volley killed him and most of the other chiefs behind him. As the two sides separated, the Hotchkiss guns went into action, each belching forth 50 rounds a minute. The exploding shells flattened the Indian camp and filled the air with deadly flying fragments. A participant remembered seeing a shell punch a six-inch hole in a man's stomach. Caught in the fire, women and children went down along with the men. In less than an hour most of the fighting had ended. The battlefield was a scene of carnage. Almost two thirds of Big Foot's band had been cut down—at least 150 dead and 50 wounded, perhaps more who were never reported. The army lost 25 killed and 39 wounded.

Wounded Knee, of course, ruined the peace initiative. Miles later preferred charges against Forsyth for the killing of women and children, but the colonel won exoneration. Both "hostiles" and "friendlies," alike outraged by the slaughter of their people, united in White Clay valley, north of Pine Ridge Agency. Their encampment contained four thousand people, including some eight hundred to a thousand angry, vengeful warriors. On December 30 some of them ambushed the 7th Cavalry at Drexel Mission and exacted a slight measure of revenge before black cavalrymen of the 9th came to the rescue. But the fugitives were hesitant and undecided.

Expertly Miles exploited the confusion and divisions among the Sioux leaders. He sent in conciliatory messages urging surrender and promising decent treatment. At the same time he drew his circle of troops—by now a formidable concentration of thirty-five hundred men—closer and closer around the big village. Slowly they moved toward Pine Ridge as the chiefs debated and quarreled over whether to trust the general and do his bidding. Thus combining force and diplomacy in just the right proportions, Miles turned the deadly incident of December 29 into a complete surrender on January 15, 1891.

On January 21, 1891, a grand review rang down the curtain on the Ghost Dance campaign—and on the Indian wars of the West. With Sioux stolidly watching from the hills, and with a winter gale whipping the brightly colored capes of the soldiers, regiment after regiment passed before an animated General Miles. Sabers flashed, rifles were presented, guidons snapped in the wind, a band played Custer's old battle air "Garry Owen" as the decimated 7th Cavalry trooped by, and the deadly Hotchkiss guns, their carriages riddled by Sioux bullets, brought up the rear. "It was the grandest demonstration by the army ever seen in the West," wrote a correspondent; "and when the soldiers had gone to their tents, the sullen and suspicious Brûlés were still standing like statues on the crest of the hills."

Yet it was not the formal parade at Wounded Knee that symbolized the disappearance of the Indian frontier so much as a poignant scene that had been enacted at Fort Yates, near Standing Rock Agency, on December 17, 1890, two weeks before Wounded Knee. While in the agency cemetery an infantry company fired three volleys over the graves of slain Indian policemen and a bugler sounded taps, at the Fort Yates cemetery a detail of prisoners unceremoniously shoveled dirt into an open grave. In it was a rough wooden box containing the canvas-wrapped remains of Sitting Bull.

SITTING BULL IS DEAD.

The Old Chief and Seven of His Followers Killed in an Engagement with Police.

Sitting Bull was Preparing to Start for the Bad Lands and His Arrest was Ordered.

The Indian Police Start From Yates, Followed by Two Companies—Cavalry and Infantry.

When the Arrest was Made, Sitting Bull's Followers Attempted a Recapture.

In the Fight That Ensued, Sitting Bull, His Son and Six Indians were Killed.

On the Other Side, Four of the Police were Killed and Three Wounded.

The Cavalry Then Arrived on the Scene, and the Indians Fled Up Grand River.

A Lengthy Account of Major McLaughlin's Last Trip to Sitting Bull's Camp.

He's a Good Indian Now.

CHICAGO, Dec. 15.—At 9 o'clock to-night, Assistant Adjutant General Corbin of General Miles' staff received an official dispatch from St. Paul, saying Sitting Bull, five of Sitting Bull's men and seven of the Indian police have been killed. Thirteen casualties were the result of the attempt by the Indian police to arrest Sitting Bull.

HOW IT HAPPENED.

ST. PAUL, Dec. 15.—The report was received in this city this afternoon that Sitting Bull had been killed by the Indian who ha~ him a~

Newspapers (here, the Bismarck, North Dakota, Daily Tribune) hailed the death of Sitting Bull, whom they had feared as a menace.

The Sioux medicine man Yellow Bird, who had exhorted his braves to fight the bluecoats, lies frozen in the snow where he fell at the western warriors' last stand at Wounded Knee.
NATIONAL ANTHROPOLOGICAL ARCHIVES, SMITHSONIAN INSTITUTION

Acknowledgments

The Editors wish to thank the following for their generous aid in pictorial research.

American Museum of Natural History: Dorothy Fulton, Joseph Saulina

Amon Carter Museum, Fort Worth: Frances Gupton

Arizona Historical Society, Tucson: Margaret Bret Harte

J. N. Bartfield Galleries, New York City

Merrill Beal, Pocatello, Idaho

B. Benschneider, Colorado Springs

Buffalo Bill Historical Center, Cody, Wyoming

Ed Carpenter, New York City

Geoffrey Clements, New York City

Culver Pictures: Robert Jackson

Deerfield Memorial Museum, Deerfield: Timothy Newmann

Denver Art Museum: Richard Conn, Patricia Stocker

Thomas Gilcrease Institute of History and Art, Tulsa: Susan Nine

Gulf States Paper Corporation, Tuscaloosa, Alabama: Doris Fletcher

Rosemary Klein, London, England

Paulus Leeser, New York City

Frank Lerner, New York City

Library of Congress, Prints and Photographs: Jerry Kearns

Metropolitan Museum of Art: Fred Gordon

Mr. and Mrs. James Meyer, East Haddam, Connecticut

Museum of the American Indian: Vincent Wilcox, Ruth Wilcox, Carmen Guadagno

Museum of New Mexico, Arthur Olivas

National Anthropological Archives, Smithsonian Institution:
    James Glen, William Sturtevant, Herman Viola

National Archives

National Collection of Fine Arts, Smithsonian Institution: Eleanor Fink

National Museum of History and Technology Smithsonian Institution:
    Geraldine Sanderson

National Park Service: Harold Peterson

Honorable and Mrs. Robert Newbegin, Washington, D. C.

New York Public Library, Photo Services Division; Prints Division:
    Elizabeth Roth; Rare Book Division: Maud Cole

Pacific University, Forest Grove, Oregon: Carl Kemp

Karen Petersen, St. Paul, Minnesota

Royal Ontario Museum, Toronto, Canada: Mrs. E. Routh

St. Louis Art Museum: Louise Walker

Arthur Silberman, Oklahoma City, Oklahoma

Stark Museum of Art, Orange, Texas: Anna Caffey

State Historical Society of Colorado: Judith Golden

Peter Tillou, Ridgefield, Connecticut

Time, Inc.: Nell Juliand

"21" Club: Peter Krindler

Wadsworth Atheneum, Hartford, Connecticut: Abbie Hodges

West Point Museum, West Point, New York: Michael McAfee

Whitman College, Walla Walla, Washington: Lawrence Dodd

Mr. and Mrs. James Ryan Williams, Cincinnati, Ohio

Yale University, Beinecke Rare Book Library: Joyce Hoffmann

NATIONAL ARCHIVES

Index

Numbers in italic type refer to illustrations.

D

Dull Knife, Chief, 302
Dunlap, Brig. Gen. R. G., 151
Dunmore, earl of, 115–16
Duquesne, Fort, *84*. 87–88, 90–93, 104
Dustin, Hannah, *74*. 75–76
Dutch, 45–46, 52
Dyar, L. S., 290

E

Eagle from the Light, 293–95
Easton treaty conference, 92
Ecuyer, Capt. Simeon, 112
Edge Hill, Battle of, 113
education, 45, 55
Egan, Chief, 304
Eliot, Rev. John, *44*
Elliott, Maj. Joel H., 256
Ellis, Fort, 267
encomiendas. 18
Endecott, Capt. John, 45–47
English, 16, 22–35, 46–61, 70, 73–80, 82–93, 95, 105, *114*. 115–17, 135, 173, 180
Erie, 112
Eskiminzin, Chief, 246
Eskimos, *38*
Etherington, Capt. George, 109
Evans, Maj. Andrew W., 256
Evans, Gov. John, 234
Ewell, Gen. Richard S., 195–97

F

Fallen Timbers, Battle of, 121, 123, 130, 137
Falmouth, 74
Fetterman, Capt. William J., 240–41, 243
Fetterman, Fort, 265–67
Fillmore, Fort, 224
Fitzpatrick, Tom, 192–96, 205–6, 236
"Five Civilized Tribes," 168
Flatheads, 177
Fleet, Capt. Henry, 27
Florida, 20, 62, 65, 68, 77, 82, 115, 133, 140–46, 237, 265, 327–29, 332
Fly, C. S., photograph by, *327–28*
Flying Crow, 117
Forbes, Gen. John, 90–93
Ford, Capt. John S. "Rip," 208, 210
Forrest, Edwin, *58*
Forsyth, Maj. George A., 255, *257*
Forsyth, Col. James W., 340–41
forts. *See* individual place names
Four Lakes, Battle of, 204
Fox Indians, *48*
Franklin, Benjamin, 110, 113–14
Frémont, Capt. John C., 192, 226
French, 20–21, 33, *40–41*. 45–46, 70–80, 83–93, 95–96, 102, 105, 108,

114–15, 167
French and Indian Wars, 70ff. *See also* Great War for Empire
Frontenac, comte de, 71–74, 94–95
Frontenac, Fort, 90
Fuller, Capt. Matthew, 56
fur trading, 52, 71, 102–3, 164, 167, 172–77, 206

G

Gadsden, James, 143–44
Gage, Gen. Thomas, 115–17
Gaines, Gen. Edmund P., 148
Gall, Chief, 272, *272*. 273, 334
Galloway, Rebecca, 131
Gálvez, Adm. Bernardo de, 119–20
Gardiner, Lt. Lion, 46–47
Gary, William, painting by, *171*
Gates, Gen. Horatio, 118
Gates, Sir Thomas, 23–25
Gatewood, Lt. Charles B., 326–29
Generall Historie of Virginia (Smith), *14*. 26
George, Chief, 202
George II, King, 84–85, *89*
Georgia, 77, 82, 92, 119, 133, 138, 151
Geronimo, Chief, *2–3*. 311, 313–30, *326–29*. *332–33*
Ghost Dance religion, 335–41, *338–39*
Gibbon, Col. John, 267–71, 276, 296
Gilliam, Col. Cornelius, 180–81, 201
Gipson, Lawrence Henry, 85–87
Gladwin, Maj. Henry, 104, 106–8, 112, 114
gold rush, 178, 194, 201, 203–4, 206, 223–24, 232, 236–40, 266, 293
Goyahkla, Chief. *See* Geronimo
Grant, Ulysses S., 236, 246–47, 258–61, 266, 288, 293–95
Grant, Camp, 246
Grant, Fort, *278*. 279, *280–81*
Grattan, Lt. John L., 205
Greasy Grass, 269, 276. *See also* Little Bighorn, Battle of
Great Comanche War Trail, 208
Great Lakes, 102–4, 108–9, 167
Great Sioux Reservation, 244, 334
Great Swamp fight, 58–60
Great War for Empire, 85–86, 95, 105, 115. *See also* French and Indian Wars
Greenville Treaty, 122, 123, 131
Gresham, Lt. John C., 341
Grey Beard, Chief, 238, 264
Grierson, Col. Benjamin H., 236, 262, 312–13
Gros Ventres, 192–93
guns, 83, 102–3, 105–6, 166–67, 169, 173, 210, *214–15*. 230–31, 241, 254–55, 340–41. *See also* weapons

H

habitants. 103, 108
Haldimand, Gen. Frederick, 121
Half-King, 87
Hallalhotsoot. *See* Lawyer
Hamilton, Capt. Louis M., 256
Hancock, King, 82
Hancock, Maj. Gen. Winfield Scott, 241–44, 255
Harkner, Fort, 259
Harmar, Gen. Josiah, *120*. 121, 122, 130
Harney, Gen. William S., 205–6, *244*
Harney, Camp, 246, 306
Harris, Caroline, *207*
Harrison, Gen. William Henry, 131–34, *132*. 136–38
Hartford, Treaty of, 53
Hatch, Col. Edward, 312
Haverhill, 75
Hawikuh, 170–71
Hayfield fight, 241
Hays, Col. John Coffee, *210*
Hays, Fort, 259
He Dog, 240
Hendrick, Chief, 89
Herkimer, Gen. Nicholas, 117
Hidatsas, 175
High Forehead, 205
Hill, Col. Edward, 29
Hoar, John, 57
Hodgson, Lt. Benny, 273
Holmes, Ensign Robert, 109
Hopis, 170
horses, 166–70, 193
Horseshoe Bend, *139*. 141
Howard, Gen. Oliver O., 246–47, 295–98, 303–6, 311
Huachuca, Fort, 327
Hudson Bay, 70, 80
Hudson's Bay Company, 180–81
Hull, Brig. Gen. William, 135–37
Hundred Dazers, 234
Hunkpapas, 265, 272, 302, 334, 338
Hunt, Capt. Thomas, 43
hunting, *65*. 165–66, 172, 255, 265–67, 331
Hurons, 33, 40, 46, 49, 68–69, 103–6, 109, 112–13

I

Idaho, 246, 293–95, 304
Illinois, 115, 133, 146–48
Indiana, 109, 122, 131
Indian agents, 104, 118, 140, 144, 170, 193, 197, 226, 247, 261, 263, 265, 304, 331–34, 336, 340
Indian Bureau, 156, 255, 263, 289, 311, 325, 330–31